Postcolonial Urban Outcasts

Extending current scholarship on South Asian Urban and Literary Studies, this volume examines the role of the discontents of the South Asian city. The collection investigates how South Asian literature and literature about South Asia attends to urban margins, regardless of whether the definition of margin is spatial, psychological, gendered, or sociopolitical. That cities are a site of profound paradoxes is nowhere clearer than in South Asia, where urban areas simultaneously represent both the frontiers of globalization as well as the deeply troubling social and political inequalities of the global south. Additionally, because South Asian cities are defined by the palimpsestic confluence of, among other things, colonial oppression, anticolonial nationalism, postcolonial governance, and twenty-first-century transnational capital, they are sites where the many faces of empowerment and disempowerment are elaborated. The volume brings together chapters that emphasize myriad critical approaches—geospatial, urban-theoretical, diasporic, subaltern, and others. United in their critical empathy for urban outcasts, the chapters respond to central questions such as: What is the relationship between the politico-economic narratives of globally emerging South Asian cities and the dispossessed? How do South Asian cities stand in relationship to the nation and, conversely, how might South Asians in diaspora construct these cities within larger narratives of development, globalization, or as sources of authentic ethnic identities? How is the very skeleton—the space, the territory—of South Asian cities marked with and by exclusionary politics? How do the aesthetic and formal choices undertaken by writers determine the potential for and limits to emancipation of urban outcasts from their oppressive circumstances? Considering fiction, nonfiction, comics, and genre fiction from India, Pakistan, Bangladesh, and Sri Lanka; literature from the twentieth and the twenty-first century; and works that are Anglophone and those that are in translation, this book will be valuable to a range of disciplines.

Madhurima Chakraborty is Assistant Professor of Postcolonial Literature in the Department of English, Columbia College Chicago, USA.

Umme Al-wazedi is Associate Professor of Postcolonial Literature in the Department of English and Co-Program Director of Women's and Gender Studies at Augustana College, USA.

Routledge Research in Postcolonial Literatures

For a full list of titles in this series, please visit www.routledge.com.

Edited in collaboration with the Centre for Colonial and Postcolonial Studies, University of Kent at Canterbury, this series presents a wide range of research into postcolonial literatures by specialists in the field. Volumes will concentrate on writers and writing originating in previously (or presently) colonized areas, and will include material from non-anglophone as well as anglophone colonies and literatures. Series editors: Donna Landry and Caroline Rooney.

Postcolonial Urban Outcasts

City Margins in South Asian Literature

Edited by Madhurima Chakraborty
and Umme Al-wazedi

Taylor & Francis Group

NEW YORK AND LONDON

First published 2017
by Routledge
711 Third Avenue, New York, NY 10017

and by Routledge
2 Park Square, Milton Park, Abingdon, Oxon OX14 4RN

Routledge is an imprint of the Taylor & Francis Group, an informa business

© 2017 Taylor & Francis

Library of Congress Cataloging-in-Publication Data

Names: Chakraborty, Madhurima, editor. | Al-wazedi, Umme, editor.
Title: Postcolonial urban outcasts: city margins in South Asian literature / edited by Madhurima Chakraborty and Umme Al-wazedi.
Other titles: City margins in South Asian literature
Description: New York: Routledge, 2017. | Series: Routledge research in postcolonial literatures; 55 | Includes bibliographical references and index.
Identifiers: LCCN 2016024649
Subjects: LCSH: South Asian literature (English)—History and criticism. | South Asian literature—History and criticism. | Cities and towns in literature. | Marginality, Social, in literature. | Outcasts in literature. | Postcolonialism in literature.
Classification: LCC PR9570.S64 P67 2017 | DDC 820.9/954—dc23
LC record available at https://lccn.loc.gov/2016024649

ISBN: 978-1-138-67723-4 (hbk)
ISBN: 978-1-315-55964-3 (ebk)

Typeset in Sabon
by codeMantra

In memory of Professor A. F. M. Rezaul Karim Siddique,
Who was brutally murdered on April 23, 2016.

You believed in the redeeming qualities of civilizations and all
human beings.

Contents

List of Figures

Acknowledgments

This project is partially supported by a Faculty Development Grant from Columbia College Chicago and similar funds from Augustana College. We would like to thank both these institutions for their help, financial and otherwise. We also greatly appreciate the opportunity given to us by the South Asian Literary Association to co-chair the conference in Chicago in 2012, which started our editorial partnership. This book would not have been possible without the contributors who very patiently accepted our critiques and worked hard over several drafts.

One of the chapters included in this collection have been published elsewhere: Chapter 6: "*Lahore Lahore Hai*: Bapsi Sidhwa and Mohsin Hamid's City Fictions" (original title: "'The heart, stomach and backbone of Pakistan': Lahore in novels by Bapsi Sidhwa and Mohsin Hamid") by Claire Chambers, *South Asian Diaspora* 6:2 (2014): 141–59. We wish to thank the journal for permission to reproduce the copyright material. We also thank Harper Collins, India for granting us permission to use the images from Vishwajyoti Ghosh's *Delhi Calm* in Chapter 4, "'Stuck at Pause': An Interview with Vishwajyoti Ghosh on *Delhi Calm*" by Amit R. Baishya.

Finally, many thanks to our families for their patience and support during this process.

Introduction
Whose City?

Madhurima Chakraborty

> When you have city eyes you cannot see the invisible people, the men
> with elephantiasis of the balls and the beggars in boxcars do not impinge
> on you, and the concrete sections of future drainpipes look like dormi-
> tories. My mother lost her city eyes and the newness of what she was
> seeing made her flush, newness like a hailstorm pricking her cheeks.
> —Salman Rushdie, *Midnight's Children*

Postcolonial Urban Outcasts: City Margins in South Asian Literature is an
edited collection of literary criticism that, as an anthology, examines the
position and role of South Asian Cities' discontents. It is an attempt to investigate how South Asian literature and literature about South Asia attend to
urban margins, whether we define those margins spatially, psychologically,
sexually, or sociopolitically. For this reason, *Postcolonial Urban Outcasts*
brings together chapters that emphasize myriad critical approaches—
geospatial, urban-theoretical, diasporic, and subaltern, to name a few. These
diverse chapters are nonetheless united in their critical empathy for urban
outcasts, which is to say in losing the "city eyes" that narrator Saleem Sinai
in Rushdie's *Midnight's Children* says allows our blindness to urban hardships (92), and because they are implicitly underpinned by the same questions: why are cities an important category for South Asia, where discussions
of the nation and of nationalism have been assumed to be the dominant
organizational logic? And, what are the consequences of literary representations and investigations into urban outcasts in South Asia?

If in 1999 Edward Soja examined in detail the cultural turn in urban studies writ large, then the significance for, inversely, an urban focus in South
Asian cultural studies has also gained traction in recent scholarship, where
we have seen a shift away from the late twentieth-century theoretical focus
on nation and nationalism. This is, of course, not to say that South Asian
cities themselves are somehow new or newly important, but that the importance of urban centers as geospatial entities in the formation of South Asian
cultural lives is receiving more critical attention. Renu Desai and Romola
Sanyal have argued that even though urbanization grew in leaps and bounds
in post-Independence India, Indian scholarship and development plans took

on a particularly "anti-urban bias" (2), thus generating and sustaining a gap between the lived and academic significances of cities. Similarly, in his convincing and compelling introduction to the two-volume *Oxford Anthology of the Modern Indian City*, Vinay Lal argues that although critical attention has not always reflected this, the importance of the city is not, in fact, a modern or relatively new happenstance: "the city in India is as old as Indian civilization" (xvi–xvii). For Lal, urban existence has always been the defining feature of Indian life, but it is only recently that scholarship has made attempts to catch up.

Postcolonial Urban Outcasts: City Margins in South Asia acknowledges the work that many such critics in the field of urban studies and South Asian studies have done both in establishing the historical and current importance of South Asian cities as well as in correcting the lack of critical attention that persists despite the importance of urban centers (Lal; Nair; Prakash "The Urban Turn"). Our volume implicitly builds on this corrective trend, assuming rather than declaring the importance of cities in South Asia. However, while we agree that a focus on cities rather than on nations provides some needed realignment in scholarship, this is not to say that we find cities as cultural organizational logics to be inherently more progressive, utopian, or emancipatory than the nations that had held the focus of the South Asian cultural imagination before it. In fact, *Postcolonial Urban Outcasts* is fueled primarily by a critical skepticism—one that is invested in interrogating the margins of cities, convinced that there are many urban exclusionary practices that find expression in South Asian literature.

We also do not mean to suggest that such exclusionary practices are characteristics of South Asian cities only in their contemporary lives, but, instead, that long-standing practices of stringent hierarchizing have been further sharpened in the neoliberal moment wherein the intense demands of the private sector have exacerbated, for instance, poverty conditions (Lal xi; Bayat 534). Our focus on marginalized urban communities is related to, but ultimately different from, gauging a city's "developmentalism"—the primary characteristic of the "not (yet) city," usually a third-world megacity, that is understood to be "lacking in the qualities of city-ness" such as effective governance, service production, etc. that might presumably characterize a more so-called First World city (Robinson 531). We agree with Ananya Roy that such developmentalism is inherently part of the emergence of such cities into the world of global capital, and that the megacities of the global south, with their attendant and rampant underdevelopment—"poverty, environmental toxicity, disease" (224)—only have in concentration what other global (north) cities, or "urban modes that are seen to be command and control points of the world economy" (224), need and rely on. In other words, while the megacity of the global south might seem to own the underdevelopment and developmentalism associated with it, the global city relies on exactly this same cheap labor and resources for its own success. The entanglement that Roy draws between, on the one hand, the financial success of and, on the other, uneven development and economic gains within cities, seems to us clear, if profound.

Yet, whereas Roy characterizes such developmentalism as a necessary *condition* of the city of the global south, especially the South Asian megacity, we find it more productive to emphasize, instead, the *practices* that underlie urban inequality. Our emphasis simultaneously expands on this notion of developmentalism by contemplating various practices of marginalization beyond economics, and narrows the focus on the process and production of such inequalities. It is by paying particular attention to process, practice, and action that we hope to prevent reproducing what Gyan Prakash has noted as being a characteristic feature of contemporary cultural-critical examinations of the city: a tendency to conclude that it is intense moments of emergencies rather than the everyday effects of historical situations that plague such urban centers ("Imaging the Modern City, Darkly"). Prakash argues that at least in part, the depiction of the depressing and dire straits of modern urbanity in literature—for instance, being "engulfed in ecological and social crises, seduced by capitalist consumption, paralyzed by crime, wars, class, gender, and racial conflicts"—is a mode of representation that is not entirely new, that, instead, "[s]ince the turn of the twentieth century, dystopic images have figured prominently in literary, cinematic, and sociological representations of the modern city" ("Imaging" 1). To be clear, it is not at all that the dystopia and darkness of cities is entirely created and has no substantive referents, but instead that, given their ubiquity, such bleak city imagery must be examined for its consequential literary-representative mode. This becomes especially important because the ubiquitous portrayal of dark cities has resulted in a "mode of interpretation," an interpretive protocol, that examines such image productions of the city that "ratchet [...] up a critical reading of specific historical conditions to diagnose crisis and catastrophe" ("Imaging" 1). Although *Postcolonial Urban Outcasts* recognizes the urgency of addressing and solving the problem of city peripheries and unequal citizenships, our general focus is on sustained diurnal practices rather than on erupting crises.

Urban Outcasts

We use the term outcast to describe those on the receiving ends of exclusionary practices for multiple reasons. First and foremost, in using a homonym for the term outcaste we mean to highlight the relationship between contemporary marginalizing acts and the long-standing practice of alienating entire communities from access to social, economic, and political power that has prominently been part of the Hindu caste system in India, although of course there are iterations of outcastes elsewhere. Although only some of the chapters in our collection deal directly with Dalit representations, we find in the term outcast a useful aural link to outcastes, a phonetic emblem of the longevity of exclusion and marginalization. Second, the term outcast is our deliberate preference over subaltern, despite the latter term's critical caché. Given the shifting meanings of subaltern even within the work of the Subaltern Studies collective, it is tempting to consider any group victimized by institutionalized and formal exclusion as a kind of subaltern; certainly, our collection is invested in thinking about as many forms of urban marginalization as possible. Moreover, as a collection, *Postcolonial Urban Outcasts* is invested in recognizing the agency of the disenfranchised, in our case the urban disenfranchised, continuing the one impulse that has remained unchanged in the iterations and vicissitudes of Subaltern Studies over the years (Chaturvedi). However, we refrain from describing the urban outcasts investigated in our collection as urban subalterns because, even recognizing the plural definitions of the latter term, we understand subaltern communities to be communities of people who are alienated from power along multiple axes—through combinations of, say, social, political, gendered, economic, epistemological, or representative rubrics that compound separate forms of disempowerment. So, for instance, middle-class women who are oppressed by patriarchy but continue to have significant access to economic resources, or diasporic returnees who are psychologically alienated from their "home" cities but have nonetheless significant mobility because of easy access to money and gendered public spaces cannot and must not be understood as subalterns. Third, the term urban outcast encompasses not only people who are alienated from power in and through cities, but cities themselves that remain consistently marginalized in literary imaginaries of South Asia. Consequently, some chapters in our collection turn to sociopolitically significant South Asian urban centers that have nonetheless been largely absent from literature of and about the area. And fourth, the coincidence of outcast as both a noun and verb embodies our focus, mentioned above, on practice and act. That is, we understand outcast in multiple ways: as noun, or the subject or object of marginalization; as verb, or the practice of exclusion; and simultaneously as noun plus verb, or the positionality of urban outcasts and not mere, static identities.

In fact, given that our investigation focuses on the literary examination of *processes* of exclusion and marginalization, our inquiry of the agency of urban outcasts similarly underscores the *practices* whereby those who are excluded seek to change their peripheral status. Collectively, the diverse set of chapters here argue that through literary representations of urban outcasts, writers conceive of the resistance to marginalizing praxes as being correspondingly grounded in a set of diurnal and quotidian practices. In this way, the contributors to this collection are implicitly responding in their literary analyses to the call by urban theorists such as Asef Bayat to shift in urban studies from the identity movements that reflect the "sentiments of middle-class intellectuals" to, instead, the "everyday practices of the ordinary people" (534), noting the urge to transition in focus not just from middle-class to "ordinary" but also from static conditions, identities, and thoughts to acts. In examining the representation and construction of fictional actions that can launch an effective resistance to marginalization, *Postcolonial Urban Outcasts* analyzes a heterogeneous set of practices. Following the theories of Edward Soja and Michel Foucault, whose respective concepts of thirdspace and heterotopia insist on binary-confounding understandings of cities, our collection argues that urban outcasts are similarly and increasingly characterized in South Asian literature not always as victims or revolutionaries, but as negotiators and strategists of these complex cityscapes.

To argue as we do that urban outcasts are agents is to allow for and articulate both the various degrees of such agents' success in mounting effective resistance as well as a fluctuating degree of complicity with existing structures of power. In this, our collection follows the critical terrain that is rife with myriad interpretations of the political potential and character of the urban disenfranchised, especially in so-called developing, third world, or global south cities. For instance, Joan Nelson, intending to quell the fear that new migrants into cities from rural spaces in developing nations are essentially disruptive to existing urban political structures, hypothesizes instead that, among other things, the material demands of everyday lives forestall any true long-term commitment to radicalization among the urban poor, although there is potential for them to stave off alienation and be integrated into the political system. Consequently, though "the political mobilization of the urban poor does [...] challenge the political system of developing nations," this challenge "is not the containment of extremist or anarchic outbursts, but the evolution of means to respond to concrete and usually moderate demands" (414). This sense of the political moderation of the newly arrived rural immigrant into the city also finds its echoes in Georg Simmel's understanding of the new migrant, or "stranger," a hybrid form "of living on the margin[s] of two cultures without being a full member of either" (AlSayyad 9).

On the other hand, Homi K. Bhabha has repeatedly argued, most famously in *The Location of Culture*, that hybrid and ambivalent spaces have, in fact, a profound potential for meaningful resistance and restructuring the very center. More cautiously, Partha Chatterjee describes the governed (his examples are largely Indian), or "specific population groups" who are characterized by being influenced and controlled by state policies but are nonetheless not true citizens because they have little access to the equal rights that citizenship confers. Chatterjee argues that these populations are outside their law—their livelihood, as their domiciles are largely illegal—yet they are not quite without the oversight of governance altogether, because they have relationships with regulatory state agencies. Their marginal status often necessitates their resistance to official moves to, say, relocate them, but their resistance does not necessarily question the existing power structures, and such an ambivalent status can be empowering even if not fully revolutionary:

> These groups on their part accept that their activities are often illegal and contrary to good civic behavior, but they make a claim to a

habitation and a livelihood as a matter of right. They profess a readi-
ness to move out if they are given suitable alternative sites for resettlement, for instance.

(Politics of the Governed 40)

In recognition of such variances within popular agency, the chapters in
Postcolonial Urban Outcasts examine degrees of political progressiveness
and conservatism among urban outcasts in South Asian literature; careful
as they are in highlighting the agency of the marginalized, they nonetheless
collectively conclude that to truly recognize the agency of a population is
to acknowledge that even the marginalized will not always be as radical as
one would hope, that they may even reproduce restrictive structures of their
own even as they navigate the exclusionary systems they face.

Literature and the Margins

In line with the efforts of this collection to investigate the question of outcast
agency in plural perspectives, we also adopt different critical frameworks—
sometimes even opposing ones—in order to open up the field of South Asian
urban literary studies as much as possible. So it is not just that we have
made a special effort to make the primary texts under examination as plural
as possible, generically and linguistically (although that is true as well), but
also that the essayists collected here inhabit differing critical perspectives in
their analyses of South Asian literatures. Through these differences, though,
we see in these chapters a unifying commitment to a progressive politics,
which is fundamentally opposed to the hierarchized access to urban citizenship along any identity markers. We identify this particular political-critical
impulse as realism; to be more specific, we understand our project to be
following what Satya Mohanty has described as a postpositivist realist theoretical lens.

We fully understand that this is a controversial, perhaps even unpopular,
critical label to adopt within postcolonial studies today given that field's
dominant poststructuralist underpinnings; in the case of our collection especially it may at first seem to be a misfit. After all, several chapters contained
in *Postcolonial Urban Outcasts* are influenced by the heavyweights of poststructuralist postcolonial theorists who have long held realism in disregard.
Perhaps the most famous of these reminders is Gayatri Spivak's criticism of
realism as the theater where the political (as-proxy) and artistic (as-symbol)
meanings of representation conflate and consequently hide the workings
of the author. Among other later subalternists, Dipesh Chakrabarty characterizes the life of the subaltern as nonsecular and nonmodern; therefore,
to think of subalterns in literature through the very secular and modern
lens of realism may appear to capitulate to a reading protocol which would
necessarily refuse to take them on their own terms. Even in Meenakshi
Mukherjee's famous study of realism in Indian literature, where she is not

particularly antipathetic to that genre, she points out that because realism was an invention of nineteenth-century Europe, the demands of that form were largely incongruous with the social circumstances in India despite being the dominant mode of Anglophone literature in circulation, and consequently the most reproduced, in that South Asian country. The very consistency between context and form that supposedly formed the strength of realism in its European iteration could not be maintained in this new literary and social situation; it was fundamentally foreign.

To claim this critical perspective for our twenty-first century and specifically South Asian-focused collection, especially given the fact that some of our chapters specifically embrace non-realist, genre-defying, and otherwise experimental forms as having the most potential for inclusivity, may seem ill fitting, at the least. However, it is because rather than in spite of the above-mentioned limitations of the nineteenth-century realism, coupled with the explicit progressive politics of this collection, that we align ourselves with Mohanty's postpositivist realist mode. (Mohanty is speaking of a philosophical realism rather than a literary form.) To be clear, we do not claim that the non-realist or otherwise genre-defying literatures are in fact realist. Such a move would extend the boundaries of realism so far as to make the term meaningless. Rather, our argument is that the critical impulse largely represented in these chapters, even when it is being deployed to examine and encourage different forms of literary production, participates not in some new critical analytical mode but in a literary politics that is attempting to comprehend the cultural expressions of exclusion of and resistance by urban outcasts. In order to do this effectively, and this is a key element of Mohanty's postpositivist realism, there is generated within this volume something fundamentally different from the poststructuralist deep disbelief of objective knowledge altogether, from a belief that "nothing is ever epistemically reliable" (Mohanty 13).

The intellectual struggle common to the essays in *Postcolonial Urban Outcasts* is in finding a cultural politics that can, one the one hand, make room for the heterogeneity of those we describe as urban outcasts and of their discursive formations (which is to say of the way that they form discourses as well as the way they themselves are formed through various discourses of gender, class, caste etc.), and, on the other hand, recognize and use political categories that may be constructed but are nonetheless extra-textual, adhere to some sense of objectivity that can direct political action, and, most importantly, embrace the optimism that the status of the marginalized can be changed. It is this particular combination of self-conscious objectivity and hope for political change that forms the bedrock for Mohanty's postpositivist realism. Mohanty's delineation of postpositivism takes into account the best of that which postmodernism (and its literary branch of poststructuralism) has had to offer—namely the much needed questioning of foundationalist theories or grand narratives that characterized, for instance, nineteenth-century realism, and of positivist declarations about the universals that bound humanity in a way that was characteristically absent any self-consciousness of its own context and construction in and through theory. Mohanty's commitment to realism then, is in light of and taking into account this very important critique. It combines such skepticism with a progressive politics that is grounded in the belief in a critical objectivity and a "radical universalism" that, while self-conscious of its own theoretical mediation, nonetheless argues that culturally diverse groups are still bound by an ultimate commonality: "No matter how different cultural Others are, they are never so different that they are—as typical members of their culture—incapable of acting purposefully, of evaluating their actions in light of their ideas and previous experiences, and of being 'rational' in this minimal way" (198).

Our commitment in this collection to heterogeneity and plurality—of critical perspectives, of literary texts, even of who might be understood as an urban outcast—is similarly expressed in a unification behind the concept of agency and self-conscious, deliberated action, especially of those that have been marginalized. And, like Mohanty, we understand the negligence of the disenfranchised to be the particular concern of cultural and literary politics. Religious fundamentalism and authoritarianism continue to thrive in South Asia—fanatical acts of India's pro-Hindutva groups, military repression of India's borderland communities, the treatment of Rohingya muslims in Myanmar, and the assassination of secular intellectuals in Bangladesh, including the brutal murder of Professor Rezaul Karim Siddique, the former professor of my co-editor Umme Al-wazedi, as this introduction was being written. Given the significant criticism of the governments of these nations for their general inefficacy in curtailing this trend, including denying the severity of these acts, the majoritarian violence against minority communities is, for all intents and purposes, state sanctioned. In such a politically oppressive climate, it is essential to mine literary and artistic productions to gauge their commitments to social justice, and their contributions to a "reasonable social hope" (Mohanty xii) that such aggressive exclusionary tactics must end.

In an interview with me some years ago, Bengali writer and activist Mahasweta Devi asserted that the separation of creative-literary work and social conscientiousness is a contemporary invention, that writers in India have historically been committed to matters of public good and political equality (Chakraborty 285–6). In fact, she characterized her own literary work as fueled by a compulsion to tell the stories of the most marginalized tribes, comprised of lower-caste communities, in India:

> Once I started to know about the denotified tribes, I felt compelled to write their stories. There was this woman, Chuni Kotal of the Lodha tribe, who was the first woman graduate of her tribe. She has an awful story of the prejudice she faced at the university ... Basically, she was told that her tribe was a criminal tribe and she did not deserve an

education ... One day [her husband] returned to his house, and found that she had committed suicide there, because of the abuse she faced in college. These things happen to tribal people all the time. We do not know these things are happening, so I write stories. (285)

We see in her response an equation with the desire to write and the desire to write on behalf of the marginalized. Although she had been writing fiction for many decades before the incident, which occurred in 1992, Chuni Kotal's suicide clearly distills the urgency she feels drives her creative endeavors. It is not lost on us that the suicide of Rohith Vemula in January of 2016 is an echo of Kotal's and proves, tragically, how much of caste politics have remained absolutely unchanged. Vemula had fought against casteist practices at the University of Hyderabad, an economically thriving urban campus in, further, a city that is historically, socially, and financially significant to India. Ironically, it was Vemula's anti-casteist activism that became the rationale for his expulsion from the University as he was ultimately accused of fostering caste-based divisiveness on campus. (This sort of reversal of politics so that the victim of a particular oppressive structure is accused of participating in exactly the same divisive behavior is unfortunately too familiar for those who are invested in the importance of deeply contextualizing the systems of oppression. In fact, the ease with which the progressive potential of multicultural endeavors translates into upholding the status quo is another reason Satya Mohanty is ultimately dissatisfied with postmodern theories that do shirk extra-textual political categories.) Vemula's suicide note underscores the unattainability of the fantasies of an objective personhood, which is the implicit promise of a liberal higher education, in the face of unrelenting and oppressive identity-based discrimination ("My Birth is My Fatal Accident"). The failure of social systems to be just and equitable is profoundly linked to the failure of intellectual practices; further, given that Vemula repeats in his note that all he had ever wanted was to be a science writer "like Carl Sagan," he despairingly shows how creative writing, even about something ostensibly as nonpersonal as science, is always under the influence of attendant exclusionary and marginalizing processes.

It is also through this lens of the necessary link between creative practice and the advocacy of the margins in South Asia that we understand the controversy with the Indian Sahitya Akademi awards. In the fall of 2015, there was a spate of Indian authors, including Shashi Deshpande, Nayantara Sahgal, Uday Prakash, Ashok Vajpeyi, Ghulam Nabi Khayal, Gurbachan Singh Bhullar, and Krishna Sobti, who returned the awards that been given to them by the national literary organization, the Sahitya Akademi, in protest of the growing national climate of hostility and violence against dissenting writers and other intellectuals. Some of these writers also resigned their positions at the institution, others returned awards given to them by other state literary organizations, and many additional artists voiced their support of this movement to criticize state sponsored literary organizations such as the Sahitya Akademi. As a collective, they were responding to the absence of any official condemnation of what Rushdie has called the "thuggish violence" of fanatical Hindus ("Salman Rushdie Rubbishes Criticism"), seen, for instance, in the murders of writers and dissenters such as Sahitya Akademi award recipient M. M. Kalburgi, whose progressive and anti-Hindutva stances had been met with escalating threats, violence, and, ultimately, assassination. (It was, in fact, Kalburgi's murder that provoked the first Sahitya Akademi writer, Uday Prakash, to return his award.) Writers such as Nayantara Sahgal also expanded the object of the protests to include the clear and present threat not just to intellectual dissenters, but also to everyday members of minority communities, such as Mohammad Akhklaq, a Muslim man in the Hindu majority area of Dadri, Uttar Pradesh, who was lynched by a mob for supposedly having beef in his fridge.

In protesting the silence of state agencies such as the Sahitya Akademi and other national arts organizations in the face of such violence, the writers' movement raises multiple interrelated objections that are relevant to the kind of work we try to do here in this book: in the particular case of the Sahitya Akademi, writers who had received accolades from that institute assert that the Akademi's role cannot simply be to recognize artists according to some purely aesthetic rubric of excellence, but instead must be to vocally and aggressively promote the right of artistic and intellectual expression and political dissent. Also, in criticizing the Sahitya Akademi for its silence regarding the violence towards not only other awardees but also other political and intellectual dissenters such as socialist Marathi writer Govind Pansare who was killed by members of a right-wing Hindu organization, these artists hold the literary organization as at least a symbolic leader for national culture writ large. Similarly, in including violence against ethnic and religious minority communities who may not have been engaged in any explicit intellectual dissent as motive enough for their rejection of state awarded accolades, writers such as Nayantara Sahgal connect political ideologies espoused by the extreme right-wing government that had swept national elections the year before to localized incidents of majoritarianist violence. Perhaps most relevantly to this book's project, such a protest by the artists and authors speaks, simply, to the relationships between creative practice, empty gestures towards intellectual plurality, and structural privileges. In other words, in the face of an alarming trend of anti-minority, pro-Hindutva, and other violent, culturally-doctored trends, the writers' protest reminds us that literary practitioners whose works have earned them tributes and accolades have to be the voice of true political dissent; one of the ways this can be undertaken is by urging the very agencies that celebrate plurality, in name, by granting awards, to recognize the stakes of political dissent in practice.

More than twenty years ago, Partha Chatterjee suggested that India was an example of how nations in the region, affected by their internal anticolonial nationalist movements, were determined by the fragments of populations who did not fit, ideologically or politically, within the larger nationalist project (*Nation and Its Fragments*). In compiling this collection, we argue that the South Asian city, given both its precolonial history as well as its specific contemporary illusion of access to wealth and full political citizenship, nonetheless continues the exclusionary practices of the nation.

The chapters in *Postcolonial Urban Outcasts* are grouped into four broad themes, although most could have easily been collected under multiple parts and there is broad thematic imbrication between the parts themselves. Part I: Urban Outcasts, Urban Subalterns assembles critiques that interrogate the very nature of the urban margin in South Asian literature—what does it mean to be outcast from South Asian cities? How do the cities participate in such marginalization, and how may they themselves be victims of other kinds of marginalization? How do subaltern communities—usually associated with ruralscapes—fare in urban environments, which make illusory promises of more opportunity? Ultimately, what is the relationship between the politico-economic narratives of globally emerging South Asian cities and the dispossessed?

To this end, the first chapter in that part and in the collection is Nazia Akhtar's "Recasting the Outcasts: Hyderabad and Hyderabadi Subjectivities in Two Literary Texts" which, in looking at the literature of the city and princely state of Hyderabad, names the key investigative spirit of *Postcolonial Urban Outcasts*. Akhtar's chapter encompasses multiple critical approaches to the relationship between the South Asian city, marginalization, and literary representation. She both investigates whom the city includes and excludes in Hyderabadi literature, as well as examines why it is that Hyderabad itself has been largely excluded from narratives of the Partition of India, despite the very key political role it played at that time. Akhtar's analysis of Zeenuth Futehally's novel *Zohra* argues that Futehally's text is a departure from typical depictions of Hyderabad, one that attempts to more fully represent the political spectrum of the princely-state's inhabitants, resituating the centrality of Hyderabad in partition narratives. In her analysis of Ian Bedford's *The Last Candles of the Night*, Akhtar examines the significance of the author's outsider status, which, she argues, allows for a particularly strategic literary critical approach to Hyderabad.

In "The Margins of Postcolonial Urbanity: Reading Critical Irrealism in Nabarun Bhattacharya's Fiction," Sourit Bhattacharya argues that Michael Löwy's concept of critical irrealism is particularly useful for representing the margins of postcolonial South Asian urbanism, especially given that theoretical framework's distinction not just from critical realism, but also from other forms more typically associated with postcolonial literature such as magical realism. In this, Sourit Bhattacharya turns to the fiction of Nabarun Bhattacharya in whose tales of the urban fantastical he finds an intense commitment to representing subaltern experiences. Fundamentally, Sourit Bhattacharya's chapter is about the form of the literary commitment to urban margins; he posits that whereas, on the one hand, critical *realism* (perhaps most famously adopted by Nabarun's mother Mahasweta Devi) falls short by refusing to centralize non-rational experiences that mark and identify subaltern urban classes, on the other hand, magical realism, especially in postcolonial contexts, is often more invested in outlining a historical condition rather than adopting a critical or analytical approach to such experiences. The power of critical irrealism, then, lies in its ability to disrupt notions of order and logic, and consequently, to confront capitalist projects that create the conditions that generate the urban subaltern. Specifically, Bhattacharya investigates Nabarun's use of filth which, he argues, confronts middle-class respectability in exactly this productive and disruptive mode.

Yet, if Bhattacharya compellingly argues that critical irrealism is a better tool for examining the life of the urban subaltern, this is by no means a settled debate. In "'Someone Called India': Urban Space and the Tribal Subject in Mahasweta Devi's 'Douloti the Bountiful',". Jay Rajiva demonstrates that the literary form taken on by Nabarun's mother Mahasweta Devi, a form that Bhattacharya argues cannot adequately attend to the full complexity of subaltern life, is, in fact, supple enough to expose the falsehood enmeshed in development narratives. In particular, Rajiva examines the relationship between the tribal and the cosmopolitan, two figures who we might assume have divergent rather than overlapping lives. Instead, Rajiva argues that the growing industrialization of rural spaces and the consequent inclusion in these spaces to more urban characteristics are deeply relevant to tribal communities, not in the least because the industrial exploitation that characterizes tribal urban experiences resonates through all spaces. In this way, the city itself outcasts other places. Through a thorough examination of Benedict Anderson's ideas of eternal as well as modern, calendrical time, Rajiva posits that both these senses of time are necessary in understanding the urban trauma of the tribal subject. Rajiva's focus is on Mahasweta Devi's story "Douloti the Bountiful," which he uses to argue both that urban spaces, through industrial exploitation, cripple the tribal's sense of self, and, relatedly, that the operation of capitalism in South Asian cities depends very much on the trauma of the (female) tribal subject.

Ending the first part is Amit Baishya's interview and analysis of Indian comic book artist Vishwajyoti Ghosh, "'Stuck at Pause': Representations of the Comatose City in *Delhi Calm*." Ghosh uses "middle of the road" protagonists in order to examine the significances of New Delhi during the Emergency, a period when then Prime Minister Indira Gandhi severely curtailed many civil rights and liberties by, among other things, suspending elections and restricting the press. In Baishya's analysis of *Delhi Calm*, Ghosh characterizes the entire city as suffering a profound but seemingly subtle psychological alienation. Baishya understands Ghosh's description of the consequences of the Emergency in Freudian terms—for instance, the daily lives of Delhiites was marked by the uncanny; whereas little variance from routine acts provided a sense of normalcy, the ubiquitous suspicion with which citizens treated their neighbors and casual acquaintances as potential spies for the government instead meant a lingering unfamiliarity. Through an analysis of the themes as well as the aesthetics and formal disruptions of the graphic novel, Baishya argues that, in *Delhi Calm*, the city is disassociated from itself.

Part II: The National, The Global, and the Diaspora contains chapters that analyze the role of South Asian cities in their nations, in more global contexts, and within diasporic currents. They ask, how do South Asian cities stand in relation to the nation? In what ways are these relationships characterized as synecdochal? How do they encourage or inhibit relationships with the diaspora? Conversely, how might South Asians in diaspora construct these cities within larger narratives of development, globalization, or as sources of authentic ethnic identities?

Ragini Srinivasan's "Unmoored: Passing, Slumming, and Return-Writing in New India" is a well-crafted essay that considers the self-representation of diasporic subjects in a body of creative nonfiction that Srinivasan identifies as "return-writing," a body that includes the works of Amit Chaudhuri, Rana Dasgupta, and Amitava Kumar. Acknowledging that diasporic returnees are often more financially and politically secure than other outcast urban populations, Srinivasan nonetheless argues that their abstraction from the everyday lived realities of the cities they return to is a significant form of urban outcasting. In negotiating changes in the face of speedy globalization and modernity, which come into sharp relief in the cities of New India and is a common theme for return-writing, the returnees reveal their own tenuous relationship to urban spaces. Srinivasan also argues that these writers often emphasize their relationships with tour guides and informants, usually from other urban outcast communities, and in combinations of passing (as authentically native to the respective cities) and slumming (and therefore legitimizing their knowledge of aspects of city life that remain elusive to middle- and upper-class urban dwellers), diasporic returnees explore ways to compensate for the economic, social, and cognitive dissonance they experience from their urban "homes."

Claire Chambers turns to the city of Lahore in her chapter titled, "*Lahore Lahore Hai*: Bapsi Sidhwa and Mohsin Hamid's City Fictions," in order to address the gap in South Asian studies surrounding analysis of that Pakistani city—even within Pakistan, Chambers argues, discussions of Lahore are second to the more dominant ones of Karachi. For Chambers, this needs particular attention because, she argues, Lahore functions most effectively as a synecdoche for Pakistan, and a close study of the issues that are commonly expressed in Lahore literature—such as the uneven development of Lahore—present a keen gateway into a better understanding of Pakistan as well. This is especially true in fiction such as Mohsin Hamid's *How to Get Filthy Rich in Rising Asia*, which critiques the paradoxical approach to, and consequences of, globalization.

Payel Chattopadhyay Mukherjee et al. contribute to this part's more global perspective on the South Asian city through a seemingly counterintuitive focus on the individual. In "Between Aspiration and Imagination: Exploring Native Cosmopolitanism in Adib Khan's *Spiral Road* and Mohammed Hanif's *Our Lady of Alice Bhatti*," Mukherjee et al. find DiBattista's notion of native cosmopolitanism as a particularly useful analytic in teasing out the relationship between roots and routes, which is to say between the fixedness of individuals in particular places and their emotional and ethical (if not physical) movements between spaces. Following Arjun Appadurai, they focus on cosmopolitanism as a worldview or an ethical perspective rather than a collective movement, and identify figures in literary representations of urban South Asia as particularly embodying this identity. In Khan and Hanif's fictions about the paradoxical opportunity that South Asian cities provide to be both spatially native and ethically cosmopolitan, Mukherjee et al. argue, protagonists that attempt this dual identity, which is to say try to be a native cosmopolitan, find that the process is not an easy one, and that the oppositional demands of fixity and a global, ethical openness often make them outsiders to both native and cosmopolitan communities.

Whereas previous chapters in Part II focus on the way diasporic, cosmopolitan, and other global subjects might (mis)fit with South Asian cities, Maswood Akhter's chapter "Portrayal of a Dystopic Dhaka: On Diasporic Reproductions of Bangladeshi Urbanity," thinks instead of how the diaspora actively constructs South Asian cities like Dhaka. We can understand Akhter's analysis as the mapping of the overlaps and distinctions in two forms of representation—the artistic, and the political. Akhter seems to ask, what are the limits of literary representation when the author is by definition removed from the daily complexities of his or her subject, as the diasporic Bangladeshi writer is necessarily abstracted from Dhaka? Given that diasporic Bangladeshi writers such as Monica Ali and Adib Khan write fiction with a thriving global circulation, how does this limited understanding of Dhaka develop into the dominant narrative about the city? On the other hand, Akhter also argues that because they experience a fragmented relationship with Dhaka, writers such as Ali and Khan reject the more common nostalgia for the imagined home city, opting instead for a dystopic view. Further, these writers use their dystopic imaginaries to move beyond enmeshed social codes and, instead, envision altogether new social possibilities for Dhaka.

Whereas chapters in other parts of the book, like Akhter's described above, explore the idea of South Asian urban centers as hyperreal cities, important for their imagined status versus their precise spatiality, the ones in Section Three: The Space of the Margins focus on the situatedness of outcasts in specific places. They investigate the particular structures of South Asian cities—public spaces, buildings, slums—and link the paradoxical experience of being marginalized in ostensibly plural environments to these specific markers of urbanity. Collectively, these chapters invoke urban theories writ large, examining the possibilities and limitations of using ideas centering, say, European cities, to their South Asian counterparts. In doing so they ask, how is the very skeleton of South Asian cities marked with and by exclusionary politics? How can spaces within cities provide possibilities of emancipation from oppressive practices?

In "Imag(in)ing the City: A Study of Ahmed Ali's *Twilight in Delhi*," Nishat Haider attempts to resituate Delhi Muslims in the city where they have been marginalized; her particular focus is of such marginalization since the Revolt of 1857 under British occupation. Through her analysis of Ahmed Ali's *Twilight in Delhi*, Haider attempts to correct the discursive outcasting of Muslims, and identifies Bakhtin's chronotope as the central concept that can help us examine both the complexity of Delhi Muslim's urban experiences as well as the variety of historical, social, and spatial contexts that determine Muslim urbanism. She reads in Ali's novel the characters' simultaneous local and metonymic purposes and places, in turn, her analysis within larger discussions of urban literary and philosophical inquiries, the particular significances of postcolonial cities, South Asian cities, and Muslim urban experiences. This extensive and thorough examination of the figurative role of Ali's novel and contained characterization both establishes how Muslims have been cast as peripheral to Delhi, and attempts to establish a more accurate history and depiction of them.

If Nishat Haider uses Bakhtin's chronotope as the central theoretical linchpin, Lauren Lacey and Joy Ochs, in their chapter, "Gendering Place and Possibility in Shashi Deshpande's *That Long Silence* and Kavery Nambisan's *A Town Like Ours*," similarly find in Foucault's idea of heterotopia a meaningful theoretical framework to help tease out how gender roles are negotiated alongside urban experiences in South Asian fiction. Concentrating on Deshpande's and Nambisan's urban novels, Lacey and Ochs explore how South Asian cities, characterized as they are as heterotopic spaces, both circumscribe and enable women's empowerment. In the case of both novels, Lacey and Ochs examine gendered acts that work through, rather than around or outside of, the limitations posed by the normative-ideological constraints of cities; similarly, the emancipatory potential of South Asian cities is also qualitatively different from any utopian urban narrative. For instance, Lacey and Ochs argue that it is in the description of the domestic sphere, generally assumed to be the locus of oppressive traditions, that the female protagonists find the ability to escape their respective shackles.

Continuing this work of reimagining the discourse on South Asian cities through the Foucauldian lens of heterotopia is Sanjukta Poddar's "Delhi at the Margins: Heterotopic Imagination, *Bricolage*, and Alternative Urbanity in *Trickster City*." However, whereas Lacey and Ochs had focused on the middle-class experiences of urban women, Poddar turns to a text written by working-class youth (originally in Hindi) in order to argue that such voices from the margins can truly change how cities are represented. The text at the center of her analysis, *Trickster City*, is a translation of a collection that, among other things, testifies to the experience of being made homeless because the authors' neighborhoods were threatened with, or actually experienced, demolition as part of the "beautification" process in preparation for getting New Delhi ready for the Commonwealth Games. Foucault's concept of heterotopia is particularly useful for Poddar because of the way it articulates the slums of New Delhi as exactly the counter city to the myth of the more "modern" and liberalized city that insists on the propertied bourgeoisie as being its true denizens. In her examination then, Poddar appears to answer the question: what happens when the subaltern speaks, specifically for him or herself? Her investigation of *Trickster City* answers that question with the argument that such a text would necessarily encompass heterogeneity embedded in its title, form, authorship, and content.

Part IV: Forms of Urban Outcasting turns to the style, aesthetics, and formal structures of South Asian literature that is invested in the examination of both what it means to be outcast and what it means to outcast. Although the chapters in this part may appear to debate the formal strategies in play and their respective appropriateness and effectiveness, they are nonetheless united in their observations that texts that can be characterized by their commitment to inclusive politics also explore plural and heterogeneous aesthetics.

In "Carl Muller's Palimpsestic Urban Elegy in *Colombo: A Novel*," Maryse Jayasuriya examines one of the most formally complicated and hard-to-pin-down novels written about the Sri Lankan city. Even the title of Muller's text, *Colombo: A Novel*, is deeply ironic and a deliberate paradox because it is neither singular ("a"), nor recognizable as a novel. Jayasuriya argues that in embracing nonfiction, reportage, and editorial comments in addition to fictional narratives, Muller's text explores and represents the very palimpsestic nature of Colombo in its form, paying special attention to the outcasts of the city: those caught in between governmental forces and various insurrectionary forces, as well as those marginalized due to poverty, social status, age, gender, or some combination of the above. Yet, although Jayasuriya sees much accomplished by Muller's complex form, she is equally attentive to the text's limitations. In her critique of *Colombo: A Novel*, she notes that Muller omits the specific politics of the insurrectionary forces, and how, in this decontextualized text, even the pluralist form cannot keep it from slipping from a deserved critique of the city's exclusionary practices into a less developed nostalgia for a colonial and precolonial past.

Kelly Minerva, in "The Fiction of Anosh Irani: the Magic of a Traumatized Community," argues that the author's narratives of Bombay expose the fissures in that city's citizenship. (Her use of Bombay versus Mumbai is deliberate.) Even though she largely places Irani's work within the tradition of Bombay novels that both turn to the city's most dispossessed as well as do so in varying experimental literary forms, Minerva nonetheless convincingly claims that Irani's fiction stands apart from these more familiar traditions because of its departure from their more traditional creative strategies; she does so largely by focusing on the narrative choices that make

Irani's distinction from other Bombay novels particularly clear. For instance, Minerva argues that Irani's use of magical realism is distinct from other famous examples, used for instance by Vikram Chandra or Salman Rushdie, that use this genre to capture the many paradoxes of Bombay. Instead, Minerva argues, Irani's magical realism as used in his novel *Cripple* couples magical realism with trauma fiction and is most particularly interested in using the former as the tool of the latter. Such strategies make it particularly clear that it is the physical trauma of dismembered bodies of beggars that underpins the city's character and economy.

If Minerva's analysis focuses on a new understanding of a South Asian city that is a traditional favorite in South Asian fiction, namely Bombay, Anna Guttman turns, in "New Capital? Representing Bangalore in Recent Crime Fiction," to Bangalore as the emerging urban focus of South Asian literature, undoubtedly to match its rise in international importance. Rather than argue that recent representations of Bangalore establish this importance to global capital, however, Guttman argues instead that recent crime and detective fiction set in Bangalore questions the logic of local and global capitalism. As Minerva points out, the genre of the crime novel as well as its cousin, detective fiction, focuses on marginalized and outcast characters in order to "access and narrate the truth of the city;" then, when these same genres turn their focus to Bangalore, they undercut and compromise neoliberal utopian representations of the center of consumer globalization.

Works Cited

Bayat, Asef. "From Dangerous Classes to Quiet Rebels: Politics of the Urban Subaltern in the Global South." *International Sociology* 15.3 (2000): 535–7. Print.

Bhabha, Homi K. *The Location of Culture*. London: Routledge, 1994. Print.

Chakrabarty, Dipesh. *Provincializing Europe: Postcolonial Thought and Historical Difference*. Princeton, NJ: Princeton UP, 2000. Print.

Chakraborty, Madhurima. "'The Only Thing I Know How to Do': An Interview with Mahasweta Devi." *Journal of Postcolonial Writing* 50.3 (2014): 282–90. Print.

Chatterjee, Partha. *The Nation and Its Fragments: Colonial and Postcolonial Histories*. Princeton, New Jersey: Princeton UP, 1993.

———. *The Politics of the Governed: Reflections on Popular Politics in Most of the World*. New York: Columbia UP, 2004. Print.

Chaturvedi, Vinayak, Ed. *Mapping Subaltern Studies and the Postcolonial*. London: Verso, 2000. Print.

Desai, Renu and Romola Sanya, eds. *Urbanizing Citizenship: Contested Spaces in Indian Cities*. New Delhi: Sage Publications, 2012. Print.

Express Web Desk. "My Birth is My Fatal Accident: Full Text of Dalit Student Rohith Vemula's Suicide Letter." *The Indian Express*. n.p. January 19, 2016. Web. January 20, 2016.

Foucault, Michel. "Of Other Spaces: Utopias and Heterotopias." *Diacritics* 16 (Spring 1986): 22–7. Print.

Lal, Vinay, comp. and Ed. *The Oxford Anthology of the Modern Indian City: Making and Unmaking the City. Politics, Culture, and Life Forms*. New Delhi: Oxford UP, 2013. Print.

Mohanty, Satya. *Literary Theory and the Claims of History: Postmodernism, Objectivity, Multicultural Politics*. Ithaca, NY: Cornell UP, 1997. Print.

Mukherjee, Meenakshi. *Realism and Reality: The Novel and Society in India*. New Delhi: Oxford UP, 1985. Print.

Nair, Janaki. *The Promise of the Metropolis*. New Delhi: Oxford UP, 2005. Print.

Nelson, Joan. "The Urban Poor: Disruption or Political Integration in Third World Cities?" *World Politics* 22.3 (1970): 393–414. Print.

Prakash, Gyan. "The Urban Turn." *Sarai Reader 02: The Cities of Everyday Life*. Eds. R. Vasudevan et al. New Delhi: Sarai SCDS and The Society for Old and New Media, 2002. 2–7. Print.

———. "Imaging the Modern City, Darkly." *The Spaces of the Modern City: Imaginaries, Politics, and Everyday Life*. Eds. Gyan Prakash and Kevin Kruse. Princeton, NJ: Princeton UP, 2008. 1–18. Print.

Robinson, Jennifer. "Global and World Cities: A View from off the Map." *International Journal of Urban and Regional Research* 26.3 (2002): 531–4. Print.

Roy, Ananya. "Slumdog Cities: Rethinking Subaltern Urbanism." *International Journal of Urban and Regional Research* 35.2 (2011): 223–38. Print.

Rushdie, Salman. *Midnight's Children*. London: Vintage, 1981. Print.

"Salman Rushdie Rubbishes Criticism by 'Modi Toadies,' Says He Is Against 'Thuggish Violence.'" *The Indian Express*. October 13, 2015. Web. January 21, 2016.

Soja, Edward. *Thirdspace: Journeys to Los Angeles and Other Real-and-Imagined Places*. Oxford: Blackwell, 1996. Print.

Spivak, Gayatri Chakravorty. "Can the Subaltern Speak?" *Marxism and the Interpretation of Culture*. Eds. Cary Nelson and Lawrence Grossberg. Urbana: U of Illinois P, 1988. 271–313. Print.

Part I

Urban Outcasts, Urban Subalterns

1   Recasting the Outcast

Hyderabad and Hyderabadi Subjectivities in Two Literary Texts

Nazia Akhtar

Introduction: Necessary Orientations[1]

For many decades now, Anita Desai's English novel *Clear Light of Day* (1980) has been a canonical text that has offered possibilities for discussions about Hyderabadi Muslims and urban citizenship and belonging in the long shadow of Partition. However, while the novel helps to bring within the same frame Hyderabad, Partition, and the politics of the city, it also exemplifies classic narratives of lavish Hyderabadi Muslim lifestyles by evoking static Orientalist stereotypes of decadence and excess in its representation of Hyderabadi Muslims. Arguably, it was only in the early 2000s that literary texts in English with more complex Hyderabadi urban subjectivities began to appear. Some of the novels that fictionally engage with the issue of urban outcasts in the context of Hyderabad include Samina Ali's *Madras on Rainy Days* (2004), Huma R. Kidwai's *The Hussaini Alam House* (2012), and Ian Bedford's *The Last Candles of the Night* (2014). Another very important development in this regard has been the revision and reprinting of Zeenuth Futehally's 1951 novel *Zohra* in 2004.

In this chapter, I will demonstrate how two of these novels, Bedford's *The Last Candles of the Night* and Futehally's *Zohra*, establish of what and whom "the city" consists, whom it includes or excludes, whom it humors or harbors, and whom it legitimizes or rejects. In other words, the texts outline the scope of the city's historical, sociocultural, geographical, political, and imaginative landscapes and boundaries. In doing so, they also interrogate standard, official, mainstream Indian notions about Hyderabad in the troubled last years of the Asaf Jahi dynasty, explicitly and implicitly replacing these notions with a problematized understanding of the politics, society, cultures, and people of Hyderabad. As I argue in this chapter, while these texts are certainly complicit in perpetuating the distorted depiction or invisibility of certain groups, such as the urban working classes, both are distinguished by an important achievement: they restore to memory Hyderabadi subject positions that are neglected or forgotten in canonical, hegemonic narratives of not only the princely state of Hyderabad but also the city after which the state was named.

Furthermore, I show how the subsequent fictional restoration after this hegemonic forgetting is achieved in two ways: first, at the level of metaphor and, second, at a more literal level. I demonstrate how Hyderabad state/city itself and Hyderabadiness as a concept, which were demonized after the turbulent 1940s, are vindicated in the literary texts through a more inclusive and historically located depiction of Hyderabad city and its citizens. And in the literal sense, the texts ensure that urban subject positions which are/ were not considered legitimate are restored to the city, offering a fictional counterpoint to an exclusionary historiography. By recasting these urban outcasts—both Hyderabad city itself and different groups and communities as well—in creative writing, the authors of both texts implicitly and explicitly create a platform for readers to question the hegemonic notions of what it is to be Hyderabadi and who is entitled to this citizenship.

In fact, Hyderabad has had a tense history of urban mobility and citizenship, much of which goes back to the politics of Partition. Contrary to earlier notions of southern India not being affected by Partition turmoil, increasingly vocal voices today emphasize how Hyderabad—the largest and wealthiest princely state in India—was in fact completely transformed as a result of Partition-related politics. The players and ideologies that definitively shaped Hyderabadi politics during the 1940s are well known in Hyderabad today: the minority ruling class of feudal and aristocratic Muslims and Hindus, led by the seventh Nizam of Hyderabad, Mir Osman Ali Khan (1886–1967) of the Asaf Jahi dynasty (1720–1948); the peasants, workers, and progressive groups who participated in the Telangana Armed Struggle (1946–1951), an uprising against the feudal, political, and cultural hegemony of the ruling class in Hyderabad; Razakars, a Muslim paramilitary offshoot of the Majlis-e-Ittehad-ul-Muslimeen who terrorized the populace in general and non-Muslims in particular; and the Hyderabad State Congress (HSC), which claimed to represent and align the democratic aspirations of Hyderabadis alongside those of people in British India.

Citing the inequalities of communal representation, the intensifying peasant struggle, and the absence of administrative checks and measures against the Razakars, the Indian National Congress leadership had consistently demanded that the Nizam must unconditionally accede to India. After many difficult negotiations between the two parties, Indo-Hyderabad relations had deteriorated to such an extent that India invaded Hyderabad on September 13, 1948, ignoring the fact that Hyderabad had approached the United Nations Security Council with an urgent appeal to put the matter on its agenda for September 15. Ill-equipped to handle a four-pronged military invasion, Hyderabad surrendered in less than five days. The subsequent crackdowns by the Indian army and police as well as local groups against peasants, workers, and progressive individuals, many of whom were Muslims and/or had participated in the Telangana Armed Struggle (Sunderlal Committee 373; Smith 20–1; Sundarayya 9), are well known in Hyderabad but not elsewhere in the subcontinent. But the discussions of these realities about the situation in Hyderabad during and after the 1940s have arguably increased since the intensification and subsequent realization of the

Telangana statehood movement, which created a sense of "openness" and space for conversations on communalism, class/caste, and regional politics. And as I have mentioned above, a direct consequence as well as contributing factor of/for these new/renewed conversations has been the fresh approach that creative writing and reading communities now show in discussions of Hyderabad and questions of citizenship and belonging.

Given the history I have outlined above, a literary analysis of the politics of the city with reference to Hyderabad in the context of Partition needs to address the differentness of Hyderabad and other princely states from British Indian territories. The princely states were not administered directly by the British and were, instead, supported by their own indigenous or hybrid mechanisms of power and patronage; this fact entails that literary texts that revisit this history too have to be approached somewhat differently than the usual course taken by studies of urban or cosmopolitan landscapes and questions of citizenship, boundaries, and belongings.[2] As historian Karen Leonard has consistently pointed out in the course of a life-time of work on Hyderabad, the culture, society, politics, and history of the erstwhile princely states must be examined from a framework that is separate from that of British colonialism and standard notions of postcolonialism and postcoloniality.[3] Leonard argues that questions and debates about colonialism and postcolonialism do not answer nor address the specific concerns and issues connected to the princely states. In the process, I argue, they also render invisible the historical processes by which urban belongings and affiliations come to be confirmed and legitimized in princely states such as Hyderabad. Keeping this in mind, my situated interpretive approach in this chapter to the two literary texts that depict life in early and mid-twentieth-century Hyderabad takes into account the special circumstances of the princely states. In the process, I privilege historically situated "contrapuntal" (Said 66) readings of literary texts that not only swim against the current of official, mainstream determinations of urban citizenship but also the colonial–postcolonial narrative thrust of much of our contemporary scholarship about the city.

Hyderabad Writes Back/Talks Down: Elite and Subaltern Subjects in Zeenuth Futehally's *Zohra*

Although *Zohra* was published amid some critical recognition in 1951,[4] the only focused, serious academic attention it has received has come in the form of Ambreen Hai's essay "Adultery Behind Purdah and the Politics of Indian Muslim Nationalism in Zeenuth Futehally's *Zohra*" (2013). Given the fact that hers is currently the only in-depth study of the novel, it is vital to evaluate the premises on which Hai situates her understanding and interpretation of the depiction of citizenship, culture, and identity in *Zohra*. For example, she asks important questions about the context in which *Zohra* was published and why Futehally chooses not to directly address Partition, the position of Muslim minorities, and the integration of Hyderabad into the Indian union.

> "[H]ow indeed," she asks, "does *Zohra* desire to remember and memorialize Hyderabadi culture and history prior to those years, to offer a different (forgotten) narrative of the 1920s and 1930s and suggest an alternative, more complex reading of at least some of its Muslim intellectuals and their families?" (323)

Hai argues that the poignant absences in Futehally's text are made meaningful by the text's foregrounding of an alternative narrative of Indian Muslim nationalism, one that "insists on the right to belonging of such Muslims who fought against the British for a secular India" (324). However, I contend that, in spite of her fine analysis, Hai's essay does not address how Futehally's *Zohra* responds to the particularities of Hyderabad as both a princely city as well as a princely state in British India.

As I have already explained, Leonard cautions scholars against using a generalized, pan-Indian analytical framework to address questions about princely states, such as Hyderabad, because these states were definitively shaped by political and social configurations that were often quite different from the factors that defined urban demographics in other parts of the subcontinent. This is precisely the problem with Hai's otherwise astute and insightful analysis of *Zohra*. She conflates Indian Muslims and Hyderabadi Muslims as she discusses Futehally's representation of "the progressive potential of Indian Muslims" and "a minority community's right to belong to the nation" (319). Such instances in her analysis reveal a critical lack of informed and contextualized understanding of the discourses surrounding Hyderabad and Hyderabadiness from the contrapuntal perspectives of Hyderabadis and scholars of Hyderabad. Indeed, Hai's assertion that "the novel also seeks retrospectively to carve a different historical space for Indian Muslims who chose to stay in India as citizens of that nation, claiming belonging *based less on heritage* than on self-sacrifice and involvement in the independence struggle as well as a history of harmonious coexistence" (318, emphasis mine) risks seriously undermining a long and illustrious heritage of indigenous Hyderabadi progressive, socialist, communist, and yes, nationalist politics. Moreover, Hai's statement not only undermines the democratic struggles of Hyderabadis of all walks of life against princely rule, but also in fact, undermines the diverse socio-political engagements and cultural syncretism that were the heritage of the small, urban Hyderabadi ruling elite.

Addressing the specific and distinct context of Hyderabad is also something that Futehally distinguishes as the larger aim and broader focus of *Zohra*, which is, as she writes in the Preface, a record of "that little world of ours, in Hyderabad … for owing to the passage of time it was fast disappearing" (262). Nevertheless, having marked the sense of distinctiveness and value that Hyderabad holds for the author, this statement seems rather unremarkable because, at first glance, *Zohra* appears to be little more than a mid-twentieth-century reformist novel that questions the institution of *purdah*, emphasizing higher education and greater agency for young *purdahnashin* women, and chronicles the disappearing world of the sophisticated, city-based elite of Hyderabad. However, when we read *Zohra* more carefully and, above all, bear in mind the temporal as well as political climate in which it was written and its plot is implicitly embedded, a more complex text begins to emerge that has considerable significance for the way we approach Hyderabad's past today.[5] As I will show in this section, two aspects of the novel have particular bearing on our present-day reading of this text. These aspects are: the representation of elite Hyderabadis, which goes against the grain of official, mainstream Indian conflations of "Hyderabadi" with "Muslim" and, ultimately, "Razakar"; and the treatment of subaltern characters, which reveals insights about the practice of class among elite Hyderabadis by establishing whose perspectives know and narrate the city and the groups who live in it.

First published in 1951, Futehally's novel *Zohra* depicts the life of the eponymous young protagonist from an aristocratic Hyderabadi family. Zohra enjoys her ongoing high-school education in languages and fine arts, but soon finds herself reluctantly agreeing to an arranged marriage to a distinguished, British-trained Hyderabadi physicist. Bashir, her brusque and matter-of-fact husband, does not quite understand nor relate to Zohra, who has an artistic and romantic sensibility. Zohra has three children, whom she adores. However, married to a man whom she respects but cannot love, she falls in love with her brother-in-law Hamid, who reciprocates her feelings. Hamid, a nationalist, leaves Hyderabad to join the Gandhian freedom struggle, motivated both by his political leanings as well as the futility of his love for his sister-in-law. Zohra, who as a young girl had toyed with the idea of participating in the Gandhian struggle, wishes in vain that she could accompany Hamid as he courts arrest during the civil disobedience movement. The sensitive Zohra alternately pines for Hamid and is wracked by guilt for her love. Unable to find a solution to her problems, Zohra falls ill, her health steadily worsens, and she dies.

The political climate to which, I argue, *Zohra* implicitly responds, was dominated by hyperbolic pronouncements about the Razakars, the paramilitary group that became influential in Hyderabad state from 1946 to 1948. The Razakars vandalized many localities in Hyderabad city as well as parts of the countryside, destroying or seizing property, raping girls and women, and cracking down on anyone—Hindu, Muslim, communist, nationalist—who offered any resistance or gestures of dissent against what they saw as "Muslim rule" in the Deccan. Indeed, the Indian government's *White Paper on Hyderabad* (1948) estimated that by 1948 there were seventy thousand armed, well-equipped, and well-funded Razakars (31–2). However, after the invasion of Hyderabad, British newspapers reported from New Delhi that there was "a strong suspicion that the magnitude of [the Razakars'] aggressive acts [before the invasion] ha[d] been grossly exaggerated in order to provide some kind of excuse for an Indian invasion" (*Morning Advertiser*). Indeed, *The Times* reported that "not more than 5 percent of their total number (which was also wildly exaggerated) were armed with firearms, mostly old muzzle-loaders, while the remaining 95 per cent carried staves and spears." Furthermore, the fact that the number of casualties was exponentially larger on the Hyderabadi side placed under scrutiny the rhetorical thrust of Indian press and radio pronouncements about "strong opposition" and "stern resistance" with regard to Hyderabad's military response (qtd. in *The Times*). Other sources, such as Osmanabad collector Mohammed Hyder's nuanced account *October Coup: A Memoir of the Struggle for Hyderabad* (2012), also corroborate the revelations from journalists, which indicate that India's step to invade Hyderabad was based on an exaggeration of the capabilities of the Razakars.[6]

But the damage was done. Not only was the Nizam held responsible in the court of Indian public opinion for the actions of the Razakars, but so were most Hyderabadis who were Muslims and/or communists, as the many instances of individual, collective, and systemic discrimination show.[7] Besides completely undermining and misrepresenting the history of the armed struggle, which at its height involved three million people in three thousand villages, such narratives constantly erase the prolonged resistance by students, workers, and other urban groups against the Nizam's government, the arms of the state, as well as the Razakars. This erasure of specific instances and the particular goals of urban protest also extends to the political mobilization generated by different but connected trade, students', and women's organizations. It was also in cities such as Hyderabad, Secunderabad, Warangal, Aurangabad, Nanded, and Gulbarga that the most influential propaganda was released, and practical and ideological mechanisms, such as the formation of unions and execution of strikes, were created (Hyder 145–6; Gour 7). Contemporary communist leader P. Sundarayya concedes that the cadres in Hyderabad, Warangal, and the mining areas were very important because they helped organize underground offices, maintain communication with neighboring regions, and supply essential items and arms and ammunition to guerrilla squads (300, 136). This activity was very dangerous, and underground centers were blown up repeatedly, and communist cadres were arrested, tortured, and shot (136–7). Such narratives of engagement, struggle, and sacrifice from Hyderabadis belonging to different cross-sections of society and situated in different urban locations either have been co-opted in homogenizing Indian nationalist narratives or entirely demonized and/or elided. That both subaltern and elite Hyderabadis participated in significant ways in these pro-democracy, anti-Razakar struggles was completely forgotten, a fact that has relevance for the way I read Futehally's *Zohra* as a fictional text that disrupts this forgetful national memory with its plural, contesting voices.

In fact, it is in this context that *Zohra* makes its biggest contribution: through its representation of Zohra, Bashir, and Hamid, it marks a literary attempt to reinstate a multitude of historical Hyderabadi urban subject positions which does not coincide with the dangerous, rabidly communal Razakars. It represents the Hyderabadi urban aristocracy in a much more complex and multifaceted manner than the stereotypes and caricatures put forth by media and government sources in the mid-twentieth century, ensuring that the complicated logic and the many contradictions of those lives are effectively rendered for Anglophone readers both internationally as well as in India. The significance of this idea is underscored when we remind ourselves that *Zohra* was originally published in 1951, at a time when Hyderabadi Muslims of many class backgrounds were still struggling to survive in a post-1948 world that had overlooked—with disastrous consequences—the diversity of the category "Hyderabadi" and conflated it with "Muslim," which in turn became synonymous with "Razakars" (Sunderlal Committee 374; Ali 43).

Futehally's restoration of complex Hyderabadi urban subjectivities emerges most clearly in her portrayal of Zohra and her brother-in-law Hamid as nationalists and progressives ideologically invested in the Gandhian independence struggle. Indeed, the clash between Bashir and Hamid on the question of Gandhian ideas of freedom and progress and western European notions about the same can be read as a literary depiction of the different ideological currents sweeping Hyderabad during the 1930s. Whereas Hamid has revolutionary and socialist leanings that he invests in the Gandhian struggle and calls for the subsequent integration of Hyderabad into India, Bashir initially represents the highly privileged, somewhat dry, westernized armchair intellectual whose ideas of progress are solidly and unrelentingly rooted in modern ideas of the scientific. Later, he goes on to profess a religious sense of affiliation as he naïvely claims that, unlike Hinduism, Islam has an egalitarian social order in which there is no caste system and everybody is equal (202–3, 124). While Hamid waxes eloquent about the "noble and friendly" Romanian and Hungarian peasants, whose handicrafts have "a beauty of their own, a certain dignity, a distinction" (125), Bashir rejects Gandhi's methods and puts his faith in the constitutional process, expressing his conviction that "swaraj will come gradually" (124). Indeed, in an almost caricatured manner, Bashir and Hamid act as foils for one another, as their views are situated in binary opposition, and Futehally devotes equal space to both.

The ideological clash between Bashir and Hamid comes to a head when both are older and Bashir's thought has undergone some change, so that he now affiliates himself with Muslims who were against "Hindu rule" in the subcontinent. In fact, Zohra dismisses Bashir's religiosity and points out that "[i]t's only after politics brought religion to the fore that you even started thinking of yourself in terms of Islam" (230). But although he displays his reductive stereotypical perceptions of both Muslims ("conquerors") and Hindus ("yogis"), Bashir also points out genuine concerns and anxieties of Muslims that arguably contributed to the demand to partition the subcontinent. He asks: "How can we [Muslims and Hindus] come closer to each other when they [Hindus] won't even eat with us?" (205) Hamid in turn had pointed out earlier:

> Muslims can have their majority provinces with safeguards at the Centre. The British Raj can't last indefinitely. World opinion is already against them. And on the same basis, Hyderabadi Muslims have no right to rule the Hindu majority. We must all be prepared for changes. (204)

This intense conversation marks a fictional enactment of the fraught and multi-dimensional debates that were current in Hyderabad city during Partition. In doing so, it creates a window not only into the customs of the world that Futehally was so keen to preserve for posterity, but also the nuanced political investments of its urban elites in contemporary politics in both princely Hyderabad as well as British India.

Fighting back against Bashir's caustic interventions about his "impractical ideas" (137), Hamid passionately proclaims: "I love Hyderabad and value much of its old-time charm. But our ancient feudal order, however benevolent it might be in some ways, must change if we are to value human dignity more" (137). In expressing his views thus, the character of Hamid represents the young generation of Hyderabad city's progressive and radical intellectuals, who played an important role in the democratic struggles in the state. This view is further highlighted in all its internal contradictions and complications when Hamid tells Zohra: "During the past months, I have been trying to resolve where my duty as an Indian lies, whether even though I am a Hyderabadi, I should not go and join the Satyagraha movement" (207).

Furthermore, Hamid is engaged in writing a romantic novel, "an effort to rouse Muslim nationalism against communalism" (189). Although the story is a transparent reference to the tragedy of Hamid and Zohra's love, the plot is also an implicit literary gesture to the future rise of the Majlis and the Razakars in the 1940s. Additionally, in response to his mother's severe disapproval of his unseemly (because un-aristocratic) wish to open a bookshop selling progressive literature, Hamid exclaims in what historically turns out for Hyderabad to be a positively prophetic pronouncement: "[O]ur sort of life cannot go on for ever, and the sooner we realize it the better!" (138) In turn, frustrated by Hamid's insistence to follow Gandhi's satyagraha and wear coarse *khaddar*, Masuma Begum asks him: "What have we in Hyderabad got to do with it?" (179). What Futehally achieves with this depiction of the tension between voices that attempt to question as well as reinforce the existing status quo in Hyderabad is that she fictionally replaces the Razakar stereotype that was so assiduously created by Indian state apparatuses and journalistic sources with a more complex narrative, thereby generating the platform on which questions of democracy, freedom, and egalitarianism can be debated.[8]

Another significant feature of *Zohra* is that it offers creative possibilities to discuss how class operated in mid-twentieth-century urban Hyderabadi society. Such possibilities can be seen not only in the novel itself, but also in the aforementioned preface, in which Futehally uses "Hyderabad" to refer interchangeably to the city as well as the state. In this way, she subsumes the interests and perspectives of urban almost exclusively elite Hyderabadis, whose world views she depicts in her novel, with the concerns of *all* Hyderabadis. The city has been (and remains) a synonym or metonym for writers as well as scholars who have worked on Hyderabad since the early twentieth century because, before the 1956 trifurcation of the princely state, "Hyderabad" referred both to the state as well as its capital city. To a great extent, mainstream, official, and scholarly Hyderabadi as well as non-Hyderabadi sources see the state as interchangeable with the city. This is a very problematic slippage that does not recognize and is, in fact, one of the reasons for the vastly disproportionate amount of official attention bestowed on Hyderabad city vis-à-vis other urban or rural parts of whatever state it has belonged to.[9]

And not only does the preface suggest it, the novel itself only confirms these exclusionary politics of representing Hyderabad. While there are strikingly progressive and critically nuanced depictions of class interactions, overall, the general representation of class in the novel predictably establishes not so much who is a part of the capital city, but whose perspective on certain groups forms the knowledge of and about the city. On one hand, the novel contains the dominating working-class character Unnie, who has been nurse not only to Zubaida Begum but also to her children and grandchildren, and often portrays the intricacies of class relations between "masters" and "servants" in a very careful and critical way. A case in point is the observation that during Ramzan, "[i]n the democratic fashion that a few Muslim homes still preserved, Unnie and the other women-servants and maids joined them [Zohra's family] in the repast" (33). Other similarly inclusive gatherings in the novel include wedding parties (20), where maids sing wedding songs and mingle "with mistresses freely joining in the fun" (42). Another example of a valuable class-related observation happens when Zohra discovers that, in a marked contrast from her natal home, none of the maids sat with their mistresses for meals in her husband's family (65). The resentment of Unnie, who accompanies Zohra to her husband's home, is registered in the text, as she tells Zohra, "In your mother's home, unlike here, servants are treated as human beings" (66). The fact that the novel contains peripheral yet revelatory insights about the practice of class among elite Hyderabadis makes it truly a remarkable text of its time.

On the other hand, in spite of highlighting enlightened Hyderabadi traditions in connection with class, the novel generally replicates feudal and upper-class notions of the working classes, creating its own structure of visibility and invisibility with reference to the urban aristocracy. For instance, although every major woman character and matriarch in the novel has a detailed personal history, Unnie has no independent history of her own.[10] In this regard, the narrator provides us with another telling insight when she tells us, "If the *unnie* had a name, it had long since been forgotten. She ... held a very special position of trust and privilege in the household and was affectionately known by the entire family simply as Unnie" (1). Thus, the absence of Unnie's personal history is glossed over by emphasizing how the affection from the family more than makes up for it.

As a gendered subaltern character, Unnie's subjectivity is relational in its recovery/reconstruction and never autonomous because it is recovered (conditionally, partially, problematically) by an elite gaze through many refractions (O'Hanlon 87). This is also why her history is inseparable from that of the family; readers never learn anything about her as an individual in her own right, and we only have the exaggerated words and hysterical exclamations that Futehally assigns to her from which to construct her as a person. In fact, the uncritical construction of Unnie's and the other maids' speech consists of inevitably adoring and self-abasing phrases and becomes a celebration of the condescension of the nobility towards other people. This kind of representation can be sharply observed in Unnie's slavish response to Zohra's concern for her health by remarking that "you think of nothing but us poor folk; we, who are more worthless than your shoes" (65). This hyperbolic nature of working-class women's speech in the novel confirms Kamala Visweswaran's notion that subaltern agency is dependent and does not have "originary autonomy: it is the underside of the subject which seeks to contain it" (125). In this way, the gendered subaltern character exists largely as an endorsement or affirmation of the status quo which favors and legitimizes the elite and its exclusive/exclusionary lifestyle. Unnie becomes a foil for the upper-class nobility of Zubaida Begum and her daughters, and although her authority and power in the family are constantly being constructed by the narrator and Zubaida Begum and also dismantled by the younger characters, such as Zohra and the maids, her stereotypical speech is meant to reinforce the legitimacy and desired continuity of the feudal aristocratic lifestyle of the ruling class of Hyderabad, which was based out of the capital city.

However, in its occasional but significant distortions of working-class perspectives on urban social life in Asaf Jahi Hyderabad, *Zohra* is not unique and only points to a much wider trend of representative politics in literary depictions and academic discourses. Like many literary texts from Hyderabad and India and across the world, it is written by and for the elite.

It might be useful here to recall Visweswaran's formulations about the twin nature of elite projects that contribute towards retrieving a subaltern voice. Visweswaran writes:

> If we agree that the point of retrieval marks the subaltern's silencing in history, and that it is at the point of erasure where the emergence of the subaltern is possible, then this analysis transits the lines of enfranchisement and disenfranchisement, oscillating between nationalist agency and subaltern agency. (125)

Put differently, the subaltern voice is heard even as it is being erased through the mediation of the elite voice that writes it into the text. Visweswaran's words offer us an insight into the possibilities of *Zohra* in terms of its partial retrieval (albeit problematic and relational) of gendered subaltern voices. Furthermore, Rosalind O'Hanlon's assertion that the subaltern is "no less 'real' for our having said that it does not contain its own origins within itself" (87) helps us to situate *Zohra* as a text that retrieves the subaltern voice even as it seeks to or simply cannot avoid erasing it. Thus, the peripheral insights into class interactions, as well as the portrayals of Unnie and the other maids, contribute in some measure to locate the working-class outcast in Hyderabad, even as the power to know and narrate the city remain with her masters, whose interests are ultimately better served by Futehally's text through the nuancing and complication the author reserves for their voices.

Hyderabad through Australian Eyes: The Outsider–Insider in *The Last Candles of the Night*

Like Futehally's *Zohra*, which undermines hegemonic narratives by fiction-ally restoring complicated elite Hyderabadi subject positions, Australian writer Ian Bedford's novel *The Last Candles of the Night* (2014) too dis-rupts standard narratives of the urban political landscape of Hyderabad during Partition. Bedford achieves this end by using the literary device of the outsider–insider protagonist. The white Australian headmaster is not quite an urban outcast in Hyderabad city/state, but is certainly not an insider either. As I show in this section, his liminal positionality means that the outsider–insider protagonist is perfectly poised to ask difficult or contro-versial questions. Such questions become fictional prompts that enable the revisiting and re-examination of the urban landscape of 1940s Hyderabad, effectively allowing difficult socio-political and historical scenarios and real-ities to be debated meaningfully.

The plot unfolds through flashback, and we are shown how twenty-three-year-old Philip comes to Hyderabad in the 1940s as part of the Nizam's attempts to reform key problem areas in the state: education, health, and the welfare of marginalized communities. While he works in Warangal, Philip befriends Ragini, an anti-Nizam activist with communist sympathies, and Anand, a Hyderabad State Congress worker who believes that the Indian Army will bring freedom to the Hyderabadi people. Anand and Ragini are clearly fascinated with each other, and a jealous Philip resents Ragini's pref-erence for their mutual friend. When the narration returns to the present, we see that Philip and Ragini, who is now known as Jenny, have been married for more than fifty years and are now estranged. They look back at the events that took place in 1940s Hyderabad from the context of multicultural Sydney in 2001. Jenny/Ragini hesitates to open her house and heart to a man who married her, brought her to Sydney, and left her to return to India, where he worked as a teacher for more than five decades. Philip returns to Australia only because he has been forced to retire. It is their re-acquaintance and mutual struggle to acknowledge as well as come to terms with what may have happened to Anand that forms the central preoccupation of the plot.

What is significant about Philip's outsider–insider position in the novel is that it not only applies to him in Hyderabad, but also to his life in

Sydney, where he feels out of place, out of touch, and unwanted by his family. However, his recollection of events in 1940s Hyderabad acquires legitimacy in Sydney, providing insights into political agitation and a useful point of departure for his young and impressionable grandson, Jim. The novel connects Philip's exposure to politics in Hyderabad state to Jim's own activities, which are set during the 2001 protests against the Australian government's refusal of entry to a Norwegian freighter carrying more than four hundred Hazara refugees from Afghanistan. Ironically, Philip becomes a source of inspiration and authority on 1940s Hyderabad for Jim, and it is his own urge to recall as a way of gaining emotional access to Jenny/Ragini and Jim's insistence on wanting to know what happened that compels Philip to remember what he saw from the sidelines in Hyderabad.

Although Philip works for the Nizam's government in the 1940s, his subject position is liminal on account of his nationality and race, and by extension, the assumption that he is not invested in the various politics around him. This ensures that he constitutes a critical counterpoint in the text to the politics of his friends, especially Anand's nationalism. Philip asks uncomfortable questions, such as whether anyone has actually seen the infamous Cotton brothers of Australian origin, who were sensationally reported to have smuggled arms and ammunition into Hyderabad during the blockade imposed by India. "No-one has seen them. Have you seen them?" he interrogates Anand (34). Naïve and often unquestioning, Anand also speaks at length with Philip about India as the panacea for all of Hyderabad's ills, and how the Indian Army will liberate "the people." Philip wonders what Anand means by "the people" and probes the depths of his reverence for peasants, searching for meaning beyond the superficial and uncritical idealism of his socially privileged friend (35). Such interruptions by Philip are vital because they unsettle and disrupt the strident Indian nationalism that Anand espouses. They critically examine the many premises and promises nationalist politics entails and which Anand wholeheartedly accepts and believes in. Indeed, Philip's fictional interventions acquire even greater significance when we remember that the nationalist narrative of the liberation of Hyderabad by the Indian Army has hegemonic status today in Indian historiography and public memory.

At various junctures in the text, Philip's outsider status is made physically and publicly apparent when the body politic that is Hyderabad city vividly and physically denotes or "wears" its various political currents and meaningful social divisions. In the process, Philip's apartness from it all is emphasized. For example, because Philip is conscious of his status as both a foreigner and an office-bearer of the Nizam's government, he had

> resolved not to set foot in the Old City, south of the bridges. He would do so in his own good time: when he was invited. For Philip was not a tourist. He was an office holder in the Nizam's administration. (38)

He is aware, thus, of how ongoing politics and governance plays itself out on the cartography of the city. On the same occasion, Philip encounters what he thinks is a gathering of Razakars: "Dispersed voices blended into one rhythmic shout of a few syllables, repeated over and over" (39). Later, as the procession actually comes into sight, Philip is confused and struggles to understand whether this is actually a Congress rally or a trade-union procession. He tries to separate the different strands of ongoing political and social movements that are taking place in Hyderabad at the time. In its most revealing moment, the text informs us in a long passage that is worth quoting at length:

> [N]othing, in Hyderabad, was intelligible in the usual sense. Hyderabad was a folly. It was, of course, destined for ruin. This did not make it more intelligible. All swept away now. How could it count, to anyone, if he were to recover those meanings, which no longer "meant"? What was the purpose of all those undisputed errands and unblinking procedures, the bazaars, the obscure crafts, the bewildering pageantry of holidays that arrived out of nowhere, the Abyssinian guard, the troupes of musicians in livery, the female armed warriors whom he had watched, in all their regalia but never on parade, lounging like ordinary shoppers on the stone benches of the Moazzam Jahi vegetable market? Why was a quarter of the population in triumphal dress? Was this the deceit of memory? ... History had pronounced its verdict on the Nizam. Wasted effort. An unjust social order. That order had vanished, like water-vapour, and nobody in India regretted it for one moment. (40)

To an older Philip trying to isolate and place different memories and impressions half a century later, the city seems to have been an absurd and fleeting façade towards the last years of the Asaf Jahi dynasty, where the established players publicly and spectacularly played their empty roles, which signified nothing and led to nothing. This staged political illusion, as it were, is bracingly experienced, recognized, and remembered in its full magnitude by Philip the outsider–insider, young as well as old. What is also ironic about this recognition is that Philip is himself part of the façade as an unbelievably young headmaster brought in at the last minute to introduce reform. And the transformation of the façade through violence and regime change, only to be replaced after 1948 by another false exterior of equality and liberty, is depicted as quietly devastating to Philip as the plot unfolds.

Another example of the difficult questions Philip is able to ask as the outsider–insider through metaphors of the city's layout is about the invasion of Hyderabad by India, which as 1948 wore on, became imminent. Describing the hostel where both Anand and another student called Parvaiz stay, Philip thinks to himself:

> The place was ideal, safe and high – though the day would come when many would climb so high. By then Anand would be far away, enlisting

on a war front, bugling in the invading Army. But what would it mean for Parvaiz, for a blind Muslim student, on the day they climbed high, searching, whoever "they" were, for whoever they sought? All might depend on who got to him first. (98)

To Philip, then, the battle for the city as well as citizenship will be written on the stairwells and rooftops of places of symbolic as well as real political significance, such as the Osmania University hostels where Parvaiz and Anand live. Osmania University has always been historically and symbolically significant as a launch pad for student agitations. Additionally, it also represented the institutionalized initiative of the Nizam as well as Muslim intellectuals from all over the subcontinent towards constructing a proud, secular indigenous education through the medium of a robust, fortified Urdu language resource.[11] In light of these facts, Philip's thoughts convey that people who gain control of these critical locations and institutions in the days to come will be the ones who will exercise the right to keep in and cast out whomever and whatever they deem fit. Ultimately, his reflections about what an Indian invasion might mean for Parvaiz suggest that it is the weak and the Muslim that might find itself outside the ramparts as the city changes hands.

Bedford's novel is replete with such literary devices as the architectural metaphor of the university and its hostels, so that an alternative reading emerges that resists or does away with the mainstream, official stereotyping or homogenization of 1940s Hyderabad. The most iconic and definitive example occurs when Anand asks Philip to listen to the sounds around the Charminar area on a hot afternoon. The sounds of the hammering of edible silver into paper-thin consistency by the famous *warq* makers of the Charminar area become a metaphor for the state in which Hyderabad finds itself in 1947:

> There was a rhythm. Furtive, bottomless, unmistakable. People were chipping away in the little dark booths where life went on all day ... Quite against his will, Philip was flummoxed by an oddness, an incompleteness in the rhythm – as if some mobile object, a kind of vehicle, was trying to run on its own wheels but could not get it right. That unstable object, which lived wholly in the realm of sound, was striving to gather its parts around it to proceed in an orderly direction. (85)

It is as if Hyderabad state's struggle to remain independent and, therefore, reform problematic areas of governance, representation, and administration is written into the very living architecture of Hyderabad city, its citizens, and its industry. And it is Philip, the outsider–insider, who later makes his memory of Hyderabad a medium through which the present can glimpse and grapple with some of the confusions of this past. In fact, in spite of his self-effacing nature and perhaps because of the privilege his race gives him in Hyderabad, Philip is able to successfully (albeit slightly clumsily) negotiate his way through different Hyderabadi circles, through Osmania University hostels where both Muslims and Hindus stay; through small villages, towns, and forests adopted and dominated by communists; and through palaces where the high politics of reform, communalism, Deccani nationalism, and *purdah* culture play out. In doing so, Philip becomes, for both Jim as well as the reader, a vehicle to carry questions from the present to the past; his outsider–insider status becomes a literary strategy that enables the recovery of a fraught and multi-dimensional understanding of Hyderabad and its inhabitants.

Conclusion

Although the sense of belonging and citizenship associated with the different kinds of outcasts are qualitatively different, both the literary texts I have examined in this chapter make similar points about Hyderabad as an urban space. Futehally's *Zohra* and Bedford's *The Last Candles of the Night* revisit the idea of the princely city of Hyderabad, implicitly as well as explicitly suggesting that we discard the official, mainstream view of Hyderabad that prevails in many literary and scholarly discussions. As I have shown above, both appropriate the figure of the outcast and the idea of outcastness in their fictional narratives. While the privileged text of *Zohra* is certainly complicit in fictionally and textually perpetuating the subalternity of the urban working classes, it also creates a platform for us to re-imagine and *re*-member a princely Hyderabad hitherto outcast from official and mainstream discourses. It is possible, in other words, to read the novel as a text that reintroduces through literary representation the forgotten subjectivities of Hyderabadi Muslims who subscribed to a variety of ideological and socio-political positions. In this way, I have used the word outcast in connection with this text in both literal and figurative senses. This nuanced, complicated Hyderabad is much more than a den of potential Razakars; it is a place where Hyderabadis professed multiple, heterogeneous socio-political identities and beliefs during the late 1940s, unlike the exclusionary and violent politics associated with the Razakar.

Furthermore, while Futehally departs from static, stick-figure stereotypes of the Hyderabadi elite, Bedford, as I have shown above, focuses on the unusual subject position and strategic literary device of the outsider–insider protagonist. His novel takes these discussions about Hyderabadi politics and society further, as the recollections of the white Australian protagonist act as a powerful device through which we can critically interrogate and disrupt the mainstream Indian neglect/silence over Hyderabad and reinsert a more problematized narrative of history, memory, and belonging. Bedford's Philip forces us to think of unsettling things and often roots his vivid, profound, and thought-provoking contemplations through the very geography and architecture of Hyderabad city, thereby compelling us to organically evaluate and question what we know about the city. In exploring these aspects of the two texts, this chapter has uncovered significant insights for the study of urban outcasts in literature. How does the princely city claim and celebrate its own? How does it simultaneously appropriate, co-opt, include, and erase the Other? How does it come to be known, remembered, and forgotten by outsiders as well as insiders when it is a thing of the past? In attempting to address these questions in the context of Hyderabad, this chapter has shed light on issues that encroach on the present but have thus far not received the attention that they deserve.

Notes

1. I borrow the subtitle for this section from Karen Leonard's book *Locating Home: India's Hyderabadis Abroad* (2007).
2. My understanding of "the usual course" proceeds from texts that have contributed significantly to our perceptions of how we imagine, document, and contest the city and notions of the urban from postcolonial perspectives: the seminal introduction and essays in Volume 8 (1996) of *Public Culture*, which was edited and introduced by James Holston and Arjun Appadurai; *Democracy, Citizenship and the Global City: Routledge Studies in Governance and Change in the Global Era* (2000), edited by Engin F. Asin; *The Postcolonial City and its Subjects: London, Nairobi, Bombay* (2011), written by Rashmi Verma; and *Urbanizing citizenship: Contested Spaces in Indian Cities* (2012), edited by Renu Desai and Romola Sanyal.
3. See, for example, Leonard's seminal article "Reassessing Indirect Rule in Hyderabad: Rule, Ruler, or Sons-in-Law of the State" in *Hyderabad and Hyderabadis* (2014).
4. E. M. Forster wrote the introduction for the first edition.
5. I agree with Hai that this complex text inextricably intertwines both questions of gender and other contemporary politics, such as progressive and nationalist politics, but in the interests of economy, this chapter will focus on the urban, politicized Hyderabadi subject and not on *purdah* and other vital questions about patriarchal social norms raised in the novel.
6. This does not mean that the Razakars were not dangerous, but that the extent of their supposed military preparedness or organization was exaggerated in order to justify the invasion.
7. See communist leader P. Sundarayya's *Telangana People's Struggle and Its Lessons* (1972) and the Sunderlal Committee's report "The Sunderlal Committee Report on the Massacre of Muslims" (1949) for extensive documentations of oppressions and discriminations against Muslims and communists of all backgrounds.
8. An additional nuance that Futehally captures is the empty ideals of Hamid's progressive friends, who are unlike him because they are freeloaders whose commitment to political action and social justice is only verbal. They take advantage of Hamid's hospitality and, ironically, live the easy lives that the landed gentry lived in their wealthy *deoris* (mansions) in Hyderabad city.

9. To resist falling into the same trap, I have tried to distinguish "Hyderabad city" from "Hyderabad state" wherever I can in this chapter without making its reading tedious or cumbersome for the reader.

10. The histories of Zubaida Begum and Masuma Begum are delineated in fine detail and intertwined with the themes and bent of the text. In fact, Zubaida Begum's entitlement and claim to citizenship in the princely state comes from her family's history at the Mughal court, which is represented with great sympathy; this sensitive, historical narrative of nostalgia and loss along with her nobility and blue blood legitimize her citizenship in princely Hyderabad. Indeed, Zohra's nobility in the novel is constructed more through her mother than from her father. In a similar fashion, Masuma Begum's history as the defensive and resentful second wife of a childless aristocrat, who marries her only because he wants children (preferably boys), brings to the fore critical issues connected to upper-class patriarchy, such as polygamy, son preference, and arranged marriage. But no such history, however brief or sketchy, is available for Unnie in the text.

11. For more on the Osmania moment and the attempted construction of a secular Urdu language resource that was intended to replace English as the language of education, governance, and administration, see Kavita Datla's impressive book *The Language of Secular Islam: Urdu Nationalism and Colonial India* (2013).

Works Cited

Ali, Samina. *Madras on Rainy Days.* 2004. London: Piatkus, 2005. Print.

Ali, Syed. "'Go West, Young Man: The Culture of Migration among Muslims in Hyderabad, India." *Journal of Ethnic and Migration Studies* 33.1 (2007): 37–58. Web. May 23, 2012.

Bedford, Ian. *The Last Candles of the Night.* Westgate, New South Wales: Lacuna, 2014. Print.

Datla, Kavita Saraswathi. *The Language of Secular Islam: Urdu Nationalism and Colonial India.* Hyderabad: Orient Blackswan, 2013. Print.

Desai, Anita. *Clear Light of Day.* 1980. New Delhi: Random House, 2007. Print.

Futehally, Zeenuth. *Zohra.* 1951. New Delhi: Oxford UP, 2004. Print.

Gour, Raj Bahadur. "Hyderabad People's Revolt Against Nizam's Autocracy: A Diary of the Struggle." *Glorious Telengana Armed Struggle.* By Raj Bahadur Gour et al. New Delhi: Communist Party of India, 1973. 1–125. Print.

Government of India. *White Paper on Hyderabad.* 1948. Print.

Hai, Ambreen. "Adultery Behind Purdah and the Politics of Indian Muslim Nationalism in Zeenuth Futehally's *Zohra.*" *Modern Fiction Studies* 59.2 (Summer 2013): 317–45. Web. Accessed 7 Apr. 2015.

Hyder, Gulam. "Anti-Nizam Struggle: Participation of Muslims." *Glorious Telengana Armed Struggle.* By Raj Bahadur Gour et al. New Delhi: Communist Party of India, 1973. 136–53. Print.

Hyder, Mohammad. *October Coup: A Memoir of the Struggle for Hyderabad.* Ed. Masood Hyder. New Delhi: Roli, 2012. Print.

Indo-Hyderabad Relations: Press Cuttings April 1948–1948 Sept. India Office Records (IOR L/P&S/13/1241). National Archives of India, New Delhi. 5. Microfilm.

Kidwai, Huma R. *The Hussaini Alam House.* New Delhi: Zubaan, 2012. Print.

Leonard, Karen. "Reassessing Indirect Rule in Hyderabad: Rule, Ruler, or Sons-in-Law of the State." *Hyderabad and Hyderabadis*. New Delhi: Manohar, 2014: 90–109. Print.

———. *Locating Home: India's Hyderabadis Abroad*. Stanford: Stanford UP, 2007. Print.

Morning Advertiser. "Aggression." September 15, 1948. *Indo-Hyderabad Relations: Press Cuttings April 1948–1948 Sept*. India Office Records (IOR L/P&S/13/1241). National Archives of India, New Delhi. 61. Microfilm.

Noorani, A. G. *The Destruction of Hyderabad*. New Delhi: Tulika, 2013. 361–75. Print.

O'Hanlon, Rosalind. "Recovering the Subject: *Subaltern Studies* and Histories of Resistance in Colonial South Asia." *Mapping Subaltern Studies and the Postcolonial*. Ed. Vinayak Chaturvedi. London: Verso, 2002. 72–116. Print.

Said, Edward W. *Culture and Imperialism*. New York: Alfred A. Knopf, 1993. Print.

Smith, Wilfred Cantwell. "Hyderabad: Muslim Tragedy." *Hyderabad: After the Fall*. Ed. Omar Khalidi. Wichita: Hyderabad Historical Society, 1988. 1–25. Print.

Sundarayya, P. *Telangana People's Struggle and Its Lessons*. Calcutta: Communist Party of India (Marxist), 1972. Print.

Sunderlal Committee. "The Sunderlal Committee Report on the Massacre of Muslims." 1949.

The Times. "Cease-Fire in Hyderabad—Nizam's Order to Troops—Surrender Troops." September 18, 1948.

Visweswaran, Kamala. "Small Speeches, Subaltern Gender: Nationalist Ideology and Its Historiography." *Subaltern Studies IX*. Eds. Shahid Amin and Dipesh Chakrabarty. Delhi: Oxford UP, 1997. 83–125. Print.

2   The Margins of Postcolonial Urbanity

Reading Critical Irrealism in Nabarun Bhattacharya's Fiction

Sourit Bhattacharya

This chapter discusses the dynamics of marginal space in the postcolonial city. It looks at the way marginalized humans utilize the urban space and resist in significant ways the postcolonial state's imposition of the capitalistic logic of clearing the space for multinational investment and development. It situates what it considers to be the central contradiction within postcolonial urbanity: the thesis of rationality as against the practice of "irreal" activities. It takes the term "irreal" from the Marxist scholar, Michael Löwy, who separates it from the domain of "unreal" and "anti-real" and argues for a case of dissent and critique in the term's use. Through a reading of work on Indian modernity, anthropological findings by postcolonial scholars, and recent literary criticism on urban space, the chapter argues that "irreality" is integral to the dispensation and practice of space in the postcolonial urban world. The literary writings on postcolonial urbanity that specifically highlight this contradiction can be meaningfully read through the lens of critical irrealism which combines irreality with the element of authorial critique. For the literary part, the chapter reads the fictional work of Nabarun Bhattacharya (1948–2014), son of Mahasweta Devi and Bijon Bhattacharya, whose work centers around the margins of postcolonial society; the domain of the urban poor—beggars, prostitutes, small-time crooks, freaks, drunkards, rickshaw-pullers, hired assassins and others—who are stampeded by the joint forces of multinational capitalism and consumerism. It is argued here that Nabarun Bhattacharya provides the urban poor with the "armory" of the spectral and the mysterious to fight the bourgeois weapon of instrumental rationality and class dominance. The deliberate narrative effort at blurring spaces, times, and processes of reason-making contributes to his empowering of the subaltern and the outcast, and pushes for a rethinking of the matrices of postcolonial urbanity and modernity.

Critical Irrealism and Magical Realism

A discussion on the concept of critical irrealism is useful here. Critical irrealism, as the term suggests, is a re-reading of Georg Lukács' concept of critical realism. For Michael Löwy, Lukács' model, which is important for many reasons, nonetheless appears "exclusive and rigid" (193). If Lukács states that the literature of realism is a "truthful reflection of reality," Löwy argues that Lukács' sense is very "narrow" in defining what "truthful" is (195). Here Löwy has mainly the later Lukács in mind, especially the Lukács of *The Meaning of Contemporary Realism* who finds in Balzac, Dickens, Stendhal and Tolstoy the ideal presentation of his concept of "type," and disdainfully dismisses the "modernist" art as subjectivist, confining, ahistorical, and suffering from "anti-realism" (qtd. in Löwy 195). Although Lukács was much moved by the "extraordinary immediacy and authenticity" of descriptive details in ETA Hoffmann and Franz Kafka, he found it difficult to categorize the realism of these writers which mixed elements of the "ghostly" and the "spectral" with the realistic and the actual (*Meaning* 52–3). Raising this issue in Lukács, Löwy asks: "Are there not many non-realist works of art which are valuable and contain a powerful critique of the social order?" (193). By non-realist Löwy does not mean un-realist or anti-realist, but those works of art which do not follow realism in a strictly narrow Lukácsian sense of the term. Through a reading of Hoffmann and Kafka, Löwy argues that the elements of distortion of reality as-it-is or the blurring of the "real" and the "irreal" should be read as modes of aesthetic register under a pressing capitalist and imperialist world order, where the "actually existing real" creates a permanent sense of disenchantment and dissociation (195). He informs us that both these terms, real and irreal, should be seen to some extent as "ideal types," because irrealist art has many aspects of realism within it. But where it opposes realism is in showing art's emancipatory possibilities. He defines irrealism as "*oeuvres* that do not follow the rules governing the 'accurate representation of life as it really is' but that are nevertheless critical of social reality" (196). For him, the utopian, dystopian, oneiric, or fairytale narratives can be good examples of critical irrealism, as often the description of social reality is minute and accurate in them; but there is a powerful tendency to question, critique, protest against the existing hegemonic forms of reality, seek alternatives and find ways to liberate the characters from the oppressive social contingencies: "Critical irrealism can contain a powerful implicit negative critique, challenging the philistine bourgeois order. The word "critique" should in this context not be understood as relating to a rational argument, a systematic opposition, or an explicit discourse; more often, in irrealist art, it takes the form of protest, outrage, disgust, anxiety, or *angst* (the feeling so thoroughly dismissed by Lukács)" (Löwy 196). It is apparent that both Löwy and Lukács seek for an aesthetic register that can meaningfully represent and help launch a critique against capitalist social order.[1] Yet Löwy's reading appears more sophisticated as it allows for a further critique and opening up of the rigidity of bourgeois social and critical realism and helps us think of many further possibilities within the dynamic matrix of realism. Also, Löwy's criticism informs us that the critic has to be alert in using this model, as many of the irrealist narrative forms such as the fairytale traditions hide strong conservative attitudes within them and are not fundamentally "critical" (196).

As an avid reader of Lukács,' Löwy's critique appears to be a significant revaluation of the theorist's model. Literary critic Benita Parry has used Löwy's readings to formulate an understanding of postcolonial realism. In an article titled "Aspects of Peripheral Modernisms" (2009), Parry argues that a certain affinity in the aesthetic registration of capitalist modernity could be found in the peripheral regions, from the once-colonized countries to the Eastern European, Middle Eastern, and South East Asian regions. Characterized by the "incongruous overlapping of social realities and experiences from radically different historical moments" (30), the aesthetic of the peripheral world could be read productively with Löwy's mode of "irrealism" (39). Parry proceeds to read Tayeb Salih's *Season of Migration to the North* with an eye to the narrative juxtaposition of "the mundane and the fantastic, the recognizable and the improbable, the seasonal and the eccentric, the earthborn and the fabulous, the legible and the oneiric, historically inflected and mystical states of consciousness"—which she calls the stylistic irregularities of irrealism (39).

It is important to note that Parry does not use the term "magical realism" here. She does acknowledge the similarities in the use of these terms, but also tells us that before the term "magical realism" received purchase in the literary-critical circles, many noted writers and critics in Latin America and the Caribbean world such as Alejo Carpentier, Wilson Harris, Édouard Glissant, and Roberto Schwarz used the concept of the "marvellous real" or an aesthetics of "the temporal and spatial unevenness" to critique the social conditions under imperialist subjection. Magical realism, gaining a celebratory status in the academic and publishing world, has lost the predecessor's critical-analytical edge and vigor and become a tool for ready-made, commercially successful literary production. In a recent study, Sharae Deckard, following Michael Denning's work on the cultural logic of magical realism, makes a similar argument: "Latin American magical realism, while it may have hailed from economic semiperipheries, was far from culturally peripheral, having assumed market dominance in the literary world field" (353). Deckard finds in Roberto Bolaño's work a disparaging dismissal of this trend and a deeply critical engagement with the social reality through the mixing of the realistic and the fantastic (352, 372). Christopher Warnes, in a study on magical realism and the postcolonial novel, finds "the endlessly repeated potted histories of the term" and wants to clear grounds with a reading that is sensitive to specific cultural contexts and the overbearing presence of the colonial and neo-colonial histories (7, 12). Although Warnes' study is analytical in its use of causality as a paradigm and faith and irreverence as important factors for the production of magical realism, the question of critique and anger as integral to narrative remains unstated. This is what pushes me to think of a fundamental distinction between magical realism and critical irrealism. The former seems to outline a historical condition of being. It is a form born out of the uneven social logic of the Latin American postcolonial world where the oral traditions sit side by side with the modern and the contemporary. The form became widely popular in the postcolonial literary landscape because of the similar social experiences resulting from the histories of feudalism, European capitalism and colonialism.[2] On the other hand, the fundamental element in critical irrealism is its criticality. The author uses a blurring of time, space, and the logic of narrative to reproduce the uneven and composite nature of postcolonial society and make a conscious case of "protest" in the prose, both against the bourgeois/colonial domination and the hegemonic nature of "actually existing reality" of social realism. Through a technique of "showing" the compounded nature of time and space in postcolonial societies, the author tends to represent and even "take part" in the domain of perception and resistance by the subaltern and the outcast. This distinction will be useful as we engage with the specific character of the Indian postcolonial urban space and modernity.

Modernity, Urbanity, and Postcolonial India: Situating Nabarun's Work

Discussions on what constitutes Indian modernity have been prolific in recent years. Partha Chatterjee's call for a study that focuses on "ambiguity" (*Modernity* 20) and Sudipta Kaviraj's argument that Indian modernity is necessarily "plural and historically diversifying" for the nation's multilinguistic formation, are but only two noted contributions ("Modernity" 157). Dipesh Chakrabarty's findings appear particularly useful here. In *Provincializing Europe* (2000), Chakrabarty attempts to outline a theory of "historical difference" in the postcolonial world. Raising the issue that the "Eurocentric" history writing by the bourgeois-nationalist and Marxist scholars in India has relegated the colonized world into an imaginary "waiting room of history" (8), Chakrabarty proposes that a postcolonial intervention must take into account the anti-rational, non-modern, and supernatural elements that are subsumed by the linear-progressive, rationalist, "transition" narrative of capital (or what he terms *History 1*). He gives us examples from Ramabai Ranade's reminiscences (38), of the various diaries, letters, chronicles, memoirs written by the middle-class Bengali women (143), of the technically irrecoverable minority histories and subaltern pasts (103), what he together calls the effective "antihistorical constructions of the past" (40). These are useful observations and findings, but unfortunately neither Chakrabarty nor the other interlocutors of Indian post/colonial modernity go beyond the urban middle-class metropolitan centers. Modernity in such studies appears to be a highly class-filtered domain of the urban-educated middle-class elite, with books, diaries, memoirs, and deconstructive techniques for an uncovering of the officially unspoken word as constitutive components for the non-modern and anti-rational. Suburban life, urban poor in the late colonial India, or capitalist aggression in and industrialization of the rural during the two world wars and the mass exodus from villages to the city during famines and epidemics, aspects that appear powerfully in the literary representations of

Tarashankar Bandyopadhyay, Kamala Markandaya, Manik Bandyopadhyay, Premchand, Rashid Jahan, Ismat Chughtai, Kalindicharan Panigrahi, A Bapiraju, Gojananda T. Madkholkar, Nanak Singh, or in Raja Rao, receive relatively lesser importance for studies in Indian late- or postcolonial modernity. Giving considered attention to these factors can help understand a subaltern's or relatively lesser known writer's use of the non-rational or the superstitious in a significant way, pushing us to think of a materialist framework that does not see these acts, the act of projecting the non-modern into the logic of the "real," as necessarily anti- or ahistorical, but historically mediated "conjunctural" elements of modernity. This aspect merits further attention.

In a study on zombies and immigrants in millennial capitalism, anthropologists Jean Comaroff and John Comaroff tell us that the fall of the Berlin Wall, the disintegration of the Soviet Union, and the official end of apartheid in South Africa in the early 1990s created a huge promise of the greater social distribution of the wealth in the third world. But the introduction of neoliberalism and the accumulation of resources at a world-scale have rather

> Intensified market competition … set many people in motion and disrupted their sense of place; dispersed class relations across international borders; and widened the gulf between flows of fiscal circulation and sites of concrete production, thus permitting speculative capital to appear to determine the fate of postrevolutionary societies.
>
> ("Alien-Nation" 797)

This has, according to them, further widened the gaps between the rich and the poor beyond comparison, making on the one hand a consumerist, comfortably settled and visibly rich middle class, and raw inequality and "desires" of imitation by the lacking on the other. Such desires, they argue from their ethnographic findings in South Africa, have forcefully brought back the "occult economies" of witch-hunting, black magic, or zombie-labor in the urban spaces, the use of which by the lower class points to the efforts both at understanding the hidden logic of demand and supply (the speculative capital), caricaturing the free market enterprise, and helping acquire a vast amount of wealth without much labor costs. Magic in this process re-encodes the value system of surplus labor: wealth created out of nothing (786). Literary critic Upamanyu Pablo Mukherjee uses these findings and insight to a productive study of "the uneven city" in the contemporary postcolonial world. He argues that the various contemporary literary and cultural examples of black magic and "alien refugees" in a global city like Johannesburg "point to the historical tendencies through which they operate under conditions of uneven development" (Mukherjee 473). Thus, unlike Achille Mbembe or Sarah Nuttal, he refuses to read the essential unevenness in the spatial production of South Africa, especially the co-existence of the modern glitzy towers and the archaic modes of life in the slums and around, only as aspects of adaptability and creative energy but also indications of long histories of dispossession and dehumanization of the national and local forms of life by forces of transnational capitalism. He asks us to understand the successful cultural expression of the contradiction of capitalist modernity or the dynamism and creativity of contemporary modernity's human subject in his or her resistance "to the *enforced* and *involuntary* conditions of migration, circumlocution and 'flexible existence'" (Mukherjee 476, emphasis in original). Another critic of postcolonial space, Rashmi Varma reads in the literary-cultural registrations of spatial unevenness in the postcolonial Bombay, Nairobi, and London the relations, imprints, inheritance of imperial and colonial power structures. The postcolonial city, for her, needs to be read as "conjunctural space," that "produces a critical combination of historical events, material bodies, structural forces, and representational economies that propel new constellations of domination and resistance, centres and peripheries, and the formation of the new political subjects" (1).

What is suggested here is not that the specific features of postcolonial urbanity in Johannesburg can also be found in or applied to another postcolonial city such as Nairobi or Kolkata. Rather, the contention is that these studies not only enable a situating of capitalism's effects in the dialectic of the rational-modern and irrational-non-modern in the postcolonial urban world, they also make us aware of the way writers either consciously or unconsciously frame the registrations of such in their work. In his fiction, Nabarun Bhattacharya appears to be conscious of the postcolonial urban modes of living and the way multinational and consumerist capitalism have created the illusion of freedom for the middle class or crushed the aspects of physical resistance from the lower. His use of the urban poor as capable of mobilizing the supernatural and non-rational powers against the instruments of rationality—law, order, reason, and the bureaucratic state—can be seen as a way of re-empowering the subaltern and the outcast in the urban world. The steady mixing of the realistic and the non-realistic in this appears to be the registration of the unevenness in postcolonial capitalist urbanity and a forceful critique of such conditions. The rest of the chapter will test these arguments through a discussion on the aspects of temporal and spatial unevenness, the ghostly and the spectral, and the concept of filth in Bhattacharya's novels, mainly *Harbart*, but also *Kangal Malsat*, and the "fyataru" stories.

Harbart: Temporal and Spatial Unevenness

Nabarun Bhattacharya's fictional work is marked by two types of urban characters: the visible-yet-negligible and the largely invisible ones. Crafted mostly in his stories and later imported to some of his novels, the first category characters include Kalmon and Moglai, the small-time thieves ("Kalmon and Moglai"), Foyara, a prostitute who has a mysterious disease and drinks petrol to alleviate the pain ("Foyara'r Jonyo Duschinta"), a police inspector and the hired assassins of the Naxalite times ("Khnochor"), a mad man who is bombed in a park and speaks through his dead body ("Bhashan"), a poor failed writer who decides to write a story about a blind cat in a hotel where he stayed in the past ("Andho Beral"), the four dead-body bearers who are deaf and carrying a mysterious corpse through the heart of the city ("4+1"), or an old man who fears that he might die any day ("Amar Kono bhoy Nei Toh").[3] These characters are culled from everyday life and can be seen inhabiting the third world postcolonial urban space in its streets, in the dark and forbidden alleys, in the whore houses, morgues, police stations, or on the footpaths and in the slums. They are everywhere and are an indispensable force of labor for the neoliberal state, which Chatterjee has influentially called the "political society" (2004). The other group of characters also belongs to this "society" but is marked by the motivational factor of resistance and insurgency. Since the people in this latter group also hail from the lowest rungs of society and do not have sufficient resources of resistance to the state, Nabarun seems to provide these characters with the armory and mobilization of the unreasonable, the fantastic, and the spectral. Harbart Sarkar in *Harbart* (1993, 2011) and the fyatarus (the flying humans) and choktars (the black magicians) in *Kangal Malsat* (2003/2010) fall in this group.[4]

Harbart is the story of Harbart Sarkar. Born in a once-rich "babu" (colonial gentry) family in Southern Calcutta and losing his parents as an infant, Harbart grows up lonely, uncared for, and abused by his cousin, Dhanna-da. The only place he finds safety and peace is a defunct water-tank on the "chil-chhād" (attic roof). Lacking in friends and sunk into his own world of reading ghost-stories and other-worldly communications, he develops a strange vocabulary and an isolated form of living which lead him often to insults such as "freak" from the street-urchins. After the death of his beloved nephew, Binu, in the Naxalite police violence, Harbart tells his aunt and the family his dream of Binu informing him of a diary hidden in the house. Although fabricated (as Binu spoke about that on his death-bed), this leads him to declare his "discovery" of the super-human powers of "conversations with the dead" (61). Readily approved of by the society and turned into good "business" in short time, the power makes Harbart temporarily arrogant. He accepts the challenge thrown by the Rationalist Association of West Bengal which exposes his "trickery" in the end. In sheer anger and defense of innocence, Harbart commits suicide keeping a mysterious note on the table that he (a small guppy fish) is now leaving home ("fish-tank") for the outer world ("ocean"). As his dead-body is burnt in an electric stove, it suddenly detonates smashing the modern crematorium into pieces and bringing the police and the State into great panic.

Although such a summary does not do justice to the highly crafted quality of the narrative, it does give us a fair notion of how a marginal, humiliated, and ignorable person attempts to empower his position by taking recourse to black magic and supernatural practices. But why does society so easily accept his call? Within a short period of time after his "declaration" that he can communicate with the dead and tell people which plane of extra-terrestrial life those dead are on, we see his place crowded with people seeking his visit for both peace-making with the dead and some "profitable" knowledge of the future. The category of "people" here is not delimited and cuts across class and caste boundaries, both the rich, upper caste middle class and the lower poor working class. Why such a ready acceptance? Is it because he is considered a "freak," or also because the supernatural or the non-rational is inherent in the constitution of postcolonial urban modernity? The contemporary Indian social-political experience contains a potential answer. The novel begins with a flash-forward to May 25, 1992, the day Harbart dies, and then goes back to his birth and develops the bildungsroman. The year 1992 is important for India. It is the year India opened its doors officially for multinational capitalism in trying to recuperate the debt-and inflation-ravaged economy by deregulation, huge tax exemption, and other lucrative deals for foreign companies. This is also the year that saw the demolition of the 1527-built mosque Babri Masjid over the Ram Mandir issue, resuming the bloody communal violence between the Hindus and the Muslims.[5] To put these two issues into perspective, if the year propagated globalization and deregulation as the ultimate progressive form of governance and business for the postcolonial "rational" subject, the dark and "unreasonable" events of communal violence also made clear that we live in a society which is still at least partly feudal and partly neo-colonial. These "events" suggest that a system of knowledge-gathering and community-building, based on instrumentalist and bureaucratic forms of rationality, is highly impractical and contingent. This will have serious consequences for the society and the people. To extend these arguments more topically for the novel, an incident in Kolkata in 1993, the year *Harbart* was published, bewildered the State and the people. Birendra Charkraborty, aka Balak Brahmachari, the leader of religious sect Santana Dal, died, and his followers declared the death as a *Samadhi* (the last stage of meditation without physical consciousness). They said he would rise again as he had on a previous occasion, and thus guarded his dead body closely, allowing no one to enter the *ashram* (where his body was kept). After multiple skirmishes between the followers and the police and the condemnation by the civil society about the State's deliberate political lobbying, the rotting body of the "saint" was finally coerced out.[6] This incident not only indicates firmly the rooted belief in, and the retention of practices of, various rituals and non-rational activities in the heart of the urban space, it also corresponds powerfully to the larger pictures of contradictory forms of living in India—the call for rationality in governance and democracy and the inculcation of deeply communal, religious, and ritualistic activities in everyday life.

A publicly marked "weird" body, Harbart, then can suddenly and persuasively declare that he can talk with the dead and be a medium between the out-worldly and the worldly. At the same time, this is also the same country where such acts are seen with suspicion and disgust by a community, which is heavily invested in the "Anglicized" ideals of hyper-rationality. Thus, Harbart loses ground to scientific inquiry by the Rationalist Association, but with rage and sarcasm replies to Pranab Ghosh's challenge of seeking out every fraudster like Harbart and putting them to custody: "Fine. That's fine. We'll take care of you too." The narrator then adds, "It had not been clear who Harbart was referring to as 'we'. When they were leaving, Harbart was chanting as he danced around the room—oh my god how I humped them! Cat bat water dog fish! Cat bat water dog fish!" (114). Harbart utters the phrase "cat bat water dog fish" whenever he encounters anything English, in language or in culture and architecture; this phrase is his self-congratulatory admission to the world of Anglicized gentry. To the use of English by Pranab et al. of the Association, Harbart has his own vocabulary. Throwing a counter-challenge at the Association that the likes of him will also take care of the former, he feels empowered. He dances around in joy while uttering that nonsensical phrase, suggesting a verbal triumph over reason, science, and the borrowed Anglicized manners and practices. In the next scene, Harbart is found dead in his house with a cryptic note that he is on some sort of a pilgrimage. These uneven factors, the religious, ritualistic, non-rational, non-modern elements co-existing with the rational, inquisitive, scientific aspect, fundamentally constitute our society, which is a result of colonial education, capitalist exploitation, and a long-existing feudal social and cultural coding system. Nabarun, through sketching such a narrative, asks us to acknowledge this unevenness and address that for a meaningful engagement with postcolonial urbanity.

His use of unevenness becomes aesthetically richer and more appealing in his powerful use of space and time in the novel which helps us understand better the aspect of, if we may call it, "uneven aesthetic." Nabarun represents space in at least four different ways in order to emphasize their over-lapping, but sometimes contradictory, natures. The first is the isolated but enclosed and intimate space of Harbart's attic roof: "The attic roof used to be Harbart's space. All his realizations had come to him there" (*Harbart* 33). It is this space with which he connects to the outer world, which consists of beautiful kites in the sky, the flying cranes, the rising smoke, the discovery of bodily pleasure, and such. "The attic roof," as the narrator puts it, "had never betrayed Harbart" (38). This small and confined space acts as a sur-rogate mother, allowing Harbart his independent romantic connections with the world and protecting him from threats and abuses from outside. Against this space is the horizontal space of the external world, which plays across wealth and poverty. About twenty minutes from Harbart's house, we are told, are the wealthy localities whose street-names, Loudon, Rawdon, Robinson, and Outram, make Harbart feel like a "sahib." He always walks this space wearing a long ulster coat, black trousers and an old tattered hat, and instantly utters a number of words in English, "cat bat water dog fish" (81). He sometimes visits the Park Street cemetery and the antique glass house, where he finds the blonde nymph of his dreams, a stone carving of a beautiful girl who reminds him of his first love Buki, and of the naked Russian woman chased by German soldiers in a film he watched as a child (90–1). Ostensibly, this is Harbart's space of desire and imitation—his clothes, his activities in, and associations with, the space transport him to a cultural world of late Victorian meaning and sensibility. This bourgeois space with its colonial-metropolitan dimension is juxtaposed with another space of consumerist violence, of "multi-storeyed structures put up by real-estate promoters to replace the old buildings," of new video-renting shops, fast food stores, new cars and the TV (55). Compounded with this uneven world of colonial and the consumerist capitalist space is a relatively poor and old neighborhood where Harbart lives—a world of decrepit houses, close buildings, flashy signboards, tea shops, groceries, whore alleys, portico pillars, lepers on the pavement, and the familiar smells of smoke and piss (91). Taken together, all these spaces appear to be what Rashmi Varma theorizes as the "conjunctural space" of postcolonial society where forces of global capitalism exist with the relatively old and residual forms of living (1). Fredric Jameson's poignant image in *Postmodernism* comes to mind: "handicrafts alongside the great cartels, peasant fields with the Krupp factories of Ford plant in the distances" (307). In using different but connected representations of space, where the ideal-idyllic (roof/flying kites) is forcibly pressed into with the "late capitalist" multi-storied structures and real estates, Nabarun speaks of a highly uneven yet combined nature of development and spatial distribution in the postcolonial societies. We traverse the terrain of this highly uneven society on an everyday basis and adapt to its aspects of disjunction and asymmetry, sometimes without necessarily carefully noting them. Nabarun's observation and representation suggest the possibility of registration of such into the domain of the aesthetic.

A further possibility of such aesthetic registration is suggested in the novel's use of time. There are several temporal dimensions in the novel—all of which correspond to the aspect of uneven aesthetic and Nabarun's particular penchant for "explosion." One temporal dimension is the description of the wealthy localities and Harbart's desires to imitate the Anglophone metropolitanism that implicate him in the late Victorian "cultured" (decadent) world. Closely connected to this is the current temporal reality, his neighborhood, his rowdy friends, his alcoholism, cursing etc. Compounded with these two is Harbart's search for and solace in the other world constituted by his readings of books such as *All About the Afterworld*, *The Mysteries of the Afterworld*, and *The Infestation of Ghosts in the Circus* (41–3, 106–7). They transport the narration and temporal reality to a mid-nineteenth-century Victorian world of letters and interest in supernatural aspects, engineering at the same time Harbart's deep appetite for materializing communications with the dead. Harbart's dream of Binu's diary hidden in the prayer-room and the "business" of "conversations with the dead" derive primarily from such "preoccupations." He confronts a moment in the novel when the first man in his family-history, Dhnui, "shows" him the whole genealogy of male descendants and their dissolute practices in life and death. One of his grandfathers, Banarasilal, who used to "supply native whores to randy Englishmen," is seen playing Ludo with Queen Victoria (110). We are also told of Harbart's dead parents looking over him with a film camera as if producing a film on the life and times of Harbart. All these different temporal realities are brought face to face in the last scene following Harbart's death. This funeral scene is participated in by his friends and local admirers who chant his name in celebration, "Long Live Harbart-da!," the police and journalists, by Satpati Marik, who assured Harbart of quick success in business, and the old obsolescent world of Dhnui and the other great-grandfathers and parents. As Harbart's dead body explodes in the crematorium, all these aspects of different temporal realities cross their paths in the haste of escaping the detonation scene. This is a very important scene for an understanding of irrealism. Nabarun juxtaposes here all the different paradoxical realities in the postcolonial world: the carnivalesque celebrations of the bizarre (the death of a local hero) by the subaltern, the rationalist-bureaucratic world of surveillance and reasoning by the police and news reporters, the world of capitalist consumerism based on duping people in a utilitarian-rationalist sense as represented by the character of Satpati Marik, and the ghostly but overbearing world of dead parents and grandparents, a genealogy that we carry with ourselves every day in remembrance or in forgetting. Nabarun appears to suggest that the everyday of a postcolonial urban space is marked by all these different temporalities. They compete with each other for temporal domination. But this domination is relative as the existence of the subordinated or the displaced enables the recognition of the dominating. Thus, when Harbart is shown shivering in fear against the Rationalist Association and yet declaring his innocence, the suggestion seems to be that, not only are aspects of the non-rational an equally relevant and referential point of entry to answering critical questions in society, but also that our society is characteristically composed of various alternative lifeworlds and beliefs. A belief based on reason-making and proof-showing, or using English in discussions and doubting every native cultural practice as a form of deception, as done by the Rationalist Association, happens to be the dominating form of reality in our postcolonial hyper-rationalized society. But this is also the same society that harbors the dark, puzzling, and unreasonable elements of communal violence; puzzling because one paradigm of thought cannot respond convincingly to questions and crises set by the other. This is why the aspect of detonation becomes an important ploy for Nabarun. By allowing Harbart's body to be exploded, the author keeps the elements of puzzle and mystery as a point of disquiet and unease within rational argumentation. He then forces a justification from the world of the bureaucratic. The police conclude that the body explodes because Binu, Harbart's Naxalite nephew, placed the dynamites underneath the bed to hide them from the police. This appears to be the only "rational" conclusion for the explosion. But we are never confirmed whether such a thing ever happened. Nabarun's power as a writer is that through this open-endedness and suggestive multiplicity he deftly indicates that the rational world, which an urban-educated human subject so overwhelmingly embraces, also has its point of force, confusion, dogma, and contingency. This is why to the response of a member of the Rationalist Association who compares the "country bumpkin" Harbart to a clever urban trickster, this answer by the head, Pranab Ghosh will be followed by deep silence: "Isn't Harbart urban too?" (131). Urbanity and modernity are thought to be the domain of the rational-pragmatic. But the domain contains characters such as Harbart as well. The puzzle and incomprehensibility in Harbart's suicide note, or the narrative content and framing at large, appear to be the author's trenchant critique of the hyper-rationalized basis of postcolonial pro-development homogenized society that is either feared by or cares less for the alternative practices of survival. This takes us back to the insightful observation by the South African anthropologists, Jean and John Comaroff that the rise of, what they call, the "spectral" army of "labor," i.e. the use of illegal immigrants and unofficial bodies for wage labor or night work, or the rise of fraudulent activities of "making money out of nothing," is associated with a "discontent" and "anger" of the lower class with current reality of joblessness, poverty, and the discrepancy in wealth. These practices thus, they argued, should not be seen as an attestation to "magical realism" in society which is sold by the media in the global literary-cultural marketplace for postcolonial exotica; rather, a more "serious" and "critical" engagement is necessary to comprehend the discontent and the rise of contradictory logic of capital in postcolonial societies ("Occult Economies" 284; "Alien-Nation" 789). Nabarun's highlighting of a "freakish" person and his weird activities and the framing of the unevenness in the narrative's layout are but one such serious mode of critical engagement with the social conditions.

Kangal Malsat and the Use of Filth as Critique

Kangal Malsat (War-cry of the Beggars) is a more forceful critique of reason, order, and establishment politics.[7] It is a novel about the entente between fyatarus and choktars, who threaten the police, the ministers, and the industrialists for corruption, political inefficacy, and capitalist greed. For lack of translation and limitation in space, the discussion here will be focused on a particular aspect: the production of fear through the public filth-making by the subaltern. The fyatarus first appear in a short story called "Fyataru" in the mid-1990s where one of the narrators defines them as the lower-class flying humans whose supernatural flight at night creates panic in the police and the upper-class people. Madan, the narrator in that story, tells D.S., the would-be fyataru:

> "Not everyone can be a fyataru ... One needs proper qualifications for that. You go to big offices, and the officers don't meet you, make

you wait, you just don't sit there peacefully, do you? – you curse him in your mind, stick the dirt from your nose to the arm-chair handles, scratch the soft cover of a sofa, say, haven't you done that?"

"Yes, I have."

"Damage. Damage whenever you can. That has to be kept in mind. We recruit only those who do that. All those hopeless cases, half-dead, abused, humiliated, we select a few from that lot."[8]

They are shown to fly to an aristocratic midnight party in a floating hotel on the river Ganga and attack people with brooms, dog shit, rotten food, alcohol bottles, human excreta, unused flesh, etc. Their function in *Kangal Malsat* is very much the same. The choktars, Bhodi, Sorkhel, Benchurani, and others, are black magicians who stay in the shanty towns and slums and give safety space for various dubious activities to take place, from voodoo to framing a chase with ghosts to make someone sick to the "game of pillow-exchange" (political negotiations), etc. ("Kangal Malsat," *Upanyas Samagra* 245). As they launch their joint guerrilla warfare against the state, assisted by an old, gigantic, speaking raven, the ghost of a fat woman from eighteenth-century colonial Bengal, Begum Johnson, and a dead major general from the army, they make clear that their intention is not to kill the enemies but to shoot discarded or abominable objects and defile the public body and space. The novel has an astonishing preoccupation with filth throughout the narrative which provokes us to think of its specific historical purchase for postcolonial Kolkata.

Sudipta Kaviraj, in an insightful essay "Filth and the Public Sphere," tells us that the wave of refugees after the Partition created a public space problem for the city of Calcutta. Most of the refugees as well as of later migrants had to take shelter in municipal parks and state-maintained public places. These places were built by the early bourgeois nationalists and upper-middle-class members who both imitated the colonial concept of cleanliness, hygiene, and order in public space, and also separated them in giving it a native color by holding festivals, cultural programs, and sports there. Refugees and migrants, who were looked down upon by this class for their disorderly and irreverent nature, started using those spaces for personal and community purpose for making everyday livelihood in the city. Gradually, filth started entering the domain with small puddles, dead grass, black smoke, food left-over, busts used for drying clothes, and such, compelling a loosening of the grip over these spaces by the bhadralok. Kaviraj writes,

> Filth and disorder, one might suspect, acted as a real barrier erected by the people inside, the new inhabitants of the Calcutta parks, to symbolically establish their control over that space. Since their tolerance of garbage was much greater than the upper-middle-class groups, the filth itself marked their making the place their own, a declaration to the middle classes of their unwelcomeness.
>
> ("Filth" 107)[9]

During the early 1990s when the ruling Communist Party of India (Marxist), which had initially supported the refugee-settlement and looked after the well-being of the slums through the means of various non-governmental agencies, started campaigning for the demolition and uprooting of the slums, street-hawking, and temporary shacks on the pavement by the pressure from the agents of global capitalism, the colonial and postcolonial history of filth and cleanliness in the public space, started resurfacing. Nabarun, who has been as much influenced by the principles and ideals of Marxism and Communism as he is disappointed by the Stalinist Russia and the parliamentary Left in Bengal, seemed to suggest such a state of condition in his conception of the fyataru characters in the mid-1990s. In this novel, on numerous occasions, the raven speaks of the problems of capitalism (that the world is run by the World Bank), the political importance of the early Communist activities in Bengal and widely in the 1930s and 1940s Soviet Russia, the element of corruption in postcolonial society, the class consciousness of the proletariat, the Russian Revolution, Marx, Hegel, Plekhanov, Trotsky, Charu Majumdar, the Naxals, and a host of writers and thinkers who question aspects of production and value in society (*Upanayas* 334–59). Choktars and fyatarus initiate the war because they want to teach upper classes the lesson that the lower class is always conscious of its power and can take recourse to spectral armies and labor power that the instrumental rationality of bureaucracy can hardly understand. Even later, in another novel based on the removal of dogs from the streets of Calcutta, *Lubdhak* (2006, Bengali for the dog-star Sirius), Nabarun's narrator says that "the megacity that is beautifying itself in the new millennium in the manner of a gigantic female monster has no room for the dogs" (*Upanyas* 388). *Lubdhak* ends with the dogs' decision of mass-exodus, with scattered mutterings that hint at the imminence of a disaster for the city. Through the fyatarus, choktars, and the dogs and their supernatural, fantastic powers, through their filth-making and ominous hints of a disaster, Nabarun seems to critique the shameful aspect of dispensing with the integral elements of postcolonial society for accommodating multinational capitalism, condemn the practice of hiding and removing the slums and the dogs from the streets for their disorderly and filthy ways of living, and point finger at the apparent bankruptcy in political and ideological faith (as these are done by the Communist government in power). A politically committed writer, Nabarun does not envision a revolutionary overthrow of the ruling classes in any near future, neither does he write for that (because it inevitably leads to reactionary power negotiations by the subaltern [as the novel *Kangal Malsat* suggests in the end]). His writing is about the way consumerist capitalism crushes the existence and social and cultural practices of the margins in a postcolonial city (Kolkata here). It is also about the everyday joys and celebrations of life by these marginal beings amidst all hardship. In framing the everyday of the marginal, in questioning the basis of rationality and governance in a composite society, and in bringing out the ghostly and scary aspects of the subaltern world for the urban gentry, Nabarun's critique seems to powerfully lay the grounds of a critical irrealist mode of writing and reading. As Anindya Sekhar Purakayastha (2015) correctly notes,

> when the elitist cult of the writer is being valorised and appropriated by the ideology of the market, Nabarun through his prose work has foregrounded the originary dissident *avatar* of the writer whose sole objective is to unmask the processes of shameless reification of the life-world. (91–2)

Conclusion

These discussions and arguments strongly indicate that postcolonial urban space cannot be comprehensibly studied or understood without referring to the way the non-modern and the irrational practices or aspects have surfaced or survived over time. The rooted existence or the rise of the non-rational is compounded with the historical factors of colonial–imperial subjection and the current practices of multinational capitalism. Such coexistence has allowed a social and cultural logic of unevenness. Critical irrealism as a formal mode not only registers that unevenness in the crafting of the narrative but also paves the ground for mobilizing a forceful critique of such conditions of being. Nabarun Bhattacharya's novels *Harbart* and *Kangal Malsat* respond powerfully to the uneven sociocultural logic in the crafting of temporal and spatial compoundedness in the narrative and in their use of filth as critique. Also, Nabarun's emphasis on the spectral, the non-rational, and the macabre contributes significantly to building the logic of unevenness in the narrative. Supriya Chaudhuri, in her short but comprehensive assessment of the history of the Bengali novel, notes in the end that the Bengali novel "has developed by constantly transforming the realist terms of its initial premises, challenging the representational and referentialist illusion, yet never losing faith in the genre's commitment to 'reality'" (122). Nabarun's work, which she refers to here, relates to this argument, as it challenges the premises of representational reality-as-it-is but never moves away from critically documenting reality-as-such. His irrealism is appealing because of his use of critique and dissidence in the narrative as a mode of registering protest against both the bourgeois social elite and the hegemonic use of realism as actually-existing-reality. This also stands close to the aspect of the recurrence of "explosion" in Nabarun's work (the detonation scene in *Harbart* or numerous accounts of mini-explosions by the subalterns in *Kangal Malsat*). Nabarun wrote in an introduction to the collection of his short stories, "Andho Beral" (Blind Cat) that it is the explosion of logic and sense that all writings must be destined to: "What I understand about writing is that it is not a process of offering entertainment, but a much deeper alchemy which has a risk of explosion" (qtd. in *Shrestho Galpo* 9). The explosion in content, then, seems to meet the explosion in form to produce the uneven, fiery, irrealist aspect of lived reality constitutive of the postcolonial world.

Notes

1. Löwy has long written on Lukács, since the early 1970s, so such a charge against the theorist is not a sudden discovery for him. See his *Georg Lukács: From Romanticism to Bolshevism*.
2. Fredric Jameson's observation appears useful here: magical realism is primarily a "formal mode" that is born of a "content which betrays the overlap or the coexistence of the precapitalist with nascent capitalist or technological features" (1986, 311).
3. These stories appear in *Srestho Galpo* (2006). In rough translation, their titles stand as "Kalmon and Moglai" (95–102), "Anxiety for Foyara" (110–15), "Spy" (30–41), "Immersion" (21–4), "Blind Cat" (184–9), "4+1" (146–50), and "I don't have to fear, do I?" (263–7). Some of them have been translated into English in a recent Nabarun Bhattacharya issue in the journal, *Sanglap: Journal of Literary and Cultural Inquiry*, 2.1 (Sup).
4. *Harbart* (1993) was translated into English in 2011. All quotations and page numbers are taken from this English translation. The rest of the translations and transcreations of quotations and citations from the Bengali texts, *Kangal Malsat* and the stories, are mine. *Harbart* won the Bankim Award in 1996 and the Sahitya Akademi Award, India's highest recognition in literary achievement, in 1997, and was made into a film by Suman Mukhopadhyay in 2005 which also won the National Film Award. *Kangal Malsat* has also been filmed by the same director in 2013 to much critical acclaim.
5. See Barbara D. Metcalf and Thomas Metcalf, *A Concise History of Modern India*, especially chapter 9 (265–94).
6. Partha Chatterjee covers the story extensively for a reading of political society. See Chatterjee, *The Politics of the Governed* (41–6). This incident will largely inspire Nabarun's satirical (mini)novel, *Mausoleum* (2006).
7. A central object of critique here is the phenomenon of literary establishment in contemporary Bengali urban society. The prominent presence of the narrator, who through a network of intertextual references and use of acerbic wit and satire criticizes the publishing industry, effectively reminds us of the mode's narrative link with critical realism.
8. "Fyataru," *Sanglap* 2.1 (Sup), p. 142.
9. I'm thankful to Anwesha Ghosh for referring me to the Kaviraj essay. A distinction between filth-making as agentic for the subaltern and "dirt" as a passive-descriptive category for it and inflicted by the State, could be further useful for an understanding of postcolonial urban space.

Works Cited

Bhattacharya, Nabarun. *Srestho Galpo*. (Best Short Stories). Ed. Rajib Chowdhuri. Kolkata: Dey's Publishing, 2005. Print.
———. *Upanyas Samagra* (Complete Novels). Kolkata: Dey's Publishing, 2010. Print.

———. *Harbart*. Trans Arunava Sinha. Chennai: Tranquebar P, 2011. Print.

———. "Kangal Malsat." *Upanyas Samagra*. 229–380. Print.

———. "Lubdhak." *Upanyas Samgara*. 381–417. Print.

Bhattacharya, Sourit. "Fyataru." In "Nabarun Bhattacharya Supplement." Eds. Sourit Bhattacharya and Arka Chattopadhyay. *Sanglap: Journal of Literary and Cultural Inquiry* 2.1 (Supp) (2015): 136–49. Web. January 29, 2016.

Chakrabarty, Dipesh. *Provincializing Europe: Postcolonial Thought and Historical Difference*. Princeton, NJ: Princeton UP, 2000. Print.

Chatterjee, Partha. *Our Modernity*. Kuala Lumpur: Vinlin P, 1997. Print.

———. *The Politics of the Governed: Reflections on Popular Politics in Most of the World*. New York: Columbia UP, 2004. Print.

Chaudhuri, Supriya. "The Bengali Novel." *The Cambridge Companion to Modern Indian Culture*. Eds. Vasudha Dalmia and Rashmi Sadana. Cambridge: Cambridge UP, 2012. 99–123. Web. April 8, 2015.

Comaroff, Jean, and John Comaroff. "Occult Economies and the Violence of Abstraction: Notes from the South African Postcolony." *American Ethnologist* 26.2 (1999): 279–303. Print.

———. "Alien-Nation: Zombies, Immigrants, and Millennial Capitalism." *South Atlantic Quarterly* 101.4 (2002): 779–805. Print.

Deckard, Sharae. "Peripheral Realism, Millennial Capitalism, and Roberto Bolaño's *2666*." *Modern Language Quarterly* 73.3 (2012): 351–72. Web. August 2, 2015.

Jameson, Fredric. *Postmodernism, or, The Cultural Logic of Late Capitalism*. Durham: Duke UP, 1992. Print.

———. "On Magic Realism in Film." *Critical Inquiry* 12.2 (1986): 301–25. Web. July 31, 2015.

Kaviraj, Sudipta. "Filth and the Public Sphere: Concepts and Practices about Space in Calcutta." *Public Culture* 10.1 (1997): 83–113. Print.

———. "Modernity and Politics in India." *Daedalus* 129.1 (2000): 137–62. Web. July 28, 2015.

Löwy, Michael. *Georg Lukács: From Romanticism to Bolshevism*. Trans. Patrick Camiller. London: NLB, 1979. Print.

———. "Currents in Critical Irrealism: 'A Moonlit Enchanted Night'." *Adventures in Realism*. Ed. Matthew Beaumont. Oxford: Blackwell, 2007. 193–206. Print.

Lukács, Georg. *The Meaning of Contemporary Realism*. Trans, John and Neck Mender. London: Merlin P, 1963. Print.

Metcalf, Barbara D, and Thomas Metcalf. *A Concise History of Modern India*. Cambridge: Cambridge UP, 2012. Print.

Mukherjee, Upamanyu Pablo. "Ivan Vadislavić: Traversing the Uneven City." *Journal of Postcolonial Writing* 48.5 (2012): 472–84. Print.

Parry, Benita. "Aspects of Peripheral Modernisms." *ARIEL* 40.1 (2009): 27–55. Web. July 25, 2015.

Purakaystha, Anindya Sekhar. "Fyatarus and Subaltern War Cries: Nabarun Bhattacharya and the *Rebirth of the Subject*." *Sanglap: Journal of Literary and Cultural Inquiry* 1.2 (2015): 90–102. Web. January 30, 2016.

Varma, Rashmi. *The Postcolonial City and its Subjects: London, Nairobi, Bombay*. London: Routledge, 2012. Print.

Warnes, Christopher. *Magical Realism and the Postcolonial Novel: Between Faith and Irreverence*. London: Palgrave Macmillan, 2009. Print.

3 "Someone called India"

Urban Space and the Tribal Subject in Mahasweta Devi's "Douloti the Bountiful"

Jay Rajiva

In recent years, scholarship in both the humanities and social sciences has positioned urban space as the site of cosmopolitan, transformative experience for women. In an interdisciplinary study of gender in urban space, Kamran Asdar Ali and Martina Rieker note that "although women, the poor, children, and minorities in most cities have not been granted full and free access to the streets—they are not complete citizens—industrial life has brought them into public life" (2). Women, Ali and Rieker suggest, "may use the urban space for mobility, transgression, and different pleasures that they seek, in the process navigating the everyday in favorable and unfavorable terms," a process that allows them to "survive and flourish in the interstices of the city" (2) as they "negotiate" the "tensions" of "contemporary urban landscapes" (2–3). In these assertions, there is a significant slippage between capitalist production ("industrial life"), political discourse ("public life"), and physical space (the urban). As this account of urban experience unconsciously associates spatial mobility with the advent of industrialization, it also presumes a cosmopolitan mobility based on a privileged relationship to industrialization. In other words, the subjects who seek out "different pleasures" are already able to navigate urban space with relative autonomy; a similar view of urban mobility has also surfaced in notable examples of contemporary South Asian fiction.[1] Absent from these discussions, though, is the tribal subject's relationship to the cosmopolitan narrative of Indian development. Drieskens and Mermier, for example, argue that "[t]he specific cosmopolitism of each city becomes a universal characteristic of cities in general" (17), without putting much pressure on the potential exclusions of such a formulation.[2] If public life is contiguous with industrial life, what are the consequences of such a formulation for tribal subjects who lack the material resources and cultural capital to negotiate the industrial urban environment on equal terms?

In this chapter, I read Mahasweta Devi's novella "Douloti the Bountiful" as a counterpoint to the contemporary urge to privilege urban space, an examination of the material effect of industrialization on tribal bondslaves who cannot access the city as the site of transformative potential. This reading is informed by the economic and social marginalization of tribals in postcolonial India, where "development ... especially the growth of the core sectors, including power, mining, heavy industry, irrigation, and related infrastructural developments" has come "at an enormous cost, borne by millions of [tribals] who were displaced involuntarily or otherwise deprived of their livelihood" (Lobo 285). As Gayatri Spivak notes, if industrial development is one of the cornerstones of postcolonial India's "regulative logic," the tribal population, which "had no established agency of traffic with the culture of imperialism," cannot benefit from this logic, and by association, post-independence capitalism (97), particularly when they are caught in an inheritable, exploitative system of bonded labor (Carswell and De Neve 112). I will focus primarily on Douloti's experience of the environment of Madhpura, interrogating the family as a naturalizing symbol in nationalist discourse, before examining the novella's use and representation of narrative time. Douloti's bondslavery undermines Benedict Anderson's distinction between pre-nationalist eternal time and "modern" calendrical time, showing how both forms of time operate simultaneously within contemporary Indian nationalist discourse to ensure the deregulated exploitation of tribal subjects in urban spaces, masked by the rhetoric of capitalist development. Furthermore, this exploitation is shaped by a *discourse* of urban space that transcends the city as a specific locale; the deadly logic of tribal enslavement characterizes rural space as the periphery of urban space, providing "the cheap labour and necessary consumers for the globalised centre" while also playing "an active role as essential constituent of the city" (Drieskens and Mermier 16–17). Douloti is thus absorbed into postcolonial India's urban shadow economy, which is "outside of organized labor, below the attempted reversals of capitalist logic" (Spivak 97) and thus evident even in locales, such as the Madhpura town where she is exploited, that are not large urban spaces as such. Essentially, the discourse of urban development marginalizes the tribal subject in city, town, and village. In this way, the novella positions the tribal as part of a group whose fate, within urban space, is "predetermined by a logic of productive sacrifice" (Mbembe qtd. in Rao 269). On the one hand, the story offers the traditional representation of the tribal bondslave: homeless, valueless, treated as inanimate matter, a "nonself" exiled to the edges of representation. On the other hand, it also constitutes a challenge to that marginalization and reduction: Douloti's body articulates a form of affective "knowing" in which an embodied awareness of her abuse as a bondslave becomes both the narrative and thematic means of implicating urban space in the trauma of tribal subjects. Ultimately, the female tribal body underwrites the process of urban industrialization.

Published in 1995, "Douloti the Bountiful" offers a profound critique of the industrialization of post-independence India through an examination of bonded labor, a condition that, as Nivedita Majumdar notes, is "still prevalent in many parts of the country (Patnaik and Dingwancy) [and that] constitutes the narrative crux of the story" (156). Bonded labor hinges on low-caste South Asians borrowing money from landlords or moneylenders, then paying off that debt and its interest via labor; as Siddharth Kara notes, it is "the most extensive form of slavery in the world today," with roughly 20 million bonded laborers worldwide as of 2011, most of whom live in South Asia (3). In theory, the agreement lasts until the worker has paid off her debts; in practice, however, the landlord almost invariably exploits the powerlessness of the workers, inveigling them into contracts that are unlimited in term, with exorbitant interest rates that they will never be able to pay off. As a result, bonded labor is not fair labor but an unending cycle of servitude that typically enmeshes the laborer's entire family, who become "collateral" when the laborer is unable to keep up with her payments. Mahasweta's novella begins with a lengthy genealogy that dramatizes the hegemony of this cycle, revealing how Douloti's father Ganori comes to be a bonded laborer. Moreover, although her uncle Bono is able to break the cycle of slavery—he murders a man while working in the mines of Dhanbad, then uses the money he finds in the dead man's wallet to purchase a house and bribe the family's slave-owner Munabar Singh Chandela—he soon finds that wage labor in the city is no better than the bonded labor of the village. This familial pattern of exploitation forms the frame for Douloti's "arranged marriage" to Paramananda, actually a sex trafficker who uses marriage as a cover to kidnap Douloti and sell her into a life of forced prostitution in an unnamed market town in the district of Madhpura. This arrangement echoes Kara's accounts of the sex trafficking trade in *kothas* (brothels), which is closely allied to institutionalized systems of bonded labor: in landless families that take loans, the women and children are "coerced" into performing labor that frequently involves sexual exploitation (175). After contracting tuberculosis and various venereal diseases, Douloti travels from Madhpura to Tohri, seeking medical treatment, but the doctors, citing a lack of proper facilities, advise her to journey to Mandar. Instead, Douloti decides to return on foot to her home village of Seora, but only makes it to a schoolyard in a Tohri village before passing away on a map of India just as the country is celebrating Independence Day.

"Mother India" and the Family

As Graham Day and Andrew Thompson observe, terms such as "Mother India," "mother tongue," and "homeland" associate the "intimacies and warmth of the family home" (123) with the nation. Just as the family is seen as an inevitable, "natural" unit of human organization, the nation uses the family metaphor when it wishes to "take on the same air of disinterested solidarity" (Anderson qtd. in Day and Thompson 119). However, this metaphor relies on a division between so-called public and private spheres (civil and domestic). From this division, nationalism can then "delineate supposedly separate sets of identification and agencies throughout the subject and nation's mediating spheres of civil society" (Schultheis 73). In other words, these divisions allow the nation to regulate political functions without appearing to do so, concealing their operations within seemingly "natural" fault lines in social organization.[3] However, the image of Mother India describes not the state actors themselves, but rather the territory of the nation which the post-independence state is always already "guarding" from threatening outside forces. The land becomes a female body, which must be protected within a discourse of post-independence Indian nationalism. The formative notion of India and Pakistan as states, Veena Das notes, arose through "the rightful reinstating of proper kinship by recovering women from the other side" (21), exemplified by the Inter-Dominion Agreement of 1947 and the Abducted Persons (Recovery and Restoration) Act of 1949 (24–5). The distinction between male state actors and female national territory arises partly from what Pheng Cheah refers to as "the nationalist desire to inspirit and transform the existing state structure in the nation's image" (5). In other words, the state must be male and its territory female in order to justify the goals of the nation. Moreover, the bourgeois state element, Fanon observes, "turns its back more and more on the interior and on the real facts of its undeveloped country, and tends to look toward the former mother country and the foreign capitalists who count on its obliging compliance" (157). To attain freedom and individual fulfillment, the nation constructs an image of the territory of "Mother India" characterized by industrial progress, modeled on the former mother country. This construction demonstrates the malleability of the family image, which is used to naturalize the political configuration of capitalism: Mother India, the supposedly inviolable and pure territory, is actually the unspoken site of industrialization.

Such an idea of the nation arises from the re-creation of the private sphere within the context of Indian nationalism. For middle-class Indian women, the new national identity both constrains and enables their subjectivity. On the one hand, they are bound by a "new patriarchy [...] different from the 'traditional order' but also explicitly claiming to be different from the 'Western' family" (Chatterjee 220). On the other hand, some of the qualities that constitute their sense of place within the national imaginary— "orderliness, thrift, cleanliness, and a personal sense of responsibility, the practical skills of literacy, accounting and hygiene, and the ability to run the household" (247)—presume a privileged place within a private household, securing their bodies from unrestrained use by the market. In other words, the household itself, for middle-class Indian women, is a physical and social shield against extreme forms of systemic exploitation.

I do not, of course, mean to suggest that middle-class subjects are never the target of exploitative violence; rather, I want to draw our attention to how the family, as a symbolic aspect of the national imaginary, presumes and retrenches the Indian female subject along lines of caste and class. Such a retrenchment, significantly, omits the tribal subject, who gains no protection from this unit of social division. Instead, her body is "the last instance in a [capitalist] system whose general regulator is still the loan: usurer's capital, imbricated, level by level, in national, industrial, and transnational global capital" (Spivak 101–02). Douloti's family is entirely provisional (and thus unsafe) in its structural integrity. The family's life is one of unremitting toil. The bondslave condition pays nominal heed to capitalist phraseology in its use of terms such as wages, labor, and interest; in reality, it is an inheritable slavery from which Ganori is unable to escape. Far from being secure from the intervention of the state, members of Douloti's family are trapped in a continuous and omnipresent caste hierarchy that mocks the distinction between public and private spheres; the latter terms have no relevance because hegemony intrudes into every aspect of their lives, public or private. The landowner is naturalized in his oppression of bondslaves:

> On the high-caste boy's forehead he writes property, land, cattle, trade. Education, job, contract. On the outcaste's forehead he writes bond-slavery. The sun and the moon move in the sky by Fate's rule. The poor boys of Seora village become kamiyas [bondslaves] of the Munabars, Fate's rule. (22)

The family unit offers the tribals no protection from exploitation, just as it offered no protection from British colonial occupation; in both instances, the tribals remain below the register of public discourse, excluded from any participation in nationhood or the material prosperity of independence. Tellingly, Douloti herself does not surface until the reader has accessed the lengthy history of the Nagesia family, and thus, the structural condition of oppression into which she is born: the novella ironizes the presumed individuation of its own title by demonstrating the material and social constraints on Douloti herself. In other words, Douloti's story is coextensive with the story of her family's structural oppression as tribals. Conditions for her uncle Bono in the mines and in town are no different from being a bondslave:

> Government—unine [union]—contractor—slum landlord—market-trader—shopkeeper—post office, each is the other's friend. Down in the mine! How dark down there! And at week's end, *double* darkness above the mine as well. The contractor's hoods stood with guns. They snatched the money. We got it only after they took their cut.
>
> (Devi 25)

The collusion between industries demonstrates the problem with development projects in India: growth in "core sectors" such as mining has increased "the gap between the haves and the have-nots [tribals]," who have borne "the brunt of the development paradigm of the first four decades in India" (Lobo 285). Neither Bono, the fugitive, nor her father Ganori "Crook" Nagesia, his back broken by the cruelty of Munabar, has any hope of escaping the cycle of bondslavery.

Douloti's lack of protection from the industrial exploitation of post-independence India is magnified when Paramananda takes her to the Madhpura district, ostensibly to marry her but actually to entrap her in a life of bondslavery. When she arrives in Madhpura, she encounters elements of urban living that have remained completely unknown to her thus far. Ill from the "stink of *diesel*," she has "never seen such an arrangement … for relieving yourself, that is too surrounded by a *tin* wall" (51). Douloti's unfamiliarity with urban life dramatizes the gap between rural and urban experience, foreshadowing her eventual entry into urban subjecthood as violent, not emancipatory. Industrialized images symbolize Douloti's alienation, instances of "worked" or processed material that has undergone a radical transformation in order to be "useful" within the economy of material consumption. Diesel, a liquid fuel that powers engines of various kinds, is commonly distilled from petroleum, whereas tin is a chemical used in many alloys, such as cans and walls. To be useful, each must be transformed through a specific industrial process; it is to these details that Douloti's cognition is drawn, not any sense of cosmopolitan possibility within the urban environment. Moreover, this description anchors Douloti's experience to bodily sensation, both in explicit and implicit form: the body, sick from the stench of diesel, is also the body that will excrete within a confined space made of tin, before eating the kind of rich food that outcasts can only afford on national holidays. More broadly, the scene evokes the industrial waste wrought by global capitalism in India, which Rana Dasgupta describes in *Capital*: urban space populated by "abandoned buildings with broken windows" and steps that "jut out like rusty teeth" within a "wasteland" of brick houses, permeated by "toxic black smoke" (427, 447). While Dasgupta is writing of Delhi, the resonance with Douloti's experience demonstrates the reach and impact of industrialization even outside the city: although the town where Douloti is held prisoner is not large, it bears the hallmarks of the industrialized urban space, juxtaposing physical isolation and enclosure with the open flow of human "goods" in the bonded labor industry. Where she was once merely an aspect of her childhood household, Douloti is now in the process of changing into an "individual" within the urban symbolic register, but an individual marked exclusively by market exploitation and subjective erasure.

The modernity of global capitalism, which middle-class Indian citizens presume they can inherit without consequence (Dasgupta 435), here gives way to nothing but the detritus of industrialization that marks Douloti's own violent transformation. As is characteristic of Spivak's translation, English words for which there are no easy equivalent in Bengali appear in italics (*diesel, tin*), a way to call out the absorption of capitalist rhetoric into the schema of bondslave oppression: the visibility of these words in the text corresponds to their intrusion into Douloti's narrative experience. The tin wall that has previously inspired wonder now takes the form of the tin box that Paramananda hands to her, along with saris, necklaces, bangles, and other items of dress (56). At this point, Douloti begins to question the plans of Paramananda, just as the third-person narrative voice provides Douloti with a sense of the larger social context as conceptually impenetrable, a thing from which she stands apart and in which she can find no image of herself: "It's hard to understand this god's plans. Will he keep Douloti here after marriage? In this kind of room with brick walls all around and clay tiles on the roof?" (52). Later, Douloti's body becomes the object of transformation: her hair is knotted, "white stuff rubbed on her face, on her hands, and feet designs with red dye, finally that fine sari, fine blouse" (57). The narrative drops into the imprecision of "stuff" to indicate Douloti's lack of comprehension, then switches to a form of irony through the mocking repetition of "fine sari, fine blouse." The novella invokes the language of daily commerce while also reinforcing the pervasiveness of the discourses at work, shaping Douloti, in this moment before her trauma. When the process of dressing is complete, Douloti is handed a mirror, but cannot recognize herself (57). Douloti, the raw material, has undergone the first stage in industrial transformation, faced with the abiding alienness of the image that mirrors and doubles her, an image clothed in a wedding sari, linking marriage with the act of rape. The image of herself in the mirror, which she has failed to recognize a short while ago, now becomes the target of assault, as she is raped by Latia, the wealthy government contractor whose "sexual hunger is boundless" (58):

> Douloti the daughter of Ganori alias Crook Nagesia of Seora village seemed to look upon another Douloti, dressed up in a peacock-blue silk-cotton wedding sari, staring in such dread. Latia pulled off her sari, he has torn off her blouse. He has taken off his own top, is he going to be naked? Lips trembling, tears in her eyes, what is Douloti saying? (58)

The violence of urban transformation surfaces in the juxtaposition of the old Douloti, from the rural village of Seora, with a new self that she does not recognize, produced in the environment of Madhpura where the logic of urban exploitation is now brought to bear directly on her body. Although the space is not itself urban, it partakes of the same discourse in which tribal bodies are part of a national-wide capitalist "flow." The rich apparel, the wedding sari, is both the symbol of Douloti's entrapment—Paramananda represents himself in Seora as a wealthy philanthropist—and coextensive with her status as a commodity to be exploited through sexual violence. Moreover, this violence alludes to her family history, the economic and caste hierarchy of the Nagesia family, in which her father acquired the name "Crook" through an act of cruelty on the part of his owner. Through this allusion to the family history of bondslavery, the novella allows Douloti, in her "dread," to recognize the violence of her abduction by Paramananda, and thus her presence in this unmarked urban environment where she will be the repeated target of routine sexual assault; this is a trauma that, as a low-caste subject, she is expected to endure as a matter of course (Kara 174). The narrator asks: "Are the spectator Douloti and the tortured Douloti becoming one?" (Devi 58). Immediately, we receive the answer: "The two Doulotis became one and a desperate girl's voice cracked out in terrible pain" (58). No dissociation is possible for Douloti, as urban discourse allows the elite to use money to enact and naturalize the trauma of the tribal kamiya: "Here everybody fears him. Latia has behaved like this before. This way is natural for him" (58). Latia, the wealthy contractor, is able both to "redefine social frontiers within the city" and to create "exclusive spaces for the rich and powerful" (Drieskens and Mermier 16).

Both Latia and Paramananda use the symbol of the family as a cover for the maintenance of unrestrained market capitalism in the relative anonymity of the Madhpura brothel. No trace exists here of urban space as "the site of personal autonomy and political possibilities" (Ali and Rieker 3). Instead, Douloti's dislocation becomes evidence of the cultural and economic possibilities that are mutually exclusive of rural tribal subjectivity. In other words, she is exiled to non-presence, enmeshed in a deregulated system of urban traffic in which her body circulates freely as a commodity. Both her body, in the function of prostitute, and the *circulation* of her body within a closed system of traffic between male "customers," are part of the unstated foundation for the material prosperity that informs the narrative of urban development. In this configuration, the town of Madhpura acquires the urban "character" of a city space. Following Douloti's first rape, Rampiyari, the administrator of the brothel, naturalizes the exploitation of tribals: "They catch you to make you a kamiya ... This is called bonded labor" (59). This conversation takes place in a room "*reserved* for the valued clients" (59), the same space in which Latia has just violated Douloti, but which subordinates, in the text, to the equivocating language of capitalism, using the client-server exchange to describe rape. Douloti thus falls outside of the nationalist discourse of productive development; she cannot situate herself within a benign family collective that would normally allow the ideal urban citizen-subject to constitute herself, in her elite consumer status, as the "definitive citizen" (Spivak 99). The tribal men are severely oppressed but have some limited access to the social registers as consumers; however badly Douloti's uncle Bono suffers in the mines (Devi 24–5), he is still able to escape. By contrast, the female bondslaves of Mahasweta's story have no money of their own, and are consequently invisible as citizens in the urban consumer economy. Moreover, they do not have homes distinct from their place of "work": the same place that would normally constitute the "private" sphere of a family dwelling is now a place where the woman's body is completely exposed to unrestrained market forces. Effectively, their bodies are "the last instance on the chain of affective responsibility" (Spivak 102). This exposure works in conjunction with coercion at the level of the experience of time, which is crucial to the naturalization of bondslavery.

In *Imagined Communities*, Benedict Anderson famously traces the formation of national consciousness to the eighteenth-century rise of print culture (specifically, the novel and the paper). For Anderson, this formation involves a break from an older, medieval notion of "messianic" time in which "the here and the now is no longer a mere link in an earthly chain of events" but instead "*simultaneously* something which has always been, and will be fulfilled in the future" (Auerbach qtd. in Anderson 24). By contrast, the new time is homogenous, empty, and blank, defined by "temporal coincidence, and measured by clock and calendar" (Anderson 24); in this way, it is "a precise analogue of the idea of the nation, which also is conceived as a solid community moving steadily down (or up) history" (25). The novel, for Anderson, amply demonstrates the pervasiveness of empty time in its tacit assumption of shared cultural and national knowledge, as well as "the absence of those prefatory genealogies, often ascending to the origin of man, which are so characteristic a feature of ancient chronicles, legends, and holy books" (26, ft. 39). Arguing that modern nations progress sequentially from eternal time to empty time, Anderson engages in a close reading of the opening page of Rizal's *Noli me Tangere*, in which he notes that the

> casual progression ... from the "interior" time of the novel to the "exterior" time of the [Manila] reader's everyday life gives a hypnotic confirmation of the solidity of a single community, embracing characters, authors and readers, moving onward through calendrical time. (27)

My reading of "Douloti the Bountiful" demonstrates that in the context of postcolonial India, *both* forms of time are key components in the urban trauma of the tribal subject, the means by which the national narrative consigns the body of the kamiya (bondslave) to non-presence. This demonstration surfaces both in Douloti's experience of time as a kamiya and in the novella's narrative mode, which formally undermines the comfortable sense of progress that undergirds Indian nationalism. Eternal time is not, as Anderson suggests, an outmoded form of apprehending history that modern nationalism has eradicated, but rather in active partnership with empty homogenous time, providing the unspoken yet crucial means of conducting the business of industrial exploitation in urban spaces. Paramananda, Latia, and Munabar, representatives of the new capitalist regime, consciously deploy the rhetoric of divine ordination within eternal time to justify tribal enslavement, a notion that the tribals themselves internalize: "It's fate's decree to become a kamiya. Our Lord Fate comes to write fate on the forehead of the newborn in the dress of a head-shaved brahman. No one can evade what he writes down" (Devi 22). When the women of the brothel discuss Bono's exhortation to end bondslavery, Rampiyari claims that "it is written in the great epics Ramayana and Mahabharata that ending bonded labor is against religion" (81). Here, we see supposedly antiquated notions of eternal time operating side by side with notions of progress, education, and the calendrical march of the nation through history. When asked why he does not take his business into town, Latia scornfully retorts: "What an idea! In the jungle area everything is profit. Tribal and outcaste labor is so cheap" (65). However, it is quite clear that Latia does indeed take "his business" into town by consuming tribal bodies in anonymous urban spaces; moreover, the logic of unrestrained capitalism—exploitative profit from tribal "labor"—is itself a product of the industrialization of urban space. Douloti and the rest of the female bondslaves are conditioned to perceive time as eternal, rather than sequential, even though it is precisely the sequential progression of events that leads to her abduction and trauma.

Urban Space and Tribal Effacement

If industrial exploitation is the means by which urban space disables the tribal subject's sense of self, it also demonstrates the extent to which the rhetoric of urban space—unrestrained market capitalism—suffuses and contaminates *all* spaces. After Douloti becomes a kamiya, the story goes on to offer "an uncompromising and harrowing portrayal of systematized gendered exploitation" over the sixteen remaining years of Douloti's life (Majumdar 158). As Majumdar notes:

> The brothel caters to its clientele with the free labor provided by women like Douloti, who are all bonded to Paramanand. Apart from rare instances when a rich client pays enough for maintaining exclusive rights to one woman, the women are made to serve numerous clients every day. The only payment that they receive in return is their poor quality of room and board. In a few years when the women prematurely age with overwork and venereal diseases, they are thrown out of the brothel, leaving them with the only option of becoming beggars. (158)

Douloti is exiled from the calendrical progress of history, and from the nation itself. However, this exile is not merely a straightforward critique of the violence of nationalism; the novella dramatizes the plight of the tribal subject at both thematic and formal levels. When the text comments directly on Douloti's place in the larger system of bondslavery, it frequently detaches both from Douloti's focalization and the unnamed third-person narrator. For example, Rampiyari's mocking rejoinder to Douloti that "you too are a whore now" (59) is followed by an unattributed stanza of poetry in which the fate of kamiyas is naturalized and explicitly tied to the land. The stanza occurs twice, leaving the reader unclear as to who is speaking. Repeatedly, the text moves in and out of realist convention, slipping into the psychic space between narrator and speaking subject, that, quite appropriately, is not part of the ostensible narrative. Thoughts, assertions, reflections on myth and fate, and bitter satire of the dynamics of bondslavery all appear in the narrative margin, accentuated by Spivak's italics to indicate industrial words borrowed from English in her translation of the Bengali text. The dispersal of ethical commentary is another aspect of the kamiya, alienated from her surroundings in the context of Indian capitalism: in the market town, only the male purveyors of human goods can freely circulate, whereas the kamiya are imprisoned in partitioned rooms until age and disease lead to expulsion and then death.

Urban space is thus not the city as the site of subjective potential, but rather the violent containment, both within and outside cities, of an anonymous partitioned room, where raw material is concentrated and molded into the desired shape, then cast away once it is no longer useful. Douloti's experience is not unique to the unnamed market town in which she is captive (most likely Madhpura town itself, although the novella omits direct mention of the name). The violated body of the tribal kamiya is isolated in an unmarked room, within the maze of streets that evince no cosmopolitan sense of possibility. Rather, the mobility and fluidity of the masculine subject—Paramananda, the slave trafficker, Latia, the contractor—enable a profound dislocation, the destruction of subjective integrity as well as a series of everyday traumatic violations for Douloti, who becomes the replacement for Somni, an older bondslave now too ill to "work" as frequently as Paramananda wants. Within this confined space, the subject disappears into the annihilating logic of market capitalism, to the exclusion of all sense of nationalist rhetoric or any distinction between forms of time. When Somni wanders around asking if famine will come soon, it is an indication of desperate poverty: if a famine occurs, she can send her children to the orphanage and out of bondslavery. But it is also a figuration of her withdrawal from "civilized" market relations into a state of being that acknowledges only the primacy of nature: the cycle of famine and plenty is eternal and has no place in nationalist discourse. Consequently, Somni is unable to identify with the construct of the Indian nation, a dislocation that gains a particular traumatic resonance in the anonymous semi-urban space of the market town. One day, she overhears that "someone called India" is "fighting some China" (65), a reference to the India–China war of 1962. However, the concept of India as a nation is unintelligible to Somni and the other kamiya, condemned as they are to the cycle of bondslavery. India and China are reduced to individuals in physical combat, personifying the only relation bondslaves can fathom: face-to-face aggression between two people, an echo of the direct, interpersonal violence of the customer–kamiya relation. Here, relationality does not evoke the cosmopolitan narrative of self-discovery, with urban space as "the site of modern citizen-making" (Ali and Rieker 3), but rather the absorption of the subject into the hegemony of capitalist relation, producing a disposable body "whose existence in the city is underwritten by forms of degraded and destructive labour" (Rao 269).

By implication, the trauma of industrialization has created a different "someone called India" in the person of the bondslave, for whom violence marks entry into a state that eradicates personhood through repeated, naturalized trauma:

> "Douloti the Bountiful" reveals that women become an exploited material resource—raw material and labor folded into one—in the economic formation of the postcolonial nation as well as its graphically physical symbol of colonial and postcolonial exploitation. Positioned at the specular surface of the nation's imaginary and also at its material and ideological core, Doulouti illustrates how ideologically embedded an image of a traumatized woman is to the postcolonial nation.
>
> (Lamm par. 25)

In "Douloti the Bountiful," the urban trauma of the female tribal subject is the precondition for the operation of capitalism in postcolonial India. In other words, the urban locale is the site of the "new" person called India who experiences both the violence of sexual assault and the violence of transformation from raw material to "product." Douloti's position articulates the vexed tribal relationship to nationalist modernity, best exemplified by the narrator's dilemma in Hazari's *I Was an Outcaste*: "I could not make up my mind, whether to fight for the freedom of India or to fight for the freedom of untouchables from the degradation of the caste system" (qtd. in Jatin Gajarawala 129). However, the text also challenges the cosmopolitan idea that one can preserve the structural hegemony of urban space but still fight caste injustice. Douloti's lengthy encounter with her uncle Bono, years after her abduction, features a number of ironies built into the grotesque inequality of their respective positions. In conversation with Bono, Douloti says that her life contains only "[g]reat sorrow, oh my, great sorrow" (73); her acceptance of her situation and refusal to believe she can be freed through changes in legislation underline her conviction that she will be always be a bondslave, even as her vocabulary displays the infiltration of capitalist jargon into her conception of bondslavery: "Uncle Bono, if a kamiya woman becomes a whore the boss makes a lot of profits. No clothing, no cosmetics, no medicine. You have to borrow for everything and the boss adds all the loans to the first loans. No whore can repay that debt in her lifetime" (73).

After Douloti gives Bono money, at which he weeps and decries the kamiya system, the text aligns Bono's realization with a departure from "faith in the *law*, in *officers*, in the *police*" (88). This realization marks the end of the text's lip service to cosmopolitan notions of individual agency or social reform based on a modification of existing laws or conditions; shortly afterward, Douloti's experience as a kamiya concludes, as the outward symptoms of venereal disease drive clients away from her room and cause the new boss, Baijnath, to cast her out of the brothel, just as Somni was cast out years before. The "interior" time of the novel, to use Anderson's term, has become impossible to discern from the "exterior" time of the reader, whose enmeshment in the relentless, quotidian representation of Douloti's trauma is bereft of the "ironical intimacy" that, for Anderson, marks the modern novel's relationship to national identity (28). Interiority disappears for good just as Douloti is expelled from the enclosure of the brothel, the formal solidification of the text's thematic critique of the urban language of unrestrained market exploitation. Mahasweta juxtaposes references to the Indian Emergency of 1975–1976 (during which the government suspended civil rights on the pretext of defending the nation's security) with Douloti's abject state of withdrawal into her own bodily trauma: sick with venereal disease, unable to eat much or "take clients" (90). The diseased tribal body, now no longer useful within the circuit of exploitation that first molded it into a "suitable" shape, is summarily discarded; although the tribal farm-workers agitate for fair wages, "Douloti didn't know this news" (90). Instead of the seamless passage from interior novel time to exterior reader time, the novella skillfully disrupts all sense of progressive time, drawing the reader into an intimacy that is at once visceral, aestheticized, and traumatic. Brothel, bus, Tohri hospital—all locales blur together within the narrative, which pauses from unmarked conversations between those around Douloti only to offer chilling descriptions of more things being done to her: while she is unconscious at the hospital, the sweepers rob her of the little money she has, and the doctors and nurses discuss her condition in her presence, before revealing that they do not have the facilities to treat the tuberculosis and unspecified venereal diseases from which she suffers (91–2). Urban space is thus the site at which the body of the tribal is known and yet effaced.

In tracing the connection between industrial exploitation, urban space, and forms of time in "Douloti the Bountiful," I want to reposition the story as more than simply the product of Mahasweta's decades-long activism on behalf of the tribal community in India. Spivak, as one of Mahasweta's major translators, is careful to note that she has made little or no attempt to soften the edges and transitions from Bengali to English. As a result, the prose style of "Douloti the Bountiful" risks being subsumed to the story's activist concerns in the genres of testimonial and protest fiction. My point is not to imply that testimonial has no aesthetic resonance or instability as a medium of representation, but to remind us that critical interpretations of texts centered on tribal or Dalit concerns tend to treat such literature as transparent expressions of identity, with aesthetics and form absent.[4] Moreover, the challenging representation of Douloti's experience of time is part of how Mahasweta's story resists the attempt to erase tribal experience within the development rhetoric of contemporary Indian nationalism; such a representation, I have suggested, is as aesthetic as it is political. If postcolonial Indian nationalism elides the conceptual space to imagine the experience of tribal women in relation to the machinery of urban development, "Douloti the Bountiful" recuperates that space in its critique of the market logic of industrial capitalism, culminating in the dead body of Douloti spread across a map of India, "putrefied with venereal disease, having vomited up all the blood in its desiccated lungs" (93). One could certainly express discomfort with the parallel between the violence done to the body of Douloti by her captors and rapists and the violence that the narrative foregrounds in its closing pages; Mahasweta may be at risk of instrumentalizing Douloti as the paradigmatic tribal body and providing no way forward for the tribal figure herself. But it is precisely this hegemonic erasure that the novella is so invested in challenging. If rural and semi-rural spaces can be contaminated by the rhetoric of urban development, this closing scene demonstrates the potential for an inverse effect: the resurgence of the rural body, the refusal of that body to be contained and effaced within urban logics. The novella, I suggest, rejects the non-selfhood that awaits the tribal woman, transferring Douloti's body from the anonymous urban realm into the national narrative by returning her body to *rural* space—to the village in which she grew up. Douloti, the tribal kamiya for whom the image of the nation as family is neither natural nor naturalized, is unable to become the citizen-subject of postcolonial India. However, her death signifies the extent to which the uncontained corporeality of countless "Doulotis" is already in the process of creating a different version of India, in which the inequities of industrialized urban life can no longer be concealed. Ultimately, the novella establishes a connection between the disruption of the tribal subject's experience of time, on the margins of postcolonial Indian nationalism, and the pervasive capitalist logic of urban space, the unrelenting penetration of market forces into all facets of tribal experience. In this penetration, bonded labor negotiates the subjection of the tribal using the language of industrial exploitation, creating an India that is unintelligible to Douloti, Somni, and the rest of the bondslaves, when they wonder *who* India is, and who this person is fighting. Their exclusion from the national narrative denies them conceptual access to the idea of a national collectivity, implicating cosmopolitan individual agency in the production of urban trauma.

Douloti's corpse dramatizes and exposes the end result of the "processed" tribal body, the detritus of industrialized urban development, which assumes that "the rights of the urban poor … are a kind of wealth that can be spent in the process of creating the market for space" and within which "[t]he wasted lives of the poor, their expendability and debasement, constitutes this foundational logic of the future" (Rao 275). In contrast to the idealized Mother India figure, Douloti is not fertile but dying, reproducing not offspring but disease, a radical challenge to the sanitized history taught in the primary school where her body is discovered: the market logic that processed and destroyed Douloti now has "no room … for planting the standard of the Independence flag" (93). The empty homogenous time of modern nationhood encounters a direct challenge in Douloti's corpse, which emerges as "something eternal, something omnitemporal, something already consummated in the realm of fragmentary earthly event" (Auerbach qtd. in Anderson 24). Paradoxically, this clash between empty and eternal time gestures to the future: Douloti, the rural kamiya destroyed by urban exploitation, gains meaning by dying in a village, not in a city, becoming the paradigmatic example of "an ecology of new spatial forms that have created new layers of obsolescence, decay, vacancy, and a sense of temporariness underneath the skin of the existing built fabric" (Rao 271). Douloti's body, "all over" the nation, reveals her own corporeality and irreducibility of experience, replacing cosmopolitan mobility with the traumatized body of the tribal bondslave, the product of urban logic that has become, in the end, "someone called India."

Notes

1. Salman Rushdie's *Midnight's Children*, for example, positions the city as the nostalgic site for a multicultural plurality that is both masculinist and culturally elitist. Bharati Mukherjee's *Miss New India* dramatizes the domestication of violence within the family unit, but offers Anjali the implausible mobility of a rich white benefactor, Peter Campion, who allows her to escape the intolerable arranged marriage to her rapist within the urban landscape of Bangalore: the world of call centers, potential, and (the novel uses the term repeatedly) "light and angles" (39).
2. In both *Midnight's Children* and *Miss New India*, urban experience is critiqued but ultimately recuperated by the national narrative: Saleem Sinai laments the downfall of the plurality of Bombay, exiled to the pickle factory from which he narrates India's emergence as a nation, while Anjali finds herself working as a debt collector, marveling at the endless web of possibilities that constitute "the wonders of the world" in which she has somehow managed to survive (Mukherjee 325).
3. Even writers who use the concept of the family to challenge the nation—Amitav Ghosh, for example, asserts that "writing about families is one way of not writing about the nation (or other restrictively imagined collectivities)" (Ghosh and Chakrabarty 147)—accord this configuration power by virtue of focus. Furthermore, one could argue that a novel such as *The Shadow Lines* privileges a form of cosmopolitan urban experience that depends on the gendered silencing of the female subject within the family. Ghosh outlines a subjectivity predicated on the self's ability to imagine different worlds outside the family without having to engage in physical travel; as the cosmopolitan world-traveller, Tridib moves freely through various spaces, cultures, and times, retaining his sense of self because "a place does not merely exist" and "has to be invented in one's imagination" (21). By contrast, his cousin Ila is little more than a pathetically defiant figure whose attempts to negotiate an independent self are never more obviously futile than when the narrator declares to her: "You can never be free of me [...]. If I were to die tomorrow you would not be free of me. You cannot be free of me because I am within you ... just as you are within me" (89). Ila's place, then, remains within the family, but this place gestures to a broader problem: it is difficult to speak of the "private" sphere of the family as an autonomous haven for individuality, because it has never actually been a free space for women.
4. As Jatin Gajarawala observes: "Dalit literature is largely understood as the unmediated expression of Dalit identity, now legible in modern narrative and poetic forms. Aesthetic and formal considerations of such texts, therefore, have been subordinated to these political aims, if not evaded entirely" (3).

Works Cited

Ali, Kamran Asdar, and Martina Rieker. "Introduction: Gendering Urban Space." *Gendering Urban Space in the Middle East, South Asia, and Africa*. Eds. Martina Rieker, and Kamran Asdar Ali. 1st ed. New York: Palgrave Macmillan, 2008. 1–16. Print.
Anderson, Benedict. *Imagined Communities: Reflections on the Origin and Spread Nationalism*. London: Verso Books, 2006. Print.

Carswell, Grace, and Geert De Neve. "From Field to Factory: Tracing Transformations in Bonded Labour in the Tiruppur Region, Tamil Nadu." *The Underbelly of the Indian Boom.* Eds. Stuart Corbridge, and Alpa Shah. London and New York: Routledge, 2015. 96–120. Print.

Chatterjee, Partha. "The Nationalist Resolution of the Women's Question." *Recasting Women: Essays in Indian Colonial History.* Eds. Kumkum Sangari, and Sudesh Vaid. New Brunswick: Rutgers UP, 1990. 233–53. Print.

———. "Whose Imagined Community?" *Mapping the Nation.* Ed. Gopal Balakrishnan. London: Verso, 1996. 214–25. Print.

Cheah, Pheng. *Spectral Nationality: Passages of Freedom From Kant to Postcolonial Literatures of Liberation.* New York: Columbia UP, 2003. Print.

Das, Veena. *Life and Words: Violence and the Descent Into the Ordinary.* Berkeley, CA: U of California P, 2007. Print.

Dasgupta, Rana. *Capital.* New York: The Penguin P, 2014. Print.

Day, Graham, and Andrew Thompson. *Theorizing Nationalism.* New York: Palgrave Macmillan, 2004. Print.

Devi, Mahasweta. "Douloti the Bountiful." Trans. Gayatri Chakravorty Spivak. *Imaginary Maps: Three Stories.* London: Routledge, 1995. Print.

Drieskens, Barbara, and Franck Mermier. "Introduction: Towards New Cosmopolitanisms." *Cities of the South: Citizenship and Exclusion in the 21st Century.* Eds. Barbara Drieskens, Franck Mermier, and Heiko Wimmen. London: Saqi Books, 2008. 10–22. Print.

Fanon, Frantz. *The Wretched of the Earth.* Trans. Constance Farrington. New York: Grove P, 1963. Print.

Ghosh, Amitav. *The Shadow Lines: A Novel.* Mariner Books, 2005. Print.

Ghosh, Amitav, and Dipesh Chakrabarty. "A Correspondence on Provincializing Europe." *Radical History Review* 83.1 (2002): 146–72. Print.

Jatin Gajarawala, Toral. *Untouchable Fictions: Literary Realism and the Crisis of Caste.* New York: Fordham UP, 2013. Print.

Kara, Siddharth. *Bonded Labor: Tackling the System of Slavery in South Asia.* New York: Columbia UP, 2014. Print.

Lamm, Kimberly. "Seeing Feminism in Exile: The Imaginary Maps of Mona Hatoum." *Michigan Feminist Sudies* 18 (2004): 1–34. Print.

Lobo, Lancy. "Land Acquisition and Displacement Among Tribals, 1947–2004." *Tribal Development in Western India.* Eds. Amita Shah, and Jharna Pathak. 1st ed. India: Routledge, 2013. 285–309. Print.

Majumdar, Nivedita. "The Nation and Its Outcastes: A Reading of Mahasweta Devi's Douloti the Bountiful." *South Asian Review* 30.2 (2009): 157–71. Print.

Mukherjee, Bharati. *Miss New India.* New York: Houghton Mifflin Harcourt, 2011. Print.

Rao, Vyjayanthi. "Post-Industrial Transitions: Citizenship and Historicity in Mumbai's 'World Class' Makeover." *Cities of the South: Citizenship and Exclusion in the Twenty-First Century.* Eds. Barbara Drieskens, Franck Mermier, and Heiko Wimmen. Lebanon: SAQI, 2007. 265–79. Print.

Rushdie, Salman. *Midnight's Children.* Toronto: Vintage Canada, 1981. Print.

Schultheis, Alexandra W. *Regenerative Fictions: Postcolonialism, Psychoanalysis, and the Nation as Family.* New York: Palgrave Macmillan, 2004. Print.

Spivak, Gayatri Chakravorty. "Women in Difference: Mahasweta Devi's 'Douloti the Bountiful.'" *Nationalisms and Sexualities.* Eds. Andrew Parker, Mary Russo et al. New York: Routledge, 1992. 96–117. Print.

4 "Stuck at Pause"

Representations of the Comatose City in *Delhi Calm*

Amit R. Baishya

Vishwajyoti Ghosh is one of the most prominent graphic novelists in the alternative trajectory of comic books in India (other prominent names include Orijit Sen, Amruta Patil, Parismita Singh, Sarnath Banerjee and members of the Pao Collective). I use the word "alternative" here because knowledge about, and scholarship on, Indian comic books and graphic novels have generally tended to focus on the well-known Amar Chitra Katha series (see McLain), comic book companies like Diamond, Indrajal and Raj, and a few vernacular comic book series. More recently, Virgin Comics (renamed Liquid Comics), which produces "commercial" comic books, and noir-ish productions like Saurav Mohapatra's *Mumbai Confidential* have also had an impact, albeit limited, on the Indian and international markets. Discussing this recent "commercial" trend, Creekmur writes:

> While such examples have met only with limited success, as products of the Indian diaspora they represent what is likely to be a continuing attempt to infuse comics designed for international audiences with "exotic" Indian characters and content while adhering to mainstream generic conventions. (356)

The oeuvre represented by Ghosh and the others mentioned along with him above, however, moves away from these dominant trends in the Indian comic book scene. Creekmur argues that "… texts most often identified as Indian graphic novels seem not to derive from earlier Indian comics, except perhaps in an oppositional way, positioning earlier or even contemporaneous mainstream Indian comics as counter-examples rather than precursors or peers" (349). While Ghosh is correct when he says in the interview below that the publication of ten books is not enough to talk about a "contemporary scene" for the Indian graphic novel, a few common elements can already be discerned in this emergent body of work: a meticulous observation of everyday life in urban centers (Sarnath Banerjee's *Corridor*, Ghosh's *Delhi Calm*), a concern with representing events of historical or socio-political significance in comic book form (Orijit Sen's *River of Stories*, Ghosh's *This Side, That Side*, Parismita Singh's *The Hotel at the End of the World*), experimentations with non-linear and experimental forms of storytelling, techniques of collage, and a deft exploration of the interconnections between interior and exterior landscapes (Amruta Patil's *Kari*). At the same time, the language and references used by these graphic novels are also culturally specific, which, as Creekmur says, "perhaps explains why no individual work has yet enjoyed international 'crossover' success" (349). However, although not commercially successful, this alternative trajectory has already distinguished itself through its engagement with socio-political issues and its divergent, experimental styles.

Both *Corridor* and *Delhi Calm*, especially, are Delhi-based narratives (although *Corridor* also moves to Calcutta) that explore the topography of the city and the multifaceted dimensions of its everyday life by choosing middle-of-the road protagonists: the second-hand bookseller Jahangir Rangoonwalla in *Corridor* and the "junior writer" for a newspaper named Vibhuti Prasad in *Delhi Calm*. By focalizing on these characters, these graphic novels also provide us brief glimpses of the populations or areas that often exist on the fringes of urban life in India.

A former student of the Delhi College of Art, Ghosh has published two major graphic novels—the solo effort *Delhi Calm* (2010) and the anthology titled *This Side, That Side: Restorying Partition* (2013)—besides publishing a book containing twenty-five postcards titled *Times New Roman and Countrymen* (2009). Ghosh is also involved with Inverted Commas—a group working in the realm of social communication in the Delhi area that often uses comics in their public endeavors (see Holmberg). While *This Side, That Side* has received a sufficient amount of attention for its depiction of stories about partition in South Asia in the graphic format, this short introduction and the interview below refers to it only tangentially. The central focus of this piece is *Delhi Calm* where Ghosh narrates a story set in Delhi and its environs during the period of the Emergency (1975–1977), when Indira Gandhi's Congress government suspended civil liberties, imposed a notorious regime of censorship and adopted harsh disciplinary measures against the citizenry.[1] The Delhi that Ghosh represents here is not a plush megapolis inhabited by wealthy people; instead, as Vibhuti Prasad says: "The Delhi I live in is not the Delhi of white Ambassadors, leather briefcases, English-speaking convent schools and stable salaries. It is a city of pot-bellied enterprises and petty cash, fueled by insecurity" (10). The brutal effects of the Emergency were experienced at full-strength in such locales. Therefore, I argue that the Delhi represented in this graphic novel is a view of life from the urban fringe, a virtually invisible city for the upper classes and the well-to-do urban bourgeoisie. The populations inhabiting this city are represented as constantly living in the shadow of potential emergency regimes.

A particular version of Delhi, therefore, is the primary protagonist of *Delhi Calm*. As Ghosh says in the interview below,

> *Delhi Calm* is not really about the characters … I tried to extract every little pore of the city that I remember, that I think existed, the type of milieu it must have had … I have also talked about Delhi the city in

many ways … about these three main characters who are not from Delhi, how they negotiate Delhi, how they look at Delhi.

A good example of this is evident in the conversation depicted in the full page spread on page 97 (see below) between Vibhuti Prasad and his former comrade and friend, Parvez Alam, after they suddenly meet in a small eatery. Both of them are migrants to the "powerpolis." While Vibhuti Prasad lives in Lajpat Nagar, one of the upcoming localities in the southern part of the city at that time, Parvez lives in Daryaganj, an older neighborhood in the north. The conversation between them in this single-page spread reveals different negotiations that outsiders conduct with the city:

Figure 4.1 Conversation between Vibhuti Prasad and Parvez.

Besides the class and locational aspects emphasized in the full page spread above, food emerges as a crucial psycho-social marker of a subject's personal itinerary of the city, especially for cash-strapped denizens like students from other cities and floating, struggling professionals. The older, more traditional areas of the city, like Daryaganj, are often considered to be havens of cheap and tasty food. No wonder then that one of the major topics for conversation between the two friends in this full-page spread centers on food. Vibhuti enviously asks Parvez whether he is having delicacies like "biryani." At the same time, both of them also indulge in social stereotyping. Vibhuti's question (and Parvez's answer that "ghettos" like Daryaganj sell cheap, good food like "kababs" and "phirni") obviously alludes to the religious composition of particular segments of the city. Furthermore, Vibhuti's rebuttal of Parvez's comments that the south is an "upcoming" part of the city and that he must be "getting good food" from the "sensitive souls" who reside there, stereotypes the predominantly lower-middle-class "partition refugees" resident in the area as people who open shops "all the time" and "make merry." This exchange of stereotypes between the two characters— predominantly Muslim areas as havens of good, cheap food, and former refugees who constitute the lower-middle class in particular sections of the city as people only interested in making a fast buck—reveal crucial attitudes through which a certain class of outsiders often frame their own itineraries of the city and how they negotiate with local populations in the areas they inhabit. Clearly, as Parvez's use of "my" city indicates, there are multiple versions of the city that coexist simultaneously with each other.

While these everyday negotiations with a subject's psycho-social versions and itineraries of the city create a sense of the intimately known and the ordinary, the imposition of the Emergency disrupts this familiar order of things. The disruption of the ordinary and the mundane is the crucial cog of this graphic narrative. I will address this by exploring two dominant narrative strands that convey the terror, fear and also the sheer banality of urban life lived under an emergency regime.

a How the abstract entity called "the state" is experienced by people at the level of everyday life during a period of emergency, and how such experiences are represented by the *narrative strategies* of the text.
b The phenomenological experiences of time and temporality experienced by the ordinary citizen during this same period and how they are conveyed by the *visual style* of *Delhi Calm*.

Influential theorizations of comics (Eisner, McCloud) focus on sequentiality as one of the central narrative features of this art form. However, even a cursory perusal of *Delhi Calm* reveals a critical modification in its distinctive narrative strategy: the sudden interruption of sequential narrative by multi-modal narratives (three of them are short pseudonymous biographies of Indira Gandhi, Jayprakash Narayan and Sanjay Gandhi) modeled on the Films Division documentaries that used to play before a feature film in theaters in India from the 1960s to the early 1990s. While at one level these interruptions show how the "private" narrative of the major protagonists in *Delhi Calm* meshes with the larger "public" events of the Emergency, Ghosh says that this juxtaposition was a conscious strategy deployed to show how propaganda operates in actuality:

> You talked about the panels in between, the disruptions of narrative time ... that was also often coming from the fact that that's how propaganda works. You get disrupted by propaganda. You are thinking that you are having a good time, you are watching a film, and then suddenly you hear a sound effect and you see something like "India is Rising." It is also reminiscent of the fact that when we went to watch movies as kids, the films would always begin with a Films Division documentary: Bokaro Steel Plant, Air India, India is moving forward ... And then you would have an Amitabh Bachchan type of *dhishoom dhishoom* movie which has no relation to these films. These narratives would have no relation to the real film, but they come in between and give you a different perspective. They are framed like propaganda pieces.

Ghosh's statements above are in line with recent anthropological theorizations of the state (Gupta and Sharma, Hansen and Stepputat) where the sphere of everyday practices emerges as the central field through which "ordinary" people learn about the state. Routine and repetitive everyday practices like standing in line to cash a pension check, paying taxes, and so on substantiate the state as an institution in people's lives.

However, what Ghosh says here about "propaganda" and its effects adds an additional spin to the depiction of the disruption and reformulation of everyday life in an urban setting under an emergency regime. While in ordinary circumstances, the banalization of state propaganda erupts as a form of disruption provoking boredom, anger or frustration, its very normalization in a state of emergency results in the production of other affects like paranoia, suspicion or fear. The familiar spaces of the city become uncanny as one's trust in the world vanishes. Ghosh emphasizes this during our interview when he says: "... where does the state come in during such situations? How do we negotiate the familiar everyday that includes the people we trust? Who is looking over your shoulder? Who is not? How are the vegetables selling that day?" While the interruption of the sequential narrative by the "propaganda" pieces in *Delhi Calm* shows how the principle of disruption and the attendant shocks it produces becomes almost a banal feature of everyday life in a state of emergency, the dissipation of the subject's trust in the world s/he inhabits is also emphasized through the repetition of the self-conscious visual motif of the theatrical mask. The segment in the narrative that probably encapsulates this best is the following series of panels.

The onus shifts in this segment from the performers on page to the audience that transforms into participants and internalizes the disruption caused by the fear of the emergency as a feature of everyday life. This shift is concretized in the move from five self-contained panels to an open-ended one

Figure 4.2 The masked character.

where a masked character, almost in Brechtian fashion, dominates a hazy background and directly addresses the audience about the absurd theatricality of the situation. Furthermore, there is a direct symmetry between the masked face in panel five (a masked man occupying center stage among a medley of faces) and the lone face in the last panel. The faces of others, including that of Parvez, are blotted out here as the anonymous masked face seems to directly address the audience. The implication is interesting to consider—the face of the familiar other appears to the observing self as a sinister mask, disrupting and returning our gaze and, thereby, making us vicariously experience the terror of surveillance during this period. Ghosh emphasizes this uncanny capacity when the familiar metamorphoses into something fearful in the interview: "What are the *chaiwala*'s plans? Is he a police informer or is he on your side?" What *Delhi Calm* explores, I wager, is how the abstract entity called "the state" infiltrates almost every fiber of the city during a state of emergency. Negotiating the city then is akin to negotiating a warzone with invisible barbwires strewn everywhere—every nook and cranny is potentially a danger zone, everyone you encounter could potentially be an agent of the state.

If the narrative strategies of the text, then, emphasize the banalization of disruption and shock, the visual style of *Delhi Calm* gestures towards another important dimension: the experience of the passage of time in a period of emergency. At the narrative level, this move towards the exploration of emergency temporality is bookended by two important first-person narrative statements. The first occurs ten pages into the narrative, after the initial coda establishes the setting and introduces us to the central protagonist, Vibhuti Prasad. On page 10, we come across a full-page spread introduced by an actual headline from the newspaper, the *Indian Express* from June 26, 1975 (the day the Emergency was declared). The headline—"Delhi Calm"—blares out at us. Towards the middle of the page, we come across the following narrative segment, a brief section of which I already quoted earlier:

> The Delhi I live in is not the Delhi of white Ambassadors, leather brief-cases, English-speaking convent schools and stable salaries. It is a city full of pot-bellied enterprises and petty cash, fueled by insecurity. This Delhi runs on a nagging post-partition fear shift from 8 in the morning to 8 in the evening, when it finally hits Pause. From there on, it slowly fades to Stop, and then Dead. Every day.
>   But this morning it has been stuck at Pause. (10)

Whereas this statement concretizes the position that Vibhuti Prasad occupies in the "powerpolis," what is also central in this passage is the manner in which the Emergency disrupts everyday temporality. Everyday time is figured as the banal repetition of certain actions, emphasized by the "Pause ... Stop ... Dead ... Every day." But on June 26, 1975, it seems as if this machinic assemblage is stuck at a permanent pause.

I suggest that this narrative of time being "stuck at pause" or freezing and lurching during a state of emergency actually ends not on the last page (page 246), but slightly earlier. On page 228, we come across a single panel showing Moon (the pseudonym for Indira Gandhi) addressing a faceless mass. This panel occupies around three-fourths of the page. Just below the panel, there is another narrative segment, "Delhi has never been so unsure of its breath as in the recent past. Mind your breath, mind your step, mind your words, mind your mind. Slowly, let the silence in the buses convert to whispers, careful but free. Let democracy appear democratic ..." (228).

Prior to this page, we come across another important date: January 18, 1977 (the day the Emergency was lifted). When we juxtapose these two passages, the city, for the bulk of the narrative, is figured as a machinic/zombie-like body. In the first passage, the repetitive, predictable actions of the machinic city seemingly come to a halt as its architecture seems to be thrown out of joint with the imposition of the Emergency. In the latter section, the "body" of the city seems to be re-animated and re-infused with life after the Emergency

Figure 4.3 Moon addressing the audience.

is lifted. Yet, like a zombie from whom the spell of the *bokor* has been lifted, the re-animated city totters as it walks, "unsure of its breath."[2] One of the primary figurations of the zombie is through the trope of automation—in a Cartesian sense, the zombie is a machinic body bereft of a soul or the power of cognition.[3] Here, as the zombified period of the Emergency is suddenly lifted, the city totters around trying to recalibrate its bearing.

Building on this conjoined trope of machinism/re-animation, I suggest that the bulk of the narrative between pages 10–228 explores the vicissitudes of everyday life conducted in "zombie time." Drawing on Terry Harpold's work, Boluk and Lenz define zombie time as "the absolute menace of [a] perpetual present, in which history (uninfected, serial time) is held apart from posthistory … by a period (missing time, time in crisis)" (12). Uninfected, serial time here is the invocation of mundane repetition ("Pause … Stop … Dead … Every Day"). In *Delhi Calm*, the Emergency infects the body of the city and makes time lurch and freeze. The bulk of *Delhi Calm*, then, is an exploration of this sense of time in crisis once the city gets "stuck at pause." Besides the motif of the theatrical mask and the interspersed "propaganda" narratives (all of these narrative "disruptions" occur within these pages), Ghosh explores this crisis with a wide, experimental mélange of visual styles. Panels often tend to be skewed or curved at the edges to convey this sense of temporal disorientation. Images are often superimposed on the gutters to convey that clear lines of spatial demarcation are virtually impossible. The speech of individual characters within panels is often counter-pointed with actual slogans and headlines deployed during the Emergency ["Work More" (128), "Avoid Loose Rumors" (131), "Mood of confidence in Country" (132)]. Full-page spreads often incorporate official propaganda messages with images that allude to the violence and terror wrought during that period. For instance, the full-page spread on page 172, can be divided into two visual planes. In the background, we notice government documents like "Certificate of Responsible India" placed at an upwards-facing angle on an empty hospital bed. Above it, and still in the background, are a group of grinning masks staring fixedly at the image of a fetus. Images of razor blades with specks of blood on them are superimposed on the masks and the bed in the background. The grey watercolors in the background allude to the peeling walls of a decrepit government hospital. At the extreme corner on the bottom-left, we notice another government slogan—"Simple-Operation and Cost is Nil!! Get sterilized at your own will!—Dept. of Family Welfare." The ironic juxtaposition of these images and icons chillingly recreate some of the most terrifying episodes of this period.

Similarly, pages 182 and 183 allude ironically to one of the iconic sequences from the famous film *Sholay* (1975)—itself a victim of the censorship regime during the Emergency. Gutters are dispensed with almost completely as a Gabbar-like figure wearing a theatrical mask interrogates Kaalia and Sambo (sic) about their success at sterilization. Instead of a gun, the Gabbar-like "Saviour" carries a giant syringe. As punishment, this Gabbar/"Saviour" castrates his three minions. The individual images in these pages bleed into each other, much like the movement in a cinematic reel. The only exceptions are the three panels at the middle of page 183 where the moment when the three minions are castrated is dramatically highlighted by boundaries that look like the two edges of a filmic reel. While this sequence obviously parodies a well-known moment in post-Independence Indian popular culture, its sudden irruption within the narrative and the lack of differentiation between its individuated narrative moments once again takes us back to the period where time is in crisis. Like the "propaganda" sections, this "cinematic" fragment interrupts the sequential flow of the narrative and "shocks" us with its invocation of sterilization and castration. Moreover, it also seems like spatial demarcations between the "real" and the "reel," between "reality" and "nightmare" become untenable. This period of zombie time that Delhi endured seems like a horror movie without end, where shocking disruptions are not an exception to the norm, but have, instead, been transformed into a banal rule.

Through a complex mélange of visual and narrative strategies, therefore, *Delhi Calm* brackets the period of the Emergency almost like the experience of a surreal fantasy. As the last page of the graphic novel shows, however, this bracketed period of zombie time is not a mere aberration. Instead, 1975 is inserted into a chain of events also including 1984 and 2002. The sentence—"From there on, it slowly fades to Stop, and then Dead"—seems to take a new, ominous cast here. These shocking events seem to repeatedly interrupt the temporal flow of events that define the everyday and the ordinary in the city. It's almost as if the experience of the ordinary in the city is shadowed by the uncanny, "fading to stop" from time to time, but periodically erupting and coming back from the dead with unprecedented ferocity. But, maybe this view of interruption, the narrative suggests, is just a view from the hegemonic center. For the denizens of the fringes of the city it may be a case of "terror as usual" (Taussig); repetition with minimal difference.

Interview

(This interview was conducted in Delhi on June 14, 2015)

AMIT R. BAISHYA: Let me begin with the standard questions first. Please tell me a little about yourself, your interest in comic books and about your background in general.

VISHWAJYOTI GHOSH: I have been a Delhiite all through. The interest in art and painting was always there from childhood. Comic books … I think came into the scene in 1979 when Amar Chitra Katha (ACK) came into the school book fair. The difference was that the children's books from National Book Trust (NBT) cost Rs. 1.50 whereas the Amar Chitra Kathas were Rs. 1.75. My parents would prefer to buy the books from NBT because they had more words and more stories, whereas ACK had more pictures. But the kids would prefer ACK. So there was a lot of haggling back and forth. Then my mother bought me my first comic book. It had to be Rabindranath Tagore because of, you know, the whole Bengali thing. I don't remember much about that book other than the fact that I read it five to six times. So, ACK became a whole new world of interest for me. In school if we were caught reading comic books, then they would be taken away from us and the parents would be called in the next day. We would read it under the desk because the school authorities had the notion that comic books will hamper your reading habits. Now, of course, the same schools call us to talk about comics. So, yeah, that's how it began. Then life happened, girlfriends came in, comic books went out for a while. Then, I think it was around 1989–1991 when I was in art school. I used to go to the People Tree shop, which Orijit Sen used to run. I used to paint T-shirts to support myself. He was working on his first comic book and I said "Wow!" I used to hang out there and read comic books like *Barefoot Gen*. I found that very interesting and thought that that can be done here as well. That got me really interested.

The first comic book I really wanted to do was about my life in art school because no one really knows what happens in an art school, right? But that book never really happened. By the time I finished art school, photoshop arrived. Whatever we'd learned in art school had changed. Then there was no real involvement with comic books for a while, but this book remained like a mill-stone around my neck. I had to do that book one day, but I didn't know what to do about it. Then I was assisting a friend of mine in college who was making a film on the Emergency. When I was assisting him, I learned that there was so much that could be done visually with this interesting phase in history. I tried to remember what I could from that period. That's how *Delhi Calm* began. It stayed in my head for about eight years. But somewhere in the middle of the 2000s, I felt that I had to complete this book in about two years. I finished it in 2009.

ARB: Just to backtrack a little bit, when you were younger was your reading limited just to ACK or did you read stuff like Phantom, Indrajal etc.?

VG: It was basically ACK which was available in English. Phantom ... one had no real access to except in the Bengali magazine called *Desh*. There was one page of Phantom there. My mother would often read it out to me. I always thought that Phantom was a Bengali character, Aranyadeb. It's only later that we came to know that it's Phantom. I also read a bit of Diamond comics. There were a lot of government school kids in the area I grew up in. They would read a lot of Hindi comics, and Diamond comics were the favorite. We could go to the bookstore and hire a comic for 25 paisa. So we would all pool a bit of money, read Diamond comics and give it back. Somewhere later in school, in the middle years, Tintin and Asterix came along. My first major achievement was winning an inter-school cartoon competition in Class X. I got a prize of two Asterixes and two copies of Laxman's *You Said It*. That was actually the time when political cartoons came into my life, and I got inspired by that. That became a passion for a couple of years. Political cartoons opened up a whole different way of reading the world and probably led the way to *Delhi Calm*.

ARB: Moving on from childhood influences, were there other types of comic books or styles that influenced you as an adult? You mentioned *You Said It* and political cartoons, but were there other influences on you? Any international influences?

VG: I think *Maus* was one because that was the only one I was exposed to. Orijit was working on his first graphic novel. Those pages were there. I saw him working on the finished book (*River of Stories*). That was definitely an influence. Other than that, not really, no!

ARB: No Joe Sacco?

VG: No Joe Sacco. All of that came much later, in 2000 or so when *Palestine* came out. Then I attended a workshop in the French Center here at Delhi which had people like Guy DeLisle and Frederik Peeters. Peeters was this rock-star Swiss-French comic book artist and he had done this fantastic book called *Blue Pills*, which was about him and his girlfriend. So these guys were there and that definitely influenced me. A little bit of Crumb had already come in during the mid or late 1990s. They also exposed me to David B., Satrapi and that really shot up things. Then French comics became very influential for my work.

ARB: Do you read French as well?

VG: I don't read French. But I follow a lot of their work. In 2003, I went for a fellowship there. So I saw work happening there at L'Association. I met people like Baudoin, went to the Charlie Hebdo office, attended a board meeting there. All those were definite influences.

ARB: I understand that this is difficult to answer precisely, but at what point did you decide that *Delhi Calm* was the comic book you wanted to write?

VG: See, the first comic I wanted to write was about the art college. Then I wanted to write a book on partition in 2002. That didn't really take off because I thought "What's my voice?" But I did a few pages of that. Then the emergency book happened because it was sitting on my head, I started digging through the material, talking to people …

ARB: Can you tell me how you began to get interested in the Emergency as a narrative?

VG: What happened was that I was assisting my friend who was working in Jamia Millia Islamia. He was doing his diploma project on the Emergency. A student project has its own limitations: you can only do it within a certain number of minutes, you can't go out of Delhi, it has a shoestring budget and so on. When he was sharing his research, we realized that there was so much he was missing out on because he did not have the resources to talk about it. I just thought that it was such a visual narrative. So much could be done with it visually. So, yeah, I kept a lot of the research material and I read up a lot about it. Then, when I was in my office … I was working in an advertising agency for a social communication unit. I used to talk to my boss who was also an inspiration for this book. I have acknowledged that in *Delhi Calm*. He used a lot of comics in advertising and was a big follower of comics. I used to talk to him as he had a few experiences. If you remember Vibhuti Prasad, the journalist in the book … he was based on my former boss. He used to talk to me a lot about his references. If you remember the main incident in the book—the guys are caught with underground magazines in their bag—it's actually him. They were actually caught and then they negotiated *charas* over the content. Those oral histories were very important in giving the book its shape.

ARB: Let's move on to the question of the style in *Delhi Calm*. One thing which fascinated me was your use of panels. Panels often bleed into each other. Another interesting aspect about the work is the evocation of the idea of being "stuck at pause" ... of the city being "stuck at pause". So, could we begin talking a little bit both about your stylistic choices and your use of archival material in the work?

VG: The archival material was something that had to be brought into the book. One of the things that has happened with the Emergency is the disappearance of the archival material. All the files on the Emergency are missing from the National Archives. A lot of the press was censored which meant that a lot of things were not said. Thus, what has survived is a little bit of archival material, but primarily oral histories of the city. I had to bring in the archival material to show that despite a lot of censorship, a little bit of it had survived. It had to be artistically woven into the narrative because it was something that was out there and was not simply a monolith of what had happened. I obviously tweaked a lot of text in incorporating those, most of it photoshopped. It's like a palimpsestic narrative. One also had to bring in the fact that these things happened coincidentally. For instance, let's say that you and I are talking in a café. The newspaper happens to be there coincidentally, not as a matter of design. You pick up some random news which eventually is not that random. But that's how news spread. That's how underground guerrilla propaganda spread. That aspect had to be brought in, whether it was a poster on the wall, a pamphlet that was being circulated, a newspaper ... the archival material has to blend in.

ARB: Just in terms of the visual narrative, let's return to the question of the panels. One of the fascinating aspects of *Delhi Calm* is the superimposition and angularity of panels. The other aspect, of course, is how the major plotline is often interrupted. You have stand-alone stories on Sanjay Gandhi, one on Jayaprakash Narayan, obviously with fake names. Could you take us through the process of creating the narrative, both visually as well as the continuities and the discontinuities in the narrative?

VG: What was important for me was the first visual. I always think of it in terms of film—what will be your first shot? Whenever I see a new filmmaker working, I ask them, what will be your first shot? The first page of *Delhi Calm* is a full-page spread. It takes you into this world through a zoom and that's it. That was what was important for me. I did not think about the panels as I began. I just thought about that first page. Then it happened that the protagonist gets up in the morning, listens to the radio, reads his Marx, listens to his Mohammad Rafi ... they are all meshed into each other. I did not want to do straight box-ish panels with gutters in between because I did not think that this was the kind of style I could do justice to or if that could do justice to my work. When I begin a work what is really critical for me is that the form is an extension of the content, and is not an ornamentation of the latter. So, till I crack the form I am very nervous. I am rude to people, I don't take calls and I don't get out of the room. I try and do every comic in a new style because it's a new story and requires a new way of drawing it. So it was very important for me to get that style. One thing I was sure of was that I wanted to use water colors because it was one way of going back to my college years and paying a tribute to my investment of time. So all I was sure of was the use of water colors. The panels evolved over time.

You talked about the panels in between, the disruptions of narrative time ... that was also often coming from the fact that that's how propaganda works. You get disrupted by propaganda. You are thinking that you are having a good time, you are watching a film, and then suddenly you hear a sound effect and you see something like "India is Rising." It is also reminiscent of the fact that when we went to watch movies as kids, the films would always begin with a Films Division documentary: Bokaro Steel Plant, Air India, India is moving forward ... you know, that type of thing. And then you would have an Amitabh Bachchan type of *dhishoom dhishoom* movie which has no relation to these films. These narratives would have no relation to the real film, but they come in between and give you a different perspective. They are framed like propaganda pieces. So, that was basically a tribute to the documentaries one saw or was made to see. That was where the state came in. Even the Soviet documentaries used to work like that. They are completely black and white, large chunks of text, low in visuals. So those were influences on the narrative overall.

ARB: What about the figuration of city in the work? You create a certain sense of place of Delhi in between 1975–1977. Obviously it's not the same city now. What were the images that you were drawing on in the individual panels? Did you recall these images from memory? Did you recreate that through research?

VG: *Delhi Calm* is not really about the characters. Delhi is the protagonist. At the same time, as an author it's my catchment area. I tried to extract every little pore of the city that I remember, that I think existed, the type of milieu it must have had. A lot of it is from memory. A lot of it from the images I framed in my head from the oral interviews I conducted. A lot of it is also constructing the city in my head. For example, I have also talked about Delhi the city in many ways ... about these three main characters who are not from Delhi, how they negotiate Delhi, how they look at Delhi. This is something that, you know, as a Delhiite, I have seen all through. People come, people leave, people talk about Delhi, people bitch about Delhi and move on. So how they negotiate Delhi fascinates me. So, for me, it's important to see how I place myself in the city, how the city places itself. So, for me a lot of the visual representations, even the ambient representations, come not so much from archives, but from memories and interactions.

ARB: So besides oral interviews, what were some of the archives you consulted?

VG: Usually for the clippings, a lot of citizen's and activist's reports which were there. *Delhi Calm*—the term itself came from an Indian Express report that came out. It was a later idea. My editor said "Delhi Calm" is a good idea. That's how it came about ... mostly that.

ARB: Let me backtrack to a point that fascinated me a lot about *Delhi Calm*—that phrase that talked about the city being "stuck at pause." You also end with a full-page spread where you show specific dates like 1975, 1984, 2002. These dates recede into the distance while the palimpsestic city seems to keep moving on. When we consider such phrases and the repetition of such major historical markers, what is the sense of time and temporality that you want to capture? The "stuck at pause" phrase, with its allusion to the VCR, seems to bring up strong associations of rewinding and repetition as far as the experience of time is concerned. Could you tell us something about the possible connections between phrases like "stuck at pause" and the closure of the graphic novel?

VG: The last (page) was basically a cut to now. The book ends in 1977, the day before the end of the Emergency. The characters are talking about a rally the day before the Emergency is lifted. The characters, of course, don't yet know that the Emergency has been lifted. But the fact that they don't know that Emergency has been lifted and they talk about how things move on from here, it's like a cut to the now. The central question is "What happens now?" It was an afterthought. We discussed it and thought that a page on now is very relevant because we don't talk about these things. We are not supposed to talk about these things. That's how Delhi negotiates its everyday.

ARB: I felt I should take your opinion on the word "Emergency" itself. It's a fascinating word to think about—it's something apart from a "normal," something based on a state of high alert, almost like a cut away from a sense of the mundane everyday etc. I was very interested in your evocation of everyday life within that cut. It's almost as if a sense of "normal" life has been suspended for a period, there is a cut in time, everyday life begins again, then there is another cut when the Emergency is lifted, only for it to "pause" during another Emergency. From your work, it seems as if the city seems to lurch from one state of Emergency to the other. Yet life is lived within the folds of such lurches. So, how did you try to capture that sense of lived experience and also the sense of the passing of time within these folds and creases in *Delhi Calm*?

VG: See, that was very important ... to get the pulse of everyday life. The fact remains that there is an Emergency. That means nothing—it's just an abstract, overarching thing! But the fact remains that the man has to go and earn his bread, the wife has to go and teach in a school, the kids have to go to school ... life keeps moving on. But they are negotiating Emergency somewhere. The wife is worried that I might get sterilized. The father is worried that my balls might get punctured. The fact remains that within whatever they are doing, they also have the sense that other kinds of things are also happening. People can come and you can be pushed into a sterilization camp. If you say anything against the government, you don't know if the *paanwala* is with you or against you. You don't know whether the guy next to you in the bus is a state agent or not. How do we negotiate these things? These are everyday, real issues. There is nothing called the state eventually. The state is a construct. I am not meeting anyone. Only when I am meeting the Prime Minister or the Chief Minister am I getting close to the concept of the state. But if I am meeting someone next to me in the bus, chances are that he has also transformed into the state. So, where does the state come in during such situations? How do we negotiate the familiar everyday that includes the people we trust? Who is looking over your shoulder? Who is not? How are the vegetables selling that day? What are the *chaiwala*'s plans? Is he a police informer or is he on your side? Those are the things we have to negotiate. So it was very important for me to get into all these things and get the pulse of how the people dealt with it. So, the *chaiwala* who is always on the side of Vibhuti, for example, becomes a state agent later. That also is a negotiation. People tried to work the atmosphere of fear and anxiety in their favor.

ARB: Besides the palpable sense of fear, anxiety, terror and paranoia in *Delhi Calm*, what also struck me was the humor in the narrative— both humor as a means of getting by in a state of constant terror and also the satirical elements in the plot and the narrative asides in general. Can you comment a little bit about the role of humor in the work?

VG: Humor pulls you through such moments. Without it, it gets difficult to survive. There is a dark humor about the city. Something on the lines of—"*Beta kuch mat bol varna …*" It's the reverse of "*Beta so jaa, varna Gabbar aa jayega.*" If you say something, the police will catch you and take you away. As far as the sarcasm is concerned, it wasn't conscious. But when the book came out, people said that they loved the sarcasm. Well, it wasn't intentional. But probably that's the only way I know how to tell a story. So, it certainly wasn't intentional, but I'm glad that it worked. There is also a certain amount of humor about how we deal with our own politics. The humor there is directed at characters who are being very politically correct and who want to change the world. Those frictions come up in the second part of the book where the characters, being the activists they are, take the bus to the village and sing there. There is the whole clash between being pragmatic and being politically correct. That friction also leads to a lot of humor. How do we deal with the police?—there is also a lot of humor there. Humor actually pulls a movement through. The underground movement, pretty much everywhere in the world, actually survives on humor. This was indeed a dark, gory period in Indian history. But what's the point of writing yet another dark, gory book about a dark, gory period in Indian history? There are a lot of books like that out there anyways. If I had to do it my way, then it would have to mix the absurd and the dark together. Black humor has always fascinated me and I think it shows in *Delhi Calm*.

There are two books I really avoided while I worked on Delhi Calm—the first was Rohinton Mistry's *A Fine Balance* and the other was *V for Vendetta*. I was in the danger of chugging into the same territory if I read those two. I could have constructed a narrative of the state being an oppressor, of the state being an overarching character, or I could have made the book about the state being a concept and about life in Delhi negotiating around itself. I chose the latter option.

ARB: Did you collaborate with anyone in the project or was it primarily a solo effort?

VG: It was primarily my own. Collaboration … no! The friend I worked with—his research helped a lot. Plus there was my own research. But primarily it was a solo effort.

ARB: How long did it take you to finish it?

VG: Technically the book stayed in my head for two years. However, the actual work took around two years, from start to finish.

ARB: Let's move on to your next project (*This Side, That Side*). That's more of an anthology of a sort than a stand-alone work. Could you take us a little bit through how you came about that project, how you got all the collaborators to write for it, and the artistic process involved in it.

VG: See, the partition book was something I wanted to do before *Delhi Calm*. But, as I told you, I couldn't do it at that time because my voice wasn't adequate enough. The idea came from my publisher. She was looking at stories on partition from India, Pakistan and Bangladesh. She asked me whether I wanted to do it and I said that I was probably the best guy to do it because it had been in my head for quite a while. So, I sat down and started thinking about it. It was something that I had been working on, researching on, thinking about and doing nothing about it. I'd been to places, I'd shot videos; but I did nothing with those videos either. We started off with an open call for entries to make it accessible to a lot of people we didn't know. That was step one. I also chased a few stories I'd heard over the years. I had been to Lahore in 2008. I heard a few stories which I tried chasing down. I had a few friends in Delhi and Kolkata who told me a few stories over time. It was a mix and match. A lot of people sent in a lot of work. A lot of people were skeptical about how Partition would be represented in a comic book, which shows how comic books are looked at and how less we deal with the event itself. So, those people had to be convinced. Some sent in their Ph.D. theses. I told them that I wouldn't be able to publish their theses because they were long form narratives. I just had ten pages for each person. Therefore, those stories had to be sacrificed. So there was a lot of to and fro.

There was an additional novelty to this project besides this being a giant endeavor for me and for partition studies. We have never actually dealt with stories from the other side in the same book with stories from this side. I have never seen a book with stories from Pakistan and Bangladesh in the same book with stories from India because the different sides could not see eye to eye. The idea was to bring it together. The interesting part about partition for me is not what we have left behind, but how we connect now, how we deal with each other. That's why we subtitled it "Restorying Partition" because this is not about partition, not about what happened, but about how we deal with one another. So we opened up a call for entries. A lot of stories came in, a lot of stories changed hands, a lot of stories changed character ... that was how it worked. The important thing for me was to consciously cover as many aspects of partition as possible. For example, the Bangladeshi Hindu or the Pakistani Hindu is as much of a victim as the Indian Muslim, whether they moved or didn't. What about the Bihari in Dhaka, for instance? These were things I was conscious about after having picked them up over the years interacting with people. For instance, I met this fascinating guy in Dhaka. He was a Bangladeshi who had been in Karachi for all his working life. He was in Karachi when Bangladesh happened, and he did not move back. He was a Bengali Pakistani. He finished his tenure there, retired, got his money, came back to Bangladesh, and became a Bangladeshi. So he actually negotiated his citizenship many times. Likewise, there was a Bihari Muslim stuck in Dhaka who still dreams of going to Pakistan one day. The Cooper's camp, for example, in West Bengal ... people are still waiting for citizenship there. So, for me, it was important for me to get as many aspects as possible.

It was also important for me to do that because we are still bound by the nation-form in the subcontinent. We have, say, ten comic books in India, none in Pakistan, none in Bangladesh. I would like to believe that people make and read comics there. So how do we get them interested? A lot of them were artists and we convinced them to try this form. We have a miniature painter from Islamabad in the collection. She worked on one of the stories. I gave her the story on dastangoi. She had never seen that. I sent her a few youtube videos and told her that this is the form in which it happens. I asked her—"Why don't you try miniatures to talk about it in the graphic novel?" I was lucky that she gave it a shot and a good piece came out of it. Similarly, I asked an art professor. I asked a poet to lend his poem and see how it worked in a visual. I was lucky to get great contributors. I had a lot of people saying no because they weren't sure of the form. But the fact remains that to bring more novel readers into graphic novels, we need more writers. To convert readers into graphic novel readers, we need to convert writers of other forms into graphic novel writers. That was important for me. So, we got poets, theater persons. Tabish Khair wrote, Mahmood Farooqui did a section on Intizar Hussain's piece, Kaiser Haq, a very well-known poet from Dhaka, contributed a piece. I convinced Rabbi Sher Gill, a rock star, to give it a shot. I tried to get a few filmmakers as well, but it didn't work out. They were interested, but couldn't manage the time. So the idea was to get different types of people because partition has affected us all. Why focus only on graphic novelists? I'm glad that it worked at the end.

ARB: What do you think about the reception of your work?

VG: I wasn't thinking that I would become a Chetan Bhagat. But I was pleasantly surprised by the reception of *Delhi Calm*. People still talk about it. In a few days, we will do five years of *Delhi Calm* and forty years of the Emergency. The book's still in circulation; so I'm happy about that. *This Side, That Side* has been phenomenal. I've travelled all across the country and South Asia with it and the reception has been very good. Students, old people who never read graphic novels ... some old people came up to me in

Dhaka and said that they had never heard of graphic novels. But they were buying this book. That's a great thing—converting a seventy year old into a graphic novel reader.

ARB: What do you think of the contemporary graphic novel scene in India?

VG: We've just had ten books. I think we need more to have a contemporary scene as such.

ARB: Are there any particular ones you like?

VG: Besides my own books? (laughs). What really works for me is good drawing. If the content is good and the drawing isn't, then it puts me off because that's probably the way I am tuned. The drawings of DeLisle or Satrapi are so simple, but there is something endearing about them. The draughtmanship of Peeters, the stroke of Baudoin—there is something so fascinating about that. They pull the brush with sheer confidence. That is what I look at when I read a graphic novel. I am always looking for the next instalments of how Orijit does his treatments, how Amruta works out her pages or how Sarnath works his pages. He really doesn't want to draw, but he still does, and he still wants to negotiate that page and that is interesting for me. They are completely different types of works. These works stand out for me. Besides that, I haven't seen a lot more actually. There is a lot of work that comes out from the mainstream, like *Devi*. I don't really follow that. So it would be unfair for me to comment on those.

ARB: Finally, what are your future projects? Is there anything that you are working on currently?

VG: There is a book on Lahore I want to do. There is a project on the growth of Gurgaon that I am interested in doing. I don't know if I will get to do those. Maybe some romance books sometime ... who knows? For the longest time I told people that I was working on the partition book, but then I came out with *Delhi Calm*. So, who knows?

Notes

1. See Tarlo.
2. In Haiti, the *bokor* refers to the *vodoun* sorcerer who creates and controls zombies.
3. See Lauro and Embry.

Works Cited

Banerjee, Sarnath. *Corridor: A Graphic Novel.* New Delhi: Penguin, 2004. Print.

Boluk, Stephanie and Wylie Lenz. "Introduction: Generation Z, the Age of Apocalypse." *Generation Zombie: Essays on the Living Dead in Modern Culture.* Eds. Stephanie Boluk and Wylie Lenz. Jefferson, NC: MacFarland, 2011. 1–17. Print.

Creekmur, Corey K. "The Indian Graphic Novel." A History of the Indian Novel in English. Ed. Ulka Anjaria. New York, London: Cambridge UP, 2015. 348–58. Print.

Eisner, Will. *Comics and Sequential Art: Principles and Practices from the Legendary Artist*. New York: W.W. Norton and Company, 2008. Print.

Ghosh, Vishwajyoti. *Times New Roman and Countrymen*. New Delhi: Blaft PublicationS, 2009. Print.

———. *Delhi Calm*. New Delhi: Harper Collins, 2010. Print.

———. *This Side, That Side: Restorying Partition*. New Delhi: Yoda P, 2013. Print.

Gupta, Akhil and Aradhana Sharma Eds. *The Anthropology of the State: A Reader*. New York: Wiley Blackwell, 2008. Print.

Hansen, Thomas B. and Finn Stepputat Eds. *States of Imagination: Ethnographic Explorations of the Postcolonial State*. Durham: Duke UP, 2001. Print.

Holmberg, Ryan. "Inverted Calm: An Interview with Vishwajyoti Ghosh." *tcj.com*. Pub. October 23, 2013. Web. June 25, 2015.

Lauro, Sarah J. and Karen Embry. "The Zombie Manifesto." *boundary2*, Spring 2008, 35(1). 85–108. Print.

McCloud, Scott. *Understanding Comics: The Invisible Art*. New York: William Morrow Paperbacks, 1994. Print.

McLain, Karline. *India's Immortal Comic Books: Gods, Kings and Other Heroes*. Bloomington: Indiana UP, 2009. Print.

Mohapatra, Saurav. *Mumbai Confidential: Good Cop, Bad Cop*. Mumbai: Archaia, 2013. Print.

Patil, Amruta. *Kari*. New Delhi: Harper Collins, 2008. Print.

Sen, Orijit. *River of Stories*. New Delhi: Kalpavriksha, 1994. Print.

Sholay. Dir. Ramesh Sippy. Perf. Amitabh Bachchan, Amjad Khan, Dharmendra. Mumbai: Eros International, 2003. DVD.

Singh, Parismita. *The Hotel at the End of the World*. New Delhi: Penguin, 2009. Print.

Tarlo, Emma. *Unsettling Memories: Narratives of the Emergency in Delhi*. Berkeley: U of California P, 2003. Print.

Taussig, Michael. "Terror as Usual: Walter Benjamin's Theory of History as a State of Siege." *Social Text*. No. 23, Autumn–Winter 1989. 3–20.

Part II

The National, The Global, and the Diaspora

5 Unmoored

Passing, Slumming, and Return-Writing in New India

Ragini Tharoor Srinivasan

[Bombay] is a city hostile to outsiders or nostalgia stuck returnees. We can muscle our way in with our dollars, but even when the city gives in, it resents us for making it do so ...

—Suketu Mehta

I have some admiration for the rat that, unlike me, hasn't fled Patna and has found it possible to live and thrive there.

—Amitava Kumar

The first two decades of the twenty-first century saw a veritable international publishing boom in English-language nonfiction works about the rise of India, including a substantial sub-genre of works on the global Indian city.[1] This chapter considers a sub-species of that sub-genre: literary nonfictions that simultaneously narrate the emergence of the Indian city's global form and a formerly diaspora-based author's return to that city in the era of what is known, in popular parlance, as the liberalized "New India": Rana Dasgupta's *Capital: The Eruption of Delhi*; Amitava Kumar's *A Matter of Rats: A Short Biography of Patna*; Suketu Mehta's *Maximum City: Bombay Lost and Found*. Despite key differences, such nonfictional works match the grandiose, expansive sweep of historical estimations of India's rise with intimate accounts of the returned author's memories, family history, and everyday life. Each also offers a narrative triangulation of the author's return to India, India's rise, and the author's encounters with other, ostensibly more rooted Indians, whose personal itineraries illuminate the nation's experiments with globality in ways otherwise unavailable to the diaspora-returned.

To what extent were these nonfictional accounts of the New Indian city adequate to a nation in the throes of its own narrative reimagining? To whom did the "nostalgia-stuck returnees" turn in order to authorize their texts? The problem presented by urban "return-writing," as I propose we term the genre, is one of accessing the contemporary: of apprehending and writing the present that is India under the conditions of globalization. This is not a problem unique to nonfiction; as Ulka Anjaria notes in an essay on the Indian Anglophone novel, "contemporaneity implies ... an uncontrollable mess of synchronous elements that are ever-unfolding and, by their very nature, impossible to contain and classify" (20). However, the problem of contemporaneity takes on heightened significance when the writers in question are returnees from diaspora, drawn back to India by the facts of birth and heritage and confronted with the nation's global transformations. For these writers, the constitutive unruliness of the contemporary is coupled with the perspectival blinders of personal enmeshment. They must cope with the eruptive and disruptive presence of "memory mines," sudden and jarring recollections of the past that make it particularly challenging "to deal with the India of the present" (Mehta 38).

Traversing the New Indian city for these returnees means looking in vain for a house that has been built over or seeking a temple that has since become a shopping mall. It means struggling to see the city for what it is, despite the inevitability of seeing it "in terms of their own lives" (Kumar, *Rats* 106). By consequence, each returnee eventually concludes, implicitly or explicitly, that his own experience of India's rise is not sufficient material for the book he seeks to write, whether he conceives of it as a work of travel writing, memoir, life-writing, or journalistic reportage. Return-writing thus unfolds through a series of portraits and micro-biographies of individual figures whose life trajectories better parallel that of India's ascent—or so the story goes: people like Ramadas, a sixty-year-old Dalit cow-broker, driven out of his profession and into the ranks of the aspiring entrepreneur, whose story "was a quintessentially Indian [one] ... of ruin and reinvention" (Kapur 285).

Individuals are rendered in this genre as types, which in turn appear across texts. New India has its Gatsbys, its do-gooders, its professional women, its suiciding farmers; there are poet-revolutionaries, artists-in-exile, CEOs, and petty politicians. Siddhartha Deb's Abdul Jabbar, an activist in Bhopal who runs an organization for widows, is Rana Dasgupta's Meenakshi, the self-appointed representative of Bhalswa settlement. For a moment, or a few pages, each figure embodies "the new sense of hope gusting through India" (Giridharadas 32). Contrary to prevailing criticisms, then, return-writers are not clear-cut native informants; rather, they are more accurately passing the proverbial baton of informancy on to other, more supposedly authentic, global Indians even as they, the returnees, continue to be interpellated as informants in the West.

This chapter seeks to unpack the relationship between the returnee's precarious inhabitance of the Indian city and his turn to other New Indians as informants and tour guides, whose critical purchase on India's realities are intended to redeem the limitations of the returnee's own perspective. In what follows, I will suggest, following a provocation from Snehal Shingavi, that this quest for authenticity leads the returnee to go "passing" and "slumming," practices which enable him "to come to terms with the dividedness of the city while confronting his own feelings of internal fracture and displacement" (Huggan 46). In *Maximum City*, for example, Mehta attempts to pass as an Indian insider, on the one hand, while indulging a predilection to slum, on the other—that is, he consorts with and writes about people of lower castes and classes whom he never would have encountered before leaving India.

Maximum City is conventionally credited as the inaugural text in the return-writing tradition, although the coinage is mine. As one critic writes, Mehta discovered "a mode in which Indians could write about place without going abroad ... The Indian city is exotic enough, grotesque enough, even for those who live in it" (Krishna). Of course, Mehta was not the first to employ his "return to India" as a narrative occasion. In the early and mid-twentieth century, Dhan Gopal Mukerji, Santha Rama Rau, Dom Moraes, Ved Mehta (no relation to Suketu), and V. S. Naipaul all produced nonfictional accounts of, in the elder Mehta's words, the process of "[finding their] way back to the heart of India by walking and talking and listening to friends" (19). *Maximum City*'s key innovation was to foreground the *city* (specifically, Mumbai) as both the diasporic return-writer's specific locus of attachment and the primary spatio-territorial, conceptual, and cultural site in which to observe the processes of capitalist globalization unfolding in the Indian nation after the economic reforms of the early 1990s.

If the rise of global India is the performance enacted and observed, then the city in each return-writing text comprises its actors, setting, and stage. Each book marries an account of "personal geography" (Mehta 3) to semi-ethnographic reporting on the post-liberalization condition of the particular Indian city to which the writer returns from his diasporic perch in the United States or the United Kingdom. Even Akash Kapur, whose *India Becoming* narrates his return to rural Auroville in Tamil Nadu, travels frequently to the big cities in order to take the pulse of the New India: "The future was in places like Bangalore—in cities that heaved with ambition and entrepreneurship and opportunity" (44).

My use of the masculine pronoun in the above paragraphs has been deliberate, for the majority of return-writers, and not only those under discussion in this chapter, are male. This has less to do with the demographic phenomenon of reverse migration itself than with the specific narrative form of the return-writing genre and the "walking and talking" methodology of encounter employed in its production. It is almost too obvious to note that women and men, not only in India but around the world, "do not share equal access to public space" (Phadke et al. viii; Butcher), nor do women experience the same freedoms as their male counterparts. This includes the freedom that is most necessary for the apprehension of New India: the freedom to walk unmolested in the city. We might ask, then, in response to Kapur: Ambition, entrepreneurship, and opportunity—for whom?

India's cities are, on the one hand, the nation's most legibly and normatively cosmopolitan spaces, where Baristas and Café Coffee Days serve English-speaking, jeans-wearing customers, including returnees like Mehta and Kapur, who are subjects of gendered, linguistic, and occupational privilege. For the majority of Indians, however, the cities can be the least accommodating spaces in New India. As scholars studying India's emergent middle class have shown, the comfortable inhabitance of the Indian city is an achievement to which the upwardly mobile continually aspire (Gooptu). Ordering a coffee in Barista is itself a challenge for many newcomers to the city; aspiring New Indians have to be instructed in and habituated into such "bodily performance[s] of competency ... which [signal] belonging within a particular social geography" (McGuire 113). In *Calcutta*, which is both a work of return-writing and a commentary on the genre, Amit Chaudhuri likens mall-goers who hesitate before stepping onto the escalator to "inexperienced swimmers by a poolside, wanting, but hesitant, to take the plunge ... averted with an inured sigh by the veteran escalator-users" (216).

The reterritorializing diasporic subject does not need to be instructed in practices like latte-ordering and escalator-riding. Nevertheless, he, too, has to come to grips with a lack of "embodied knowledge" (McGuire 122) about the transformation underway in India's cities. Ved Mehta eventually found "elbow room" (144) in the 1950s Delhi crowd, but Bombay in the 1990s is neither legible nor hospitable to those whom Suketu Mehta dubs, to return to the first epigraph, "outsiders or nostalgia-stuck returnees" (23).[2] Attending an art auction in Mumbai, Kapur is comforted by the feeling that he "could be anywhere in the world" (171). A bearer of the dominant ideology of globality, he not only expects, but is also relieved that the East should appear as a derivative form of the West. And yet, Kapur must eventually leave the auction and step out onto Mumbai's potholed, frenetic city streets: "I didn't know which India was the real one," he says, voicing in naïve terms a predicament shared to varying degrees by all the return-writers (173).

Return-writing is fundamentally an ambivalent genre, in which the writer attempts to square his affection for an India-past with his frustrated desire for accommodation in and by the city in question. "It would be too simple to say that I fell in love with Delhi," Dasgupta writes, "it is just as true that I fell in hate" (36). "I don't actually like the Calcutta of today," Chaudhuri says, and yet it is "the world that I (for some obscure but dogged reason) love" (44–5). For Mehta, moving to Mumbai means confronting the fact that the city "that has a tight claim on my heart" (3)—the city formerly known as Bombay— has been effectively "ruin[ed]" (97). These lines reflect an implicit conflation of city and nation that is intrinsic to the genre, for what is at stake in each disavowal of the city-present is a critique of the neoliberal New India. If India's cities were once the playgrounds of affluent, English-speaking, cosmopolitan elites, now, the same cities have taken in millions of rural migrants, entrepreneurial New Indians, who are vying to establish *their* rights to the city. "This is the new breed," Chaudhuri marvels at the Kolkatans who occupy his Calcutta (216).[3] Kumar, quoted in the second epigraph, suspects that even Patna's rats are more at home in the city than he will ever be.

These are not triumphant returns "home" after long, self-imposed periods of diasporic "exile." Rather, as I discuss in the next section, the genre posits return as a challenge, both to the reverse migrating subject and to the New Indian city that stands to embrace or cast him out. The readings of

Maximum City and *A Matter of Rats* which then follow show that diasporic returnees internalize the idea of Indian globality as a challenge to encounter the "real" India, as if for the first time. The result has been the production of the generically hybrid return-writing genre of Indian Anglophone non-fiction, characterized by an at once novelistic and ethnographic disposition evident on the level of narrative (through the importation of unreliable narration into the nonfiction work) and politics (the ambivalent embrace of social criticism as the imperative of all writing on New India). It is a genre that rises to the challenge of apprehending the real New India by problematizing the very notion of the real. And it is one which I will ultimately show offers stories of two kinds of outcasts: those on the margins of the New Indian city, and those who return from diaspora to write about them.

Of Exiles and Outcasts

Postcolonial literary discourse has long prioritized the epistemic violence and material consequences of writers having left, or been made to leave, their nations of origin—first, through the dislocating experience of being instructed in the languages and literatures of the colonial metropole, and then, by emigrating for economic opportunity or higher education in the West. To that end, scholars of Indian Anglophone literature have conventionally discussed the writer in diaspora as an exile, one whose precarious purchase on Indian realities is compromised not only by his location, but also by his dual reliance on the English language and Western audiences for the legitimation of his literary production. These assumptions span critical writings on both Indian Anglophone fiction and nonfiction. For Tabish Khair, the rhetoric of exile masks the constitutive alienation of writers of "babu fictions," who, he argues, have more in common with Englishmen than with the Indians they attempt and fail to represent in their "stylized English" (109). For Rob Nixon, writing on Naipaul's travelogues, an exilic, dislocated posture exaggerates Naipaul's "distance from mainstream Anglo-American traditions, literary and political alike," enabling him to speak as an authority on the non-West (14). For Khair, exile is a delegitimizing location; for Nixon, it is a disingenuous one.

The insistence on the exilic nature of postcolonial writing is in part borne of Edward Said's influential writing on the subject. For Said, exile could be cultivated as a perspective; the exile's "plurality of vision" would give rise to a "[contrapuntal] awareness of simultaneous dimensions" (*Reflections* 186). Exile has its "rewards," Said famously wrote, "and, yes, even privileges" (*Representations* 59). The exilic intellectual is free "to see things not simply as they are, but as they have come to be that way" (*Representations* 60). By that same token, however, Said was critical of the exilic posture. Homelessness could become an affectation, "dissatisfaction bordering on dyspepsia, a kind of curmudgeonly disagreeableness," characteristic of a jaundiced writer like Naipaul (Said, *Representations* 53).

Even when Indian Anglophone literature and criticism are alive to the dynamics of return—recall, for instance, the iconic line from Salman Rushdie's *The Satanic Verses*, with which critics have made hay: "Exile is a dream of glorious return" (212)—the popularity of the trope of exile, whether construed as enabling or disabling, freeing or blinding, has overshadowed consideration of the consequences of return: of what happens once the dream is fulfilled and found wanting. The contemporary phenomenon of reverse brain-drain from West to East that has attended the rise of India and China in the "Asian" twenty-first century provides new occasion to consider the implications and literary signature of authorial repatriation, as well as to plumb the tenacity of diasporic subjects' corporeal and territorial attachments to their nations of birth or heritage (here, India). It also makes it possible for us to pose the question of how India generally, and the Indian city specifically, performs its attachment to or rejection of those same subjects.

The figure of the urban outcast who occasions the chapters collected here is someone on the margins of the city; the reasons for that marginality, however, and the affective experience of it can vary tremendously. The diasporic returnee is, as I have been suggesting, a privileged subject—a member of the club of India's "rich people, English-speaking people, foreign-returned people" (Mehta 34)—and yet he is not immune to the exclusions the city enacts against newcomers: those who do not belong, who are not in the know, and are often not fluent in the vernacular. "A city has its secrets," Mehta writes, detailing the many indignities Bombay visits upon his family in the early days of their return. They have difficulty finding a flat and end up in one with terrible ventilation; they try to shop and are repeatedly fleeced. "You are not from here," the city says, "you are not Indian, so you deserve to be ripped off" (29–30). Nor are Mehta's children immune to the illness all around them: "The food and the water in Bombay, India's most modern city, are contaminated with shit ... We have been feeding our son shit" (28).

Reviewing *Maximum City*, Amitava Kumar calls this passage an example of "hysterical realism," a self-reflexive mix of exaggerated panic and irony ("Enigma"). But it is also the returnee's sincere, if distressed, attempt to grapple with the question of his belonging in New India and the dawning realization that neither India nor the city of his birth owes him anything. As Rau realized after returning "home" to Bombay from London in 1939, it is not that India has to "prove itself" to the returnee, so much as the returnee has to have "something to contribute to Indian life" (189, 143). Failure to contribute means being ignored or rejected, for, put simply, one need not be forcibly "cast out" of the city in order to find oneself outcast, homeless, and unmoored upon return. By that same token, a contrapuntal, exilic perspective is not a vantage that the diasporic subject can ever fully adopt until his attempt to return to India is thwarted, or until he discovers his marginality upon return.

In contrast to "exile," might the term outcast more adequately politicize and situate the figure of the diasporic returnee in New India's global cities?

To couch this move as a riposte to Khair, alienation is a two-way street. It is not only that those who leave India for the West become alienated from the conditions of Indian life because of physical and psychic distance; rather, it is also that those who return to India from the West are alienated from the conditions of living there because of the obstacles thrown up by the New Indian city, which, in its global form, repeatedly stages the "volatile relationship between insiders and outsiders" (Huggan 39). "India is the Country of the No," Mehta observes. "['No'] is India's Great Wall; it keeps out foreign invaders" (18). Is it any wonder, then, that the return-writer-invader must join forces with other outcasts in their attempt to scale India's Great Wall?

Passing, Slumming, and the Ethnographic Disposition

The returnee's "joining forces with other outcasts" in order to gain entrance to India is, of course, a generous construal of the slumming to which I've already made mention. Slumming narratives began to appear in London in the sixteenth and early-seventeenth centuries. They took on a "moral dimension" in the 1830s, when journalists in London and Paris became interested in exposing inequality and poverty in order to effect meaningful change on the level of urban planning and policy (Seaton 28). Tony Seaton's account of slumming as "part of a modern quest for identity in the city," one that serves as "a kind of existential rite of passage, an accreditation of the [leisure classes'] authoritative grasp on modernity and the 'real world'" (43) is instructive. The two things I want to emphasize following Seaton are the fact that slumming is by definition an urban practice, and that it is also a technology of authorization for the return-writing subject, who uses his encounters with other outcast Indians as a way to legitimize his own marginality from New India and, eventually, find his way back into the elite fold.

Here, I want to take a detour through fiction, and turn to a well-known novel that dramatizes, albeit hyperbolically, the phenomenon of urban outcasting in which I'm interested: Aravind Adiga's *The White Tiger*. In the voluminous scholarship that has attended this novel, critics have examined how Adiga rains on the "India Shining" parade, performs pan-Asian solidarity, and ventriloquizes India's subaltern (Mendes; Mishra; Subrahmanyam). For Snehal Shingavi, *The White Tiger* is a novel about "passing" and "slumming," one that lays bare its limits as a tale of social transformation by ultimately upholding caste as a ticket to economic advancement. Shingavi reads Balram Halwai, the entrepreneurial-minded driver, as a figure for the slumming author; through Balram, Adiga takes the reader—here addressed as the Chinese Premier Wen Jiabao—on a tour of India's "Darkness." But Balram is a classically unreliable narrator, and the story of his ascension from slum-kid to Bangalore Brahmin "transforms him into the very object of his critique" (Shingavi 5). Shingavi continues: "The problem with slumming and passing is that one can never know where the deception ends" (5).

Return-writing is also fundamentally about the co-habitance of "passing" and "slumming" as mechanisms through which the outcast returnee stages his representation of the new global India. On the one hand, the returnee attempts to *pass* as an urban insider, one with both rights and means to live in the Indian city. "We are Indian, and we will pay Indian rates!" the returnee declares, hopeful that his past belonging might eventually guarantee present acceptance (Mehta 30). On the other hand, many return-writers find that *slumming* with other urban outcasts is their ticket to acceptance in India, as well as the means by which they will eventually garner recognition in and from the literary sphere.

Whether the return-writer imagines himself to be passing and slumming as such, this is precisely what he ends up doing. In *India Calling*, Giridharadas exemplarily describes the chain of events that leads the return-writer to seek out encounters with other marginal Indians striving for a piece of the New-India pie: The diasporic subject returns to India; this India lacks "enthusiasm for [his] arrival"; he sees "only what [he has] always seen"; he is "shielded ... from India's hardships." Thus, he resolves to stop "prancing on the surface of things" and instead "[go below and confront] what [has] fascinated, angered, and humiliated [him] about India all these years" (22). Over the course of the book that details this "going below" (an apposite phrase for slumming if ever there was one), the returnee searches out figures who "distill, in a single being" the story of the New India (32).

What distinguishes the return-writer's venture into the underworld from that of, say, Katherine Boo in *Behind the Beautiful Forevers* is not only that the returnee is a former Non-Resident Indian, as opposed to a Resident Non-Indian, but also that Boo is an investigative journalist whose method involved four years of reporting and utilized thousands of public records, whereas the return-writer's credibility is founded on the assumption of familiarity with his subject. The returnee at first relies on a network of family and friends in order to gain access to interview subjects. Boo's explicitly political reporting project is to share what she has learned from her informants about "ordinary lives" in the Mumbai slums so that "better arguments, maybe even better politics, get formulated" (251). By contrast, the returnee's primary politics is that of the personal: "I was chasing the frontier of the future," Giridharadas writes, "Which just happened, in my case, to be the frontier of my own past" (254). Complicity and enmeshment are consequently important aspects of the narrative tone and structure, because the returnee's informants are not simply "natives" but, more challengingly, fellow countrymen.

Sonia Faleiro's *Beautiful Thing* and Aman Sethi's *A Free Man* also serve as instructive counterpoints to the works I am reading as return-writing of the emergence genre. Each of their books focuses on one specific New Indian—the young Bombay bar dancer, Leela, in Faleiro's case, and the Bihari contract worker Ashraf, in Sethi's—in order to illuminate the complexities of the sexual economy and "the mazdoor ki zindagi," or laborer's life, in New India (Sethi 7). Whereas slumming evidences a roving, even impatient sensibility and desire for "full" representation in accumulative terms, Faleiro and Sethi individually tell the story of a singular human life. In so doing, however, they also reveal the impossibility of forging an equal and reciprocal friendship with an Indian urban outcast.

The irony of nonfiction is that the first-person perspective that purports to bring the reader closer to the truth—if the truth be that of the author's perspective—is also profoundly distancing. Thus, while both Faleiro and Sethi attempt to forge ethical relations to their subjects, their relations are strained by the writers' comparative privilege and remove from their subjects. One way their narratives register this imbalance in social, cultural, and linguistic capital is through the simple fact that their New Indian informants show little interest in those who are so patently, instrumentally interested in them. "Despite the apparent difference in our worlds, Leela had no curiosity about me ... Leela wanted only to be heard" (Faleiro 7). When Ashraf tells Sethi that no one listens to him, the journalist muses, "Except for me it seems. I have been listening to Ashraf for two hours this morning, and haven't got a word in edgeways" (27). These are both frank admissions of what Faleiro terms "onesided relationship[s]" and a neat alibi for the persistence with which she and Sethi pursue their respective subjects. It is an alibi that others, like Mehta, also embrace: The bar-dancer Monalisa "has nothing to hide and is quite delighted that the world should know about her life" (300).

How we read these nonfictional narratives of one-sided relation and self-disclosure depends in part on whether our comparative frame is the novel or ethnography. Numerous critics have focused on the former generic relation. Ipshita Ghose reads *Maximum City* as a "semi-autobiographical novel" (204). Ankhi Mukherjee suggests that such narrative nonfictions "[subscribe] to the humanitarian aims and objectives we relate with the rise of English novel: social circulation and mobility, redistributive justice, articulations of equivocal forms of national belonging." Stressing these nonfictional works' novelistic qualities allows critics to focus on questions of belonging—how, in Ghose's words, such texts "[acquaint readers] with the compassionate and humane aspects of life in the city" (210). By that same token, reading these texts as novels risks absolving the writer from responsibility for the processes of information gathering and participant-observation that precede each urban-living account.

The real critical challenge is that novelistic and ethnographic genres are not mutually exclusive. And while we might read Suketu Mehta's or Amitava Kumar's "insider–outsider" narratives as offering novelistic treatments of the New Indian urban multitude, their highly textualized interpretations of encounters with other Indians equally reflect an ethnographic mode of realist apprehension. They and other return-writers exhibit what Anand Pandian describes as the anthropological imagination: a belief that, when confronted with the ordinary individual, "there are many others like him, scattered here and there ... and beyond" (164). The genre as a whole shares the narrative logic of ethnography: the researcher-narrator enters the field, apprehends the lives and cultures of a set of subject-informants, and then leaves the field in order to metabolize and write about it. The writer becomes a knower by "demonstrating distance from a reality once held in close observation" (Clough xiv).

In Pandian's own generically hybrid New India book, *Ayya's Accounts*, he translates his subject's, his grandfather's, words but also interprets them, returns to them, tries to tell the reader what they mean, and he does this "out of fairness" and professional calling (150). Instead of such mediated ethnographies, what we get from return-writers are texts that by and large allow their subjects, like Monalisa, to speak for themselves. By way of another example, Dasgupta's *Capital* unfolds through a series of interviews in which Delhi's über-rich, from a real estate scion who calls himself "the chosen one" to a shopping-mall titan with "imperial" plans for shipping Punjabi farmers to plantations in Ethiopia, are allowed to voice their tragicomic visions of the world with little to no authorial pushback (Srinivasan 2014).

Which brings us back to passing and slumming, and Shingavi's suspicion that both work together in *The White Tiger* to produce what is ultimately a narrative con in lieu of a narrative of social transformation. The returnee who has left the "field" in order to produce a work of return-writing is, like Balram, caught between his desire to "show the real India" and to indulge, slyly "his own delusional sense of self" (8). He must ultimately disavow attachment to the poor, marginal, and/or underworld subjects he encounters in order to claim to know something about them, and, of course, to assert his own ontological difference from the ranks of the New Indian outcast. This imperative also necessitates a further disavowal of the writer's desire for belonging in the New Indian city, which is the generative condition for return-writing in the first place.

It is perhaps no coincidence that *The White Tiger* also narrates New India's purgation of the diasporic returnee. In a piece of critical subplot, the "crazy" (98) organization of Delhi's urban space, where "civilization can appear and disappear within five minutes" (241), enables Balram to murder his employer, the America-returned Mr. Ashok, on the side of the road. There, on that desolate stretch of highway, one of the most populated cities in the world effectively turns a blind eye to the murder of the returnee. Those both drawn to and alienated by India's cities would perhaps do well to heed Adiga's cautionary tale.

Slumming in Bombay

Maximum City begins with a familiar question—"Can you go home again?"—and ends with an unusual answer: "You can go home again, and you can also leave again" (3, 536). In the intervening pages, Mehta offers detailed accounts of his interviews and outings with outcast Bombayites: murderers, prostitutes, corrupt cops and kept politicians; people who exist both at the edge of their own "inner extremity" and on the margins of society, where they "live out the fantasies of normal people" (538). Mehta takes pleasure in these encounters. He is propelled both by curiosity about "morally compromised people" (538), and by the validation he receives from his own social milieu, members of the creative classes who derive vicarious pleasure from his tales of sex, violence, and death. The book is Mehta's effort to "find" Bombay through the writing of its stories, and yet the people to whom he turns in his search are those on the margins of the city who are, like him, "between worlds."

What does "going home" have to do with the semi-ethnographic explorations that primarily comprise the text? Why is Mehta's "dream of return" to Bombay (13) actualized in a "shadow history of the real Mumbai" (Roy 225)? On the one hand, Mehta's family "live[s] rich" in Bombay (29); it is their only option given the English-speaking, foreign-returned demographic to which they belong. On the other hand, Mehta chooses to "write poor": The majority of *Maximum City* is about slumming in the global city, not fighting for accommodation by members of its upper crust (537). It's the middle-aged, married, father-of-two, Mehta, sitting in bed with Monalisa, a nineteen-year-old bar dancer, "the kind of girl men don't give their home numbers to" (298) and a social outcast who "can never be accepted" by Mehta's world, although she wishes to leave her own. It's Mehta meeting with a group of young hitmen in a desolate hotel, as they pass around 9mm Mauser guns and proudly recount the numbers who have died at their hands.

This is the stuff of myth, specifically, the urban myth that has historically been written through narratives of slumming. But is Mehta a "low-life [specialist]" who "trawl[s] the lower depths, dredging up terrible realities for the armchair reader at home" (Seaton 28), or does he have a nobler purpose? Is he a humanitarian or a sensationalist; a friend to those he writes about, or an agent of exploitation? I am posing these questions in binary terms, not because the book itself eschews ambiguity, but because it lays bare the fact that these seeming polarities are really only different expressions of a single narrative form. This, then, is the book's constitutive contradiction, and a contradiction that characterizes return-writing as a genre: Mehta presents his return to Mumbai as an effort to find a way for his family to be at home in the New Indian city, but most of the book documents his calculated erasure of his family's presence through his self-presentation to those underworld subjects he strives to represent. While Ghose reads this movement from elite domestic sphere to nether-world as a generative "shift of literary locales" that enables for Mehta "a recreation of the self" (205), I read it as a sign of narrative unreliability, a novelistic device that is here complicated by the text's pretensions to ethnographic presentism.

In *The Rhetoric of Fiction*, Wayne Booth memorably introduced the figure of the unreliable narrator as one who does not "[speak] for or [act] in accordance with ... the implied author's norms ... the narrator is mistaken, or believes himself to have qualities which the author denies him" (158).

The unreliable narrator is a figure who, at first blush, only makes sense in the context of fiction, because it is the very distance between author and narrator that enables the introduction of unreliability. However, nonfictional return-writing, which purports to close the gap between author and narrator, actually installs an ironic distance between the narrator as participant–observer and the author–writer who delivers his observations into story form. To this end, return-writing offers both a nonfictional exploration of the unreliability that universally characterizes human relations, and a dialectical engagement with the shared narrative forms of ethnographic and novelistic texts.

Thus, the Mehta who converses with hitman Satish is a substantively different Mehta from the author of *Maximum City*. The former Mehta describes his encounters with Bombay lowlifes and criminals as dangerous and "exhilarating," rendering his ordinary life "trivial" (233). He strives to impress and engage them, to ingratiate himself into their company, even as he also digs for sensational accounts of their lives:

> Then, holding the gun in his hand, Satish asks me point-blank, 'Are you afraid of death?'
>   My answer is crucial. My answer must be exactly right.
>   He is loading the gun. 'What do you think will happen to you after you die?' ...
>   ... 'With all the sins I've committed in this life, I'll probably be reborn an ant.'
>   They laugh and the tension breaks. I start breathing again. (228)

The latter Mehta is fully aware that Mickey and Satish would not actually hurt him, a laptop-wielding, English-speaking foreign-returnee. He is also so comfortable in his knowledge that the hitmen will never read his Anglophone literary nonfiction that he can write, "I don't like Satish ... If the police or another gangster shoot [him] dead ... I will feel no regret" (233). This discomfiting reflection by the latter Mehta—who admits the omissions, insincerity, and instrumentality that attend his research process—is not in keeping with the implied norms of the former: a subject who some critics credit with "becoming increasingly sensitive to the inconsequentiality faced by ordinary individuals who are engulfed by the multitude" (Ghose 206), but who I am suggesting is calculatingly savvy about the marketable extra-ordinariness of those same multitudes.

Throughout *Maximum City*, Mehta-the-author gives the reader access to the narrator's unreliability by thematizing the lengths to which Mehta-the-participant-observer dissembles in service of gathering material for his book: "[Monalisa] tells me she missed me ... and had gone out to catch the last show at Sterling. I don't tell her that I was there too, in the audience, with my wife" (300). Clearly, what John L. Jackson, Jr., calls "the presentation of self in ethnographic life"—a calculated attempt to build rapport by "[greasing] the wheel of comfortable connectedness" with one's informants—is operative in return-writing as well. That said, my point is not that slumming can't be both moral and prurient, sincere and insincere, interested and exploitive; rather, it's the coincidence of these motivations that make it a compelling and problematic genre. Return-writing repeatedly exposes its own Janus-face, which inevitably conditions the reader's assessment of the narrator's (sympathetic or unsympathetic) character.

"We fought with Bombay, fought hard, and it made a place for us," Mehta writes in closing (537). And yet he, Mehta, then gives up his place in Mumbai to return to the United States, while all those outcasts whose stories made his name—Mickey, Satish, Monalisa—remain on the margins of the city. Slumming, *Maximum City* reminds us, is an embodied practice in service of a narrative, textual one. The writer returns to India because New Indian outcasts make "excellent copy" (Sethi 6). If and when he leaves India again, it's for the same reason.

Passing in Patna

"Telling Bombay's story" is Mehta's alibi for hanging out with gangsters and hitmen, bar dancers and escorts, cops and robbers. "Report[ing] from the global future" is Dasgupta's. In *A Matter of Rats*, Amitava Kumar takes a different approach: Rather than "seek out the chief minister's rally or a Bollywood star's banquet," he opts for "the fullest encounter with the ordinary" (xiii). Effectively, this means that Kumar ends up "search[ing] for that which would have engaged [him] most fully" if he lived in Patna—which is to say, if he had never left.

Kumar distinguishes between three versions of Patna, the city to which he returns frequently from the United States in order to visit his aging parents. The first is the Patna of diasporic subjects who emigrated from India and now treat Patna like an unwanted "leftover": "As soon as they land at Patna airport, they show how uncomfortable they are in their hometown—such humidity! Such filth!" (50). Residents of the first Patna are non-residents like Kumar, or rather, the ugliest version of the non-resident. The second Patna belongs to those who stayed in India, who belong "nowhere else" and who alone understand daily life in the city. The third is the Patna of those for whom it is "a matter of life and death," that is, those for whom Patna either represents an activist calling or a state of abjection. If Kumar were like the other return-writers, like Mehta, for example, his short biography of Patna would be focused on this third Patna. It isn't, and what Kumar's typology brings into relief is just how odd it is that so many residents of the "first" India must go slumming in the "third" in order to locate and moor themselves in the Indian city.

A resident of the first Patna, Kumar strives to see the city as if he lived in the second. He is fascinated and compelled by those of his peers who stayed behind in India, who resisted the lure of the West, finding ways to live in and even contribute to global India. He visits a friend who started a school for low-caste Musahar children and describes the work of Samta Rai, an activist who performs street plays and organizes arts festivals in Patna. "I am struck by the fact that I left Patna in search of a life of comfort," Kumar reflects, chastened. "I am haunted by the zeal and affection of a person who came to Patna and stayed there in the hope of bringing about social change" (84).[4]

A Matter of Rats can be read as an exploration of diasporic expendability; it expresses a desire for authenticity that is also a desire for a position of legitimacy from which to speak and act. The book might equally be read as an essayistic commentary on its author's ambivalence about return-writing-as-slumming. While he does seek out low-caste Musahars, who catch and eat rats, as part of his Patna biography, Kumar also offers sustained meta-commentary on other writing in the emergence genre, broadly construed, including Naipaul's India trilogy and Sethi's *A Free Man*. For example, he accompanies Sethi to Bara Tooti Chawk, where the young journalist first encountered Mohammed Ashraf. Inspired by Sethi—whose book was animated by his commitment to finding "the joy" in working life—Kumar tries to ask the workers he meets there about "pleasure":

> But the fact was that there wasn't much to feel happy about ... And I was finding it pretty fucking depressing ... I had found it difficult to listen to the stories that the men had told me, and in response [Sethi] said that one cannot write about the poor with one's sensibilities left intact ... [nor can one] write only out of sympathy and sorrow. (58–9)

What do the men drink? What do they do for fun? Kumar is admiring of Sethi's approach and yet fundamentally "unsure" about his right, as a returnee, to retell the stories of the people he meets in Patna (59). What he is sure about is that "self-reflexivity is not a way out of this" (Huggan 31).

Kumar is right to be cautious, for those who leave Patna return to a different city from the one they remember, one filthier and less hospitable, incapable of managing its transportation system and basic infrastructure, and the relation between city and returnee is ultimately one of mutual mis-recognition. Lepers sit at Patna railway station, just as Kumar remembers, but now there are also ports for charging cell phones. How is he to tell this story? Is this a sign that India has moved forward in time despite being "frozen" in the diasporic subject's memory? Or is it an ironic, painful commentary on what the nation and its cities have prioritized, over and above the lives of all those who have been left behind? Works of return-writing are caught between offering a critique of what they depict and simply depicting what they seek to critique (Huggan 32). Kumar refuses to make this choice, opting instead to reflect on the impossibility of choosing between inadequate narrative forms in the representation of New India.

Complicity and Critique

In *Mumbai Fables*, Gyan Prakash quotes Jonathan Raban in order to argue that the myths that attend Bombay are even more real than "'the hard city one can locate on maps in statistics, in monographs on urban sociology and demography and architecture'" (4). Prakash attributes his own mythology of Bombay to Bollywood movies he saw while growing up in the 1950s and 1960s; those movies produced a vision of a cosmopolitan Bombay that "held the promise of exciting newness and unlimited possibilities" (5). Is a work of return-writing like *Maximum City* the literary equivalent of a Bollywood film, or is it an attempt to uncover the remains of the "real" Bombay? To ask the question differently, is the book itself a work of mythology, or a realist counter to the mythos of the global city?

In a related essay, I argue that the return-writer's migratory intention leads him to seek out signs of urban renewal and opportunities for the cultivation of a metropolitan ethos in New India, despite his overwhelming feelings of alienation. I call the resulting affective posture "the rhetoric of return" (Srinivasan 2015). The preceding discussion redoubles my effort to re-center the phenomenon of return in the reading of contemporary Indian Anglophone writing, but with a focus on the narrative disposition of the texts in question, over and above the affective dissonance that their writers lay bare. The question, as I hope to have shown, is not so much why diasporic writers are returning to India, or how they feel about giving up the privilege of foreign location for the agonistic confrontation of a nation to which they only precariously belong (and only sometimes "like"), but rather how, and with recourse to whom, that return is given narrative form.

Unreliable narration, the turn to slumming as method, and the tension between political diagnosis and moral prescription suggest that return-writing is part of a broader capitulation to inequality in the New Indian city. The genre is replete with dramatizations of complicity, insincerity, and ambivalence that rarely evolve into substantial interventions into the lives of New India's urban outcasts. By that same token, however, return-writing offers a timely, sustained meditation on the politics and aesthetics of literary nonfiction. If the exile in an earlier model of postcolonial literary criticism was a figure predominantly preoccupied with the vantage afforded by departure, then the outcast return-writer seeks to reclaim the Indian life he might have lived, in addition to the Indian subject he might have become. In each work of return-writing, there is a tacit self-critique of having left India in the first place, as well as a humbling awareness that the nation, India, is capable of functioning, thriving, and arriving into the future *without* the diasporic subject's presence. As Kumar both laments and concedes, "neither the *chappals* that I had photographed, nor anything else written about their wearer, were going to get toys for Shakeel Ahmad's five-year-old in time for Eid" (59). Having accepted that return-writing will not reshape New India, his question is simply how he might "endeavor to represent, with as much creativity as possible, the conditions of living" (59).

Notes

1. Think: *India Arriving* (Dossani), *India Calling* (Giridharadas), *India Becoming* (Kapur), *India Rising* (Balch) ... and that's only works with gerunds in the titles.
2. By "elbow room in the crowd," Ved Mehta means a place at Prime Minister Nehru's table (144). In *Walking the Indian Streets*, he recounts returning to India from Oxford to find a congenital "lack of urgency" in the nation (43). What restores his faith in India is a spirit-lifting lunch with the PM himself. By contrast, return-writers of the emergence genre do not typically have access to the governing elite, nor to direct political influence as a vehicle for national contribution. All parenthetical references to "Mehta" are Suketu Mehta.
3. Calcutta was renamed "Kolkata" in 2001 in a wave of nationalist vernacularization that had earlier substituted "Mumbai" for Bombay and "Chennai" for Madras. What Chaudhuri is registering here is the sense that Calcutta is not ontologically equivalent to Kolkata. Similarly, Bombay's 1995 renomination as Mumbai eroded for many the city's cosmopolitan character (Hansen).
4. Decades earlier, the Europe-returned Rau described a similar crisis of exilic perspective: "[W]e felt that [Indian] conventions were ... retrogressive and socially crippling ... We thought at the time that one needed the perspective of travel to see these things ... later we found many young Indians who had lived at home all their lives and ... were doing a great deal more toward solving [India's social problems] than we ever thought of doing" (25).

Works Cited

Adiga, Aravind. *The White Tiger*. New York: Free P, 2008. Print.

Anjaria, Ulka. "Introduction: Literary Pasts, Presents, and Futures." *A History of the Indian Novel in English*. New York: Cambridge UP, 2015. Print.

Balch, Oliver. *India Rising: Tales from a Changing Nation*. New York: Faber and Faber, 2012. Print.

Boo, Katherine. *Behind the Beautiful Forevers: Life, Death, and Hope in a Mumbai Undercity*. New York: Random House, 2012. Print.

Booth, Wayne C. *The Rhetoric of Fiction*. Chicago: U of Chicago P, 1961. Print.

Butcher, Melissa. "Distinctly Delhi: Affect and Exclusion in a Crowded City." *Urban Theory Beyond the West*. Eds. Tim Edensor and Mark Jayne. New York: Routledge, 2012. Print.

Chaudhuri, Amit. *Calcutta: Two Years in the City*. New York: Alfred A. Knopf, 2013. Print.

Dasgupta, Rana. *Capital: The Eruption of Delhi*. New York: The Penguin P, 2014. Print.

Deb, Siddhartha. *The Beautiful and the Damned: A Portrait of the New India*. New York: Faber and Faber, 2011. Print.

Dossani, Rafiq. *India Arriving: How this Economic Powerhouse is Redefining Global Business*. New York: Amacom, 2008. Print.

Faleiro, Sonia. *Beautiful Thing: Inside the Secret World of Bombay's Dance Bars*. Edinburgh: Canongate, 2011. Print.

Ghose, Ipshita. "Bombay, Multipli-city: De-Marginalizing Urban Identities and Activities," *The Idea of the City: Early-Modern, Modern and Post-Modern Locations and Communities*. Ed. Joan Fitzpatrick. Newcastle upon Tyne: Cambridge Scholars Publishing, 2009. 203–12. Print.

Giridharadas, Anand. *India Calling: An Intimate Portrait of a Nation's Remaking.* New York: Times Books/Henry Holt and Co., 2011. Print.

Gooptu, Nandini, ed. *Enterprise Culture in Neoliberal India: Studies in Youth, Class, Work and Media.* London: Routledge, 2013. Print.

Hansen, Thomas Blom. *Wages of Violence: Naming and Identity in Postcolonial Bombay.* Princeton, NJ: Princeton UP, 2001. Print.

Huggan, Graham. *Extreme Pursuits: Travel/Writing in an Age of Globalization.* Ann Arbor: U of Michigan P, 2009. Print.

Jackson, John L., Jr. "The Presentation of Self in Ethnographic Life." *The Chronicle of Higher Education.* July 15, 2009. Web. March 15, 2015.

Kapur, Akash. *India Becoming: A Portrait of Life in Modern India.* New York: Riverhead Books, 2012. Print.

Khair, Tabish. *Babu Fictions: Alienation in Contemporary Indian English Novels.* Oxford: Oxford UP, 2001. Print.

Kumar, Amitava. *A Matter of Rats: A Short Biography of Patna.* Durham: Duke UP, 2014. Print.

———. "The Enigma of Return." *The Nation.* The Nation, September 30, 2004. Web. March 15, 2015.

Mehta, Suketu. *Maximum City: Bombay Lost and Found.* New York: Alfred A. Knopf, 2004. Print.

Mehta, Ved. *Walking the Indian Streets.* Boston: Little, Brown, and Co., 1961. Print.

Mendes, Ana Cristina. "Exciting Tales of Exotic Dark India," *The Journal of Commonwealth Literature* 45.2 (2010): 275–293. Print.

Mishra, Pankaj. "Hindi or Hinglish." *London Review of Books*, November 20, 2008. Web. March 15, 2015.

Moraes, Dom. *Gone Away.* Boston: Little and Brown, 1960. Print.

Mukerji, Dhan Gopal. *Disillusioned India.* London: Dutton, 1930. Print.

Mukherhjee, Ankhi. "Interview with Dr. Ankhi Mukherjee," *Critical Margins.* January 15, 2014. Web. December 20, 2015.

Naipaul, V. S. *An Area of Darkness.* New York: Macmillan, 1964. Print.

———. *India: A Wounded Civilization.* New York: Knopf, 1976. Print.

———. *India: A Million Mutinies Now.* New York: Viking, 1990. Print.

Nixon, Rob. *London Calling: V.S. Naipaul, Postcolonial Mandarin.* New York: Oxford UP, 1992. Print.

Pandian, Anand and M. P. Mariappan. *Ayya's Accounts: A Ledger of Hope in Modern India.* Bloomington: Indiana UP, 2014. Print.

Phadke, Shilpa, Sameera Khan, and Shilpa Ranade, *Why Loiter? Women and Risk on Mumbai Streets.* New Delhi: Penguin Books India, 2011. Print.

Prakash, Gyan. *Mumbai Fables.* Princeton, NJ: Princeton UP, 2010. Print.

Rau, Santha Rama. *Home to India.* New York: Harper & Brothers, 1945. Print.

Roy, Ananya. "Slumdog Cities: Rethinking Subaltern Urbanism." *International Journal of Urban and Regional Research* 35.2 (2011): 223–38. Print.

Rushdie, Salman. *The Satanic Verses.* New York: Picador/Henry Holt and Company, 1988. Print.

Said, Edward. *Representations of the Intellectual.* London: Vintage Books, 1994. Print.

———. *Reflections on Exile and Other Essays.* Cambridge: Harvard UP, 2000. Print.

Seaton, Tony. "Wanting to Live with Common People ...? The Literary Evolution of Slumming." *Slum Tourism: Poverty, Power and Ethics*. Eds. Fabian Frenzel, Ko Koens, and Malte Steinbrink. New York: Routledge, 2012. 21–48. Print.

Sethi, Aman. *A Free Man: A True Story of Life and Death in Delhi*. New York: W.W. Norton & Co., 2012. Print.

Shingavi, Snehal. "Capitalism, Caste, and Con-Games in Aravind Adiga's *The White Tiger*." *Postcolonial Text* 9.3 (2014): 1–16.

Srinivasan, Ragini Tharoor. "Complicity and Critique." *Public Books*, October 15, 2014. Web. March 15, 2015.

———. "The Rhetoric of Return: Diasporic Homecoming and the New Indian City." *Room One Thousand* 1:3 (2015): 308–35.

Subrahmanyam, Sanjay. "Diary." *London Review of Books*, November 6, 2008. Web. March 15, 2015.

6 *Lahore Lahore Hai*
Bapsi Sidhwa and Mohsin Hamid's City Fictions

Claire Chambers

Introduction

In November 2013 an Indian television advertisement for Google entitled "The Reunion" went viral on YouTube, garnering over four million hits from India, Pakistan, and the wider world in just five days (Associated Press; Google India). The advert pivots on the friendship of two boys from different religious backgrounds who were separated due to the partition of the Indian subcontinent in 1947. Now an old man living in Delhi, the Hindu boy Baldev Mehra reminisces to granddaughter Saman about his younger years flying kites and stealing sweets in what is today's Pakistan. He recalls his best friend Yusuf especially fondly, and so, aided by the Google search engine and associated apps, Saman traces this fellow septuagenarian and brings him to Delhi to be reunited with Baldev on the latter's birthday. The ad generated largely positive reactions on both sides of the border, although Associated Press quotes one second-generation partition migrant's observation that it is not so easy for ordinary people to travel between India and Pakistan in the ongoing climate of hostility between the two countries.

For the purposes of this chapter about the city as a simultaneously material and textualized space, what is most noteworthy about "The Reunion" is that Yusuf lives in Lahore, the antique city from which Baldev and his family fled, never to return. Indeed, the way in which Lahore is represented in this tear-jerking commercial is suggestive of the nostalgic diasporic lens through which the city is often depicted. Its opening scene features the call to prayer from a red-brick, white-domed mosque, which is presumably intended to be the city's most famous monument, the Badshahi Mosque, commissioned in the late seventeenth century by the Mughal emperor Aurangzeb (1618–707). In the course of her research Saman googles Lahore's ancient history, parks, city gates, and sweet shops—rich, culturally loaded, and recollective images of the city. In this short film as in much other cultural production, Lahore is made emblematic of partition and the shared history of these two hostile subcontinental neighbors. As Gyanendra Pandey puts it, partition's legacy is "an extraordinary love-hate relationship." This relationship is split between on the one hand anger, hatred, and nationalism, and on the other "a considerable sense of nostalgia, frequently articulated in the view that this was a partition of siblings that should never have occurred" (Pandey 2). The viral video tacitly supports and helps to answer this chapter's central research questions: how are South Asian cities and regions imagined by their inhabitants—both elites and the poor—their diasporic communities, and their artists? How does partition and its aftermath continue to impinge upon such imaginings of the Punjab, the province that was most affected by the violence and population exchange that occurred after partition? In the context of this collection's concern with urban outcasts, the emphasis in the chapter is on redressing imaginings that are shaped by what Salman Rushdie terms "city eyes" (81): in other words, an inattention to the marginalized denizens of urban spaces.

This chapter also stems from awareness that the Punjab has long been an area of key importance to pre-colonial India and to postcolonial India and Pakistan. The two Punjabs experienced overlapping but distinct aftershocks from British imperialism, great trauma in partition, relative economic vitality and hegemony within their nations, and centrality in the reinventions and imaginings of the postcolonial Indian and Pakistani nation-states. In an effort to enhance understandings of Punjabi literature, history, and anthropology, I examine depictions of the Pakistani Punjab, and particularly its ancient capital of Lahore, in texts by Bapsi Sidhwa and Mohsin Hamid, two important writers who are from that city and are among its most observant chroniclers. However, these writers have also spent significant proportions of their lives in the diaspora, specifically the United States. Their perspectives on the city are therefore to some extent molded by what Dennis Walder terms "postcolonial nostalgia."[1] Sidhwa, born in 1938, is from the generation affected by India's partition and the creation of Pakistan, whereas Hamid was born in 1971, the year of a second partition after a bloody war of independence, which resulted in Bangladesh seceding from Pakistan.

As well as exploring these authors' representations of the city's topographical, cultural, religious, and linguistic diversity, the essay also examines a central but taboo locus of Lahore as depicted in the novels. The iconic red light district, Heera Mandi, stands incongruously close to a key religious site, the Badshahi Mosque. Heera Mandi is often frequented by powerful, wealthy, and religiously orthodox clientele, but the people who depend on it for their livelihood are the kind of urban outcasts with which this chapter and the broader collection are concerned. Notwithstanding the whiff of scandal surrounding it, Heera Mandi is increasingly becoming the trendy playground of the rich, liberal and not so liberal classes who are happy to pay European prices for cappuccinos and curries overlooking the Badshahi Mosque. As Louise Brown remarks, "There's something exciting and illicit about coming here, something that makes respectable Pakistani pulses race" (8). There is a marked contrast between such urban, urbane upper-middle-class flâneurs, the vulnerable streetwalkers who work there, and some conservative Sunni Muslims who castigate the arts and permissive sexual behavior but in secret frequent the district. In her book *Heera Mandi*, Claudine Le Tournier d'Ison and her translator express this diversity in non-politically correct language:

> The street resembled a court of miracles—handicapped beggars, cripples rolling in a ball on the ground, tramps in the last shreds of a shalwar

kameez, and emaciated drug addicts [...] within [the] misshapen walls looked like a junkyard for all of society's most depraved—dealers, prostitutes, pimps and of course, Shi'as, as rejected as the Christians. The only ones who dared enter here were the bourgeois in need of excitement, ready to mix with the riff-raff at the cost of their virtue, politicians who by day proudly brandished the Quran, and by night the bank notes that they showered on the dancers. (88–9)

Here Le Tournier d'Ison recognizes the almost carnivalesque intermixture in Heera Mandi of those usually considered society's dregs—sex workers and their keepers, drug users and their suppliers, many of them Shi'a (a sect increasingly despised in frantically Sunni-izing Pakistan)—alongside those at the top of the social pile: patriarchs, politicians, and the pious.

In Graham Huggan's and my essay "Reevaluating the Postcolonial City," we argue that the recent efflorescence of postcolonial urban studies research has tended to overlook rural experience and to neglect the structural asymmetries and social injustice found in what we term the "global city" (786–7). Moreover, and as the editors of this volume recognize, studies of South Asian cities have tended to focus on the urbanization of the city space but not necessarily on the urban poor. A great deal of research from various disciplines has been conducted in relation to Indian cities, such as Bombay/Mumbai (see Hansen; Mehta; Prakash; and Patel and Thorner), Calcutta/Kolkata (Chaudhuri; Dutta; Gupta, Mukherjee, and Banerjee) and, to a somewhat lesser extent, Delhi (Kaul; Dalrymple; Hosagrahar). However, Pakistani urban environments have been strikingly underrepresented, with Karachi and especially Lahore receiving a small amount of scholarly attention in comparison with the vast archive on Bombay.[2] As such, Lahore is itself an outcast city compared to others in South Asia. This chapter is an attempt, as it were, to re-cast this metropole and to make a literary contribution to urban studies. I examine Sidhwa's work, paying special attention to her acclaimed partition novel *Cracking India* (1991), alongside Mohsin Hamid's three novels. These texts are scrutinized for their textualized descriptions of Lahore as a postcolonial city and as the heart of the Punjab and of Pakistan more broadly. I then weave in the theoretical approaches of Fredric Jameson, Edward W. Soja, Michel Foucault, Michel de Certeau and others, which allow me to frame the same geographical locations as a dynamic space of social and cultural contestations. My objective in doing this is firstly to highlight the precariousness of the urban poor (working-class women, for instance, occupy a doubly marginalized position) in the global city and its rural hinterland. Second, I hope to draw Lahore into the twice-born fold of those highly scrutinized South Asian cities Bombay/Mumbai, Calcutta/Kolkata, and Delhi.

Lahore has appeared almost invisible to literary and other humanities scholars, whereas other South Asian cities, such as Delhi, Calcutta, and Mumbai, have been loudly celebrated by critics. The first reason for this neglect is that Lahore is in Pakistan, a country with a troubled and variable relationship with the West, and with its own internal problems apropos of scholarship. Ever since Zia-ul-Haq's regime, which was bankrolled by the US as part of its Cold War strategy, censorship has been at the heart of Pakistani governance. The media opened up dramatically and temporarily during Pervez Musharraf's military rule (1999–2008). But Pakistani higher education institutions, particularly their arts departments, still chafe under restrictions and a lack of funding which limit the research of the many brilliant scholars who work there. Secondly, Lahore used to be an important destination along the hippie trail (loosely mapped onto the old Silk Route). After the Iranian Revolution of 1979 and the occupation of Afghanistan by the USSR and later the US, ordinary tourists could no longer enter or exit Pakistan's western gateways with ease. This means that fewer outsiders have had a chance to be inspired by the city's history and culture in the way that Indian cities have spawned their Mark Tullys, William Dalrymples, and Dominique Lapierres. Finally, in relation to urban studies, it is Karachi that grabs the headlines, in part because its megacity status dwarfs Lahore's, with estimated populations of 23 and ten million respectively. Karachi's higher profile is also due to its disproportionately larger population of *muhajirs* (the migrants and descendants of migrants who fled from India to Pakistan during and after partition) and attendant ethnic and political conflict, which attracts much scholarly attention (see, for example, Anjaria and McFarlane 298–337).

Yet Lahore could not matter more, given its history and hold on the South Asian imagination; its location and strategic importance as a hub connecting India and Khyber Pakthunkhwa (formerly known as the Northwest Frontier Province); and its economic productivity in the manufacturing and communications industries. As I show in this chapter, the city's close proximity to the almost impregnable Wagah border means that it is uniquely vulnerable when the two nations of India and Pakistan square up to each other. Hostility between these countries periodically combusts, as in the nuclear standoff of the late 1990s and the crisis following the Indian parliament attacks of 2001.[3] More positively, Lahore is the cultural capital of Pakistan, even if it has never been the political or administrative capital of anything larger than the Punjab province. In 1940, it was in the city's Iqbal Park that Jinnah issued the Lahore Resolution, advocating the creation of Pakistan through an inchoate plan for "autonomous national States" within independent India that would allegedly "allow the major nations separate homelands" (Jinnah 55).

Lahore has long been Pakistan's social and cultural heartland. Its landmarks provide architectural testament to the many pasts that have overlaid the city, making it a palimpsest and the space of intersecting identities, and pre-dating colonial India by centuries if not millennia. The metropolis has a vibrant arts scene that is diminished because of partition but still clearly present. Lahore also matters because it acts as a barometer of the changes that are happening in Pakistan, many of them especially damaging to the urban poor. Unlike Karachi with its high numbers of *muhajirs* and ethnic violence, Lahore has until recently been a relatively peaceful city. However, the last five years have witnessed a sea change in relation to terror, sectarian violence, and international machinations. I argue that Sidhwa and Hamid trace the genesis of this transformation back to the class, gender, and ethnic divisions that have always been present in the city and which were exacerbated by the creation of Pakistan.

To anyone who disagrees with the idea that Lahore is the city which acts as the most accurate microcosm of Pakistan more broadly, it is worth thinking of Anatol Lieven. In a section of his book *Pakistan: A Hard Country*, entitled "Lahore, the Historic Capital," Lieven mistakenly writes: "Pakistan is the heart, stomach and backbone of Pakistan. Indeed, in the view of many of its inhabitants, it *is* Pakistan" (267). This tautological but revealing substitution of "Pakistan" for "Lahore" chimes with the saying Lahoris use, almost shruggingly, to emphasize their city's distinctiveness: "*Lahore Lahore hai*" (Lahore is Lahore). The northeastern city is the cultural heartland of the country, with a detailed recorded history going back to the tenth century CE, and a much longer oral, cultural, and communitarian presence. Its economic powerhouse status and the hold it has on the Pakistani imagination, channelled through the movies of Lollywood (the nation's film industry, based in Lahore), have also meant large-scale migration, from the rural areas to Punjab's capital, in order to find work.

From the dire situation of many women in Lahore (which I will explore in the later textual analysis), to the intelligence, independence, and creative power of the city's women's movement, the picture revealed is extremely complex. Lahore is often seen as a pleasure city,[4] and Mohsin Hamid in particular is interested in millennial Pakistan's voluptuary, ecstasy-taking social whirl, as well as more familiar scenes of violence and stark class divisions. His debut novel *Moth Smoke* (2000) was viewed by Anita Desai as a turning point for subcontinental literature, in that it was one of the earliest twenty-first-century novels to depart from the Indian magic realism fashionable in the 1980s and 1990s and venture into darker and generically indeterminate territory inspired by his hometown Lahore (Desai n.p.). Indeed, for many, the metropolis represents pain, exploitation, and danger. Or, as Bapsi Sidhwa puts it in her anthology, *City of Sin and Splendour: Writings on Lahore* (2005), this is at once a city of sin and splendor. Even the Lahore of the late 1970s and early 1980s, under the viciously Islamizing Zia ul-Haq regime, is portrayed in Sidhwa's fourth novel *An American Brat* as a city of "paradoxes, where bold women of a certain class often wield as much clout as pistol-toting thugs" (192).

Tracery of Urbanization

Lahore is an unevenly developed, international urban center, which productively intersects with and is cross-fertilized by the well-irrigated rural hinterland in this "Land of Five Rivers," so that the city is not easily separable from its outlying countryside. On first glance, my last statement might seem to be contradicted by Hamid's third and most recent novel *How to Get Filthy Rich in Rising Asia*, in which the text's protagonist, "you," comes from an archetypal Punjabi village. There workers genuflect to *zamindars* or feudal landlords, women carry pots on their heads, and water buffalo are milked while they chew on fodder (8–9). Yet this rural setting is not idealized. When the main character's father surveys it, far from noticing the deliberately clichéd pastoral tropes, he instead sees "the labor by which a farmer exchanges his allocation of time in this world for an allocation of time in this world. Here, in the heady bouquet of nature's pantry, your father sniffs mortality" (Hamid, *Filthy* 7–8). For these reasons of hardship and mortality, most of the novel's rural dwellers long, in the words of the opening chapter's title, to "Move to the City," where they know wages to be high but do not realize that expenses are equally lofty. The protagonist migrates to a city which it becomes clear is Lahore (although places and people are unnamed in this novel, perhaps to lend it a universality that accords with its ironic structuring as a self-help book). During his relocation to the metropolis, the focalizer witnesses:

> a passage of time that outstrips its chronological equivalent. Just as when headed into the mountains a quick shift in altitude can vault one from subtropical jungle to semi-arctic tundra, so too can a few hours on a bus from rural remoteness to urban centrality appear to span millennia. (14)

This passage suggests that even though there is only a relatively short physical distance between the forelock-tugging, pitcher-carrying, buffalo-milking villagers and the city of pollution, dual carriageways, electricity, and advertising hoardings, culturally they are as dissimilar as jungle and tundra. Despite this first impression of the book, in an interview with me, Hamid complicates such a bifurcatory picture of urban and rural Punjab:

> I think the rural/urban split is blurring, because all along Pakistan's many major roads, there's an urbanization taking place. If you drive around the GT Road, or any other large road in Punjab, little towns and shops have grown up around it. People live along those roads, have electricity, televisions, satellite dishes, and mobile phone coverage, and they watch the cars passing through. They are traders, selling things in their shops, and paying for services. They are not like the farmers. This network cuts across all of Punjab now, so it isn't as though there's an urban core and then periphery, but a tracery of urbanization that penetrates the periphery.
>
> (Chambers 182–3)

Such a sketch is filled out in *How to Get Filthy Rich in Rising Asia* when "the region that forms the economic hinterland to your metropolis" is described:

> The car approaches the outskirts of the city, passing the disinterred earth and linear mounds of vast middle-class housing developments. Rows of electricity poles rise in various stages of completion, some bare, some bridged by taut cables, occasionally one from which wires dangle to the ground. (88–9)

This portrayal of Lahore's outskirts dramatizes the "tracery of urbanization" which Hamid outlined in the interview. His description of the exposed soil and incomplete electricity pylons suggests that here we see an unfinished, in-between space that is neither urban nor rural, but fuzzy. This interstitial area of the suburbs is seen as having neither the danger nor promise of the city, nor the bucolic idyll and grinding poverty of the country but, as rents and demand for urban space soar ever higher, urbanization is encroaching on the suburbs too. Cropland in the outer suburbs is increasingly being sold off to developers (*Filthy* 90, 165, 219) and the narrator acknowledges the porous nature of the city's borderlines: "[y]our city is not laid out as a single-celled organism with a wealthy nucleus surrounded by an ooze of slums. [...] Accordingly, the poor live near the rich" (22). To some extent, then, Hamid recognizes with Ian Talbot that "Punjabi society [is] overwhelmingly rural" and that "[t]raditional rural customs and values lay just beneath the veneer of urban sophistication and culture" (Talbot 13, 15).

Similarly, in Hamid's debut novel *Moth Smoke*, we are told that Dilaram, now the madam of a brothel in Heera Mandi, was propelled to the city after having been repeatedly raped by her landlord and his relatives as a young village girl from rural Punjab, who was later sent into bonded prostitution in Lahore (50–1). Some doubt is cast over this story, however, because the protagonist Daru thinks she seems "a little too well-spoken for an unedu-cated village girl, sounding more like a wayward Kinnaird alumna to me" (Hamid, *Moth* 51). Whether Dilaram really was an innocent peasant girl who got caught up in human trafficking and prostitution, or she is in fact a sophisticated urbanite who attended a prestigious school like Lahore's Kinnaird College for Women, is never resolved in the narrative.

La Whore: Gendering the City

Nonetheless, this moment from *Moth Smoke* establishes Heera Mandi as a space in which young girls from the country and city put their bodies on display, evade the cops, and are exploited by predatory pimps. Even more extensively, in *Cracking India* Sidhwa paints a vivid picture of Heera Mandi as a place where poetry and music flourishes. The area was originally built as a sanctuary for the illegitimate sons of Moghul emperors and their *tawaifs*, also known as nautch-girls or courtesans, who during the Raj era at least were mostly Muslim women from North India. The exploitation of women, many of them from the countryside, went hand in hand with an attempt to dress this up in glamorous ways. *Ghazals*, often composed, recited, and sung in red light districts such as Heera Mandi, are also a typically Muslim poetic form. However, the association that *ghazals* make between royal courts, courtesans, and dancing girls contributed toward these poems containing recurrent, apparently un-Islamic images such as the nightingale, wine, roses, and the beloved, although these metaphors also reflect the Sufi devotee's longing for God.[5] Sidhwa's villain Ice-candy-man uses the elevated language of *ghazals* in order to shower the kidnapped Hindu Ayah with praise. This is notably ironic in the following instance, since it is he who has forced her into the dancing-girl profession he extols here: "She lives to dance! And I to toast her dancer's grace! | Princes pledge their lives to celebrate her celebrated face!" (259). Despite his most poetic efforts, Ice-candy-man's exploitation of Ayah is evident in her diminished figure and downcast glance. As feminists often point out, the flip side of idealization is abuse.

Heera Mandi is a central locus of Lahore's Walled City. The red light district is very near the Minar-e-Pakistan, a tower built in the 1960s to commemorate the 1940 Lahore Resolution. As mentioned, it is also adjacent to Lahore's most famous landmark, the enormous Mughal mosque, Badshahi Masjid. Other nearby Mughal sites include Anarkali Bazaar, Shalimar Gardens, and Jehangir's Mausoleum. By highlighting the diversity and history of this district, I want to suggest that Heera Mandi can be read as a microcosm of the city as a whole, and therefore of the Punjab more broadly, just as Lahore may in some ways be read as the nation in miniature. Unsurprisingly, few in Pakistan are willing to recognize the "female street" (Sidhwa, *Bride* 60) of Heera Mandi as a touchstone for the Fatherland. Fouzia Saeed indicates this when she writes:

> Identified by various names, it represents one of the oldest flesh markets in the land, where prostitution and the performing arts are linked in a complex web of human relations. Hardly any informed citizen can plead ignorance of the residents of this area, but they are considered the least entitled to be understood by their fellow beings. (vii)

In the red light district binaries are broken down, given the contiguity of the nearby Badshahi Mosque and also given the professed religiosity of many of the area's Shi'a sex workers. Naheem Jabbar observes that "[t]he self-conscious piety of the women [in the red light district Heera Mandi] contradicts the ideas that they are so generically typical of profanity (woman *qua* profanity)" (109). The authors' representations of the heterogeneous nature of the people who congregate in the two very different areas of red light district and mosque allow them to explore the metropole/hinterland dynamic.

References to the mosque also necessitate discussion of the important and changing role of religion—the majority faith Islam and, to a lesser extent, the minority creed of Zoroastrianism to which Sidhwa and the Parsi community belong—in contributing towards post-partition Lahori identity. In an elegiac section of *An American Brat*, Sidhwa reflects on the increasing religification not only of Muslims in Pakistan, but also of the formerly tolerant Parsi community:

> Established custodians of the Zoroastrian doctrine were no less rigid and ignorant than the *fundos* in Pakistan. This mindless current of fundamentalism sweeping the world like a plague had spared no religion, not even their microscopic community of 120 thousand. (305–6)

It is useful to keep this even-handed reminder in mind, rather than accepting the widespread contemporary assumption that the rise of religious sentiment is limited to Muslims and mosques.

A sexualization of the city (La Whore) is perhaps best articulated in *The Pakistani Bride* (1983):

> Lahore—the ancient whore, the handmaiden of dimly remembered Hindu kings, the courtesan of Moghul Emperors, bedecked and bejeweled, savaged by marauding hordes. Healed by the caressing hands of successive lovers. A little shoddy [...] like an attractive but ageing concubine, ready to bestow surprising delights on those who cared to court her—proudly displaying Royal gifts. (43)

Here Sidhwa alludes to the "succeeding lovers" who have conquered Lahore, from the pre-Mughal "Hindu kings" to the "Mughal Emperors," and implicitly from the Shivaji and Durrani Empires, the Sikh leader Ranjit Singh, and the British colonizers to the postcolonial Pakistani politicians who have ruled over Lahore and West Punjab. Personifying the city as a fading but still attractive, somewhat tawdry figure, Sidhwa evokes Lahore's loss of its multicultural identity after partition. This is also reflected in *Cracking India*: "The garden scene has depressingly altered. Muslim families who added color when scattered among the Hindus and Sikhs, now monopolize the garden, depriving it of color" (249). Elsewhere in *The Pakistani Bride*, there is a sustained passage about Heera Mandi (57–65), which contains strikingly similar motifs to those found in Sidhwa's first novel, *The Crow Eaters* (130–8). Both depict men chewing betel leaves and proffering money; women in gaudy dress (*churidar* pyjamas, ankle-bells, and heavy makeup) going through the movements of dance in a "mechanical" fashion while accompanied by harmonium, sitar, and tabla; and Heera Mandi's narrow streets, decrepit wooden buildings, trellises, and balconies. The recurring characters of a middle-aged madam, young girls of varying degrees of fair-ness, plumpness, and innocence, and sinister pimps in each text suggest that many features of Heera Mandi *qua* space have changed little in the last hundred years.

Space in Theory and the Imagination

To discover more about space and its many manifestations and constructions I concentrate on one theoretical text in particular, Edward W. Soja's *Postmodern Geographies* (1989). His claim that space has three manifesta-tions is helpful in thinking about Lahore, and I would argue that it is borne out in the novels. Soja makes a tripartite distinction between "space *per se*, space as a contextual given, and socially-based spatiality" (79). He is inter-ested in the way in which space is primordially given, yet is also an effect of social production and imaginative construction. Soja's ideas come out of a theoretical perspective starting from the mid-seventies onwards to aver that Western accounts of history are incomplete, due to an excessive concentra-tion on the temporal perspective, at the expense of the spatial dimension. Michel Foucault famously indicts Western thought as a whole for its inat-tention to geography: "Space was treated as the dead, the fixed, the undia-lectical, the immobile. Time, on the contrary, was richness, fecundity, life, dialectic" (70). He identifies a dichotomy of thinking about time and space, suggesting that since the nineteenth century space has largely been ignored by philosophers, whereas time and history have been closely interrogated. Foucault's call for greater attention to space led to what many have sum-marized as the "spatial turn" in the social sciences and humanities (Raju 1; Teverson and Upstone ix).

Returning to Soja, he argues that in commonsense perspective space is a given, relatively unchanging physical reality that has a profound effect on its inhabitants. This is demonstrated in Lahore's status as a frontier city, just thirty miles away from hostile Indian territory, which means it would likely be the first place of attack in any nuclear war between the two countries. Hamid is alert to the impact this has on the city's residents, and in *Moth Smoke* "if they nuke Lahore" is a frequent refrain (88, 91–2). Other sorts of violence in the city also have a leveling effect on Lahore's residents, both rich and poor, shaping their behavior and fears and limiting their move-ments. After his mother is killed by a stray bullet while asleep on a charpoy on the roof during a baking Punjabi summer, Daru has a recurring dream in which he "imagine[s] Lahore as a city with bullets streaking into the air" (Hamid 108). This prefigures the later standoff between Pakistan and India over nuclear tests, which is tensely felt in Lahore as the municipality on the frontline between the two:

> The entire city is uneasy. Sometimes, when monsoon lightning slips a bright explosion under the clouds, there is a pause in conversations.

Teacups halt, steaming, in front of extended lips. Lightning's echo comes as thunder. And the city waits for thunder's echo, for a wall of heat that burns Lahore with the energy of a thousand summers, a million partitions, a billion atomic souls split in half.

(Hamid 211)

The exaggeration of "entire city" and the mild comedy in "teacups extended" undercuts the implicit reference to Nagasaki and Hiroshima as well as Lahore's own holocaust of partition. Clearly even space that appears to be a stable, de facto entity is actually socially constructed. Although space is more likely to be a problem for urban outcasts, it can also turn against the tea-sipping middle classes, engulfing them in violence and terror.

Therefore, according to Soja, the second understanding of urban space is as a socially manipulated, changeable material that is produced as much as it produces and involves "social translation, transformation, and experience" (79–80). Both Soja and his theoretical forerunner Henri Lefebvre write compelling accounts of the ways in which city planning is intimately related to ideology and methods of social control. They also recognize that the attempts of the powerful to monopolize the social production of space are never entirely successful. The intentions of town planners are modified or subverted by the uses locals make of their space "on the ground" and city dwellers have varying degrees of agency to transform their surroundings.

We need only look at the depiction of Lahore's Lawrence Gardens (now the Bagh-e-Jinnah) and other locations in Sidhwa's *Cracking India* to see that space can be radically re-constructed by its residents. The nanny character, Ayah, who is in many ways a gendered personification of independent India (*Bharat Mata* or Mother India), meets her admirers in Lawrence Gardens on the Upper Mall near Charing Cross. Her beauty at first unites members of many different religious groups, so that they sit together in relative harmony, discussing current events and gossip under a Raj-era monument. In contrast to this statue of Queen Victoria, which is "cast in gunmetal, [...] majestic, overpowering, ugly," Ayah is described as resembling "the Hindu goddess she worships" (Sidhwa 28, 12). Everything about her is depicted as soft, attractive, and fertile. Ayah is an allegorical representation of the youthful promise of Indian Independence in comparison with the austere decay of the old British order, and in the park she subverts the colonial space around her. But later, when the group stops meeting under the symbol of the British Raj and instead starts to meet at an Indian restaurant, the group's unity disintegrates, suggesting that existing tensions between different groups are exacerbated once the common enemy has departed. As the accord between Ayah's courtiers breaks down and a more vicious struggle begins for her approval (and, by implication, for control over her body), it becomes evident that the city is splintering along ethnic lines. The different religious groups now make it impossible for each other to meet within the same spaces.

The third way in which Soja argues that we experience space is through its construction in the imagination. This is what Fredric Jameson terms "cognitive mapping" (89), through which he shows that we all have our own mental maps of the cities in which we live. Jameson emphasizes the social, collective nature of this mental cartography, suggesting that each of us positions our subjective consciousness within "unlived, abstract conceptions of the geographic totality" (90). These conceptions may however be "garbled" or distorted reflections of cultural biases (353). Jameson's cognitive mapping serves as a reminder that space is as much created by the imagination as by civic leaders and planners. William Glover, the preeminent scholar of Lahore as urban space, concurs, writing, "Any city is created as much imaginatively as it is physically of bricks and mortar" (xv). Anatol Lieven dramatizes this in relation to Lahore when he writes that it "is a city of the imagination, in a way that bureaucratic Islamabad and dour, impoverished Peshawar cannot be" (268).

A disjuncture between this city of the imagination and the metropolitan world of everyday lived materialism discussed earlier is illustrated in Hamid's second novel, *The Reluctant Fundamentalist* (2007). The text's protagonist, Changez, muses on the city's Mughal history and historic textures to a skeptical and materialist American businessman: "I said I was from Lahore, the second largest city of Pakistan, ancient capital of the Punjab, home to nearly as many people as New York, layered like a sedimentary plain with the accreted history of invaders from the Aryans to the Mongols to the British. He merely nodded. Then he said, "And are you on financial aid?" (Hamid 7) William Glover's research accords with Changez's imaginative view, expressed here, that Lahore is a palimpsest in which British architecture is grafted onto layers of pre-Mughal, Mughal, and Sikh history. According to Glover, there is a surprising amount of interchange between Lahore's bustling Old City and the white civil station which was supposed to be spatially quarantined from Indian areas during the Raj era. For example, from the year of the Indian Rebellion (1857) until 1891, St. James's Church found itself formally consecrated and housed in Anarkali's Tomb, the last resting place of a Muslim dancing girl (19). This woman, Anarkali, is said to have been the Mughal Emperor Akbar's courtesan, but when his son Prince Salim fell in love with her too, Akbar was so enraged that he buried Anarkali alive in a wall located within the bazaar. However, Lahore's supremely romantic and hybrid past constantly rubs against the bathos of financial realities. These are laconically introduced by the US official in the long quotation cited above when he barks, "And are you on financial aid?" Fiscal restraints are also apparent in Sidhwa's *An American Brat*, in which the young migrant Feroza has all her pride in her education and background in aristocratic Lahore undercut when she tries to enter New York's Kennedy Airport and finds a "sallow, unsmiling officer" who handles her Pakistani passport with contempt, quizzing her on her financial means and the length of time she plans to stay in the United States (Sidhwa, *Brat* 54).

There are thus barriers to the movement of even the most Mughal-prince-or-princess-like upper-class Lahori. This suggests the relevance of Michel de Certeau's theorization of "walking in the city" to an understanding of contemporary Lahore. Writing in 1980, De Certeau lyrically describes the "ordinary practitioners of the city," who are said to live "down below," and whose main *raison d'être* is apparently *flânerie* or walking. Interestingly, he begins his account of the ordinary walkers in the city down below from a panoramic vantage point at the top of the World Trade Centre. The post-9/11 reader may find chilling presentiment in his description of New York as "a universe that is constantly exploding" (91) and the World Trade Centre occupant as anticipating "an Icarian fall" (92). How can this not resonate with the famous passage in Hamid's *The Reluctant Fundamentalist* in which Changez admits that his first reaction to the twin towers' destruction was to smile, "caught up," as he was, "in the *symbolism* of it all, the fact that someone had so visibly brought America to her knees" (73)?

As soon as De Certeau descends "down below" once more, he argues that walking is "an elementary form of this experience of the city; they are walkers, *Wandersmänner*, whose bodies follow the thicks and thins of an urban "text" they write without being able to read it" (93). Hamid and Sidhwa unsettle these assumptions, showing that walking is not an "elementary form" common to the experience of all cities. In *The Reluctant Fundamentalist*, Hamid writes,

> the newer districts of Lahore are poorly suited to the needs of those who must walk. In their spaciousness—with their public parks and wide, tree-lined boulevards—they enforce an ancient hierarchy that comes to us from the countryside: the superiority of the mounted man over the man on foot. But [...] in the [...] congested, maze-like heart of this city—Lahore is more democratically *urban*. Indeed, in these places it is the man with four wheels who is forced to dismount and become part of the city. (33)

Some parts of Lahore are difficult to walk in because they are spread out and lack pavements, whereas in other places, especially the Walled City areas, the class hierarchy privilege is reversed and it becomes the envehicled person who is at a disadvantage. This is the only instance in Hamid's representations of the divided city where the poor are sometimes privileged over the rich. By contrast to this context-specific privileging, various binaries are set up in his other novels—between the classes who possess air conditioning and their own generators in *Moth Smoke* and those with access to bottled water and those without in *How to Get Filthy Rich in Rising Asia*—which are unvaryingly weighted towards the rich. As such, Lahore's Old City has a leveling effect on class distinctions. De Certeau does mention barriers to movement when he writes of "interdictions (e.g. [...] a wall that prevents one from going further)" (98). Such barriers are marked in post-colonial cities such as Lahore, with the Wagah border a short car ride away but the partitioned country of India almost impossible to get to for Pakistanis.[6]

From a gendered perspective, walking in the city is shown to be even more difficult in Sidhwa's *An American Brat*, in which Feroza observes, "there were so few women, veiled or unveiled, on the streets of Lahore, that even women stared at other women, as she did, as if they were freaks" (127). This description of the self-alienation of woman indicates that going outside is a hazardous occupation for her even in one of Pakistan's most sophisticated cities, as she encounters a cavernous gender gap on the streets. In *Cracking India*, Lenny is not only constrained in her walking in the city due to her gender, but also because of her disability. She has suffered polio and is lame, with a fallen arch in one of her feet. Ayah pushes her in a pram until well past the age for which this is seemly. Once she begins corrective surgery, Lenny worries that her foot will "emerge [...] immaculate, fault-free," thus forcing her to compete with other children "for my share of love and other handouts" (12, 18). In the context of this story concerning Independence, and considering that the girl's lameness is arguably an indirect legacy of British rule (16), it is hard not to read Lenny and her calipers as the infant Indian nation preparing for the difficulties (and rewards) of standing on its own two feet. As Clare Barker writes,

> Echoing a problematic conflation of individual and national bodies that was apparent in nationalist discourses in this period, the text becomes a discomfiting oscillation between materialist constructions of disability as a social presence and the deployment of disability as a prosthesis standing in for colonial disablement and mutilated—partitioned—body politic. (95)

Pakistan as a whole is known to be a hard place for wheelchair users and other disabled people. As well as a lack of ramps and lifts to aid their movement (Farid n.p.), there is also a widely reported lack of cultural awareness about disability. Further impediments to De Certeau's blithe Western analysis of "walking in the city" encountered in Lahore include the threat of rape and kidnapping, which becomes a central issue for women during the partition so graphically depicted in *Cracking India*. Moreover, the workers of Heera Mandi are only allowed to move around in their area between 11pm and 1am because of draconian and extortive police tactics there.

Conclusion

Perhaps spatial theorists have had a tendency to overlook barriers to walking, particularly when these relate to various forms of oppression in previously colonized countries. Just as the social sciences and humanities took a "spatial turn" approximately 40 years ago, especially since 9/11 there has been increasing interest in analyzing the postsecular city.[7] The idea behind the postsecular turn is to take more account of religion, war, and terror's impact on twenty-first-century cities. This is clearly very timely, especially in light of cities such as Cairo, Benghazi, Damascus, Homs, and Hama becoming sites for revolution—to varying degrees religiously inflected—in the Arab Spring/Winter of 2011 onwards. We wait eagerly to see what this new postsecular direction in scholarship will bring to the study of postcolonial, post-Arab Spring cities. In the meantime, it is hoped that this chapter has shed light on Sidhwa and Hamid's depictions of Heera Mandi's important place within Lahore, itself of inestimable significance to the Punjab and the Pakistani nation.

I have shown that Lahore is a highly multifaceted space, constituted by history, uneven capitalism, rural and urban continuities and discontinuities, and cultural nostalgia. Notwithstanding these noteworthy features, the city is underresearched compared with Indian conurbations (and, to a lesser degree, compared with research into Pakistan's former capital and largest city, Karachi). As a palimpsest of various accreted histories and the nation's artistic and cultural capital, Lahore is Pakistan's heart (and stomach and spine, to recycle Lieven's metaphor). However, these creative writers from the diaspora construct a complex picture of the city, refusing the binaries that are seductively omnipresent in representations of Lahore. Hamid is keen to dismantle conceptual borders between Lahore and its pastoral hinterland, showing how the city is invading the country in the guise of industrialization. At the same time, they suggest, the country encroaches on the city via the figure of the erstwhile village dweller seeking a livelihood. Sidhwa adds a gendered dimension to the city in her preoccupation with sex workers in Heera Mandi across almost all of her novels to date. Turning to theory, the article suggested that scholarship from the social sciences, literature, and postcolonial studies provides three broad understandings of space: as a physical reality, a socially constructed entity, and a place that is imagined through cognitive mapping and the textualizations of fiction, life-writing, and nonfiction. De Certeau's walking in the city helps us to see ways in which the city is imagined, but also how its physical manifestations and social manipulations can thwart the imaginer's assumptions and dreams.

Notes

1. It should be noted that Hamid returned to live in Lahore in 2009, which may affect the future trajectory of his fiction.
2. The main scholarly monographs on Lahore are Glover 2007 and Suvorova 2012.
3. Both of these incidents, the nuclear race and the Indian parliament attacks, are foregrounded in Hamid's fiction (*Moth* 88–92; *Reluctant* 121, 126–7, 143).

4. The term "pleasure city" comes from a neglected novel by Kamala Markandaya. Heera Mandi is also referred to as a "Pleasure District" in the subtitle to Louise Brown's book *The Dancing Girls of Lahore* (2006).
5. For more on the *ghazal* form, see Matthews, Shackle, and Husain 32–7.
6. This point could also be extended to Palestine and the notorious Separation Wall.
7. See, for example, Beaumont and Baker; Knott "Religion" and "Cutting."

Works Cited

Anjaria, Jonathan Shapiro and McFarlane, Colin, Ed. *Urban Navigations: Politics, Space and the City in South Asia.* Delhi: Routledge, 2011. Print.
Associated Press. "India, Pakistan agree: Emotional Google Ad a Hit, Strikes a Cultural Chord." *The Hindu.* November 15, 2013. Web. November 2013.
Bakhtin, M. M. *The Dialogic Imagination: Four Essays.* Ed. Michael Holquist, trans. Caryl Emerson and Michael Holquist. Austin: U of Texas P, 2004; 1981. 84–258. Print.
Banerjee, Himadri, Nilanjana Gupta, and Sipra Mukherjee eds. *Calcutta Mosaic: Essays and Interviews on the Minority Communities of Calcutta.* Delhi: Anthem, 2009. Print.
Barker, Clare. *Postcolonial Fiction and Disability: Exceptional Children, Metaphor and Materiality.* Basingstoke: Palgrave, 2011. Print.
Beaumont, Justin and Baker, Clare Ed. *Postsecular Cities: Space, Theory and Practice.* London: Continuum, 2011. Print.
Brown, Louise. *The Dancing Girls of Lahore: Selling Love and Saving Dreams in Pakistan's Pleasure District.* New York, NY: Harper Perennial, 2006. Print.
Chambers, Claire. *British Muslim Fictions: Interviews with Contemporary Writers.* Basingstoke: Palgrave, 2011. Print.
Chambers, Claire and Huggan, Graham. "Re-evaluating the Postcolonial City: Production, Reconstruction, Representation. Foreword." *Interventions.* 17(4) (2015): 1–5. Print.
Chaudhuri, Sukanta, Ed. *Calcutta: The Living City: Volumes 1 and 2.* Delhi: Oxford UP, 1990. Print.
Dalrymple, William. *City of Djinns: A Year in Delhi.* London: Flamingo, 1994. Print.
De Certeau, Michael. *The Practice of Everyday Life*, trans. S. Rendell. Berkeley: U of California P, 2011; 1980.
Desai, Anita. "Passion in Lahore." *New York Review of Books.* December 21, 2000. Web. November 2013.
Dutta, Krishna. *Calcutta: A Cultural and Literary History*, intro Anita Desai. Oxford: Signal, 2008. Print.
Farid, T. "Wheelchair Users Deprived of Right to Free Movement." *Daily Times.* January 14, 2012. Web. November 2013.
Foucault, Michel. *Power/Knowledge: Selected Interviews and Other Writings, 1972–1977*, ed. Colin Gordon, trans. Colin Gordon et al. Hemel Hempstead: Harvester Wheatsheaf, 1980. Print.
Ghosh, Amitav. *The Shadow Lines.* Delhi: Penguin, 2008; 1988. Print.
Glover, William J. *Making Lahore Modern: Constructing and Imagining a Colonial City.* Minneapolis: U of Minnesota P, 2007. Print.

Google India. "The Reunion." November 15, 2013. Web. November 2013.

Hamid, Mohsin. *Moth Smoke*. London: Granta, 2000. Print.

———. *How to Get Filthy Rich in Rising Asia*. London: Hamish Hamilton, 2013. Print.

Hansen, Thomas Blom. *Wages of Violence: Naming and Identity in Postcolonial Bombay*. Princeton, NJ: Princeton UP, 2001. Print.

Hosagrahar, Jyoti. *Indigenous Modernities: Negotiating Architecture, Urbanism, and Colonialism in Delhi*. Abingdon: Routledge, 2005. Print.

Jabbar, Naheem. "Symbology and Subaltern Resistance in Hīra Mandi *Mohalla*." *Interventions* 13.1 (2011): 95–119. Print.

Jameson, Fredric. "Postmodernism, or, the Cultural Logic of Late Capitalism." *New Left Review* 146 (July–August 1984): 52–92. Print.

———. "Cognitive Mapping." Cary Nelson and Lawrence Grossberg, Ed. *Marxism and the Interpretation of Culture*. Basingstoke: Macmillan Education, 1988. 347–57. Print.

Jinnah, Muhammad Ali. "An Extract from the Presidential Address of M.A. Jinnah: Lahore, March 1940." *India's Partition: Process, Strategy and Mobilization*. Ed. Mushirul Hasan. Delhi: Oxford UP, 1994. 44–58. Print.

Kaul, H. K., ed. *Historic Delhi: An Anthology*. Delhi: Oxford UP, 1997. Print.

Knott, Kim. "Religion, Space and Place: The Spatial Turn in Research on Religion." *Religion and Society: Advances in Research*, Eds. Simon Coleman and R. Sarro, 2010. 29–43. Print.

———. "Cutting Through the Postsecular City: A Spatial Interrogation." *Exploring the Postsecular: The Religious, The Political and the Urban*. Eds. Arie L. Molendijk, Justin Beaumont & Christoph Jedan. Leiden: Brill, 2010. 19–38. Print.

Lefebvre, Henri. *The Production of Space*, trans. Donald Nicholson-Smith. Oxford: Blackwell, 1991; 1974.

Le Tournier d'Ison, Claudine. *Hira Mandi: A Sensitive Portrayal of Life in Lahore's Notorious Centre of Prostitution*, trans. Priyanka Jhijaria. Delhi: Roli, 2012. Print.

Lieven, Anatol. *Pakistan: A Hard Country*. London: Allen Lane, 2011. Print.

Markandaya, Kamala. *Pleasure City*. London: Chatto & Windus, 1982. Print.

Matthews, D. J., C. Shackle, and S. Husain. *Urdu Literature*. Islamabad: Alhamra, 2003. Print.

Mehta, Suketa. *Maximum City: Bombay Lost and Found*. London: Headline Review, 2005. Print.

Pandey, Gyanendra. *Remembering Partition: Violence, Nationalism, and History in India*. Cambridge: Cambridge UP, 2001. Print.

Patel, Sujata and Alice Thorner, Ed. *Bombay: Mosaic of Modern Culture*. Bombay: Oxford UP, 1995. Print.

Prakash, Gyan, Ed. *Noir Urbanisms: Dystopic Images of the Modern City*. Princeton, NJ: Princeton UP, 2010. Print.

Raju, Saraswati, Ed. *Gendered Geographies: Space and Place in South Asia*. Delhi: Oxford UP, 2011. Print.

Rushdie, Salman. *Midnight's Children*. London: Picador, 1982; 1981. Print.

Saeed, Fouzia. *Taboo!: The Hidden Culture of a Red Light Area*, foreword I. A. Rahman. Karachi: Oxford UP, 2002. Print.

Sidhwa, Bapsi. *The Crow Eaters*. Glasgow: Fontana/Collins, 1982; 1980. Print.

———. *Cracking India*. Minnesota, MN: Milkweed, 1991. Print.

———. *An American Brat*. Delhi: Penguin, 1994. Print.

———. ed. *City of Sin and Splendour: Writings on Lahore*. Delhi: Penguin, 2005. Print.

———. *The Pakistani Bride*. Minnesota, MN: Milkweed, 2008; 1983. Print.

Soja, Edward William. *Postmodern Geographies: The Reassertion of Space in Critical Social Theory*. London: Verso, 1989. Print.

———. *Postmetropolis: Critical Studies of Cities and Regions*. Oxford: Blackwell, 2000. Print.

Suvorova, Anna. *Lahore: Tophophilia of Space and Place*. Karachi: Oxford UP, 2012. Print.

Talbot, Ian. *Punjab and the Raj, 1849–1947*. Riverdale, MD: Riverdale Company, 1988. Print.

Teverson, Andrew and Sara Upstone, Ed. *Postcolonial Spaces: The Politics of Place in Contemporary Culture*. Basingstoke: Palgrave, 2011. Print.

7 Between Aspiration and Imagination

Exploring Native Cosmopolitanism in Adib Khan's *Spiral Road* and Mohammed Hanif's *Our Lady of Alice Bhatti*

Payel Chattopadhyay Mukherjee, Arnapurna Rath, and Koshy Tharakan

WHAT KIND OF IDEA ARE YOU? Are you the kind that compromises, does deals, accommodates itself to society, aims to find a niche, to survive; or are you the cussed, bloody-minded, ramrod-backed type of damnfool notion that would rather break than sway with the breeze? – The kind that will almost certainly, ninety-nine times out of a hundred, be smashed to bits; but, the hundredth time, will change the world.
—Salman Rushdie, *The Satanic Verses*, 335

City and Native Cosmopolitans

The notion of a postcolonial urban outcast is both complex and intriguing. It is a complex position because the individual envisions freedom of movement and expression of opinions in spite of the limitations that the city imposes in time and space. It is indeed a struggle on the part of the individual to continue being among their compatriots, family, and friends, while becoming equally conscious about experiencing a sense of internal exile. These individuals, trapped in the continuing dilemmas of being torn between city and citizenship, churn out as the native cosmopolitans (DiBattista 149). The position of such individuals as native cosmopolitans is also intriguing since there is a willingness to continue in spite of the growing sense of exile within the mind. There is also, a lingering hope to live within the layered ambivalence of the city, even though they display an aesthetic resistance through a kind of self-distancing. Thus, the native cosmopolitans become urban outcasts in either ways—within their own self and also get formed by others. On one hand, they materialize their identity as urban outcasts by living with a sense of exile without isolating themselves completely from the city, whereas on the other hand, they also endure being critiqued by their own people and suffocate within their familiar surroundings.

In this chapter, we observe the emergence of individuals as native cosmopolitans in the South Asian cities of Dhaka and Karachi through Adib Khan's *Spiral Road* (2007) and Mohammed Hanif's *Our Lady of Alice Bhatti* (2011). We argue that there are, in these novels, individuals who are cosmopolitans in their own ways despite being rooted in their respective cities and cultures. We challenge the dichotomy in the understanding of the cosmopolitan as opposed to the native and attempt to emphasize the possibility of a concurrent existence of these aspects in such individuals. In Adib Khan's *Spiral Road*, there is Masud Alam a librarian who stays in Melbourne but has his roots in Dhaka. He emerges as a native cosmopolitan by participating in the homecoming as a way of relating to his roots and emphasizes the need to reconnect to the city of Dhaka. On the other hand, Melbourne promotes his understanding of the world and also enables Masud to realize a deeper connection to Dhaka. In the other selected text, *Our Lady of Alice Bhatti*, we find Alice Bhatti's identity as a native cosmopolitan evolving from within the taboos and constrictions of Karachi to a space of imagination where she realizes freedom and liberation. Even though she is a junior nurse who has never been out of her city, Alice aspires to expand her horizons as a native cosmopolitan through her generous service to those in need. At the same time, she also grows into an outcast in her own city through her conscious disregard for the categorical stereotypes of class, gender, and religion, which are stringently observed. Individuals like Masud and Alice play pivotal roles in the postcolonial South Asian literary imagination by anticipating cosmopolitanism as a way of living within individual, conceptual, and cultural differences.

In the two narratives, the postcolonial South Asian cities of Dhaka and Karachi open the ground of complex interrelations between the native's imagination of a cosmopolitan identity and local affiliations. Within the rubric of contemporary cosmopolitan dialogues, the postcolonial cities embody the tension within the nodes of global ways that penetrate individual identities and the spaces of negotiable ruptures in their cosmopolitan imaginations. According to Neera Chandoke, "The postcolonial city maps out for us the historically constructed social relations of power and domination" (2871). While the postcolonial city inherits the vivacity of a colonial influence and appears as a ground open to the experiences of a historically fraught cultural condition, there is an inherent anxiety in the act of balancing the local roots with the global routes. The urban space opens as a dialogic nexus of cosmopolitan aspirations through emerging identities of individuals negotiating their sense of belonging to native spaces with a conscious inclusion of the world. The postcolonial urban space facilitates the appearance of such identities through individuals who mobilize their position meandering across its multiple layers thereby recreating a legitimate claim as native cosmopolitans. While these native cosmopolitans participate in the processes of the hegemonic urban discourses of city and citizenship, they also simultaneously reconfigure their identities as the outcasts within their own circles. These urban outcasts forge new possibilities of cosmopolitan solidarity within the deeply contested and increasingly complex network of relationships of the postcolonial city and the world beyond.

Therefore, the postcolonial city entails a space of political geography that echoes an underlying philosophy of global citizenship where individuals inculcate an understanding of difference and a free outlook towards cultural diversity (Binnie et al. 5). The urban space not only facilitates critical responses of the individuals to a postcolonial modernity but also opens further possibilities of sustaining these emerging discussions about the postcolonial city and its individuals. At this point, it is interesting to note that postcolonial politics is not merely a reminder of aspects beyond colonialism but more unambiguously a negotiation with "the new world order" (Jacobs 25). In *The Postcolonial City and Its Subjects: London, Nairobi, Bombay* (2011), Rashmi Varma describes the postcolonial city as a "conjunctural space that produces a critical combination of historical events, material bodies, structural forces and representational economies which propels new constellations of domination and resistance, centers and peripheries, and the formation of new political subjects" (1). Varma's analysis of the postcolonial city, apart from emphasizing the socio-historical transformations and "global capitalist developments" (15), also teases out the complexity in identifying an individual as a cosmopolitan.

The identity of a cosmopolitan in the postcolonial city is often understood as limited to the elite, educated Western traveler, transnational migrant, refugee or asylum seeker (Binnie et al. 2). Scholars such as Arjun Appadurai have understood cosmopolitanism not as an "elite luxury" but as the "urge to expand one's current horizons of self and cultural identity and a wish to connect with a wider world in the name of values which, in principle, could belong to anyone and apply in any circumstance" (32). He argues that although the idea of a cosmopolitan is often shrouded with notions of being significantly well traveled, elite, and opposed to indigenous acquaintances and priorities, any individual could belong to this worldview. Interpreting a cosmopolitan in a postcolonial city also implies ruling out the stereotypes associated with the individual possessing a "cultivated knowledge of the world" (32). Thus an attempt to understand a cosmopolitan in the postcolonial city comes with the challenge of negotiating the provincial rootedness with a sense of crossing over categorical boundaries. It also expresses the difficulties of understanding the emerging individuals who attempt to maintain equilibrium between their aspirations of looking beyond the boundaries and the urge to remain an integral part of their cities.

The South Asian megacities embody the tension between the desire to "metamorphose into a world or global city" (King 2) and the complacency of going back to the roots that were once challenged and subjugated by the colonial rule. Cosmopolitanism in such cities maneuvers through the interconnected nodes that simultaneously connote a spatial limitedness in its personal geography and a permeable construct that allows diversity to survive and proliferate. The postcolonial city surfaces as a dialogical ground which supports the variety of discordant voices in the city to aspire and engage in their journeys to unravel the world. It addresses the complexities of an imagined cosmopolitan identity and the ambiguities connected to the emergence of the individuals who are natives as well as cosmopolitans. As Ulrich Beck notes, cosmopolitanism has underlying presuppositions of "individualization" (37). This individualization operates as a counterforce in some cities like Karachi and Dhaka, especially within the monologues of religion, caste, and gender. We examine these emerging identities in the post-colonial cities of Dhaka and Karachi through Maria DiBattista's concept of native cosmopolitanism.

DiBattista, in her *Novel Characters: A Geneology* (2010), while analyzing contemporary novelists like V. S. Naipaul, Salman Rushdie, and J. M. Coetzee, contemplates the emergence of individuals who allow themselves to bear multiple identities, recognizing both the world and the home. They mobilize their individual subject positions by negotiating their identities in and out of the porous boundaries of the nation and beyond. DiBattista argues for the importance of physical location and the sense of belonging to a place as a crucial ingredient for the formation of a native cosmopolitan. She points out that native cosmopolitanism emerges as an attitude with which many of the fictional characters in contemporary novels struggle to find their place in a new world, negotiating their identities with rootedness in local traditions and the yearning to embrace global citizenship. Native cosmopolitanism is understood as the way of life in which an individual is at "home in his world, even as he is fascinated and estranged by it" (DiBattista 200). The unease that comes with the realization "that one is more connected to, yet less at home in the global cities" that one inhabits, marks the birth of native cosmopolitanism. At this point, it should be noted that although the city as a locale might be complementary to a cosmopolitan realization, it is the individual who plays a pivotal role by developing "an orientation toward self, others, and world" (Hansen et al. 587). The native cosmopolitan is an individual who has an "aesthetic openness" and "a personal ability to make one's way into other cultures, through listening, looking, intuiting, and reflecting" (Hannerz 239). Cosmopolitanism in this light emerges from the intersecting grounds of the native's imaginative association with the city and the aspiration to see beyond its boundaries.

Apart from opening up a suitable framework to locate the native within the cosmopolitan discourse, DiBattista's concept of native cosmopolitanism also highlights the anxiety and curiosity of an urban native who negotiates with the different and complex aspect of identity politics while aspiring to sustain interactions with the imagination of a global world (169). With native cosmopolitanism, DiBattista underscores the significance of the native as an integral part of the cosmopolitan world that is neither contingent on any "innate" sense of belonging to a place nor is bounded by cultural or ideological orientation. Instead, she articulates the necessity of identifying the native as a "marker of origin" instead of limiting him/her to spatial locations or ideology that attempt to homogenize the "often ethnically and culturally mixed nature of 'local' characters" (164). Native cosmopolitanism, in this sense, also points out the subtle gaps in the stereotypes associated with the understanding of the native and underscores the necessity of looking into the individual narratives, as DiBattista does in *Novel Characters*:

> Such returns of the native, in their very ambiguity, are exemplary of the uncertain and confused status of the native as an integral character. They alert us to the ways in which the word native, used as a noun, is too burdened by history and its pitiless ironies to support by itself the complicated, often ethnically various and culturally mixed nature of "local" characters. The word native is more trustworthy when used as an adjective, a marker of origin, than as a noun denoting a kind of being innate to a certain region or culture. (164)

Exploring the conceptual notions of native cosmopolitanism, therefore, opens a dialogical lens to observe characters like Masud Alam in *Spiral Road*. Khan interweaves the cosmopolitan with the native in Masud, a librarian who is living in Melbourne for the last thirty years. Masud's "going away" from Dhaka, Bangladesh to Melbourne, Australia, and "coming back" from where his journey began, is the "spiral road." The shuttling between two places signifies the oscillating temperament of an individual (Masud) whose growth as a native cosmopolitan is an unsteady and complicated process. The city contributes to Masud's emergence both as a native cosmopolitan and as an outcast. Although he began his journey as a freedom fighter in the 1971 Bangladesh Liberation War, his foray to becoming a native cosmopolitan begins when he overcomes his radical commitment towards defending boundaries. Masud identifies borders as mere geographical necessities that exist because of political reasons and realizes that these dividing lines cannot be the limitations that prevent dialogues across peoples and cultures. While Masud looks forward to exploring different places in the world, it is in Dhaka that he realizes the necessity of identifying home as an integral part of his identity as a native cosmopolitan. In Khan's Dhaka, Masud's flexibility in understanding his loved ones as well as adapting to diverse cultures makes him a global character. His sense of belonging to the world grows with the importance of understanding locales as an obligatory aspect in the cosmopolitan worldview and makes him evolve as a native cosmopolitan.

In the other text, *Our Lady of Alice Bhatti*, Alice is responsive to the impediments the city thrusts on her. As an individual, she not only tackles her abject victimization within the space and place of the city Karachi, but also points to the difficulty that DiBattista articulates of "becoming a fully-fledged character in a metropolitan environment in which demographic labels abound and a single trait stands for entire personalities" (169). Alice negotiates her identity among the several interpretations she carries on her body as a Christian woman of Choohra class in Karachi. For her, it is an intertwined association of her caste, gender, and religion with the locale that facilitates her emancipation from the limitations of being a native. To understand Alice as a native cosmopolitan, one must be sensitive to the contentions she has to experience at multiple layers. In spite of a stressful and rather difficult life that she leads in Karachi, Alice is able to face all humiliations due to her moral strength and conviction that she would reach out to all through her service. Her growth as a native cosmopolitan is an intimate revelation of the bigger possibility that she realizes amidst the chaos of her life in Karachi.

Thus, the cities of Dhaka and Karachi in Khan and Hanif's texts challenge Masud and Alice to grow and sustain as native cosmopolitans within their cities. These individuals recognize their cities as intrinsic to their identities and consciously engage themselves in dialogue with the places they experience, thereby making the urban space emerge as a conspicuous challenge in their lives. These individuals tease out the chaos within the ambiance of the city, making it almost a responsive "other," contesting and determining its character in their lives. In doing so, they strive to expand their identities through the cities they inhabit and people with whom they interact on a daily basis. They possess a sense of rootedness to their cities, opening up new perspectives to communicate with the world comprising peoples and cultures unknown to them. The ambivalence in their subject positions as native cosmopolitans arises due to the fact that they are neither accepted as natives nor are they expected to become cosmopolitans. Their relation with the city fluctuates between their adherence to the cultural codes of the city and their hesitation to conform to the limitedness inherent within these cultural systems. The uncertainties of becoming a native cosmopolitan culminate into a forlorn alienation within their minds. It surfaces as a challenge restricting their freedom to inculcate a sense of belonging to the city and its spaces. Thus, in the process of aspiring to become native cosmopolitans, they also situate themselves as outcasts in their own cities and among their own people. Their individualism also inspires the understanding of cosmopolitanism not merely as a prerogative of the city, but that of an individual, and more so of native/s who begin at home and expand their visions to the world.

The Outcasts

Khan and Hanif's narratives complicate Masud and Alice's position as outcasts within their own cities of Dhaka and Karachi. Although the concept of an outcast highlights issues regarding marginality and a quest for social recognition, for Masud and Alice it also incites a poignant debate on the freedom and choice of defining an individual's identity. Historically, outcasts have been identified with the "liminality" of their subject position, suffering an in-betweenness of the self and the other (Thomassen 7). In Khan's Dhaka, the idea of an outcast is further complicated through the ways in which the outcast is cast into the imagination of friends, family, neighbors, acquaintances, and colleagues. Masud's flexibility in inhabiting multiple homes both in the foreign and the native land teases out the dilemma of the native versus the cosmopolitan debate. His native cosmopolitanism is the reception of the other as a part of his own identity. Although this dual aspect is the bone of contention for some, including members of his family in Dhaka, Masud clarifies his position of accepting home as a "place in the mind" when his brother Zia questions him about his future plans of coming back to his home in Dhaka:

> "I don't suppose you've any intention of coming back home perma-
> nently." He makes no effort to conceal his displeasure at this foregone
> conclusion.
> "Home? It's not a physical location any more. More like several
> places in the mind. I like the flexibility of such an arrangement."
> I manage to nettle Zia.
>
> (Khan 38)

Masud refuses to attribute any spatial preference to the idea of home. He possesses a sense of belonging to the world. He is open to the idea of experiencing home in different parts of the globe. This notion is however contested, both within and beyond the city of Dhaka, where Masud notices that the people there have a profound attachment to the religion and political issues such as their country's government (40). The attachment of people with the native land is such that they show a considerable disregard of the world around. Whereas he critiques the preoccupation and indifference for places and events beyond territorial boundaries, there also surfaces in Masud a sense of alienation in facing Dhaka as the city where he has grown up. Masud expresses his concern for "these people" of his city who "would not care" to understand anything beyond their day-to-day problems of life and living in the city of Dhaka: "These people would not care to know about New York or the twin towers. Afghanistan and Iraq are distant, mythical lands crawling with mechanical monsters and white sahibs. Here instead are flood-ravaged lives and peasants seeking nothing more than meager meals, shelter and something to wear" (Khan 8). While Masud recognizes the importance of being involved with the affairs of material life in one's place of living, he also considers the necessity of being aware of the world beyond. Masud evolves as a native cosmopolitan through his sympathetic understanding of locales, cultures, and people both within and beyond spatial boundaries.

Masud echoes Martha Nussbaum's idea of refining openness about the different people, cultures, and nations in the world in order to emerge as a "good citizen" of the world.[1] Masud expresses his bewilderment with the intense regionalism and local political ethos of Dhaka (8). While DiBattista argues that the native is related both to the sense of rootedness with the locale and the urge to engage in dialogue with the global audience, in Khan's

Dhaka, Masud points out the difficulties in experiencing the ambiguity as a part of his identity. The stereotypes that people associate with identity—passport, birthplace, religion—(15) and the constructions of the impermeable boundaries within these aspects also impinge the closed associations of such structures on an individual's identity. Thus, Masud's bafflement with the idea of the native in Dhaka; and the cosmopolitan desire despite the impenetrability of one domain into the other, is what DiBattista underlines as native cosmopolitanism: "Native cosmopolitans are neither mythical nor symbolic creatures; yet they, too, possess or hope to develop the ability to live in two worlds: the native and the global, the homeland (real or imaginary) and the place where they happen, through accident or by design, to abide. Note: though they can live in two worlds, they cannot do so at once" (162).

As a native cosmopolitan, Masud cultivates a critical understanding of the world both through his umbilical connection to Dhaka and the other world that he shares with Amelia in Melbourne. Although Masud identifies with the complexity in human adherence to one's roots, he is also open to the sense of plurality that allows moving to and fro across the imagined margins of emotional and geographical boundaries. Thus, cosmopolitanism evolves as innately personal. It develops as an individual's worldview that simultaneously recognizes and transcends the local, to a realization of humanity through the acceptance of family, nation, and the flux within the multiple experiential spaces of evolving identities:

> Who am I now? Born in a Muslim family, a Bangali, freedom fighter. A suspected terrorist sympathizer? An Australian, a librarian … a scarred person. An emotional nomad … Maybe I should have changed my name to John Something and converted to Christianity. Solid citizen. Right religion. Probably of a conservative mould. There are plenty of advantages when you are one of the herd. For one thing, the ground beneath your feet remains stable.
>
> (Khan 245)

Masud survives with a "double consciousness" (Chakrabarty 36), where on one hand he is a compelling native whose identity is largely shaped by his connection to Dhaka, and on the other hand, he is an outcast who is simultaneously alienated from the city, his family, and the people living there. Khan points out the irony in understanding identity as clubbed together in different aspects and the difficulty in dissociating these facets from each other. In a way, it might just be impossible to disentangle them, but the sheer helplessness connected with such associations and outright labeling is what troubles Masud most in the narrative. He meanders through various associations with the other voices in the narrative that propel him to confront his own self once again in his native land, reflecting on the concepts, places, and faces he has always known. The recurring question—"Do you feel like an alien in your birthplace?" (Khan 3) that has occurred to him since the time he boarded his flight to Bangladesh makes Masud realize the burden of being attached to "imagined homelands." His alienation in the process of becoming an outcast within his own city is perpetrated by his family and recollections of his days as a freedom fighter, entrapped in the disillusionment of insecure boundaries.

In the narrative *Our Lady of Alice Bhatti*, Alice transforms from a marginalized nurse to an outcast within the city of Karachi. Her sense of alienation might be explained as a willing detachment even from the closer precincts of her domestic circle, which she had chosen for herself imagining Teddy as her companion. The husband almost functions as one of the agents of the city of Karachi, meting out retribution to individuals such as Alice who violate the cultural codes of its space. Teddy's indifference to Alice personifies the insensitivity the city embodies through its daily encounters with her. In the narrative, Karachi does not tolerate individuals like Alice who dare to challenge the stereotypes, which the city sustains and encourages within its physical space. However, looking from Alice's perspective, both the city and her husband Teddy steadily contribute to her cumulative emancipation from a native nurse to a native cosmopolitan and to an outcast. This gradual transition showcases Alice's existence in the city as a dynamic experience quite contrary to the placid compromises of her senior nurse, Hina Alvi.

In the narrative, Alice delineates her individuality through the choice of her dress. Although other women in Karachi dress themselves in a *hijab* and most of the time choose to remain covered "in swathes of loose, man-repelling fabric" (Hanif 144), Alice explores her physicality by dressing up in shirts. Alice's aspiration to express her identity as a free individual, through the metaphor of her dress, points out both the limitation and the challenge of becoming an outcast in her own city. Alice confronts Karachi as a native cosmopolitan, opening her generous nature to people with whom she is not even acquainted. As a result, she is both violated and challenged by the city that is skeptical of her growth. However, it is the same city that contributes to her imaginative transformation from a human to a saint. Alice exemplifies, what Varma points out in her essay "UnCivil Lines: Engendering Citizenship in the Postcolonial City" as one of the "often unwelcome figures on the horizon of postcolonial cities" (Varma 34). This space that Alice carves out for herself within her liminal position makes her an outcast in the city, nevertheless leaving her newfound identity as a "lady".

Hanif discloses the discontent within the urban space of the city where Alice suffocates while trying to survive even transient exchanges while passing through the streets and bazaars. Alice struggles to negotiate both her physical and emotional presence at the bazaar with which she is acquainted partly as a native of the city and partly as an individual who desires to deal beyond the surface realities of her religion and profession. Her insistence on a cosmopolitan existence defies the spatial limitations and constricting spaces imposed by the Karachi bazaar: "It seems to her that the unspoken language that is used by men and women on the street to communicate doesn't exist in this bazaar" (Hanif 321). The bazaar posits itself as an unreceptive spirit of the city that resists the desire of individuals such as Alice to expand their sense of identity by allowing the other to be a part of them. Her sense of belonging to the city fails to limit her within the cultural construct, and instead she justifies her sense of freedom as an individual by infusing a kind of liberated consciousness in her mind from the topographical restriction of space and place.

Alice's native cosmopolitanism emerges both as a challenge and as an alternative perspective to the notion of cosmopolitanism as the enlightened ideology of a sanitized worldview as proposed by Tagore in his vision of a "creative unity."[2] Thus, through Alice, cosmopolitanism emerges as a choice that individuals might practice in the everydayness of their lived spaces and appears even though these spaces might be hostile to their ideas. Therefore, one might legitimately question the impossibility of such a wish, especially as it appears in Hanif's Karachi through Alice. Alice expresses her tenacity to carry on the dream of living a free life until her last breath, despite the "lewd gestures," "whispered suggestions," "uninvited hands on her bottom" (14), and persuasions to "suck cocks in VIP rooms" (88) that she has experienced in different phases of her life. Instead of succumbing to the several humiliations, Alice chooses to deliver her ideals through her conviction of the universality of human suffering across the overlapping terrains of life and death:

> During her house job she worked in Accidents and Emergencies for six months and there was not a single day – not a single day – when she didn't see a woman shot or hacked, strangled or suffocated, poisoned or burnt, hanged or buried alive ... And what she learned was that nobody was surprised; there were no police detectives sitting around matching clues, no parliamentary subcommittees discussing ways of saving this endangered species.
>
> (Hanif 143)

Her transcendence from being limited to an image of a marginalized individual within the structure of cultural stereotyping, to a benevolent nurse, reaffirms her ingenuity as a native cosmopolitan. She aspires for a higher, spiritual realization of life through service to humanity by helping hapless women and babies in the hospital. Also, by her inimitable approach of integrating "Musla prayers" (71) and "Lord Yassoo's" (292) blessing for "strangers" is how Alice questions and contradicts her imagined identity in her quest to be a free individual who endures her own choices.

The way Alice evolves as a native cosmopolitan in her own city and within her own people might very well border on the idea of her being an individual who is liberal and unencumbered. Perceiving Alice as a native cosmopolitan insists on a keen understanding of her circumstances and the way she enters "into a brave new world" (DiBattista 169). Unlike Masud in *Spiral Road*, Alice's journey as a native cosmopolitan begins with her urge to expand her "concentric circles" (Nussbaum 158) from her identity as a Choohra Christian woman, to the mother of an adopted baby, and ultimately into a "lady" for every individual who needed her service. The coming back to her "roots" within her own city is, for Alice, achieved through a new revelation of her own self as a benevolent human being who is an "in-house messiah" (271), available for everyone irrespective of class, religion, and social position. This transition from being "a lone soldier of Yasso" (254), who is a defiant individual fiercely safeguarding her cross, to a sympathetic individual who discovers herself by reciting "Musla prayers" to heal others, is a way by which she experiences a sense of belonging to spaces beyond her limited access and acquaintances. However, in the process, she emerges not only as an outcast to the city and to her own husband Teddy, but she also experiences the multiple transitions from an acute realization of the vulnerability of physical existence to a spiritual deliverance as "our Lady." Unlike Masud, whose identity as a native cosmopolitan is expressed through an overlapping journey across spaces, memories, and realizations, for Alice, it is a travel across her imaginations and aspirations of overcoming the stereotypes imposed by the city.

Politics of Being and Becoming

In *Spiral Road*, Khan alludes to the traveler's imagery through Masud. Like a wandering migrant who is exposed to new experiences of the unknown world, Masud opens himself to the anxieties of discovering new meanings of home/s. On one hand, Masud's cosmopolitan self seeks a fulfilling relationship with Amelia without the impositions of caste, religion, and nationalities, whereas on the other hand, his mother, his uncle Rafiq, and his nephew Omar (among others) want him to be married and settled in Dhaka forever. Masud articulates the complexity that a native cosmopolitan experiences in his or her city. He feels a perpetual tension in making choices, as those decisions are either dubbed befitting of a native or of an individual who does not conform to the ways of the city. Masud's predicament hints at the ambivalence within the conceptual paradigm of native cosmopolitanism. While native cosmopolitanism facilitates a kind of liberal individualism that balances the priorities of home with aspirations to engage beyond, there is also a nagging insecurity of experiencing failure in the process of sustaining oneself as a native cosmopolitan. While DiBattista argues that a native cosmopolitan is "consolidated in an all-embracing, warm circle of life" (166), Masud evolves as a native cosmopolitan by realizing the sense of alienation in becoming an outcast within his own Dhaka and among his own relatives and family. He unravels the dichotomies inherent in the philosophy of the concept and also sustains the struggle of negotiating between his cosmopolitan yearnings and expectations from his family in Dhaka. Ideally, Masud practices the notion his father had envisioned for his children: "'They have to broaden their minds and accommodate ideas from other cultures. They must know about people from different races', Abba argued. 'I want my children to be fluent in the language of the world. I want them to be at home wherever they are'" (Khan 56).

Masud's going back to his past, and understanding his native realities, is deeply connected to his father's Alzheimer's disease. The disease, which brings sudden bouts of unfinished narratives back to the old man's mind, is like the repressed reality that Masud consciously pretends-as lost into oblivion from the moments of his own life. He recognizes the need to connect with the shortcomings of the city, not only as a native inhabitant who survives by ignoring its inadequacies, but as a family member who in spite of being chided is never thrown away from home. Like his apprehension for Abba's condition, his concern for Dhaka also brings in a familial sympathy that extends to the city he has been a part of. The native in him reconciles with the imposed dilemma of not being able to do justice to both the roles he executes: as a native and as a cosmopolitan.

Although Masud does not share a similar mindset with his father, these individual differences do not restrain him from realizing the sorrow that the old man carries in his heart for his lost love Sumita and for his daughter, Rani. After his return to Dhaka, Masud realizes the need to observe sympathetically the city and the native surroundings. He envisions an obligation to include the city and its people in his mind in a similar way in which he aspires to connect to his Abba's diaries. Masud attempts to broaden his consciousness even to people, places, and familiar relations, which do not conform to his ideas. The way Masud empathizes with Abba's disturbed memories of the past is similar to his poignant connection to his fractured memories of the city. The city, by opening a polyphony of experiences for Masud, invites him into deeper introspection of his transition into becoming a native cosmopolitan. His philosophy of dealing with his father's disturbed past symbolically represents his relationship with Dhaka:

> I ignore the barb. "We stand on the same level. I can look him in the eyes. If we could communicate now, I'd talk to him about flaws, treachery and lies. Hurt and healing. Fallibilities in a genuine relationship. I feel for him more now than I did before."
>
> "Why is that?"
>
> "Maybe because closeness is about shared imperfections. One may admire saints, but I doubt if you can have intimate relationships with them."
>
> (Khan 310)

Masud wishes to expose himself to the "alien" even in the most acquainted space of his own city Dhaka, and he realizes the essence of being a cosmopolitan. His travel from being to becoming also has its own consequences. Masud's cosmopolitanism and the city of Dhaka are complementary to each other. The city of Dhaka in Khan's *Spiral Road* becomes the nexus of Masud's tallying of the past with the present and invokes the dilemma in the spatial recognition of home, native, and the sense of belongingness to the locale. Dhaka carries within itself the memory of Masud's life, the enigma of forgetfulness of the world. Masud, on the other hand, carries the fluidity of intercultural understanding, a quest to sympathetically get back to his roots. Dhaka and Masud are complete together, each fitting the unfinished parts of their imagined existence through a connection with the other. The city, apart from broadening his consciousness, also makes him feel the invincible limitations of an outcast that Masud experiences as a native cosmopolitan in Dhaka.

While Masud's limitation as a native cosmopolitan factors in the anxiety of balancing places and relationship, Alice and her father Joseph Bhatti in Hanif's Karachi inspire a cosmopolitan urge, despite the conflicting categories of caste, religion, and gender that are thrown upon them. Alice and Joseph both inhabit the lived space of Karachi, not only negotiating their identities through multiple interactions, but also standing as individuals in the cultural nexus of dominating regional, caste, and religious ideologies. Their voice meets with other contradictory voices that evaluate their positions as outcasts. While Masud faces religion as a dictatorial monologue of politics, further deepening his sense of alienation with his native land, Alice finds alienation in her domestic life. In both these cases, the individual in Masud and Alice are not imagined as outcasts only by others who observe them, but because of their own sensitivity, imagine themselves as the counterpoints in the dialogue of place, space, and time.

Hanif meticulously points out the obscurity of being alienated like an outcast in subtle bonds of human relationships like marriage. Even though Alice decides to marry a man of her choice, she is unable to do away entirely with the complexities that arise out of an inter-communal wedlock, especially when she is subjected to a subsidiary position in a relationship and is expected to play her role accordingly. Her dilemma in conversing about babies with her husband Teddy brings out the anxiety and repression in their domesticity. The fear of being forbidden to make a choice and discuss the names of her own children points to the extreme marginalization that Alice faces in her own home:

> She has never talked babies with Teddy and now she knows why. It would have involved a discussion about names, how the child would be brought up, in what religion. Would it be circumcised or baptised or first circumcised then baptised? Would it be easier if it were a girl? …
>
> And it would seem like a concession. Shouldn't a baby be a blessing and not some kind of half-baked deal? What kind of life begins with a compromise?
>
> Like her own.
>
> (Hanif 264)

Alice's hesitation to strike an open conversation with her husband on the prospect of starting a family indicates the lack of communication in their relationship. While she accepts Teddy as her spouse, there is a persistent uncertainty that she experiences in the relationship. With Teddy, she perceives a similar kind of dilemma as that she experiences in the streets and bazaars of Karachi, in the hospital where she works, and also in the locality she has lived her life. Like the voidness of "unspoken language" in the Karachi bazaar, Alice feels a sense of "nothingness" as an active collaborator in the marital alliance. Her relationship with Teddy gets reflected in her connection with the city where she wanders as an outcast. She stumbles on her way to becoming a native cosmopolitan despite the challenges of being imagined as an outcast even in her own city and within the intimate bonds that she hopes to develop with her husband.

For Alice, her growth as a native cosmopolitan emerges from an innate understanding of, and sympathy to, human life and values. Her prayers signify the desire to reach beyond the domains of stereotypical categorization like gender (being a woman), caste (a Choohra), and religion (a Christian). Her image as an individual immersed in prayer with hands "folded in front of her chest" (272), assuming the status of shared benevolence towards humanity, resists the imagination of people like Teddy who wish to chain down her spirit to her body. Through her prayers, she experiences an emancipated sense of life and the freedom to express her concern for people whom she does not know. Her decision to adopt "Little Yassoo" (292) without asking permission from her husband underlines her wish to challenge her own limitations within the city and in her marriage. While she resolves to accept the orphan boy as her child, she also expresses her disapproval in conforming to the image that the city of Karachi and her husband have ordained for her. Instead she inspires in herself a broader association with herself and the city through her efforts to heal people who are sick through her prayers. She becomes "Our Lady" for those people for whom she has prayed and served. The transition from being Alice Bhatti to a higher, emancipated, spiritual "Our Lady of Alice Bhatti" (337) constitutes a counterpoint in her discourse with the city of Karachi where her identity was deemed to be as insignificant as the "loose change" (142) of currency notes. This difficult process of becoming a native cosmopolitan by imagining a broader sense of connection with others, and praying for the well-being of people who have never been important to her, makes Alice a "lady." Her spirituality emerges as a defiant yet forgiving code that points to the spaces of contestations that echo "goodness" and services to humanity at large without being concentrated within Congregations and social systems.

Like Masud, Alice declares herself a native cosmopolitan by practicing benevolence and individuality through her body, service, and life. It might be noteworthy to observe that, while Alice evolves as a native cosmopolitan primarily through her service and fulfills her quest for self-recognition in the city of Karachi, Alice's accomplishment as a native cosmopolitan also hints at the possible way of legitimizing the outcast's position within the city. Her evolution as an individual from the margins of the city as a Choohra Christian nurse to a "lady" anticipates what Varma terms as the "unhomely women" (27). Being an outcast in her own way, Alice juxtaposes "domesticity's discontents" with the "crisis" of being a native cosmopolitan in Karachi (Varma 27). Her native cosmopolitanism attempts to open the subtle differences between the native cosmopolitan and the outcast, the home and the city, and the imagination of becoming a native with cosmopolitan aspirations.

Between Roots and Routes

Khan's *Spiral Road* and Hanif's *Our Lady of Alice Bhatti* discuss the complex binaries of local/global and roots/routes. Khan allows the "spiral road" to open up for Masud and his journey between two cities and two locales. The spiral road is a metaphor connecting the straying dots of his life and represents the cyclic process of Masud's going away from Dhaka and coming back to it after thirty years. While his journey begins as a 1971 Liberation War freedom fighter, desperately defending physical boundaries between nations, the Masud who comes back from Melbourne is aware of the permeable spaces within these boundaries. Although Masud returns to the city where he began his journey as a passionate native, he unearths the secrets of a wider sense of belonging to "several places in the mind" (Khan 38). The spiral road therefore is not only a metaphor of a journey that an individual makes to become a native cosmopolitan; it also indicates the intersecting spaces of home and the world, the native and the cosmopolitan. In Khan's narrative, Masud experiences the spiral road by coming closer to his city and his family after living a couple of decades outside Dhaka.

The cosmopolitan and the native intersect within the individual and Masud realizes the significance of considering both of these concepts for a life beyond the binaries of "us and them." However, Khan does not ignore the difficulty Masud faces owing to his position as a native cosmopolitan and points out the contesting space of human predicament fraught with multiple voices and numerous possibilities. He proclaims the complexity associated with holding on to both ideologies simultaneously and through the domains of his family, community, city, religion, and country. Masud legitimately questions the predicament of living in a 'third space,' a neutral zone, as a sandwich between human beings categorizing their minds in mutually exclusive groupings. For Masud, the cosmopolitan worldview and his love for Dhaka are mutually inclusive: an individual belongs to his locale and to the world through a sense of underlying interconnectedness between them. The "spiral road" represents the inevitability of coming back to the roots of native culture and connecting back to the world. An individual like Masud cannot help but walk on the spiral road. Masud realizes the flexibility of multiple homes, of connecting in depth to several people with different ideals and backgrounds after he comes back to Bangladesh:

> The indigenous man of the subcontinent and the migrant will never reconcile their differences and live as an entity. With each passing year, it becomes increasingly difficult to decide where I'd rather be. There will always be an awareness of the pieces that are missing. Now I'm unable to silence the voice of lament that whispers about denial and loss. But regret has given way to resigned acceptance.
>
> (Khan 38)

In *Spiral Road*, Khan reiterates the necessity of forging relations of the mind, not by overlooking but by simply recognizing the barriers. Masud's journey as a native cosmopolitan begins with his acceptance of the other both in his family and in the world. The ineffectuality of human ego and the tenacity displayed in keeping boundaries intact or fighting for people based only on common interest is the monologue of selfish human interest that Masud is actively voicing against. The narrative therefore does not come to a closure with Omar's death or Masud's inability to fly back to Australia. Rather, it signals a new beginning for Masud—he begins to imagine the world through his home and city. The narrative remains open-ended with Masud trying to communicate with Amelia from the Dhaka airport and assimilating himself to his "home" in the space that is the nodal point of accommodating both the native and the cosmopolitan self concurrently.

While in *Spiral Road* Khan reiterates the necessity of forging mental relations, not by overlooking but by simply recognizing the barriers, Hanif in *Our Lady of Alice Bhatti* exposes the intricacies of gender, caste, and religion that play a decisive role in the cosmopolitan imagination of a city like Karachi. The narrative begins with Joseph Bhatti's fear of the discrimination that his daughter Alice might face as a junior nurse: "'These Muslas will make you clean their shit and then complain that you stink', he had said. 'And our own brothers at the Sacred? They will educate you and ask you why you stink'" (Hanif 1). Alice's progression from her father's apprehensions of discrimination and from being "a lone soldier of Yassoo" (254) to "an in-house messiah at the Sacred" (271) is the emergence from the specificities of body and materialism to becoming a native cosmopolitan.

> And then the sweeper sees that Sister Alice Bhatti is kneeling on the floor surrounded by bloodied cotton and piles of gauze. Her hands are folded in front of her chest and she is praying. The sweeper thinks he has no option but to go down on his knees and join her in prayer ... The sweeper will tell everyone that he felt the presence of the Holy Spirit. (272)

Alice's divinity as interpreted by the sweeper and perhaps many others like him, is symbolic of accepting a broader aspect of life through service to humanity. Although she is executed brutally by her husband, Alice continues to live on in the domains of imagination and aspirations of her father and other people for whom she was "our Lady." Although Alice's death represents to a certain extent the psychological gagging of human aspiration, it also points to the gap between imagining a cosmopolitan existence and the desire to experience it.

With Masud and Alice, native cosmopolitanism in the South Asian literary world finds an expression and an indulgence from the reader who is eager to tease out the new directions of understanding individuals and their sense of identities in the world. Khan and Hanif not only make Karachi and Dhaka grow in the imagination of individuals like Masud and Alice, but also underscore the influence that these cities have on the emergence of their cosmopolitan aspirations. There is an umbilical connection that these characters have with the city despite contesting its spatial connotation with their understanding of the world through the contours of their homes as outcasts. These South Asian cities—with their typical cultural constitution and the intricate fabrication of regionalism, caste, family, religion, and politics—bring both Alice and Masud into a complex puzzle of interacting ideologies and reflexive identities. Although there is a constant tension in the rediscovery of Masud and Alice and their relations with the cities of Dhaka and Karachi, their native cosmopolitanism points to a creative liberation from the impermeability of boundaries. Emerging as native cosmopolitans, these individuals represent the new hope for character. In spite of being imagined as outcasts in their own cities and by people in their own circles, these individuals initiate the cosmopolitan call, connecting South Asian literature to the world.

Notes

1. In her book *Cultivating Humanity* (1998), Nussbaum points to the Stoic principle of the "good citizen" as a "citizen of the world" and argues that an individual's place of birth and community is an accidental fact (59). In *Spiral Road*, Masud emerges as a conscious human being who respects differences, yet understands, as Nussbaum emphasizes, the need to stand for humanity in general.
2. In *Creative Unity* (1922) Tagore's worldview corresponds to an idealized vision governed by knowledge and higher human values (30). In *Our Lady of Alice Bhatti*, Alice does not envision a cosmopolitan existence through a sublime understanding of the world as Tagore has visualized. Nonetheless, she becomes a cosmopolitan, despite being grounded in her local problems, through her service towards the unknown, helpless, and sick.

Works Cited

Appadurai, Arjun. "Cosmopolitanism from Below: Some Ethical Lessons from the Slums of Mumbai." *The Johannesburg Salon* 4 (2011): 32–43. Print.

Beck, Ulrich. "The Cosmopolitan Perspective: Sociology of the Second Age of Modernity." *British Journal of Sociology* 51 (2000): 79–105. Print.

Binnie, Jon, et al. *Cosmopolitan Urbanism*. New York: Routledge, 2006. Print.

Chakrabarty, Dipesh. "Humanism in a Global World." *Humanism in Intercultural Perspective: Experiences and Expectations*. Eds. Jörn Rüsen and Henner Laass. Piscataway: Transaction Publishers, 2009. Print.

Chandoke, Neera. "The Post-Colonial City." *Economic and Political Weekly* 26.50 (1991): 2868–73. Print.

DiBattista, Maria. *Novel Characters: A Geneology*. Massachusetts: Wiley-Blackwell, 2010. Print.

Hanif, Mohammed. *Our Lady of Alice Bhatti*. Uttar Pradesh: Random House, 2011. Print.

Hannerz, Ulf. "Cosmopolitans and Locals in World Culture." *Theory, Culture & Society* 7 (1990): 237–51. Print.

Hansen, David T., et al. "Education, Values, and Valuing in Cosmopolitan Perspective." *Curriculum Inquiry* 39.5 (2009): 587–612. Print.

Jacobs, Jane M. *Edge of Empire: Postcolonialism and the City*. London: Routledge, 1996. Print.

Khan, Adib. *Spiral Road*. Sydney: Harper Collins Publishers Australia Pvt Limited, 2007. Print.

King, Anthony D. "Postcolonial Cities." Binghamton, NY: Elsevier Inc, 2009. Print.

Nussbaum, Martha C. "Patriotism and Cosmopolitanism." *The Cosmopolitan Reader*. Eds. Garrett W. Brown and David Held. Cambridge: Polity P, 1994. Print.

———. *Cultivating Humanity*. Cambridge: Harvard UP, 1997. Print.

Rushdie, Salman. *The Satanic Verses*. London: Vintage, 1988. Print.

Tagore, Rabindranath. *Creative Unity*. London: Macmillan, 1922. January 29, 2013. Project Gutenberg Literary Archives. Web. January 12, 2015.

Tomassen, Bjørn. *Liminality and the Modern: Living Through the In-Between*. Vermont: Ashgate Publishing Company, 2014. Print.

Varma, Rashmi. "UnCivil Lines: Engendering Citizenship in the Postcolonial City." *NWSA Journal* 10.2 (Summer 1998): 32–55. Print.

———. *The Postcolonial City and its Subjects: London, Nairobi, Bombay*. New York: Routledge, 2012. Print.

8 Portrayal of a Dystopic Dhaka
On Diasporic Reproductions of Bangladeshi Urbanity

Maswood Akhter

Long before *The God of Small Things*, the Booker-winning Indian author and activist Arundhati Roy appeared in a "lunatic fringe cinema," *In Which Annie Gives It Those Ones*, where she played the role of a bright, brash, and vaguely idealistic final-year student of architecture named Radha. The screenplay was written by Roy herself in 1988 and the movie—although it was shown only once on Door Darshan, the national television of India, and that, too, in a late-night slot—became popular among the English-speaking contemporary urban Indian youth. In defending her architectural thesis, Radha told the examiners:

> Every Third-World city consists of two parts: the city and a non-city. And the city and non-city are at war with one another. Now, the city consists of a number of institutions: of houses, offices, shops, roads, sewage systems ... the non-citizen has no institutions; he lives and works in the gaps between these institutions; he defecates on top of the sewage system. He [the architect] designs them [the institutions] so that they say to the non-citizens, "stay out of here", "keep out, this is not your area."[1]

By raising issues of the existence of the non-city within the city itself as well as the elitist manipulation of the built environment—that brutally renders the millions automatic outcasts—the film prefigures Roy's "commitment to the underprivileged" (Rao 307) and her capacity to delve deep not only into the structure, design, and minute details of things within and around "the buildings," but also into the "city's truth,"[2] discovery of which remains to be a central fantasy of much modern/postmodern urban aesthetics and studies.

Radha's speech in the film is rather uncannily pertinent in understanding the essentially duplicitous profile of the growing city of Dhaka, the largest and the capital city, and arguably the *most urban* scape of a so-called developing nation, Bangladesh. Dhaka contains a non-city or an anti-city within it, manifest not only in this unplanned city's more unplanned suburban sprawl and economically debilitating human geographies, but also equally in its aggressive process of gentrification and the privileged colonies of gated communities. The cruel monopoly of the few, the affluent minority comprised of the political, corporate, and bureaucratic shenanigans, over most of the urban resources and privileges automatically outcasts the majority of the city including the poor and the women of all classes. The situation, of course, arises from large-scale and deeply embedded inequalities and discriminations built up over the years and is associated, among other things, with the continued injustices and exploitation wrought by age-old patriarchy, and colonialist encroachments in this part of the world, either by the British imperialists and the Pakistani junta or the comprador bourgeoisie in post-independence Bangladesh, irretrievably impacting its topography and mindscape.

Against this backdrop, this chapter examines fictional reproductions of the cityspace of Dhaka and its distinctive spatial features that turn different sets of its population urban outcasts, in the writings of Bangladeshi diaspora authors such as Monica Ali's *Brick Lane* (2003) as well as Adib Khan's *Seasonal Adjustments* (1994) and *Spiral Road* (2007). While Khan portrays Dhaka—in counterpoint to Shopnogonj, "a replica of the thousands of villages which confirm the rural primitivism of Bangladesh" (Khan, *Seasonal* 11)—trying unsuccessfully to hide its real poverty through a few superficial symbols of modernity, Ali's fiction conceives the city as an ironic dystopic antithesis to the idyllic "Golden Bengal" of poet Rabindranath Tagore's songs. Conceiving the city as "a complex and interactive network which links together, often in an unintegrated and de facto way, a number of disparate social activities, processes, and relations, with a number of imaginary and real, projected or actual architectural, geographic, civic, and public relations" (Grosz 244), the chapter engages with Dhaka's distinctive urban geography, built on its own dynamics of social exclusion and spatial segregation: the sexist character of the socio-spatial structure, the large population's lack of choice over the space they occupy, competing nationalisms as well as clashing views over religion, massive inequality in the distribution of justice and development, education, and governance—all contributing to the perpetuation of an insidiously powerful dichotomy between urban centrality and urban margins. While the monochromatic images of the depressing Dhaka inspire many to question the diaspora authors' grasp on the city's current topography and humanscape, their "home narratives" still succeed, as I argue, in querying the form and the nature of urbanity of Dhaka and in implying the need for transforming an unsympathetic urban space into a more equitable one.

Discussions on diaspora writings conventionally involve issues of a writer's location and the attendant anxieties, hegemony of the publishing industry, and marketing the margins, as well as debates regarding whether these narratives are mere creative elaborations of the pre-existing white stereotypes of idiosyncrasies and symbols of the non-western cultures. This chapter, however, assumes that diaspora home narratives represent reality in some important ways, and that if the representation is dystopic, it becomes significant, among other things, for the critical potential of exaggeration that such type of narration involves. It may then serve as useful interrogation, even necessary resistance, to insular/parochial romanticization of "home." In other words, I take dystopic vision of a city as a meaningful and significant representational category, as a distinctive form of urban criticism that potentially provides wider scopes to the analysis of dynamics producing and perpetuating situations of exclusion. Indeed, there is a natural connection between "dystopia" and "exclusion" since dystopia, according to *Oxford Advanced Learner's Dictionary*, refers to a state which is "extremely bad or unpleasant," and such politically and environmentally degraded condition would inevitably marginalize/outcast different sections of people.

The City of Dhaka: History's Stepchild and the Dystopic Urban

In his *Urban Outcasts*, Loïc Wacquant views urban space as a historical and political construction and pays particular attention to historical trajectories of spaces. Among many other equally influential factors, the long legacy of national slavery, humiliation, and deprivation, as well as the cultural havoc wrought by the colonial hegemony, contributes to the production of Dhaka's cityscape where a few blindly imitative "First World" architectures, and a loud collection of intimidating infrastructural specimens decorating its urban interior, come to be touted as symbol/semblance of modern development—a kind of sinister urban postcolonial modernity where the neo-colonial elite have, in effect, established several privileged cocoons of their own and left the rest with an alien, inaccessible system created and controlled by them. The city's "hyper-defended enclaves" of the rich, the "carefully-manicured residential and commercial ecologies," loudly speak of a brutal social polarization manifest in the wildly increasing gap between different social, religious and gender groups. All these point starkly to an inequitable character and management of the city that renders a vast number of its population "a cluster of undesirables" and perpetual outcasts.

Khan's and Ali's protagonists are not ready to buy myths of the once affluent, glorious Bengal concocted by nostalgic Bengalis. The truth for *Seasonal Adjustments'* Chaudhary remains that Bengal, since ancient times, has always been treated as the stepchild of history, suffering accumulated neglect of the past "right from ancient Sanskrit texts where Bengal is mentioned as a backward, hostile land of ignorance, to the rule of the Senas and Palas through to the Mughal period" (208). It was ravaged thereafter by British colonial exploitations. Finally, soon after the creation of Bangladesh from the clutches of the oppressive Pakistan, the leader of liberation Sheikh Mujib's "brief romance with the nation was brutally terminated" (262) and the military government camouflaged itself behind a civilian visage. Pertinently, Ngugi Wa Thiong'o observes that after Independence of the colonies, the elite who assumed political ascendancy in the newly liberated nations continued to function in a way analogous to colonial dominance (210). For the last several hundred years the region had never really been free from colonial encroachment, not even after the country won its blood-soaked independence from the incorrigibly colonialist Pakistan in 1971. In the newly independent Bangladesh the army, the bureaucracy, the elite, and political opportunists combined to forge a vicious nexus of power to rule the country according to their selfish whims.

The representation of Dhaka in both writers' fiction paints a living urban dystopia plagued by violent inequities and exploitations, overcrowding and disorder, social disintegration, appalling poverty, religious conservatism, and political tensions. The depiction of everyday life in the city reproduces a skeptical, dark vision of the modern urban condition of Dhaka. Extreme economic disparity itself is indicative of many injustices prevailing in the city. Regressive attitudes towards women, postwar disillusionment of freedom fighters, repressive military regimes, too, are constitutive elements of Dhaka's dystopicity.

Conceiving Home in a Dystopic Dhaka

For characters of these diasporic writers, Dhaka as "home" remains an intriguing, even elusive concept: often it is a lonely escape to an alternative reality from a defeated present, sometimes a bundle of betraying memories and longings, sometimes a wholly imagined idyllic hub and, very rarely, a practically existing, cartographic space ready for return. In fact, when home becomes a series of mental images or a mythic space of desire, it automatically ceases to be a place of any real return. Adib Khan's own words in his essay "Writing Homeland" aptly define the diasporic reproduction of home: "It is an amalgamation of remembrances, half-truths, fragmented images, gaunt shadows, snatches of conversations and yearnings, structured into a shimmering mirage by an imagination that feeds itself uneasily on an awareness of the discrepancy between the way it was and the way it possibly is" (24).

In *Brick Lane*, the male protagonist Chanu's construction of Dhaka is largely discursive and book-based rather than deriving from any direct memory or lived experience. He prepares his daughters for the journey back home through Tagore's song about Golden Bengal (incidentally the national anthem of Bangladesh):

> In autumn, o mother mine
> In the full-blossomed paddy fields,
> I have seen spread all over—sweet smiles!
> Ah, what a beauty, what shades, what an affection
> And what a tenderness. (146)

The translation renders the tenderness for the impossibly beautiful Bengal in a slightly exaggerated and parodic tone, a tone that flavors Shahana and the author's responses to "the frog-faced" (12) Chanu's grandiose lectures attempting to instill in his daughters proud legacies of Bengali culture and history, ranging from the pre-colonial state of Dhaka's weaving industry to the syncretic religious tradition of Bengal. When Chanu quotes professors of the London School of Economics and proclaims Bangladesh the happiest nation of the world, the snug answer to all confusions, Nazneen asserts quietly, "It may be written down. But I do not believe it" (290). And Nazneen's friend Razia asks: "Tell me this ... If everything back home is so damn wonderful, what are all these crazy people doing queuing up for visa?" (357). For Nazneen's daughters Bibi and Shahana, Bangladesh defines nightmares to be eternally avoided: it is an impossible place where girls get married off and have a "swelling belly" in no time, are locked up in little smelly rooms and made to weave carpets, where one brushes with a *daaton* (neem twig) and not a toothbrush and has to do without toilet paper and so on. *Brick Lane* seems determined to discard the memory-drenched golden image of home back in Bangladesh.

Chanu, however, plans to go back to his city, which symbolizes for him all that is positive: an uncorrupted sanctuary for his daughters, a proud and autonomous history and culture defying colonial dictates and curricula and, above all, a site that would grant him his due dignity and position. While Chanu views Dhaka as a safer place for his girls to grow up, Nazneen nurtures a strong distrust in Chanu's utopic reconstruction of home since her younger sister Hasina's uncensored word-maps of Dhaka project a very different picture. Hasina's life in Dhaka, as revealed by her letters, "is a pedestrian (that is to say, unexceptional) tale of outrageous misfortune" (Ali, "Where I'm Coming From"), and the city is violently *urban*, grossly iniquitous, and locked into the global capitalist system. Britney Spears is painted on a baby-taxi among a jostle of the regular peacock, tiger, elephant, film star, Taj Mahal, or mosque, and "Pantene Head and Shoulders hair contests" are held at the capital's Sheraton Winter Garden. The presence of transnational capital, and the instance and effects of what Jorg Durrschmidt has termed *microglobalization*, that is, the "integration of global difference(s) and variety into a distinctive social environment"(57) are to be noticed in Dhaka's new urbanism; unique local features are gradually being diminished, and one witnesses architectures, buildings and lifestyles that refer to situations anywhere in the world, or to be more accurate, somewhere else in the First World, rendering the majority outcast, alien to their *own* city.

While the memory of her village Gouripur—frozen at a particular time and not necessarily corresponding to the cartographic reality of Bangladesh—soothes Nazneen in crisis, Dhaka promises only an utter desolation; from the beginning, she is wary about returning to Dhaka: "Dhaka would be a disaster. Shahana would never forgive her. Chanu would be finished ... Hasina was in Dhaka but the city of her letters was an ugly place, full of dangers" (Ali, *Brick Lane* 56). The unending macabre account of suffering mediated by Hasina's letters dispels the idea of mythical Golden

Bengal. London emerges, through its comparison with the fearful situation in Dhaka, as a catalytic site of positive changes in women's lives; its status as a potentially fulfilling environment for women serves as foil to accentuate Dhaka's dystopicity.

Dhaka, in contrast to the snug female matrix controlling an entrepreneurial network in London, is represented as slandering its women who work in the *male-owned* garment factories. Women back home, as Hasina's letters suggest, are in a dismal state. Aleya's husband discourages her from going to work in the garment factory and insists on her wearing a *burkha*. He beats her on false suspicion the day she gets a sari as a bonus for her work. There are *mullahs* who play religious messages with loudspeakers forbidding men and women to work together. On the other hand, upper-class women like Lovely are glamorous puppets, liberalized only in their fashion statements, and contributing mainly, as Monica Germana puts it, to "the promotion of western capitalist models of fashion production and consumption" (81).

In *Brick Lane*, Dhaka is shown as mindlessly conservative, zealous on retaining its *tradition*, and cruel to its women. As Hasina defies her parents to enter a "love marriage," her family rejects her, and then, when the husband turns out to be a wife-beater, she runs away to join the vast army of garment workers in Dhaka. She could not, however, continue with the factory for long. She becomes a maid in a wealthy household after that, is abused by a succession of men, and is even forced into prostitution.

If the reader can overcome the comic dimension of the odd idiom—resulting from Ali's experimentation with a bizarre "pidgin" in a desperate bid to reproduce Hasina's supposedly incorrect but energetic variant of Bengali— her letters to Nazneen present Bangladeshi urbanity as a state in anomie and chaos: there, strikes or *hartals* are frequent, university students rally for the right to cheat, corruption is pervasive, politicians hire goons to win elections, and men are lynched on the street, all of which leave Hasina wondering: "Sister what is happen to police and court and thing? In England could such thing happen like this?" (221). But then, Hasina's *non-urban* language is also revealing of her location, her alienation, her non-belongingness to urban space. It is also interesting to see how the diasporic imaginary conceives an urban outcast through inventing such language.

Production of Urban Outcasts

Ali claims to have been moved by *The Power to Choose*, the Bangladeshi academic Naila Kabeer's book of case studies about Bangladeshi women garment workers in Dhaka and the East End of London. However, Ali portrays Dhaka, where Hasina struggles fruitlessly against the spatial segregation based on gender, as more repressive than Kabeer's study. Hasina eventually has to leave the garment factory and becomes increasingly powerless and socially excluded, while Nazneen undergoes such a powerful emancipation that she is finally "startled by her own agency" (*Brick* 11).

Dhaka, for Ali's urban working-class women, is thus more often an uninviting reality than a fantasized or discursive space; suffering is routine for women there, especially for the poor among them and those who transgress the pre-scripted role of the ideal, obedient Bengali-Muslim wife. Hasina's letters written from Dhaka are the one real contact with the actual geographical "home" but the contact is alienating, and they project an ironic dystopic antithesis to Chanu's dreamscape. For Hasina, Dhaka is aloof and uncaring; indeed, she becomes, to quote the epithet given to Medea by the chorus in Euripides' play, a "woman without a city" (l. 650); her letters bitterly lament her "being citiless" (l. 256). The horror described by her sister contributes to Nazneen's decision not to return to this dystopia.

The sexist character of Dhaka's cityspace indicates, to use Elizabeth Grosz's insights from her "Bodies-Cities," "the implicitly phallocentric coding of the body-politic" which "uses the male to represent the human." (247). The gendering of body/space is used as a device of control, evidenced, in this context, by the situation in garment factories. Conservative forces erect invisible but hugely formidable walls by "holding up the sacred as a justification" (Mernissi xviii). In *Brick Lane*, we see how some men call garment workers prostitutes as these girls share *mixed-sex* public space. To include women in non-domestic spaces implies sexual desegregation and many believe this to be in contradiction with the principles of *sharia* (Islam and its laws). Indeed, women's seclusion is largely due to the age-old Bengali patriarchal culture appropriating Islam and its views on women to serve its own hegemonic purpose. This hegemony is operative not only in rural areas but also equally in the urbanized middle- and lower-class population affecting women's marginalization, deprivation, and exclusion from modernity. Exclusionary spatial configuration is thus not about upholding religious ideal, rather about power relations: "The spatial division according to sex reflects the division between those who hold authority and those who do not" (138). Patriarchy is resistant in allowing women to operate as productive economic agents, in integrating them "into modern circuits of the production system" (146) since, after all, it is a question of sharing resources.

The way Dhaka's garment industry operates points to the truth that "cities and buildings are, by and large, designed by men," and they bear "only the imprint of male perceptions and male power" (Short 67). Women's mobility is curtailed, as shown through the fate of the garment girls, by the notion that the presence of the female body pollutes the moralscape of the public space, and also by the widespread sexual violence and harassment. Thus, although Hasina took her garment job for a "cure" (*Brick* 107) to her unending misery, it finally could not save her from being exploited by successive employers. *Brick Lane* thus, as Elizabeth Jackson puts it, overturns the popular perception of paid employment outside the home being necessarily liberating or empowering for women (65). Dhaka does not turn into Raban's "soft city" for Hasina, as the city negates any attempts on her part "to remake it, to consolidate it into a shape [she] can live in" and make an imprint of her identity (2). The dystopicity of the situation for women is further consolidated by the female industrial entrepreneur Alya's report in Khan's *Spiral Road* that, although "women hold important government posts now," and are "more readily" employed in the private sector, "too much ignorance and gender bias" still prevail (63–4).

Hasina's coming to Dhaka also brings to the fore the issue of rural-to-urban migrants. There is a visible urban development in Dhaka, but the fundamental question is whose growth and development is this? The city, obviously, needs to be more pro-poor, more humane to these people whose labor is crucial to the functioning of this city. The people who have flocked to the city desiring a better life are inevitably by-products of unequal growth and unplanned urbanization across the country. The spatially segregated Dhaka disavows the existence of the working-class urban poor while simultaneously relying on their labor.

Poverty and exclusion are directly connected, yet different forms of exclusion, as Andrew Fischer emphasizes, are not always related to actual lack of means, or exclusively a matter of material deprivation usually described as poverty, since people can be excluded on the basis of their race, age, or gender, etc. (146). Exclusion, thus being both a process and condition, results from a combination of intertwined forms of social, economic and power inequalities and the systematic denial of individuals' or communities' rights, opportunities, resources, and dignity (Levitas 9). Bangladeshi women face rejection in their right to space, not only because the space is discriminatory and segregative in terms of wealth and economic resources, but also because it is defined by blatant patriarchal interpretations of Islamic ethics and beliefs regarding women. The infrastructural developments in Dhaka do not equally correspond to the mental and attitudinal advancement of the citizens, and women continue to remain outcast and marginalized.

The garment industry in Dhaka both challenges and extends exclusionary practices with regard to women; apparently it defies traditional rules about gender segregation as it allows women to work there and provide them with a source of earning, but Hasina's description of the factory she works in reveals its segregated interior: "It [the factory] have three room around courtyard all new solid concrete. One place is for machine. I go there. Another for cutting and finishing. Men go there" (*Brick* 149–50). And also: "*Men and women keep separate here. No men doing machining ... So you see how it is and when we must speak it is as brother and sister*" (125; emphasis in original). For Ali's garment girls, Dhaka's textile industry thus remains nothing more than a Janus-faced space of desire and disappointment, an equivocal site of emancipation and exploitation. Lefebvre observes insightfully, "repressive space wreaks repression and terror even though it may be strewn with ostensible signs of the contrary" (144). Again, girls are only workers here and hardly on the management. True, *Spiral Road*'s Alya runs a cottage industry at Manikpur, yet there she faces opposition in the form of Mullah Hakim, who sees women's earning as socially harmful as it disrupts *order* in the family.

These diaspora narratives suggest that while there is apparently little modernization in rural areas, the city of Dhaka experiences massive transformation. However, as gendered space, there exists no difference between the city and the village, each space showing clear misogynistic tendencies disavowing women's space for articulating any position outside what is legitimized by the Bengali Muslim society. Sexist attitudes prevalent in rural areas in the name of upholding tradition and religion witness almost a verbatim reproduction in the city, perpetuating women's parasitical existence everywhere. In *Spiral Road*, while at the village Manikpur, Farida's father forces her to marry a much older man who tries to kill her, in the affluent urban household Alam's mother tolerates her husband's "fallibility" during their married life. In *Seasonal Adjustments* the protagonist's sister Nafisa's *progressive* family cannot accept her lesbian identity and her reluctance to get married, making her feel outcast at home. Her mother looks for a supernatural solution to her problems and becomes a devout disciple of a fake *Pir*. She worries about her daughter's marriage, since, for a woman, marriage is inevitable! The artificial, limited life led by the upper-class woman, Lovely, is also pathetic. Although these women belong to different classes than Hasina and Farida, and are neither tortured physically nor face financial exigencies, they too suffer from different sets of anxieties and remain marginalized in one way or other.

The outcasts in these novels thus cover women, irrespective of classes, including prostitutes, maids, garment girls, housewives, single women or lesbians as well as the holders of liberal views, the poor, the beggars, the rural-to-urban migrants and the returnees from overseas. Khan's home-returned protagonists are beset by the anxiety of "unhomeliness," a condition of "living unsettled *in* multiple places at once while being *of* none of them" (Flusty 110). With such fragmented identities, they feel alienated and outcasts in their *home city*. In *Seasonal Adjustments*, Iqbal Chaudhary returns to his ancestral land after almost two decades craving for "the security he once knew," but in vain; "the womb" is there all right, but he could not fit into it anymore. For his acquaintances in Dhaka, Chaudhary is "a traitor to the Bengali cause, an opportunist" (140), and for his relatives a misguided family member "corrupted by the hedonistic ways of the West" (16). *Spiral Road*'s home-returned protagonist Masud Alam, too, realizes soon that he not only needs to tackle the changes in people around him but also the "foreignness" of a city that he once called his own. Everywhere Alam goes the land elicits his "migrant guilt" as he finds bits of him scattered all over places. In a subtle way, the gendered subaltern's marginalization at home corresponds to these migrants' own sense of being outcast, their realization that *home* no longer remains a matter of simple identification, but is rather "fraught with ambiguities" (*Seasonal* 61).

Dhaka's Urbanity: "Overtly Dystopian"?

Adib Khan's fiction does not indulge a "chest-beating exercise about a community's superior virtue" ("Janus' Footsteps" 27); rather, his is an obviously pessimistic documentation of a country and its people. He projects the nation's trajectory as a grim catalogue of chaos, army coups, political agitations, hunger and corruption, voluntary/forced censorship of media, and "the fragile semblance of democracy" (*Seasonal* 31) as well as other varieties of "Third-World iniquity and grotesquerie": a charlatan of a *Pir* with his flow of "holy bullshit" (43), or aggressive beggars who promptly mug Chaudhary. Wandering around various locales, *Seasonal Adjustments'* home-returned narrator is overwhelmed by "the bleeding rawness of bare existence" (10), and relieved that he does not live amidst such squalor anymore.

The sketches of rural and urban locations exist as distinct, different topologies in Khan's novels. We have descriptions of six seasons, each with their distinctive flavor and color: the monsoon rains, the bright tropical greenness of paddy fields, huge water lilies crowding the water surface of a small pond, wild ducks gliding in the pond. However, against the backdrop of all-engulfing poverty, the marvelous natural beauty of Tagore's Bengal can only represent "a bad-tempered step-parent showering moments of guilt-ridden generosity on a maltreated child" (*Seasonal* 31). While urban Bengal is portrayed as unsuccessfully trying to hide real poverty through a few overt infrastructural developments—evidenced by the glossy billboards from under which the truth is exposed through a message in Bangla, scribbled in charcoal "WE ONLY WANT RICE" (257)—rural Bengal emerges as starkly primitive: "Travelling beyond Dhaka is like taking a giant leap back in time ... The *pucca* roads radiating from the city like the arms of a starfish, are the only enduring symbols of a marginally successful invasion of modernity into the otherwise impenetrable depths of an ancient way of life" (10). When Chaudhary's daughter Nadine had to travel by a crowded local bus—where a passenger insisted that his goat was his luggage—she was exposed to "the unpredictability of public transportation and a raw slice of life experienced by ordinary Bengalis" and overwhelmed by "the glaring contradiction between her comfortable living conditions and the abject poverty she confronts when she steps outside the house" (281) in Dhaka or at Shopnogonj.

In *Spiral Road*, the narrator compares the suburban boredom of Ballarat, where he presently lives, with the chaos and energy of Dhaka: on his way home from the airport he faces unruly traffic, and agitated demonstrations which are organized routinely by students, activists or mullahs. The citizens generally lack proper urban facilities; the narrator's sister Nasreen, for example, complains: "load-shedding has become a regular part of our lives" (253). The condition of various areas of "New Dhaka," like Eskaton or Dhanmondi, in *Seasonal Adjustments*, adds to the same shabby picture. Wari is described as "a sprawling suburb of sinewy lanes choked with a conglomeration of two-storied buildings" (100). "Old Dhaka," too, looms large with its dark, smelly lanes. In contrast, the suburb of Banani represents "a bastion of a lifestyle uncommon in the subcontinent. It is *carefully hidden away from the damning marks of abject poverty that plagues the country.*" The narrator marks the creek there as "*an official dividing line between the privileged few and the millions out there*" (31; emphases added). The description, evidently, is a reminder of how "the class struggle is inscribed in space" (Elden 106) and it also implies that, instead of an equitably planned environment for human life or a democratic vision of a city, what is happening here is a version of gentrification, the process which, among other things, ensures that residents with lower incomes and older ways of life find it difficult to survive, and move out of their own area.

Spiral Road, too, describes Banani as "one of Dhaka's most affluent suburbs" where "The signs of prosperity show only in the glimpses of *the houses behind high walls* ... the streets themselves don't indicate the people who live here, except by *the new imported cars that negotiate their ways among cycle rickshaws, three-wheeled auto-rickshaws, trucks, carts, cows and stray dogs, bicycles and pedestrians*" (46; emphasis mine). Clearly, the city houses a non-city within itself. "The houses behind high walls" exemplifies what Gyan Prakash refers to as "fortified privatopias" erected by the privileged (1). These gated communities, with their high-security perimeters and surveillance, seek to achieve both symbolic and physical separation from the rest of the city. Their expansive, luxury houses suggest a whole new lifestyle, and the city's development virtually becomes synonymous with the affluence of its stinking rich minority. Retaining privileged space for them is enabled through the creation of what Steven Flusty calls "crusty" and "jittery" spaces: spaces that are deliberately obstructed and spaces that are under high surveillance (72–4). Their private "city-within-a-city" stands as "a symbol of discriminatory consumption" (Raban 118) which deprives the masses of what Lefebvre calls "the right to the city," that is, "the realization of urban life [which] becomes possible only through the capacity to assert the social in the political and the economic realms in a way that allows residents to participate fully in society" (Gilbert and Dikeç 259). The way the city's more privileged factions section themselves off from their far more populous *other* manifests "a polarization in living standards between the entrenched and educated urban elite versus the bulk of city residents" (Flusty 46). The situation, characterized by such massive socio-spatial injustices and resultant social dysfunctions, is "overtly dystopian."

The diasporic fictional reproduction of Bangladeshi urbanity, in its own way, reflects the dynamics of social relations within which the dwellers of the city live. It points to the fact that the city has yet to achieve the language and gestures of substantive democratic governance; the seemingly unmanageable city reflects even the absence of local government on a regular basis. Authorities appear non-representative of people and evidently not concerned with improving the quality of life for the deprived; rather, they erect an exploitative mechanism of social exclusion and spatial segregation. *Seasonal Adjustments* exposes how democracy withers away in the hands of self-serving and morally bankrupt politicians and bureaucrats who thrive on the dictum "a good civil servant never worries because he is his own boss. Pretend to serve and continue to rule" (140). The corruption of traders and businessmen is also hinted at by the mention of rampant manufacturing and marketing of fraudulent products at Zinjira across the river Buriganga on the banks of which the city stands. The city's modernity is exclusive for these wealthy businessmen, politicians, and bureaucrats, for people in power or close to power, and it hardly trickles down to the majority in the city.

The recurrent appearance of beggars in Khan's novels exposes lack of employments in the city for its huge workforce; many in the city remain outcasts as they cannot take part in respectable, real economic activities. The situation gives birth to many other problems; in fact, problems like unemployment and poverty have connections with the proliferation of religious prejudices and superstition: "Little food means more religion," wrote Syed Waliullah in his much acclaimed Bengali novel *Lal Shalu* or *Tree Without Roots* (Choudhury ix). No wonder, *Seasonal Adjustments* portrays beggars listening with rapt attention to "well-fed" religious speakers elaborating, with lengthy quotes from the Quran, on the Islamic imperative of equality. The agitated beggars' sloganeering: "seeking alms should be encouraged by the government as a means of self-employment" (189), and the scuffle between them and the police, no doubt verges on melodrama, yet no one can deny that what is being done to address issues regarding the population's basic human needs proves far less than enough. Only the *Imams* in *jumma* prayer across the country, as the narrator describes sarcastically, preach about the Islamic solution through *zakat*, the mandatory donation by rich Muslims, as a sure means for eradicating poverty and establishing social justice.

Accentuating Dystopicity: Religious and Political Extremism

In *Brick Lane* and *Seasonal Adjustments,* Dhaka is a city where day-to-day life is full of problems; there is almost every recipe for a dysfunctional and failing, in short, dystopic, city. *Spiral Road*'s portrayal of domestic politics infected by extremism and antagonism, and its exposure of an armed Muslim group operating from the southeastern hilly region of the country and allegedly in cahoots with trans-border terrorist outfits, further accentuates the already dystopic spatiality. The protagonist Masud Alam's nephew, Omar, returns home leaving his American IT job behind to join the *jihadists*; like Karim and the "Bengal Tigers" in Ali's *Brick Lane*, Omar, too, feels outcast as a Muslim by the post-9/11 world and is bent on restoring "Muslim dignity" through fighting against what he understands as "civilized exploitation" and "recycled colonialism" (*Spiral* 301). Even at a local bazaar near his home in Dhaka, Alam is interrogated by a group of bearded mullahs who force him to recite from the Quran.

Importantly, as *Spiral Road* implies, the growth of religious extremism has rendered Bangladesh a site of conflicts over national identity issues involving rival nationalisms, one based on Bengali language and culture, the other on Islamic belief and values. Besides, the "self-righteous insularity" of the self-proclaimed "true believers" of Islam fertilizes grounds of bigotry and the politics of exclusion. In fact, Bengali's independence war in 1971 originated in their feeling of being outcast by derogatory and discrimina-tory treatment at the hands of West Pakistanis who thought Bengalis in East Pakistan impure Muslims, "the *naapak* half-Hindu" (*Seasonal* 157), and even refused them the charge of "Islamic Pakistan" when Bengalis won the parliamentary election in 1970.

But then, in postwar Bangladesh, the narrator's idealistic, freedom fighter friends are embittered and disillusioned, their "burning energy to create a new social order" (*Seasonal* 262) is extinguished. Iftiqar is dubbed traitor for not participating in "a frenzied mood of patriotism" that "terrorised the [Urdu-speaking] Biharis" (139) in the newly won country. The journalists of *The Voice* are bundled off to the cantonment for voicing disillusionment with the postwar governments and the increasing interference of the military in state affairs. Khan's narrative thus encapsulates the dystopic trajectory of a nation, and appears to be firmly critical of religious dogmatism as well as rigid political philosophies, which never fail to create misery and violence.

On Diasporic Positionality and Production

The expatriate writers' identity remains at once plural and partial; such paradoxical space, however, can still be an enabling condition, as it may provide her with a unique perspective as outsider–insider, from which certain significant critical perceptions about homeland become possible. Monica Ali states metaphorically in an interview with Dhaka's *Daily Star*, "Standing neither behind a closed door, nor in the thick of things but rather in the shadow of a doorway is a good place from which to observe." Regarding the common accusation of lack of authenticity and legitimacy of representation, the diasporic writers insist on their *right to write* whatever they choose. Indeed, these writers strive to retrieve individual experiences and memories imaginatively and put them together to constitute a meaningful narrative; to quote Rushdie: "he [the expatriate] is obliged to deal in broken mirrors ... but the broken mirror may actually be as valuable as the one which is supposedly unflawed" (11).

The diasporic vision, even if fragmentary, may act as the fountainhead of endless creative reconstructions of home. This chapter studies diaspora texts for what they are, as works of *fiction*, and is aware that the genre has been "simultaneously honourable and suspect" (Rushdie 10) as a represen-tational category; one does not expect a "think-tank report" or "news" or, for that matter, "histories" of people, place, and culture from it. Interestingly, this corresponds well to the inevitable, perhaps intrinsic, fictionality of all homes: "A place does not merely exist, it has to be invented in one's imagination" (Gellner qtd. in Anderson 6). My argument here is that since the production of urban space, too, is "simultaneously real, symbolic and imaginary" (Balshaw and Kennedy 4), fictional representations may well provide insights for urban analyses.

Another observation on diaspora writing is that it often "encashes on the marketability of the homeland" (Mishra 284). Sunetra Gupta believes that a large chunk of such writing is catering to what she derogatorily labels as the "travel market," an expanding market for armchair tourism to the East, to "exotic" places (Ghosh and Scholte 120). Along this line of argument, the exotic factor is bound to be there in Khan's or Ali's writings as they fictionalize people from a particular ethnic background not very familiar to a wide section of their readership. One may read the linguistic and cultural symbols in their texts, for example, as adding to the Bengali flavor and thus serving as "devices" in order to woo (international) audiences with exotica. But then, although there is admittedly a hegemonic niche market in the West that thrives on commodification of ethnic cultures, representations of non-westernscapes perhaps should not be reckoned as automatically exotic.

It is also argued that these writers' affiliation to the "new diaspora"—people who have left their homeland largely for "lure of the lucre"—breeds in them certain anxieties if not guilts towards the homeland, and consequentially, their texts not only describe home but also justify why it has to be left behind; this tends to render their depictions bleak, even dystopic (Paranjape10). True, both Ali and Khan's fictions seem to write off the old country in favor of an immigrant status in Australia or England which, as their narratives record, despite discouraging expatriates from developing any sense of belonging, are fairly "livable" when the livability of Dhaka is deeply doubted. I have shown however that although these authors do not experience Dhaka on a daily basis, and although their texts replicate, to an extent, negative stereotypings and rather clichéd generalizations, their portrayal is still able to offer significant insights into the urban realities of contemporary Dhaka.

Towards Envisioning an Equitable Urbanity

A city, of course, is neither identical with, nor reducible to, its representations (Balshaw and Kennedy 5); we, nevertheless, derive meanings and imperatives from those. Thus, if diasporic fictional reproductions of Dhaka reveal that on its streets marks of social injustice or gender prejudice are apparent, then the challenge is to construct a new urban spatiality where gender justice is ensured, domination and oppression are minimized, distributions of resources are more just, and above all, where the struggle for more equitable remaking of urban spaces will continue. And in this regard, it is perhaps imperative to listen to the proponents of postmodern architecture, such as Charles Jenks, who suggest that the solution to such inhuman environments, among other things, is to strip architecture of its "elitist aims of a universal aesthetic and social renewal," and to replace them with "conservative form-languages" that could communicate better with local society (87–8, 127–9). Understandably, "better cities" can only be created when all citizens are "empowered and engaged," and this requires improved socio-spatial arrangements, involvement of people in all the various activities of their public life, and a democratization of the way they arrive at social goals (Short 76). A much fuller democratization of public space ensuring a more just urban order cannot be emplaced without a transformation of the existing relations of power.

In the diasporic fictional remapping of material and human geographies, Dhaka represents, primarily, what one may identify as sort of "architectural modernism" where the urban structure, the "brick-strewn wilderness," becomes a major symbol of modernity itself, with no corresponding expansion/progress in the mindscape. The narratives offer a difficult, depressing tour of an "unhinged, wild urbanism" that the city underwent mostly during the 1980s and 1990s, of an unmanageable metropolis, an "out-of-control urban order," of a modernization gone wrong. Economic exigencies, and segregated gender and socio-political structures are principal emblems of Dhaka's postcolonial urban modernity that undercut and endlessly mock the state's official narrative of progress. The infrastructural development of the city is hollow and nowhere near the ideal human environment; it is uneven, partial, and unjust, and it is not coincided with positive changes in the mentalscape, and thereby only perpetuates the city's discriminatory and exclusionary spatiality. Besides, the dichotomous fictional representation of topographies and culturescapes of rural Bengal and metropolitan London serve as foils to the urbanscape of Dhaka, and highlight the underside of Bangladeshi urbanity. The most damning fact of life in this dystopic city is that for the poor and the women this is an essentially bad place to live. The city as a human community needs, more urgently than architectural utopias or ingenious traffic disposal systems, a more humane urban order, since a very large portion of its population remains outcast and maladjusted.

Keeping in view some fundamental insights that "cities give physical expressions of relations of power in society" (Short 54) and that space is a sociocultural reality, a manifestation in material form of social practices and of complex interconnections between physical and mental space (Lefebvre 141–7), my analyses frequently traffic between material environments and "embedded ideologies" of the city as reflected in the novels, and imply that without a paradigm shift in mentalscape—in attitudes and ideologies—no meaningful changes in the material fabric is possible since they are mutually constitutive. The glaring examples of spatial segregation in the city of Dhaka that the novels capture emerge from discriminatory ideologies and practices, and all these force different individuals and groups to "conceive, perceive and live" the city differently. In such an inequitable public space, social justice or the "right to the city" necessitates a kind of urban order that would actively consider "the needs of the poorest and most marginalized residents" (Mitchell 6). Diasporic fictional representations by

Monica Ali and Adib Khan are free from insular/parochial romanticization and remain useful interrogations into the variegated scapes of the city, and they provide, at their best, insightful textual probes into the "city's truth" and thereby imply the need for a more just and democratic urban modernity in postcolonial Dhaka.

Notes

1. I have quoted Radha directly from the visual production of *In Which Annie Gives It Those Ones* (1989), directed by Pradip Krishen, and not from the screenplay of the same name published in 2003.
2. Donald Preziosi suggests that "What urban studies is clearly after, by and large, is what does not (quite) 'meet the eye': what escapes (almost) the immediate perception (or memory) of cities and their pasts ... The city's truth: always to be found (sought) in some *place*—at the city's heart, on its margins" (qtd. in Balshaw and Kennedy 5).

Works Cited

Ali, Monica. *Brick Lane*. London: Doubleday, 2003. Print.
———. "Where I'm Coming From." *Guardian* June 17, 2003. Web. March 5, 2012.
Anderson, Benedict. *Imagined Communities: Reflections on the Origins and Spread of Nationalism*. London: Verso, 1983. Print.
Balshaw, Maria and Liam Kennedy. Introduction. *Urban Space and Representation*. Eds. Balshaw and Kennedy. London: Pluto P, 2000. 1–21. Print.
Choudhury, Serajul Islam. Introduction. *Tree Without Roots*. Ed. Niaz Zaman. Dhaka: writers.ink., 2005. ix–xiii. Print.
Durrschmidt, Jorg. "The Delinking of Locale and Milieu: On the Situatedness of Extended Milieux in a Global Environment." *Living the Global City: Globalization as a Local Process*. Ed. John Eade. London and New York: Routledge, 1997. 56–72. Print.
"Dystopia." *Oxford Advanced Learner's Dictionary*. 7th ed. 2005. Print.
Elden, Stuart. "There is a Politics of Space Because Space is Political: Henri Lefebvre and the Production of Space." *Radical Philosophy Review* 10.2 (2007): 101–16. Print.
Euripides. "Medea." *Collected Plays of Euripides*. Trans. Gilbert Murray. London: Allen and Unwin, 1954. 1–96. Print.
Fischer, Andrew M. "Reconceiving Social Exclusion." *BWPI Working Paper*. Manchester: Brooks World Poverty Institute, 2011. Print.
Flusty, Steven. *De-Coca-Colonization: Making the Globe from the Inside Out*. New York and London: Routledge, 2004. Print.
Germanà, Monica. "From Hijab to Sweatshops: Segregated Bodies and Contested Space in Monica Ali's *Brick Lane*." *Postcolonial Spaces: The Politics of Place in Contemporary Culture*. Eds. Andrew Teverson and Sara Upstone. New York: Palgrave Macmillan, 2011. 67–82. Print.
Gilbert, Liette and Mustafa Dikeç. "Right to the City: Politics of Citizenship." *Space, Difference, Everyday Life: Reading Henri Lefebvre*. Eds. Kanishka Goonewarden, Stefan Kipfer, Richard Milgrom, Christian Schmid. New York: Routledge, 2008. 250–63. Print.

Grosz, Elizabeth. "Bodies-Cities." *Sexuality and Space*. Ed. Beatriz Colomina. New York: Princeton Architectural P, 1992. 241–53. Print.

Haq, Kaiser. "Interview with Monica Ali." *Daily Star* (Dhaka) May 31, 2003. Web. November 5, 2012.

In Which Annie Gives It Those Ones. Dir. Pradip Krishen. Screenplay by Arundhati Roy. Perf. Arjun Raina, Arundhati Roy, and Rituraj. Door Darshan.1989. Film.

Jackson, Elizabeth. "Gender and Space in Postcolonial Fiction: South Asian Novelists Re-imagining Women's Spatial Boundaries." *Postcolonial Spaces: The Politics of Place in Contemporary Culture*. Eds. Andrew Teverson and Sara Upstone. New York: Palgrave Macmillan, 2011. 57–66. Print.

Jenks, Charles. *The Languages of Post-Modern Architecture*. London: Academy Editions, 1984. Print.

Kabeer, Naila. *The Power to Choose: Bangladeshi Women and Labour Market Decisions in London and Dhaka*. London: Verso, 2000. Print.

Khan, Adib. *Seasonal Adjustments*. St. Leonards: Allen & Unwin, 1994. Print.

———. "Writing Homeland." *Australian Book Review* 170 (May 1995): 24–5. Print.

———. "In Janus' Footsteps." *Australian Humanities Review* 22 (June 2001): 26–8. Print.

———. *Spiral Road*. Sydney: Fourth State, 2007. Print.

Lefebvre, Henri. *The Production of Space*. Trans. Donald Nicholson-Smith. Oxford: Blackwell, 1991. Print.

Levitas, R. *The Multi-Dimensional Analysis of Social Exclusion*. London: Cabinet Office, 2007. Print.

Mernissi, Fatima. *Beyond the Veil: Male-Female Dynamics in Muslim Society*. Bloomington and Indianapolis: Indiana UP, 1987. Print.

Mishra, Sudesh. "From Sugar to Masala: Writing by the Indian Diaspora." *An Illustrated History of Indian Literature in English*. Ed. Arvind Krishna Mehrotra. Delhi: Permanent Black, 2003. 276–94. Print.

Mitchell, Don. *The Right to the City: Social Justice and the Fight for Public Space*. New York and London: The Guilford P, 2003. Print.

Ngugi Wa Thiong'o. *Decolonising the Mind: The Politics of Language in African Literature*. London: Heinemann, 1986. Print.

Paranjape, Makarand. "Introduction: Displaced Relations: Diasporas, Empires, Homelands." *Diaspora: Theories, Histories, Texts*. Ed. Makarand Paranjape. New Delhi: Indialog, 2001. 1–14. Print.

Prakash, Gyan. "Introduction: Imaging the Modern City, Darkly." *Noir Urbanisms: Dystopic Images of the Modern City*. Ed. Gyan Prakash. Princeton, NJ: Princeton UP, 2010. 1–14. Print.

Raban, Jonathan. *Soft City*. London: Picador, 2008. Print.

Ranjan, Ghosh and Christiane Scholte. "'… nobody likes to be bracketed': Interview with Sunetra Gupta." *Critical Practice* 11.2 (2004): 117–24. Print.

Rao, E. Nageswara. "Arundhati Roy." *South Asian Writers in English*. Ed. Fakrul Alam. Farmington Hills: Thomson Gale, 2006. 305–13. Print.

Rushdie, Salman. *Imaginary Homelands: Essays and Criticism, 1981–1991*. London: Granta, 1991. Print.

Short, John R. *The Humane City: Cities as if People Matter*. Oxford: Basil Blackwell, 1989. Print.

Wacquant, Loïc. *Urban Outcasts: A Comparative Sociology of Advanced Marginality*. Cambridge: Polity P, 2008. Print.

Part III
The Space of the Margins

9 Imag(in)ing the City
A Study of Ahmed Ali's *Twilight in Delhi*

Nishat Haider

This chapter is centrally concerned with understanding the ontological pre-eminence of the imaginal, imaginary, and narrative for mapping out the rele-gation of urban Muslims through the shifting and/evolving contours of Delhi, as the locus of historical memory, in Ahmed Ali's *Twilight in Delhi*.[1] Ahmed Ali, recipient of the Sitara-i-lmtiaz Award in 1980, is "a Muslim fourth to the Indian big three of the 1930s—Rao, Narayan and Anand" (King, "From *Twilight* to *Midnight*" 244). Ali was not only one of the most active par-ticipants of the All-India Progressive Writers' Association in 1936, but also one of the signatories of its first manifesto of April 5, 1933. However, he broke away from the paradigmatic Marxist stranglehold of the Progressive ideology and pursued the elusive world of individual consciousness in his creative works (Gopal 16–17). In the introduction to *Twilight in Delhi*, Ali says: "My purpose was to depict a phase of our national life and the decay of a whole culture, a particular mode of thought and living now dead and gone already right before our eyes. Seldom is one allowed to see a pageant of History whirl past and partake in it too" (xxi). Originally rejected by the printers who viewed *Twilight in Delhi* (henceforth *Twilight*) as a subver-sive text, it was eventually published by the Hogarth Press in 1940 after the "friendly" intervention of E. M. Forster and Virginia Woolf (Coppola 21–2). The novel chronicles the life of the *ashraf* or the upper-class Muslim family living in Delhi (India) at the beginning of the twentieth century, who sees its fortunes fading as the British work to eradicate Islamic culture. Ali's narra-tive delineates the "relationships between the memorialization of the past and the spatialization of public memory" (Johnson 63) in the postcolonial context of nation-building.

Engaging with the cultural practices, actual spaces, and real politics, this chapter draws and overlaps the complex contours of postcolonial studies onto the specific space with both material and imagined dimensions of the city in order to locate in Ali's Delhi the crucible of nationhood and the site of urban marginalization of Muslims. After a preliminary discussion of the South Asian city of Delhi, through a Bakhtinian chronotope lens the chapter examines the space–time relationships in *Twilight* to explore the questions of city space, locality, and culture in order to make visible the coalescence of culture, history, and language as textual codings of a chronotopic poetics.

Although there is valuable knowledge on the political production and socio-spatial distribution of urban precariat and poor, theoretical or critical studies of the cultural variables in relation to the socio-spatial relegation and exclusionary closure of urban Indian Muslims are still hard to find. Acknowledging the dearth of specific works which explore the varied interactions between imperial culture and the production, consumption and representation of urban space that include architectural, cultural and performative aspects of lived experiences, this chapter underscores that a clearer appraisal of marginalization of Muslims in urban India can only come about through works like *Twilight* which not only privilege the elided or ignored Muslim view of the colonial encounter, but also explicate the social, political and especially, cultural processes that are responsible for the involuntary spatial containment and control of Muslims, relegating them as urban outcasts.

Can the 'Muslims' Speak?

South Asian literature in English, "an independent, powerful literary tradition on its own" and "a subcategory of postcolonial literature" (Hasan, "Marginalisation of Muslim" 184), has been receiving enormous critical attention from academics, geographers, and other scholars who have long recognized that fiction writers often are able to capture the "sense of place" or the image of the city in ways which enable researchers to expand and reform their interpretations of urban places. Ahmed Ali's *Twilight*, a South Asian postcolonial novel, is an important archive not only to excavate the complexities of the urban spaces, urbanism and its varying conditions, but also to explicate the exclusionary closure of Muslim minority, the strong local sociocultural peculiarities and spatial responses of Muslims within the city of Delhi. Although it is problematic to speak of a monolithic South Asian Islam and an Indian Muslim minority, given the extent of diversity and distinction in the formations of religious communities, the legitimate questions to pose concern: the large-scale disregard of the literary contributions of South Asian Muslim writers who produced English texts on a variety of topics, the relegation of Islamic or Islamicated cultures, and the rendering of Muslims as outcasts in the nationalist movement. While some diasporic authors like Salman Rushdie, Hanif Qureshi, and Adib Khan are adequately discussed by literary critics, other Muslim writers like Ahmed Ali, Saadat Hassan Manto, Ismat Chugtai, and Qurratulain Hyder have received little attention in critical studies on South Asian writing, perhaps mainly because of Hindu writers' dominance and literary historians' neglect of Muslim writers (Hasan, "Marginalisation of Muslim" 185). In fact, *Twilight* is "the first major work of fiction written by a Muslim ever to be published in English" in South Asia (Malak 3). The novel maps out "the perspective of a colonized culture and civilization that had hitherto been denied the opportunity to speak for itself" (Malak 19). Therefore, for Ahmed Ali, the issue central to *Twilight* and his own positioning is precisely the issue of the South Asian nationalist Muslim (essentially gendered male), who has been estranged by the various political choices accessible to him and who has been rendered as an urban outcast, politically and socially. Located in Delhi from 1910 to 1919, Ali's *Twilight* sifts through the central consciousness of the aristocratic Mir Nihal. The novel not only elaborates "a specifically Muslim perception of colonial rule as the loss of Mughal hegemony over India" (Gandhi 185) but also recuperates the voices of Delhi's Muslims who had been systematically penalized for being more "aggressive" than the Hindus in the revolt of 1857 (Nehru 460). Hence, Ahmed Ali's *Twilight* deserves renewed scholarly attention to unpack the discursive marginalization of Muslims and to unravel the trajectories of Muslim persecution, which contributes towards the continuous alienation and ghettoization of Muslim communities in Indian cities.

The Ligatures of Time and Space in *Twilight*

If the city is a text, then the spatio-temporal frame of Delhi in *Twilight* plays a key role in the production of meaning as the matrix of situated meaning-making, roles, identities, values, boundaries and crossings, cultural classes of discourse, and tools (Lorino 201). In *Twilight*, Ali projects the literary cartography onto the city of Delhi, which is analogous to Mikhail Bakhtin's notion of chronotope, to offer a representation which apprehends and gives a clearer sense of the relations between historical time and geographical space in literature, referring specifically to the political, cultural, and spatial-built forms, to unravel the systematic relegation of Muslims. Since the chronotope as a conceptual tool (Bemong 3) brings space, time, and genre together in a conceptually integrated way, it unravels how the narrative of *Twilight* functions not only as a means of mapping what Edward W. Soja has referred to as the "real-and-imagined" spaces, but also to elucidate "how texts relate to their social and political contexts" (Vice 201). The advent of colonialism put India on the verge of momentous change, and in *Twilight* a sense of this is reflected in the chronotope of the threshold, some of which are depicted as specific periods such as: the 1857 Mutiny when Indian soldiers revolted against their British officers and tried to restore the Mughal Bahadur Shah II as emperor of India (the Mutiny was brutally put down and Bahadur Shah called to Rangoon by the British); the coronation in Delhi of George V on December 7, 1911; the early subversive activities against British rule; the 1914 war as it affected India; and the passing of the Rowlatt Bills in 1919, which allowed British judges to try cases without juries and permitted provincial government to hold suspects without trial. All these events are seen from the *haveli* in the congested and decaying by-lanes of old Delhi where the family of Mir Nihal, the Muslim protagonist, lived. The unpacking of the narrative of *Twilight* is the only way to pierce the screen of discourses and to unravel the lived relations and meanings that are constitutive of the everyday reality of the urban Muslim living in alienation in the neighborhoods of exile. In the next section of the chapter, I will foreground Ahmed Ali's *Twilight* to explore the historicized and contextualized understanding of the city of Delhi and to unravel how South Asian novelists negotiate the binaries of self/other, insider/outsider, and citizen/outcast while remaining true to their calling to prioritize local perspectives and to decolonize/dehegemonize the literary enterprise.

Narrative Cartography: Representation of Delhi in Ali's *Twilight*

Ali's *Twilight* tells the story of Mir Nihal, a Sayyed, an Arabic honorific title denoting descendants of the Islamic prophet Muhammad, who lives in Delhi, and whose scion, Asghar, a modern young man, wants to marry a Mughal girl (considered inferior in rank and lineage), and the inevitable conflict that this produces in the household, their subsequent reconciliation, and the gradual decline of their homes under British rule. The central premise of the narrative is the lament of Nihal and his peers about the altered urban landscape and cultural scape of Delhi, their estrangement from the city of their birth, and the gradual loss of their bearings in the new geography of their imperial capital. In *Twilight*, Ali's engagements with the city of Delhi and Mir Nihal's family "uncover the aporias of seizing upon the third-world city as artistic material, and prise open questions of representation, representability, individual subject-positions, and class-divides" (Khanna 21). Through the gradual decline of Nihal and his family, the novel enunciates its lament for the historical erosion of Delhi and its culture. Built and rebuilt seven times, Mir Nihal's Delhi, a heroic city, capital of earlier empires of which "only some monuments remain to tell its sad story and to remind us of the glory and splendor—a Qutub Minar or a Humayun's Tomb, the Old Fort or the Jama Mosque," is truly Ali's protagonist (4). Summarizing the history of Delhi in *Twilight*, Ali says: "[Delhi] was built after the great battle of Mahabharat by Raja Yudhishtra [sic] in 1453 B. C., and has been the cause of many a great and historic battle. Destruction is in its foundations and blood is in its soil. It has seen the fall of many a glorious kingdom, and listened to the groans of birth. It is the symbol of Life and Death, and revenge is in its nature" (4). In *Twilight*, Ali establishes the urban structures of Delhi as sites, which make visible the peculiar relationship between history and territory, between the spatial and the temporal matrix.

If we map the shifting contours of literary memorialization and representation of historical traumas by Muslim writers, for example Ali's *Twilight*, Shahid Ahmad Dehlavi's *Dilli ki Bipta* (1948) and Ebadat Barelvi's *Azadi ke Saaye Mein* (1988), it is evident that these Muslim writings linked the collapse of the old world in Delhi and its rich culture to the aftermath of the revolt of 1847 in particular. Since the Muslims were the dominant force behind the revolt of 1857, the British called it "a Muhammadan rebellion"

(Khairi 26) and therefore singled them out as their most mortal enemy from among the population of India (Russel 77–8; Malak 22). Ali very evocatively describes the enormous losses that the Muslims, especially the aristocracy and the descendants of Mughal rulers, had to suffer during the British rule in India. Reduced to begging Gul Bano, the granddaughter of Bahadur Shah (the last of the Mughal Kings), says, "They usurped our throne, banished the king, killing hundreds of princes before these unfortunate eyes which could not even go blind, drank their blood, and we could do nothing … I am still alive to suffer the bludgeon blows of Time" (Ali 139). Recalling the merciless killings of Muslims, Ali says, "It was this very mosque, Mir Nihal remembered with blood in his eyes, which the English had insisted on demolishing or turning into a church during 1857" (145). The specificity of the location, the Jama Masjid, offers a symbolic emphasis that combines nationalism with religion and anti-British feelings with Islam. The ruins of old Delhi become "symbolic of the ruin of Islam" and Muslims (King, "From *Twilight* to *Midnight*" 244). In India, the decline of Mughal political power coincided with the ascendancy of the British. The city of Delhi in *Twilight* is a microcosm for the Muslim culture and civilization which had become a victim to the vagaries of history.

Twilight corroborates the centrality of cities to an understanding of historic societies, an assumption shared by most urbanists (Soja, "Writing the City Spatially" 269). The novel deals with its specific historical material at two levels. First, it portrays the life of Mir Nihal, a Muslim, and his family in Delhi during the first two decades of the twentieth century. Through this family Ali foregrounds "the political and cultural ethos of Indian Muslims in Delhi in periods when Britain was still powerfully clasping its crown jewel" (Malak 20). Blending the private with the public, the familial with the communal, the novel also interlinks the present with the past. Ali unravels the sociocultural and historical trajectory of the city of Delhi from the perspective of the Muslim protagonist, Mir Nihal. Juxtaposing a family wedding ceremony and the 1911 coronation of George V with Mir Nihal's graphic memories of the ruthless quelling of the 1857 revolt by the British, Ali says, " Here it was in this very Delhi, Mir Nihal thought that kings once rode past, Indian kings, his kings, kings who have left a great and glorious name behind. But the Farangis came from across the seven seas, and gradually established their rule … In the background were the guns booming, threatening the subdued people of Hindustan" (144). After the territorial annexation of the Indian sub-continent (from 1757 to 1857) by the English East India Company, the notion of Hindus and Muslims as two opposed and self-contained religious communities gained dominance within the Indian social system (Pandey, *The Construction of Communalism* 23–65). Thus, the latter part of the nineteenth century witnessed a period of Hindu and Muslim revivalism. In *Twilight*, Ali has made a serious attempt to focus on a spatiotemporal mode of civilizational being at a juncture in Indian history when, as Ayesha Jalal (*Self and Sovereignty* 43–5) and Mushirul Hasan

(*India Partitioned* 5) disclose, the urban community boundaries were being redrawn, leading to deterioration in inter-community relations and reduced interaction with the now progressively more dominant Hindu 'majority' community which resulted in the ghettoization of Muslims in cities. The effect of these socio-political developments, on Mir Nihal and the Muslim residents of the old city of Delhi, Ali says, was "a little too much" as non-Muslims, people from other Indian provinces, areas, and cultures had started coming into the city and the old culture was in "the danger of annihilation" (197). The new city of Delhi had become "the city of the dead," inhabited by people who had "[neither] love for her nor any associations with her history and ancient splendor" (197). In practical terms, to read the city in *Twilight* effectively is to understand how urban social processes (encompassing the socio-political, the cultural, and the economic) are constituted at particular historical moments.

In *Twilight*, Mir Nihal's attachment to the city of Delhi is coterminous with his sense of being a Muslim. Pointing out the remarkable hold wielded by the city over the imagination and identification of Indian Muslims, Jalal explains that cities were the place where a sense of identification to a non-territorial entity (the *Umma*) converged with a sense of belonging to a more circumscribed community (the *qaum*, the *watan*). It was where infinite space met finite spaces of belonging (10). In *Twilight*, the city of Delhi is imbued with Muslim practices, religious spaces, and imaginaries. The novel portrays religion, as a significant critical analytical category that "makes place," that is, "the connections between people and places, movement and urban form" (Sepe 63) in Indian cities in manifold ways and contributes to an understanding of the links between *ummah*, *qaum* (community) and *watan* (nation). The city has a crucial place in the history of Indian Muslims, as it is in the urban spaces that Muslim power arose and established itself from the latter part of the twelfth century onwards (Gayer and Jaffrelot 13). The city of Delhi, its architecture, and its buildings are closely linked to the history of Muslims. Historically speaking, under Muslim rule in Delhi, cities flourished as trade zones and became the center of Muslim politics, policies, culture, arts, and literature. Ebadat Barelvi wrote, "*Dilli Musalmanon ka shahar tha* [Delhi was a city of the Muslims]," incomparable in the subtlety and exquisiteness of its culture or the magnificence of its public displays (qtd. in Pandey, *Remembering Partition* 135). Religion, as a critical analytical category that encompasses physical, built, natural as well as its sociocultural ritualistic and performative aspects, identities and values-based manifestations, contributes to a vital understanding of how religion "makes place" in the city of Delhi in multiple ways. *Twilight* offers the first serious reflection in Indian English literature of how the material practices and imaginaries of Islam shaped urban forms and culture in a South Asian city. In *Twilight*, "the historic architecture can be read in many ways—as emblems of sanctity, as narrators of history, as milestones in art, as picturesque ruins, as interruptions in the process of laying out a new town" (Gupta, "From Architecture to Archaeology" 49).

Describing the architecture of old Shahjahanabad (Delhi), the "last and probably the greatest capital city ever designed by Indo-Muslim rulers between 1639 and 1648," Gayer and Jaffrelot say that "Persian traditions of architecture, for their part, made their influence felt in the conception of the city as a living organism, whose head was located in the imperial palace, whose backbone was found in the bazar and whose heart beat in the Jama Masjid" (17). The Mughal royals, Muslim architects and city planners were inspired by the "Islamic" imaginations of the city (Ehlers 11–12). The symbols of religiosity and a sense of sacrality of space in old Delhi frame the mundane transactions and encounters, and exert a singular effect on the everyday making and remaking of the lifeworlds of Muslims like Mir Nihal. Ali's *Twilight* represents a distinctive metonymy: Delhi was a microcosm for the colonized India and Delhi was Muslim. Hence the ruin of Delhi implied the marginalization of Muslims and decay of their culture, not only in Delhi but also all over urban India.

The Wretched of the City

In *Twilight*, Ali credibly represents religion, with its focus on place-making and developing spaces of public heritage, as the key to analyze the role/influence of religion not only in molding urban place, particularly through various forms of tangible or non-tangible religious heritage, but also in the exclusion and social backwardness of Muslims in Delhi. In *Twilight*, Ali depicts the year 1857 as the turning point for the Indian Muslims and the city of Delhi. After the failure of the revolt against the British in 1857, Queen Victoria announced Crown rule in India. During the siege of Delhi, all inhabitants of the city were ousted. When the residents reverted, they discovered that in their absence the British had confiscated much land and property of those Muslims who could not prove themselves innocent of involvement or conspiracy in the Mutiny, which left many from among the old *rais* (aristocrats) without their lands, farms, and orchards and the income from them. The demolition of a large number of houses in order to build the Cantonment and the railway line, and the necessity to compensate the owners of these houses, were all linked into a single operation (Gupta, *Delhi Between Two Empires* 12). Although some *ashraf* Muslims retained their *havelis*, with the loss in income it was impossible for the owners to sustain either the patronage or the earlier opulence. In *Twilight*, the traditional architecture of old Delhi became an arena for challenging and negotiating identities. *Twilight* evocatively describes the metamorphosis of Delhi's landscape "from the picturesque to the dysfunctional occurred through a disarray of synchronic activities—demolishing and building, disclaiming and appropriating, redefining and abandoning" (Hosagrahar 27), all engaged in building the city wedged in the vectors of specific history, colonial ambitions, and flows of cultures. Mir Nihal is distraught that the city walls have been demolished and worse than all the changes, which were so deeply resented by the people, was the disfiguring of the Chandni Chowk, whose central causeway was demolished. The city "still stands intact, as do many more forts and tombs and monuments, remnants and reminders of old Delhi" (Ali 3). But gradually these very structures of Delhi, which had resisted decay, are seen falling apart: "Yet ruin has descended upon its monuments and buildings, upon its boulevards and by-lanes" (Ali 5). Describing old Delhi's landscapes, the relegation of Muslims to the margins, and the urban decay, Nihal says, "the gutters give out a damp stink ... [b]ut men sleep with their beds over the gutters, and the cats and dogs quarrel over heaps of refuse which lie along the alleys and cross-roads" (3). For the new British bureaucracy, the city underwent massive restructuring based on the design of imperial New Delhi by Edwin Lutyens and Herbert Baker. Lutyen's New Delhi condemned the old spaces that had once fostered Mir Nihal's ways of life.

Twilight is "an irreplaceable record of the old Muslim life in Delhi at the beginning of the [twentieth] century" (Brander 77). The novel opens up debate on the nexus of religion, culture, colonialism and the development of the city for understanding the ghettoization of Muslims in Delhi. Following Loïc Wacquant's conceptualization of ghetto (49), one can conclude that the socio-spatial formation of Delhi was born of the forcible relegation of a negatively typed Muslim population. The character of Mir Nihal underscores the position of *ashraf* Muslims in Lutyen's New Delhi as urban outcasts. Decrying the new imperial Delhi that Lutyens designed for the new British bureaucracy, Ali says, "The residents of Delhi resented all this, for their city, in which they had been born and grew up, the city of their dreams and reality, which had seen them die and live, was going to be changed beyond recognition. They passed bitter remarks and denounced all the Farangis" (195). In *Twilight*, Delhi is the site of the colonial wound, "twilight struggles" (Roy 308), and heterogeneous forms of subalternity as well as exclusionary social closure through which colonial cities are lived, negotiated, and shaped. *Twilight* implicates "the sense of place and place making" (Sepe 63) as instrumental ways of constructing the multiple deprivations, communal segregation, the escalating spatial marginalization and the swelling ghettoization of Muslims as an increasingly urban phenomenon.

The city of Delhi in Ali's *Twilight* features "as the space of architectural writing" (Nalbantoglu 10). Ali's marvelous depictions of houses, *Khazanchi havelis*, and streets of the city, as they are being worked upon by time and politics in the novel, are the rich sites of Delhi's history. Jyoti Hosagrahar, who addresses transformations in Delhi in the latter half of the nineteenth century through an investigation of the ubiquitous mansions and courtyard houses of historic Delhi, includes Ali's *Twilight*, among other sources, in her interpretation of the *Khazanchi haveli* (44). Mir Nihal's *haveli* was "a microcosm of the city" of Shahjahanabad (Delhi) as a dynastic capital, in micro-perspective, not only in its Mughal grandeur, but also in its subsequent disintegration (Hosagrahar 42). The women in the novel are exemplars of the futility, emptiness, and vacuity that pervade the Muslim urban spaces of old Delhi. Describing the emptiness of life in the *zenana*, Ali says, "The world lived and died, things happened, events took place, but all this did not disturb the equanimity of the zenana, which had its world too where the pale and fragile beauties of the hothouse lived secluded from all outside harm, the storms that blow in the world of men" (39). The decay of old Delhi is analogous to the fall in the fortunes of urban elite and the concomitant deterioration of the *havelis*. Mir Nihal's eldest son died and the youngest relinquished tradition and moved out; the patriarch confronts huge problems regarding the maintenance of his *haveli* and the running of the household. As Mir Nihal lies paralyzed at the end of the novel, his condition becomes symptomatic of the gradual decay of a feudal economy and its replacement by a colonial capitalist one that creates grave changes in the private and public realms of the *ashraf*.

From Center to Margins: Muslim Urban Outcasts and Vectors of Marginalization

In *Twilight*, Ali enables an understanding of the social, political and especially, cultural processes governing the urban development of Delhi which have translated into expulsion of Muslims to the margins and crevices of Delhi. Ali has excavated the historicity of Mughal Delhi by foregrounding Delhi's lived spaces, the planning as well as the architecture, and as they came "under sway of a corrosive, corrupting, commercialized and aggressive colonial culture" (Pandey, *Remembering Partition* 135). The novel underscores that it is in South Asian cities like Delhi, which were once ruled by the Muslim royals, that the subsequent marginalization of Muslims by the British and successive governments is most blatant, as evident in "their increasing socio-spatial segregation" (Gayer and Jaffrelot 2). In *Twilight*, Mir Nihal often describes the new city of Delhi, the imperial city, as a sinister space where the colonial subject is defenseless and invisible. In the novel, this polarity is clearly evident:

> It was the city of Kings and monarchs, of poets and storytellers, courtiers and nobles. But no king lives there today, and the poets are feeling the lack of patronage, and the old inhabitants though still alive, have lost their pride and grandeur under a foreign yoke. Yet the city stands still intact as do many more forts and tombs and monuments remnant and reminders of old Delhis ... (4)

The complicated implications hidden by the image of the dual city are poignantly portrayed in *Twilight*. Mir Nihal identifies art, culture, and literature with the old Delhi and rues the building of the new city. According to Janet Abu-Lughod, Zeynep Çelik, and Brenda Yeoh, the introduction of Western urban forms led to the segregation and isolation of native towns, which left a great historiographical legacy. Veena Oldenburg and Narayani Gupta have shown how the duality of north Indian colonial urban landscapes after the uprising of 1857 was violently transgressed not only to make physical space sanitary and clean for the British, but also to make the population safe and loyal. The British were taking control of everything and displacing the once-ruling Muslims. Bemoaning the urban changes taking place with the arrival of the British in Delhi, Ali says, "The old had gone, and the new was feeble and effete. At least it had nothing in common with his ideals or his scheme of things" (240). Unsettled by "the growing indifference of the world" around him, Mir Nihal began to live more and more at home in his own world, a world which was still his own and which he could comprehend (241). *Twilight* enunciates not only Muslims' struggle to claim the urban space of Delhi but also their everyday battle for the survival of a culture, a civilization, and an identity.

Twilight implicates the sense of place and place-making as extensive ways of constructing the spatial marginalization of Muslims as an increasingly urban phenomenon. After the Mutiny of 1857, the British reprisal against Muslim populations in Delhi was one of the major causal factors in the imperial regulation of space in the nineteenth century (Nayar 135), which systematically relegated Muslims and turned them into urban outcasts. By the early decades of the twentieth century this imperial vision of architecture was paying full attention to Delhi, now the capital of the Indian empire (Irving 73). Imposing the European style of architecture on Delhi, Lutyens declared: "I want old England to stand up and plant her great traditions and good taste where she goes and not pander to sentiment and all this silly Moghul-Hindu stuff" (qtd. in Metcalf 219). However, the people of Delhi reacted with "indignation and outright hostility" towards the building of the imperial city (Hasan, *From Ghalib's Dilli to Lutyens' New Delhi* xxxix). Displaying his disquiet over this transformation of Delhi with which he shares neither connection nor values, Mir Nihal says, "A new Delhi meant new people, new ways, and a new world altogether. That may be nothing strange for the newcomers: for the old residents it was a little too much ... The old culture, which had been preserved within the walls of the ancient town, was in danger of annihilation" (197). Mir Nihal feels alienated and exiled in his own city. The dissonance that follows, however, moves from the paved spaces of the city into the Nihal household, and thence into the imaginative realm that structures Nihal's social relations. Delineating the intrusions of modernity that Mir Nihal most heatedly abrogates, Joshi says, "... [they] appear at first to be small ones: the leather shoes, English furniture, silk dressing-gowns, and hairstyles that his son, Asghar, sports—he clearly ascribes these to the British presence in India" ("The Exile at Home" 218). But Mir Nihal experiences the full import of the changes that the British have ushered in when he realizes that "they have spayed the culture of Delhi, rendering it incapable of regenerating itself or the city" (Joshi, "The Exile at Home" 219). To its old inhabitants like Mir

Nihal, the new city gradually "resembles an alien, foreign, environment in which the individual is pitted in a contest against the metropolis, a contest that, we will see shortly, takes its toll on what Georg Simmel has called the individual's mental life" (Joshi, "The Exile at Home" 218). The contrast that Ali draws between Mir Nihal's old Delhi and that of Lutyens' is analogous to Max Weber's notion of the medieval and renaissance city, whose social structures emerge from within and whose environment sustains its citizens, versus Simmel's concept of a retrograde, enervating, modern, urban space that extracts a toll on its citizens by making them seek protection from its constant and unwanted stimuli.

The inextricable link between architecture, society and culture in city studies makes it important not only to explore the relationship between the value system of Muslims and their spatial arrangement in the city system, but also to unpack the connection among the urban/social structures and the cultural variables (e.g. language) that account for Muslims' distribution/relegation in the urban centers. The unique intervention of Ali's *Twilight* is to link the fall of Delhi to the decline of Muslims, the stagnation of the city culture, and the erosion of Urdu. Talking about the general importance of the poetic imagination in the construction and understanding of nation, Alasdair MacIntyre says that one can comprehend the nation by a poetic register more completely (161). In the literary history that Ali creates for Delhi, he accomplishes this audacious project through the concurrent mappings of the trajectories of the city of Delhi, Muslims, and Urdu language/poetry. Since "society and language are part of the metahistorical givens without which history is inconceivable" (Hampsher-Monk 4), it is important to explore how *Twilight* links the forms, functions, and rising/falling fortunes of the city of Delhi to the Muslim history, the Urdu language, and literary trends. When the Muslim dynasties ruled in Delhi, they recognized Urdu language and poetry "as a major element in the master narrative of the quest for Muslim self-understanding" and identity (Malik, "The Language Issue: Urdu" 283), and hence they gave patronage and support to Urdu literature. Urdu, also acknowledged as "*zaban-e'urdu-ye mu'alla-ye shahjahanabad* (the language of the exalted court of Shahjahanabad), is among the most important languages in South Asia though academically it has lost ground" (Malik, "The Language Issue: Urdu" 282). From the eighteenth century onwards, as Urdu emancipated itself from the court language (Persian), it flourished and became a medium of communication among the royals and the wider population living in the Mughal catchment areas. Apart from its important role as the main vehicle of Islam in South Asia, Urdu has a rich secular literature, whose poetry inherited the syncretic tendencies of North Indian Mughal rule and was closely based on Persian models. Unlike Arabic, there was nothing intrinsically holy about Urdu and Persian. But gradually Urdu language and literature came to be "tied to 'Muslim literature' and 'Muslim literary tradition' thus making up an important pillar in Muslim cultural memory" (Malik, "The Language Issue: Urdu" 283). However, with the collapse of the Mughal rule, the city of Delhi lost not only its cultural supremacy, but also its hegemony in poetry as a majority of poets migrated to Awadh and Deccan. Besides, the people from outside Delhi brought with them, as Ali observes, "new customs and new ways" and the language, on which Delhi had prided herself, would become "adulterated and impure, and would lose its beauty and uniqueness of idiom" (197). Gradually the urban hegemonic forces communalized and marginalized Urdu.

The generic mechanisms that have relegated Muslims and rendered them as urban outcasts become fully intelligible when one embeds them, as Ali does in *Twilight*, in the historical matrix of religion, culture, language, and class. In *Twilight*, often as Mir Nihal lay on his bed he heard men sing in the street "new verses cheaper than any that had ever been written or recited before" (240). Decrying the "poverty of thought" and "vulgar sentimentality" that had replaced emotion and sentiments in Urdu poetry after the departure of the great poets of Delhi like Mir, Ghalib, Insha, Dard, Sauda and Zauq, the protagonist, Mir Nihal, exclaims, "Time had reversed the order of things, and life had been replaced by death-in-life. No beauty seemed to remain anywhere and ugliness had blackened the face of Hindustan" (241). The novel poignantly describes how the relation that existed between the society and its poets and its members was ruined. The poets had gone and with their departure, Ali says, "a silence and apathy of death descended upon the city" and "ruin has descended upon its monuments and buildings, upon its boulevards and by lanes" (5). The minoritization of Urdu, in turn, ghettoized Indian Muslims and reduced them to a destitute life in the congested and decaying lanes, living as urban outcasts (Malik, "The Language Issue: Urdu" 289). The society of Delhi had "perhaps moved forward" but the Urdu-speaking Muslim *ashraf* "people had been left behind in the race of Life" (Malik 240). The unity of Muslim experience and form of expression, which existed in the city of Delhi in Mir Nihal's youth, had disappeared never to return again.

The main burden of *Twilight* is the elegiac description of the intimate lives of the *ashraf*, in a period when the loss of supremacy in the political realm forced them to live as urban outcasts. The melancholia of Nihal at being reduced to a castaway, epitomizing the lament of all Muslims, seeped into the cultural domain, resulting in feelings of nostalgia and crippling powerlessness to prevent the disappearance of aesthetic values and the Urdu language treasured in the past. Despairing over the doomed decline of Delhi and the irreversible transformations underway, Nihal says, "But who could cry against the ravages of Time which has destroyed Nineveh and Babylon, Carthage as well as Rome?" (197). By staging the city as the center of subjective consciousness—indeed as subjective consciousness itself—Ali goes back to far older influences. The relationship between spatiality, language, and subjectivity operate both in the theme and tone of the novel, a characteristic that derives directly from the Urdu verse form *shehrashob* (Joshi, "The Exile at Home" 216), a lament on a misgoverned, ruined, or declining city in classical Urdu poetry (Sharma 77). *Shehrashob* or *ashobia shairi*, a genre in which poets such as Shafiq Aurangabadi, Shah Hatim, Mirza Rafi Sauda, and Mir Taqi Mir excelled, encapsulates the sociocultural turbulence of cities in the late Mughal period (1707–1857). The poets of the eighteenth century who eulogized the splendor of Shahjahanabad and bemoaned the assaults to which it had been subjected, made a distinction between their *shahr* (city) and the *khandarat* (ruins) of former Delhi (Gupta, "From Architecture to Archaeology" 51). Mir Nihal expresses this painful attachment of the poet to his city of predilection, Delhi, by articulating Mir Taqi Mir's verses, which he recited at a *mushaira* (the public recital of poetry) on his arrival to Lucknow in 1782, after the fall of Delhi:

> Why do you ask my native place,
> O dwellers of the East,
> Making mock of me for the poor plight I am in?
> Delhi, which was once the jewel of the world,
> Where dwelt only the loved ones of fate
> Which has now been ruined by the hand of Time,
> I am a resident of that storm-tossed place.
>
> (Ali 5)

The poet's lament of the city evocatively echoes Mir Nihal's disquiet over the urban decay and lost cultural legacy and aesthetic glory of Delhi. In representing a town, it was not so much its buildings that were commented on, as the atmosphere, with *raunaq* (animation) in the past and *virani* (desolation) in the present as opposite poles (Gupta, "From Architecture to Archaeology" 51). In *Twilight*, Ali examines this link between literary expression and the history of Delhi. This shared textuality—this symbiosis between literary and urban text—has an evidentiary basis in Ahmed Ali's agonizing outburst in an interview with William Dalrymple: "Delhi is dead; the city that was ... the language ... the culture. Everything I knew is finished" (*City of Djinns* 109). Akin to *shehrashob*, the undertone of *Twilight* is a grave longing for a vanished city, culture, and ethos. At the end of Ali's poetic chronicle, one is agonised by the fact that the warps and woofs of poetry and daily life have been separated in a way that could never unite them again.

In *Twilight*, Ali succeeds in merging "the office of psalmist with the function of a national bard, to associate a religious wisdom with an historic vision" (Niven 3). The city of Delhi in *Twilight* provides a palimpsest stage for the lyrical performance of personal and collective memories of the *ashraf* Muslims of north India that enable an understanding of the urban decline of Muslims at the opening of the twentieth century. *Twilight* is "*ijtimai*" narrative, a collective novel, whose hero is the city of Delhi (Askari 32). The advantage of this form is that "the collective life of a whole society can be presented through the ideas and actions of a group against the background of a revolutionary movement or war, as is generally the case in such works" (Askari 32). Linking the fall of Delhi after the 1857 mutiny to the marginalization/disenfranchisement of *ashraf* that foreshadowed the precarious future reserved for the Muslims of India, Ali says, "Delhi had fallen, he reflected; India had been despoiled; all that he had stood for had been destroyed" (*Twilight* 175). In *Twilight*, Ali derived his storytelling techniques from the oral Indian/Muslim tradition, whereby an intrusive, often digressive, teller plays such a dominant role that it licenses him or her to impede or redirect the narrative flow by recurrently reciting nostalgic poetry culled from collective memory, and injecting it (as Ali often does) into "an English that has been infused with the social and political consequences of its own indigenization" (Sadana 5) in order to reinscribe a new history of India on terms different from and even irrelevant to the versions presented by the colonial state. In *Twilight*, the narrative has a public theme which runs parallel to the family theme until the tension mounts and the public and the private coalesce and the decline of the one leads to the destruction of the other. Once Delhi had fallen, the story takes on tragic overtones when Mir Nihal begins to have bad luck with his pigeons and eventually loses them all (Brander 79). At the end of the novel, the decline of the city and culture turn into the decay of a nation, marginalization/ghettoization of Muslims and the demise of Mir Nihal.

The narrative spaces in *Twilight*, as significant cultural loci and *lieux de mémoire* (sites of memory) (Nora 7), become arenas for cultural associations and memorialization of the past, whereby the represented city of Delhi in the novel performs the acts of invention/reconstruction of "spaces that we have come to believe we know, those that we can read," but which "are often legible through the mediation of texts about them ..." (Wirth-Nesher 54). Ali conflates the fate of Mir Nihal and his family with Delhi, using the metonymy not only to represent the capital of the conquered nation but also to epitomize the common political and cultural subjection of Muslims in urban spaces. Lauded by William Dalrymple in *City of Djinns* (1993) as the finest and final evocation of a world forever vanished, *Twilight* displays or reveals the variety of discourses, the dialogues, and natural dialogic character of life that knowledge of other genres seeks to suppress. Ali has inaugurated the literary tradition of Muslim writing in English, which has given "the erstwhile inaudible, if not also invisible, subjects a voice to project the other side of the story and to prove that spunky 'subalterns' can speak for themselves" (Malak 27). Challenging Western presumptions to monopolize the fact, meaning, and content of secularism and freedom, Ranajit Guha and E. I. Brodkin in their works have elucidated the unreliability of English language historical records of 1857 by the British, a problem exacerbated by the fact that the Urdu records of the Lucknow and Delhi courts preserved in the Allahabad and National Archives are written in *shekastah*, a very difficult form of Persian calligraphy (Dalrymple, *The Last Mughal* 310; Bates, *Subalterns and Raj* 64; Farooqui, *Besieged* no page). Despite the involvement of "Subaltern Studies" in Indian national historiography, the "Muslim" role in the Indian national movement went relatively unacknowledged by many scholars; hence, there is a need to reinterpret the nationalist portrayal of Muslim history of India. Historically, Pakistan was not the sole national imagination that Indian Muslims had during the colonial period. In fact, a study of anti-British Muslim uprising demonstrates that Muslim reactions to the colonial rule and its legitimizing discourse were varied. However, most of these responses were not acknowledged in the nationalist historical narratives of both India and Pakistan. By reconfiguring this key concern within the field of postcolonial studies, *Twilight* projects "a subversive, revisionary view of history that debunks for the reader in English the official colonial description of events in the empire" (Malak 27). Writing the novel at the close of an epoch of *ashraf* Muslim culture in Delhi from the vantage point of the late 1930s, Ali betrays the diachronic realities of Delhi and the entropy of modern existence as a veritable endless *marsiya* or lamentation creating the chronotope of Delhi. The portrayal of Delhi in Ali's *Twilight* is not only a reminder of the South Asian colonial past, but also an expression of imag(in)ings of alterity and cultural negotiation in a very material sense, "geo-graphing" the spatial contours of the postcolonial experience (Sharp 124) that is part of the literary narrative and text (Teverson 10). *Twilight* unravels the triangular nexus of colonial domination, class fragmentation, and religious division in the polarizing city of Delhi at the beginning of the twentieth century to explain the political production, socio-spatial distribution and punitive regulation of Muslims through the disciplinary sociocultural and administrative policies as tools for the construction of the Muslim precariat.

Note

1. All citations in this chapter regarding Ahmed Ali's *Twilight* are drawn from the Indian reprint of *The Twilight in Delhi* (2007) published by Rupa & Co.

Works Cited

Abu-Lughod, Janet. "Tales of Two Cities: The Origins of Modern Cairo." *Comparative Studies in Society and History* 7 (1965): 429–57. Print.

Ali, Ahmed. *Twilight in Delhi*. New Delhi: Rupa & Co., 2007. Print.

Askari, Mirza Hasan. "A Novel of Ahmed Ali." *The Annual of Urdu Studies* 9 (1994): 73–84. Web. February 20, 2015.

Bakhtin, Mikhail M. "Forms of Time and of the Chronotope in the Novel: Notes Toward a Historical Poetics." In *The Dialogic Imagination: Four Essays*. Ed. Michael Holquist. Trans. Caryl Emerson and Michael Holquist. Austin: U of Texas P, 1981. 84–258. Print.

Bates, Crispin. *Subalterns and Raj*. 1st Indian Reprint. London and New York: Routledge, 2008. Print.

Bemong, Nele, Pieter Borghart, Michel De Dobbeleer and Kristoffel Demoen Ginko, Eds. *Bakhtin's Theory of the Literary Chronotope: Reflections, Applications, and Perspectives*. Ghent: Ginkgo Academia P, 2010. Print.

Brander, Lawrence. "The Novels of Ahmed Ali." *Journal of Commonwealth Literature* 3 (July 1968): 76–86. Print.

Brodkin, E. I. "The Struggle for Succession: Rebels and Loyalists in the Indian Mutiny of 1857." *Modern Asian Studies* 6.3 (1972): 277–90. Print.

Çelik, Zeynep. *Urban Forms and Colonial Confrontations: Algiers Under French Rule.* Berkeley and London: U of California P, 1997. Print.

Coppola, Carlo. "Ahmed Ali in Conversation: An Excerpt from an Interview with Carlo Coppola." 1975. Web. February 22, 2015.

Dalrymple, William. *City of Djinns: A Year in Delhi.* Harper Collins: London, 1993. Print.

———. *The Last Mughal: The Fall of a Dynasty.* New York: Alfred A. Knopf, 2007. Print.

Ehlers, Eckart and Thomas Kraftt. "Islamic Cities in India? Theoretical Concepts and the Case of Shajahanabad/Old Delhi." *Shajahanabad/Old Delhi: Tradition and Colonial Change.* Delhi: Manohar, 2003. Print.

Farooqui, Mahmood. *Besieged: Voices from Delhi 1857.* New Delhi: Penguin, 2010. Print.

Gandhi, Leela. "Novelists of the 1930s and 1940s." *An Illustrated History of Indian Literature in English.* Ed. Arvind Krishna Mehrotra. New Delhi: Permanent Black, 2003. Print.

Gayer, Laurent and Christophe Jaffrelot. "Muslims of the Indian City: From Centrality to Marginality." *Muslims in Indian Cities: Trajectories of Marginalisation.* Ed. Laurent Gayer and Christophe Jaffrelot. London: C. Hurst & Co. Publishers Ltd., 2012. 1–23. Print.

Gopal, Priyamwada. *Literary Radicalism in India: Gender, Nation and the Transition to Independence.* London: Routledge, 2005. Print.

Guha, Ranajit. "The Prose of Counter-Insurgency." *Subaltern Studies II.* Ed. Ranajit Guha. New Delhi: Oxford UP, 1983. Print.

Gupta, Narayani. *Delhi Between Two Empires, 1803–1931: Society, Government and Urban Growth.* Delhi: Oxford UP, 1981. Print.

———. "From Architecture to Archaeology: The 'Monumentalising' of Delhi's History in the Nineteenth Century." *Perspectives of Muslim Encounters in South Asian History 1760–1860.* Ed. Jamal Malik. Leiden: Brill, 2000. 49–64. Print.

Hampsher-Monk, Iain, Karin Tilmans, and Frank van Vree. "A Comparative Perspective on Conceptual History: An Introduction." *History of Concepts: Comparative Perspectives.* Ed. Iain Hampsher-Monk, Karin Tilmans, and Frank van Vree. Amsterdam: Amsterdam UP, 1998. 1–10. Print.

Hasan, Md. Mahmudul. "Marginalisation of Muslim Writers in South Asian Literature: Rokeya Sakhawat Hossain's English Works." *South Asia Research* 32.3 (2012): 179–97. Print.

Hasan, Mushirul, Ed. *India Partitioned.* 2 vols. New Delhi: Roli Books, 1997. Print.

Hasan, Mushirul, and Dinyar Patel, Eds. *From Ghalib's Dillii to Lutyens' New Delhi.* New Delhi: Oxford UP, 2014. Print.

Hosagrahar, Jyoti. "Mansions to Margins: Modernity and the Domestic Landscapes of Historic Delhi, 1847–1910." *The Journal of the Society of Architectural Historians* 60.1 (March 2001): 26–45. Print.

Irving, Robert Grant. *Indian Summer: Lutyens, Baker and Imperial Delhi.* New Haven: Yale UP, 1981. Print.

Jalal, Ayesha. *Self and Sovereignty: Individual and Community in South Asian Islam Since 1850.* London: Routledge, 2001. Print.

Johnson, Nuala C. "Cast in Stone: Monuments, Geography and Nationalism." *Environment and Planning.D: Society and Space* 13.1 (1995): 51–65. Print.

Joshi, Priya. "The Exile at Home: Ahmed Ali's Twilight in Delhi." *Another Country: Colonialism, Culture, and the English Novel in India.* New York: Columbia UP, 2002. Print.

Khairi, Saad R. *Jinnah Reinterpreted: The Journey from Indian Nationalism to Muslim Statehood.* Karachi: Oxford UP, 1995. Print.

Khanna, Stuti. "Art and the City: Salman Rushdie and His Artists." *Ariel* 37. 4 (2006): 21–43. Print.

King, Bruce. "From *Twilight* to *Midnight*: Muslim Novels of India and Pakistan." *The World of Muslim Imagination.* Ed. Alamgir Hashmi. Islamabad: Gulmohar, 1986. 243–59. Print.

Lorino, Philippe and Benoît Tricard. "The Bakhtinian Theory of Chronotope (Time–Space Frame) Applied to the Organizing Process." *Constructing Identity in and Around Organizations.* Eds. Majken Schultz, Steve Maguire, Ann Langley, and Haridimos Tsoukas. Oxford: Oxford UP, 2012. 201–34. Print.

MacIntyre, Alasdair. "Poetry as Political Philosophy." *Ethics and Politics: Selected Essays* Vol. 2. Cambridge: Cambridge UP, 2006. 159–71. Print.

Malik, Amin. *Muslim Narratives and the Discourse of English.* New York: State U of New York P, 2005. Print.

Malik, Jamal. "The Language Issue: Urdu." *Islam in South Asia: A Short History.* Leiden, Boston: Brill, 2005. 282–90. Print.

Metcalf, Thomas R. *An Imperial Vision: Indian Architecture and the Britain's Raj.* London: Faber & Faber, 1989. Print.

Nalbantoglu, Gülsüm Baydar and Chong Thai Wong. "Introduction." *Postcolonial Space(s).* Eds. Gülsüm Baydar Nalbantoglu and Chong Thai Wong. New York: Princeton Architectural P, 1997. 7–12. Print.

Nayar, Pramod K. *Colonial Voices: The Discourses of Empire.* Oxford: Wiley-Blackwell, 2012. Print.

Nehru, Jawaharlal. *An Autobiography.* London: Bodley Head, 1955. Print.

Niven, Alistair. "Historical Imagination in the Novels of Ahmed Ali." *Journal of Indian Writing in English* 8. 1–2 (1980): 3–13. Print.

Nora, Pierre. "Between Memory and History: *Les Lieux de Mémoire. Representations: Special Issue: Memory and Counter-Memory* 26 (Spring 1989): 7–24. Print.

Oldenburg, Veena Talwar. *The Making of Colonial Lucknow 1856–1877.* Princeton, NJ: Princeton UP, 1984. Print.

Pandey, Gyanendra. *Remembering Partition.* Cambridge: Cambridge UP, 2001. Print.

Roy, Ananya. "Postcolonial Urbanism: Speed, Hysteria, Mass Dreams." *Worlding Cities: Asian Experiments and the Art of Being Global.* Eds. Ananya Roy and Aihwa Ong. Sussex: Blackwell Publishing Limited, 2011. 307–35. Print.

Russel, William Howard. *My Diary in India*, Vol. II. 4th ed. London: Routledge, 1860. Print.

Sadana, Rashmi. "Two Tales of a City." *Interventions* 11.1 (2009): 1–15. Print.

Sepe, Marichela. *Planning and Place in the City: Mapping Place Identity.* New York: Routledge, 2013. Print.

Sharma, Sunil. "The City of Beauties in Indo-Persian Poetic Landscape." *Comparative Studies of South Asia, Africa and the Middle East* 24.2 (2004): 73–81. Print.

Sharp, J. *Geographies of Postcolonialism.* London: Sage, 2008. Print.

Soja, Edward. *Thirdspace: Journey to Los Angeles and Other Real and Imagined Places.* Oxford: Blackwell, 1996. Print.

————. "Writing the City Spatially." *City: Analysis of Urban Trends, Culture, Theory, Policy, Action* 7.3 (2003): 269–80. Print.

Teverson, Andrew and Sara Upstone. "Introduction." *Postcolonial Spaces: The Politics of Place in Contemporary Culture.* Eds. Andrew Teverson and Sara Upstone. New York: Palgrave Macmillan, 2011. 1–13. Print.

Vice, Sue. *Introducing Bakhtin.* Manchester: Manchester UP, 1997. Print.

Wacquant, Loïc. *Urban Outcasts: A Comparative Sociology of Advanced Marginality.* Cambridge: Polity P, 2008. Print.

Wirth-Nesher, Hana. "Impartial Maps: Reading and Writing Cities." *Handbook of Urban Studies.* Ed. Ronan Paddison. London and New York: Sage Publications, 2001. Print.

Yeoh, Brenda S. A. *Contesting Space: Power Relations and The Urban Built Environment in Colonial Singapore.* New York and Oxford: Oxford UP, 1996. Print.

10 Gendering Place and Possibility in Shashi Deshpande's *That Long Silence* and Kavery Nambisan's *A Town Like Ours*

Lauren J. Lacey and Joy E. Ochs

Gendered Spaces

To anyone walking through the streets of a modern Indian city, the concept of heterotopian simultaneity is a visible reality. Pedestrians vie with bicycles and taxis on crowded through-ways; street vendors and four-star restaurants cater to veg or nonveg diets; passengers on the metro might as well be wearing a dhoti as a business suit. In all its bustling, chaotic energy, the Indian city carries, in the words of social psychologist Albert Mehrabian, "high load" (12). The notion of heterotopia is an important tool for thinking through the ways in which urban landscapes offer plentiful plurality at the same time that they delimit and define the roles of men and women who navigate that space. For instance, in a recent scheme to combat air pollution, the municipal government of Delhi enacted an odd–even scheme to keep half of all private cars off the road on alternate days. This rule, however, only applied to male drivers, prompting the *Times of India* (TOI) to ask "Why exempt women drivers?" (TOI). The exemption, it turned out, was based on the belief that women would be endangered if they walked or rode public transportation in the city. Clearly, the gendered experience of moving through an urban space like Delhi penetrates even the bureaucrat's awareness. Proceeding from this observed notion of heterotopia, then, our reading will examine the specific ways in which gendered subjectivity shapes, and is shaped by, its relationship to urban space.

While it has long been commonplace in feminist literary criticism to talk about how spaces and places are gendered, *That Long Silence* (1988) by Shashi Deshpande and *A Town Like Ours* (2014) by Kavery Nambisan offer some important ways to think more specifically about gendered spaces in contemporary India. For the female protagonists inhabiting heterotopian spaces, their urban experiences are profoundly embodied, and the ecocritical notion that "bodies know" provides an important counternarrative to the culturally dominant one imposed on them as women and wives. As described by ecocritic Lawrence Buell, "Place connotes not simply bounded and meaningful location but also dynamic process, including the shaping of place by outside as well as internal influences" (145); "place itself is not entitative ... but eventmental" (73). To examine a city through an ecocritical lens is to shift the observational emphasis from the city as a structural entity and instead to view it as a dynamic ecosystem. Both Deshpande and Nambisan offer this eventmental experience of the city through their female narrators whose place in the city is defined by their interaction with it. Thus, insofar as an ecocritical approach treats texts as "refractions of physical environments and human interactions with those environments" (Buell 30), the particular refractions we examine have to do with women's interactions with spaces in the urban landscape. Within this interactional mode, ecofeminist criticism provides an even more specific structure for examining how women are able to "redefine terrain thought to be familiar and push into new territory" (Buell 110). Urban environments have plasticity; both authors' acknowledgment and description of this plasticity create the very defamiliarizations that allow them to stake out new territory, both physical and psychological, for themselves.

We begin with the ecofeminist notion that embodied female subjectivity is rooted in its relationship to place. The two novels we have chosen allow us to examine the dual nature of this relationship. In Deshpande's novel, the narrator Jaya has been transplanted into an unfamiliar and sterile spot in Bombay. Her quest to redefine her role as an uprooted wife is intimately tied to her ability to feel at home in the city. Nambisan presents the opposite scenario: Rajakumari, her narrator, is deeply rooted in her sense of place in the fictional Pingakshipura, but her relationship to the land is threatened daily as the town aspires to economic growth at the expense of what Buell calls "placeness." Both Deshpande and Nambisan privilege female protagonists who move from within constrained places and discourses to the rejection of those constraints as artificial and ineffectual. Sara Mills, in her 1996 essay on "Gender and Colonial Space," rehearses what was already a large body of scholarship on gendered space and makes the general point that: "Groups of women at various times in history have had to be chaperoned when in the public sphere, have seen the public sphere as a place of potential sexual attack and have been taught to consider the domestic as primarily a female space. However, this does not mean to say that women have not negotiated within the constraints" (699). The female characters explored in our analyses are involved in precisely the kinds of negotiations Mills mentions. Safety is not to be found within the confines of a home or the restraints of respectable femininity. Instead, the female protagonists, in both novels, confront heterotopian complexity and realign their relationships to the places they inhabit.

One purpose of the city is to provide a space for economic and cultural growth—especially in the case of modern Mumbai and Bangalore—to enable participation in a globalized capitalist economy. In *That Long Silence*, Bombay represents the opportunity and risk of political status gained and lost. In *A Town Like Ours*, Pingakshipura is a fictional town caught in the wake of Bangalore's rapid growth. Its preeminent inhabitant is described as a "capitalist in a dhoti," concerned only with making money. In this view of the city as a production unit, women's roles are defined insofar as they provide utility (Chandramukhee).

Constrained both by physical architecture and by hegemonic narratives of the city, the female protagonists in these two novels are physically or ideologically trapped. At the most basic level, the women in these novels are made to function as the keepers of idealized utopian domestic spheres. In *That Long Silence*, Jaya describes her own "career as a wife … [t]he woman who had shopped and cooked, cleaned, organized and cared for her home and her family with such passion" (24–5). Her functionality as an urban upper-middle-class wife boils down to the same measures of productivity by which the poor village woman Saroja in Nambisan's novel is identified: her ability to procure food, cook it, and bear children. When Jaya attempts to alter the output of her productivity by writing and selling articles, her husband infantilizes her and admonishes her not to "bring that habit of exaggeration into our life, keep it for your stories" (79). Similarly, Manohar chastises his wife in *A Town Like Ours* when she gets an invitation to sell her paintings: "How can you do this, they're the very paintings I deplore, you'll get mud on your face. Tell them no. Give them something new—and decent" (Nambisan 128). In both cases, the wives are made to understand that their first duty is to maintain a "hegemonic masculine ideal" (Crinnion) and protect the husband from any outside censure that might accrue were the women to step outside of their domestic bounds. These are the limits of the private sphere, but also the limits of the larger public spheres the characters inhabit to the extent that stepping outside their prescribed gender roles puts them in dangerous territory. One of the questions raised by both novels, then, is to what extent female subjects can negotiate their relationships with the landscapes surrounding them without sacrificing security or safety.

Heterotopian Possibilities

If ecocritics emphasize placeness as "dynamic process" (Buell 145), such a notion certainly gives us a starting point from which to begin thinking about how the protagonists in the novels are located in and through their urban surroundings. Conceptualizing the ways in which the narratives offer models of resistance in and through placeness, however, can be more fruitfully explored via the notion of heterotopia. In thinking through the concept of heterotopia, Robert J. Topinka writes, "By juxtaposing and combining many spaces in one site, heterotopias problematize received knowledge by revealing and destabilizing the ground, or operating table, on which knowledge is built" (56). The destabilization he describes is precisely what happens as narrators Jaya and Rajakumari begin to rethink their roles and realities. Kevin Hetherington emphasizes not just the simultaneity in heterotopian spaces but also the ways in which that simultaneity can lead to unsettling potential:

> This is the main principle of heterotopia … they bring together heterogeneous collections of unusual things without allowing them a unity or order established through resemblance. Instead, their ordering is

derived from a process of similitude which produces, in an almost magical, uncertain space, monstrous combinations that unsettle the flow of discourse. (43)

Both novels include examples of this "magical" quality of heterotopia as Jaya and Rajakumari continually reorient themselves as women in urban spaces. Heterotopia can be a hopeful and productive concept when simultaneity and diversity are seen as preferable to various models of utopian and/ or colonial sameness and hierarchy.

Anupama Mohan's work on utopia identifies three types of heterotopic possibilities that can push back against these hierarchical utopian narratives: heterotopic space can be territorial, textual, or social (173). The female narrators of both novels operate from within the nested spheres of all three types of heterotopia. Both are socially displaced: Rajakumari because she has chosen to live outside the bounds of society on her own terms, and Jaya because her husband has taken them into hiding to avoid a political scandal. Both tell their stories from within a sheltered space that, at first glance, appears to be a traditional one: Jaya is confined in a small B-type flat, a domestic space where she is expected to carry out her function of wife while her husband tries to save face. In the traditional, if marginalized, role of temple prostitute, Rajakumari is confined in a small, enclosed chamber. Barred from walking abroad, both narrators retreat into their spaces and transform them from putative prisons to alternative womb-like sanctuaries where they can gestate and give birth to their stories. In doing so, both narrators invert their locus of control within the city. Rather than cutting them off from public life, the private chamber becomes the site of production for a gendered narrative that transcends the mere constructedness of the city. From within these heterotopic territories, both female narrators transgress their imposed social functions, create interactional geographies, and learn how to re-inhabit public urban spaces.

In addition to exploring physical territory, both narrators navigate their textual space in ways that disrupt the possibility of a hegemonic perspective. Characteristic of the ecofeminist approach, both authors employ disruptive narrative strategies to define and create space for their female narrators in cityscapes that are otherwise designed and defined by men. In both novels, the practices of writing, storytelling, and their relationship to gendered experience are central concerns. Nambisan lays out the shifting nature of narrative and the impossibility of using language to pin down a single definition of anything. If patrimony, and the bearing of sons to carry on the father's name, are central to the social order, Nambisan's narrator doesn't think much of them: "Names don't help much, not in these modern times" (44). Worship of the local deity is destabilized, as her names proliferate: "Pingakshi is the accepted name but there is Neeladenta/Neeladantaa" as well as "Ashtaangada/Ashtaangadaa, Suchetana/Suchetanaa and Pingaksha/Pingakshi, all of which go to show that gender confusion reigns" (44).

Gender is further destabilized when an abandoned boy is discovered to be a girl (45), and in as short a period as a decade and a half, "villages reincarnate into towns" (22). Even Rajakumari's companion cow evades taxonomic categorization, having had "a mother who fell in love with a buffalo" (6). Ambiguity and the limitations of language become the raw material from which to fashion a fresh narrative not tied to the language of utopia.

If a community's notions of place, piety, and identity are all in a state of transition, the idea of a master narrative itself becomes obsolete, as both Jaya and Rajakumari discover. Rajakumari speaks from the subject position of an omniscient narrator while never gaining direct experience of anything outside her cell. Yet, through hearsay, intuition, and imagination, she is able to report on the intimate details and inner thoughts of every other character. The confines of the cell become immaterial because Rajakumari "roams free inside her mind" (Nambisan 23). The other female characters, in both novels, find similar methods to practice "waywardness of mind" (23). Kripa fills canvases that upset her husband; Jaya explores the fault lines between her current self and the self she recorded in a diary; Saroja sits in the front seat of a taxi and shares oral histories of her horrific true crimes; Kusum expresses herself through madness. Meanwhile, women who don't discover ways to navigate and claim these interstitial social spaces fall into silence and despair.

That Long Silence: Negotiating Gendered Selfhood in Heterotopia

For Deshpande, self-realization occurs at the level of the individual. Anju Jagpal describes Deshpande as an author who "thrashes out the issues of women's domestic life ... and without erasing the self, she allows each of her heroines to draw on her inner vision to achieve autonomy ... It is here that resistance, instead of shattering the socio-cultural structure, holds the transformative promise" (40). Female characters in Deshpande's novels work out their experiences of self in relation to place, often locating potential for agency by claiming a different sense of subjectivity within that place. Writing specifically about the narrator of *That Long Silence*, Amrita Bhalla describes the female subject's need "to practice restraint and control; writing as self-expression in conflict with the self-generated suppression of a woman who has to 'fit' her self to a preconceived image, 'cut' and repress her intellect to conform" (36), a task Jaya has always performed uneasily. The tension between fulfilling her husband's expectations of a good woman and being a subject and agent is played out in the novel through Jaya's struggles as a writer and, as will be discussed in detail below, in Jaya's reactions to, and interactions with, the cityscape around her.

That Long Silence depicts Bombay as a specific geographic entity, fixed in history as a site of colonial power, economic output, and cultural production. Deshpande situates her characters against the backdrop of this metropolis;

the fact that the narrator moves from one Bombay neighborhood to another is a kind of shorthand that seemingly offers everything the reader needs to know about her caste, religion, socio-economic status, and artistic tastes. Deshpande's Bombay, then, functions as a monolithic structure: a set system made up of concrete, vehicles, and attitudes that are accepted as given. What makes this setting interesting is Deshpande's focus on the particular ways that female characters form relationships to this space. The narrator Jaya's perceptions, interactions, and responses to her cityscape create a kind of parallel universe; she and her husband move through identical physical structures, but their gendered subjectivities refract the significance of that place into multiple, sometimes contradictory, facets. Writing from the female position, Jaya is more aware of these facets than her husband, who adheres to the dominant narrative. Heterotopia, in Deshpande's novel, is exclusively brought to light by a female narrator writing from a gendered subject position.

The narrative is a first-person interrogation of Jaya's life as a daughter, wife, and writer, and is occasioned by a crisis in her husband's career. Mohan has been implicated in an act of fraud, and he weathers the investigation by leaving his position and closing up his home. The couple's teenaged children have been sent on vacation with friends, and Jaya's domestic routine is suspended as she and Mohan retire to a small apartment in Bombay, where they had lived much earlier in their lives. As she comes to terms with these events, Jaya creates a narrative that jumps between the past and present, observation and introspection. Early in the novel, Jaya adopts a heterotopic narrative strategy when she describes the scene of the couple's return to the apartment as though she is observing herself from afar. She sees "a man and a woman climbing the dingy stairs of a drab building in the heart of Bombay. A trail of garbage on the soiled cement stairs, cigarette butts, scraps of paper, bits of vegetable peel. And red stains—squirts of *paan*-stained spit—on the wall, macabrely brightening up the dinginess" (7). The externalized viewpoint Jaya employs here resurfaces throughout the narrative as she tries to understand herself, her relationship with her husband, and her place in the city from a carefully constructed perspective outside of her own subjectivity. It's her position as a writer, observing her own interactions with her husband and with her surroundings, that allows for these moments of self-scrutiny.

While she positions Jaya as a self-scrutinizing narrator, Deshpande also calls attention to the interactional urban space in the microcosm of the stairwell. It is a liminal space: inside the building but not part of the family apartment. It is in the heart of Bombay, but it is closed off from the streets and the people and animals who populate them. Within the stairwell are the traces of others who share the space. The stairway exemplifies "the trope of crossing the threshold" (Bhalla 36). All of Jaya's interactions with Bombay's urban spaces will involve the presence of a threshold, whether physical or psychological, crossed or uncrossed. In the ecofeminist style, Jaya's understanding of place arises from the dynamics of interaction with it rather than from the static perception of it as a fixed entity.

This becomes apparent when we examine Jaya and Mohan's experiences of space within the stairwell. Mohan sees the functionality of the stairs: a means to get to the apartment. Jaya, however, views the stairs as a transactional space that she occupies as a gendered subject. The embodied/disembodied narrator watches herself from above as Mohan reacts, with disgust, to the garbage on the stairs and a neighbor comes into view in the narrow space:

> A woman descending the stairs, a huge garbage bin balanced nonchalantly on her head, looks at them curiously, stops and smiles. The man gives her a blank stare as if affronted by that smile, but it is not for him, it is for his companion, who smiles back. The man goes on and waits with a scarcely controlled impatience before the closed door of a flat, while the two women converse. "Poor Nayana," the woman says when she joins him, "pregnant again. Have you ever seen her not pregnant? Her mother-in-law was just the same." The man's face has the blankness of indifference. (7)

Mohan is offended by the garbage, by the traces of others whose lives are not his concern. His annoyance is brought on by Nayana's smile; the same smile that welcomes Jaya back into, what turns out to be, a small community of women in the building who, despite caste and class differences, feel a sense of connection within that domestic space. Mohan's indifference is that of a man who only sees the stairwell as a functional space: having a conversation with a neighbor is an impediment to reaching the apartment.

In his desire to get inside, Mohan plays out his traditionally defined role: to shelter and protect his wife and to keep her safely away from the chaos of the world just beyond the doorstep. Jasbir Jain describes this role through the trope of the husband as a sheltering tree, which "*That Long Silence* used in several different ways. Sheltering trees protect, insulate and isolate; they do not allow anything to grow beneath them; they act as a wall between the self and the world" (82–3). Jaya herself acknowledges "marriage as a safe hole I'd crawled into" (Deshpande 149). Even within this short passage, however, it is already clear that such marital safety is, at best, limited, and quite likely illusory as well. Nayana's pregnancies and daily struggles are no less difficult for being within the confines of the domestic sphere.

Jaya's return to the Bombay flat causes her to reflect on her reactions to place, or to *placeness*, because she is thinking about the flat precisely as the kind of meaningful, relational space that Buell describes. She calls up nostalgic, idealized memories of her childhood home: "Our house had been surrounded by fruit orchards, and the clean little ribbon of a tarred road leading to it had been bordered by tamarind trees and gutters in which nothing ever ran but rain water" (54). The organic imagery and her connection to it offer a sense of rootedness and belonging. In contrast, her first impressions of Bombay are alienating:

> But Bombay, I'd realized at once, was nothing but a grey, uniform ugliness. The buildings had seemed terrible to me, endless rows of looking-exactly-alike, ramshackle, drab buildings, the washing that flapped on their balconies giving them a sluttishly gay look. (54)

Her initial experience of Bombay is of uniformity, rather than heterogeneity; the perceived lack of difference of any kind creates a sense of deadened stasis. However, it doesn't take long for Jaya to become aware of the dynamic city and to open herself to interaction with it:

> It had taken me some time to notice the streets of Bombay; once I did, however, I had been immediately caught up by the magic of their teeming life. I had watched in utter fascination the mobs, the brawls, the drunkards, the school children, the coy newlyweds. (54)

In these Bombay observations, Jaya still keeps herself apart from the scene as a passive voyeur. Since she watches mostly from the removed and fairly safe distance of her apartment balcony, she stays isolated from the spectacle while enjoying its potential. It is only as she writes and returns to these memories later in life that she becomes aware of her desire to engage that potential.

Jaya's first sense of engagement comes in the form of an invasion. She remembers that, as a young bride unused to Bombay, she felt assaulted yet fascinated by the city:

> Almost worse to me than this constant noise had been the sense of being invaded, not just by sounds, but by a multitude of people and their emotions as well. Anger, fear, hatred, envy, tenderness, love—all of these came to me as I lay in bed, a fascinated listener ... I had taken it all in eagerly, though often there was the shamed, guilty sensation of being a voyeur. (56)

Here, Jaya articulates one of the paradoxes of her experience of life in Bombay. She is literally closed off from the city below while in her family apartment, but the walls are permeable. Her sense of place, of placeness, gives way to the possibility of heterotopia. Sounds, smells, and even emotions make their way through the barriers of her home so that she cannot be completely sheltered from them. The sense of invasion is combined with the eagerness with which Jaya embraces this access to the world beyond her home. It is a terrifying, but exhilarating, potential that heterotopian Bombay presents to a woman bound by gender roles to staying within her enclosed domestic space.

Jaya's passivity begins to bother her when she realizes that not participating in the cityscape can have consequences. This awareness comes about when she and her husband overhear a man beating a woman in the street outside their apartment. While both Jaya and Mohan are upset by it, the striking element of the scene is that neither Jaya nor Mohan act in any way. They are affected by the city around them, but they do not engage with it. The suffering woman outside is part of the otherness of the city, beyond their apartment walls, and neither moves to intervene. For Jaya, intervening would, of course, be a dangerous choice. Nancy Ellen Batty writes,

> As the recurrent images in the novel of the emaciated bodies of the poor and of seething violence in the streets remind the reader … Jaya faces … a psychological and a physical crisis in response to a threat not only to Jaya's identity as a married woman but to the potential of her own self being reduced to a naked and unprotected (by class and marital status) female body. (132)

The scene above, in which Jaya and Mohan listen to a woman being beaten just outside their window, underscores the degree to which Jaya herself is vulnerable. Without her husband's presence as a "sheltering tree" and her husband's salary that keeps them in their apartment and off the streets, the dangers of the city could close in. Here is the crux of the relationship between heterotopian plurality and gendered identity within this Indian context: the potential to resist gendered power restrictions is clearly there but so is the danger of losing the safety provided by those restrictions. Women's bodies are at stake.

Jaya has certainly tried to create the safety of the perfect domestic space, but through the telling of her own story, Jaya comes to recognize the futility of her attempts: "Close the doors, stay in and you're safe. But what happened when everyone went out and you were left alone inside?" (139). Safety is a reasonable desire within the chaos of Bombay, but it is associated with stasis and alienation. Jaya recalls an alternative response to Bombay from a more carefree period of her life. Years ago a former neighbor, Leena, provided her with a happier, riskier vision of the city beyond their balconies:

> We struggled with the bolts and bars that had been intended to keep us out of the balcony until the monsoon was over. The wind pinned us to the wall as we watched the monsoon sea dash over the parapet wall and fall in a fine spray across the road. Our faces and lips felt

salty and sticky. The lights on the road came on instantaneously as we stood there, and Marine Drive became a shimmering, gleaming river, lights moving gently on it. Bombay is not ugly, I thought, Bombay is beautiful. I laughed aloud in sheer happiness and Leena laughed with me. (141)

The freedom of opening the balcony mid-monsoon is in direct contrast to the stagnant image of Jaya and Mohan listening to the violence outside. Leena and Jaya embrace the city in a moment when the city's logic is itself being undermined by the force of the monsoon. The point, though, is that Jaya only remembers this experience after she has had to question the safety and stability of life inside the apartment. It turns out that she had grown judgmental towards Leena after learning that Leena had overstepped convention by spending time with a married man. As she remembers this, the Jaya in the present of the novel becomes remorseful. She has been trapped within "[h]omotopia, a largely static space where everyone is putatively the same" (Mohan 177), instead of understanding heterotopia as "registers of social interaction … marginal spaces … as the site for the articulation of difference and the exchange of knowledge" (177). Jaya's growing self-awareness leads her to remember when she was open to the beauty and potential of Bombay, rather than frightened by it. It is a shift from a desire for the safety of homotopia to the acknowledgment of the potential of her participation in heterotopia.

Near the end of the novel, Jaya's self-interrogation finally opens her to her sense of agency within the city and enables her to step into the heterotopic potential. While she is, as usual, observing streets of Bombay, a playful scene between two men and a young woman turns ugly:

As I watched, the girl snatched at a cigarette one of the men was smoking. He feigned unwillingness then, yielding, put it between her parted, exquisitely tender lips. She took a deep drag, eyes closed in ecstasy … One of them, I realized now, was openly fondling the girl's small breasts. She opened her eyes and the men laughed. She laughed too—a thin, ugly laugh that went on and on. The cigarette was roughly pulled away from her lips by the man. She tried to grab it … He held her and began roughly kneading at her breasts. The girl, unaware of it, still reached out for the cigarette.

I could not control myself any longer. "Stop," I cried out. "Stop what you are doing to her." (175)

The two men ignore Jaya and then laugh at her, but their predictable reaction is not really the point. Jaya has engaged. She is no longer silent. Bombay is her city, and she is a part of the heterotopian mess, as well as the heterotopian potential. Breaking her silence has not altered the young woman's fate;

it simply means Jaya has revised her understanding of her own place in the heterotopian landscape and accepted the risk of taking part in it.

This change in her perspective is driven home by a realization she has as a newly self-aware subject near the end of the novel. She recalls, almost nonchalantly, her former inability to find her place in the urban landscape:

> I think of a time when, for some reason I can't remember now, I'd suddenly walked out of home, unable to cope with anything, finding everything too much. I'd walked about, not knowing where I was going, up and down streets that were unknown to me. Once, in the midst of the drab, ugly *chawls* and smelly streets I'd come upon a garden that had pleased me with its unexpectedness. I had sat down on a bench, but within minutes a man had come down and sat beside me. I had scarcely noticed him until he had said 'Hello, sister' and smiled at me, a suggestive leer, like a villain in a Hindi movie. I'd got up then and resumed my aimless walking. Finally, totally exhausted, I'd gone back home. (190–1)

Jaya's vulnerability in Bombay, as she attempts to escape the daily trials of wifehood and motherhood, is telling: she frames it as an escape, only thwarted by a man who sees her as a kind of prey out in the open. Although she has just come to her new perspective on the world around her, all is not well. Heterotopian Bombay will never be a safe Bombay. However, in breaking her own silence, in finding ways to articulate her experiences in and of the world both inside and outside her domestic space, Jaya has found an alternative to the false safety and stifling enclosure she thought were her only options. Deshpande's novel explores how an outsider like Jaya, devalued because of her gender, literally from beyond the bounds of the city, and "protected" by the walls of class and marriage can find creative potential and make a place for herself through participation in the heterotopian landscape of urban India.

A Town Like Ours: Gendered Selves in Heterotopic Community

While Deshpande focuses on the experience of the individual, Nambisan examines how entire communities situate themselves in relation to urban spaces. Her subject is Pingakshipura, a fictional settlement about to get caught in Bangalore's gravity well; its story becomes a parable of every small South Indian town caught off guard by the impacts of globalization. Like Deshpande, Nambisan focuses on female characters and places them in liminal spaces that include a temple chamber, a taxi-cum-teashop, and a painter's canvas where a traditional wife displays her private thoughts. In Jagpal's study of Nambisan, she characterizes her as an author whose heroines "gradually learn to accept the untidiness of life" (47). This character trait is epitomized in Rajakumari, the unabashed narrator of *A Town Like Ours*.

Unlike Deshpande's historically fixed Bombay, Nambisan's fictional town of Pingakshipura in *A Town Like Ours* is in a state of transition: somewhere between its history as an autonomous village and its future as an urban tentacle of a sprawling Bangalore. Its residents are aware of, and express anxiety about, the town's catapulting trajectory into the modern global economy, and from one day to the next, newly paved roads or newly drilled borewells alter the shape of the town's geography. In this setting, heterotopia is already the pre-existing condition. Fittingly, Nambisan chooses to narrate the town's story through an unconventional female character whose subject position defies easy categorization. A self-proclaimed *chudayil*, Rajakumari has retired to a small chamber attached to the Temple of Pingakshi, the goddess to whom the town is dedicated. From here, she observes and comments on the lives of others. While the illegal practice of devadasi is still known to take place in areas of Karnataka, Pingakshipura's locale, Rajakumari is not actually a temple prostitute. She has no aspiration to the divine, serves no official function, and boasts of her past secular strategies for earning money in her business. Her position in the temple chamber, then, is particularly ambiguous. Is she a harlot or a hermit? Is she an outcast or a woman of power? Her occupation of the temple chamber places her outside the quotidian bustle of Pingakshipura's commerce and social intercourse but inside the inner sanctum of the growing town's namesake. From this liminal space, she becomes the guide who not only exposes but also actively reshapes Pingakshipura's heterotopian fault lines. Nambisan explains that she gave this insider/outsider status to her narrator to enable her to "speak her truth freely, unfettered by convention" ("Life").

Rajakumari identifies herself as the observer of "a changing world, a *changed* world, and I making what sense I can of it from my room in the temple" (Nambisan 158). However, Rajakumari's observational powers defy narrative convention. She reports what she gathers with her own senses and muses on her own past experiences, but without ever leaving her chamber, she also reports on intimate conversations taking place between interlocutors miles from the temple, private interior conflicts that other characters never express, and even the unarticulated sexual longings of other species. Her narrative perspective is neither limited-subjective nor omniscient; it comes from an embodied experience within a particular community: "All that I know ... has been received in small earfuls from various people over a length of time. I picture everything I hear and a lot that I might not hear. You can rely on most of what I tell" (129). Gretchen Legler identifies this kind of narrative position as the essential one of the ecofeminist perspective, "erasing or blurring the boundaries between inner (emotional, psychological, personal) and outer (geographic) landscapes, or the erasing or blurring of the self-other (human/nonhuman, I/Thou) distinctions" (230). Indeed, Rajakumari recognizes herself as this kind of narrator: "I wonder sometimes if I am the voice of this town rendered voiceless by the eternal babble of progress; the instrument that plays the music of strangeness" (Nambisan 66). Where Deshpande's narrator struggles to define a self against the backdrop of the city, Nambisan's surrenders herself to merge with the egos and landscapes of hers.

As Ami Crinnion notes, insofar "as there does not seem to be a female (counter-) narrative of the city, women are still marginalized in and by urban structures and practices." Rajakumari, however, embraces her marginalized position and transforms it into a position of power. By identifying herself as the voice of a voiceless town, she enters into an alternative subject position unconfined by the traditional binaries of self/other or human/nonhuman. Her counter-narrative recasts the urban experience such that "heterotopia resurfaces as a strategy to reclaim places of otherness on the inside of an economized 'public' life" (Dehaene and de Cauter 4).

Rajakumari's success as a narrator plays out in her ability to speak for the voiceless. With her usual attention to issues of environmental justice, Nambisan makes explicit the metonymy of natural landscapes represented as female bodies. The land outside the expanding Sugandha Enterprises is expected to yield its fertility to the urgent demands of capitalist growth: "Good old Mother Earth," as the narrator calls her, undergoes a physical assault as "the experts drilled into the bowels of the earth, going right through its heart or any other wretched heart if it got in the way until the water table was struck and lo, we had a spring here" (55). The first well miscarries, and "so one, two, three, four, five, six, seven, eight, nine more bore wells were dug in nine days" (55). The violent sexuality of the language here echoes Nambisan's depiction of Saroja's early marriage. Matched at thirteen to the mentally handicapped son of a landowner, the girl is appraised in terms of her utility to the men. Her husband treats her as a vessel for sating his desires, and after the first child is born, he wants "not just a second and a third but many more" (38). Despite her distaste for motherhood, Saroja endures his nightly importunities, which, like the drilling of the bore wells, disturb her insides in the quest for greater production. Just as water is drawn from the earth, babies are extracted from Saroja, and "at the mature age of nineteen, Saroja feels parched for a life of some dignity" (37). Like the land outside Sugandha, Saroja's body is valued only for its ability to produce goods demanded by those who control their destinies.

Maria Mies and Vandana Shiva critique the exploitation of "the female body's generative capacity" as an "area of investment and profit-making" (175) in a capitalist society. The further detached they become from rural patriarchal norms, the more Nambisan's female characters reject the notion that they are biological production units. Saroja bears no more children once she moves to the town, Kripa takes steps to remain childless, and Rajakumari sets her own rules as a woman of pleasure. Despite the agency these women gain claiming bodily autonomy, the female body becomes the most visible site for the environmental damage caused by urbanization in a Pingakshipura striving to become a bustling city. Not content simply to extract economic value in the form of resources from the bowels of the earth, the Sugandha factory additionally ejaculates its effluent into the stream, which, as a result, is described as having "shed its girlish sweetness and become an old woman" (Nambisan 59). The river runs black with undisclosed chemicals from Sugandha's pesticide factory, and starting in 1995, a year meant to evoke the tenth anniversary of the Union Carbide disaster in Bhopal, the women of Pingakshipura begin to give birth to children who have been affected by the chemical in the womb. In an interesting narrative move, Nambisan presents the details of the contamination in the objective voice of a fictional journal, *The International Journal of Trichology* (vol. XXI, no. 7, pp. 26–48), which finds that "children who grow up in [Pingakshipura] between the ages of nothing and four are more likely to be white-haired than black" (50). In dispassionate terms, Nambisan's researcher explains, "The reason behind the denaturing of hair is apparently a pigment called melanin naturally present in black hair, which is rendered impotent by some chemical in the pesticide. When effluents containing the substance leach into the water, the infant hair colour is altered" (50). This ostensibly objective scientific explanation is given privilege as the official story and overrides the wails of the women giving birth to the affected children.

While the financial success of the pesticide factory and Sugandha's other ventures allow the town to enter the world economic stage, the cost of the environmental damage is borne entirely by the female bodies. This outcome, too, evokes the ongoing impact at Bhopal, where thirty years after the chemical spill there, "women have had to take the lead in fighting for justice because it is most damaging to female bodies" (Pariyadath). In Pingakshipura, white hair "can be quite a disfigurement, especially in girls" (Nambisan 49). As with female survivors of the Bhopal disasters, the girls are not only physically marked themselves, but they carry the specter of passing the trait along to their future children as well. If, as Jagpal asserts, "for the Indian woman [marriage] is the *summum bonum* of her life and the worth and justification of her being depends upon the success of her marriage" (25), then the white-haired girls of Pingakshipura have been robbed of the primary economic and social function of their lives. For these girls, arranging an "alliance with another village is tricky and the dowry asked for is disgusting" (49). Girls who marry outside the town by disguising their disfigurement are soon discovered and "are sent back with the burden of shame on their heads" (49). Meanwhile, the ever more profitable Sugandha Enterprises is off the hook:

> The chance of any chemical contamination of water is so remote a possibility as to be insignificant," said the senior-most hair scientist, reading from a prepared speech. "We're conducting more trials and experiments to pin down the true cause. Till then, let us not come to any hasty conclusions and blame innocent people, particularly when it is someone noble, like the Sugandha boss. (51)

Nambisan's fictional ex culpa echoes the real ones offered by Union Carbide when they denied responsibility for the health problems that burdened its victims (Pariyadath). Whether by being made to bear children or being prevented from bearing children because of a genetic defect, the female body in this novel, as in life, is viewed as a commodity whose utility can be sacrificed to the economic growth of the city (Chandramukhee). This would be the last word if not for Rajakumari's counter-narrative. Unlike the hired Sugandha scientist reading from a prepared speech, Nambisan's narrator gives voice to the marginalized: the mothers, the shunned white-haired girls, and the despoiled land itself.

Perhaps the character who best epitomizes the promise offered by hetero-topic space is the young woman, Saroja, the main subject of Rajakumari's narration. There is nothing remarkable about the early trajectory of Saroja's early life: she is sold into an arranged marriage in a neighboring village a few months after her first menses, made to bear the cruelties of her in-laws, and to perform their domestic chores. She gets pregnant and enters the duties of motherhood. Her routine life of carrying out her prescribed gender roles is one that has been experienced by millions of village women and one that she would have continued had it not been for a freak accident. Saroja's story becomes interesting when Nambisan relates the circumstances of her widowhood from within what Mohan refers to as "textual heterotopic space" (173). The method of communicating Saroja's story offers a sharp contrast to the clear-cut delivery offered by Sagandha officials interested in privileging one particular interpretation of the facts.

Saroja tells her story, a private and intimate one, to a single listener while they are both seated in the front seat of a taxi owned by the man she now lives with. The taxi is a public place when it is moving; it hauls paying passengers through the streets of the town. When it is parked, however, the taxi becomes Saroja's private domestic space. Bedroom, living room, kitchen—the spaces traditionally reserved for female productivity—overlay seats, engine, tires: the means of livelihood for the male driver of the taxi. Saroja treats this moving/stationery, public/private space as one in which she feels empowered to speak. Rajakumari lays the scene for Saroja's story to begin: "There might as well be two Sarojas—one telling the story and the other living it" (34). At this moment, however, when one might reasonably expect a Deshpande-like first-person account of Saroja's past, Rajakumari dissolves the subject/object boundary between Saroja and herself and inhabits Saroja's memory as if the events had happened to her. What follows is a narration of Saroja's experience told through Rajakumari's lips. When young Saroja and her husband were enjoying a swim, the mentally handicapped Vasu found himself caught in a dangerous current, and Saroja swam out to rescue him. The panicked Vasu clings to her, and during the ensuing struggle, Saroja, depending on one's point of view, either fails to save her husband from drowning, or succeeds in saving herself from being drowned by him. In either interpretation, Vasu is dead at the hands of his wife, and

Saroja flees to Pingakshipura to hide in the blanket of anonymity the town provides.

What is extraordinary here is not the specific content of the narration, but the fact that both narrators have succeeded in carving out and claiming secure heterotopic places within urban public spaces where such a story can be spoken, shared, and ratified by a listener. Saroja, in her taxi-home, and Rajakumari, in her temple cell, do not fear the reprisal, repression, or rejection other wives in our novels have faced when expressing themselves. The death of her husband may free Saroja from her conscripted role of village wife, but the telling of the story liberates her to become a full, unfettered human being. This could never have happened in the homotopic village (Mohan 177), where even the roles of widows are scripted. Extending Deshpande's choice of allowing her narrator to speak freely in a private diary, Nambisan lets her women speak out loud within a community. It takes the heterotopic promise of the city and the courage of women speaking their truth, listening to one another, and erasing the boundaries between them to create a space where they can inhabit public spaces freely.

Ecofeminist Re-workings of Space

Nambisan's Pingakshipura and Deshpande's Bombay conform to the logic of patriarchy and male honor on the one hand and to economic growth and capitalism on the other. In both novels, the female protagonists are physically and ideologically trapped in these versions of the city. Their gendered narrations, however, shift focus from what Legler terms "mind-centered ethos" and instead posit an epistemology of "bodies that know" (230). Insofar as ecofeminist criticism deconstructs the conflation of female bodies with exploitable natural resources, it allows the female narrators to speak back to patriarchal notions of the city through their own embodied experiences of it. Legler describes this "embodying" as "writing nature out of a position as a passive mirror of culture into a position as actor or agent" (229). In both novels, the narrators leave behind a past where they were acted upon (as wife or prostitute, as mirrors reflecting patriarchal desire) and tell their stories from a position of agency, where their experiences and observations redefine the space of the city in their own terms. These narrators navigate gender constrictions in city life and take on roles of active tellers of stories, rather than recipients of normative narratives, using the potential of heterotopian urban landscapes to articulate an expanded vision of space and place.

Works Cited

Batty, Nancy Ellen. *The Ring of Recollection: Transgenerational Haunting in the Novels of Shashi Deshpande*. New York: Rodopi, 2010. Print.
Bhalla, Amrita. *Shashi Deshpande*. Horndon, UK: Northcote, 2006. Print.
Buell, Lawrence. *The Future of Environmental Criticism: Environmental Crisis and Literary Imagination*. Malden, MA: Blackwell, 2005. Print.

Chandramukhee. "Dowry Practices and Gendered Space in Urban Patna/India." *Gender and Urban Space*, Gender Forum (42), 2013. Web. November 12, 2014.

Crinnion, Ami. "The Slutwalks: Reappropriation Through Demonstration." *Gender and Urban Space*, Gender Forum (42), 2013. Web. November 12, 2014.

Dehaene, Michael, and Lieven de Cauter. *Heterotopia and the City: Public Space in Postcivil Society*. New York: Routledge, 2008. Print.

Deshpande, Shashi. *That Long Silence*. New Delhi: Penguin, 1989. Print.

Hetherington, Kevin. *The Badlands of Modernity: Heterotopia and Social Ordering*, London: Routledge, 1997. Print.

Jagpal, Anju. *Female Identity: A Study of Seven Indian Women Novelists*. New Delhi: Prestige Books, 2012. Print.

Jain, Jasbir. *Gendered Realities, Human Spaces: The Writing of Shashi Deshpande*. Jaipur: Rawat Publications, 2003. Print.

Legler, Gretchen. "Ecofeminist Literary Criticism." *Ecofeminism: Women Culture Nature*. Ed. Karen J. Warren. Bloomington: Indiana UP, 1997. Web. November 10, 2014.

Mehrabian, Albert. *Public Places and Private Spaces*. New York: Basic Books, 1976. Print.

Mies, Maria, and Vandana Shiva. *Ecofeminism*. London & New Jersey: Zed Books, 1993. Print.

Mills, Sara. "Gender and Colonial Space." *Feminist Postcolonial Theory: A Reader*. Eds. Reina Lewis and Sara Mills, New York: Routledge, 2003. 692–719. Print.

Mohan, Anupama. *Utopia and the Village in South Asian Literatures*. New York: Palgrave Macmillan, 2012. Print.

Mohanty, Chandra Talpade. *Feminism Without Borders: Decolonizing Theory, Practicing Solidarity*. Durham, NC: Duke UP, 2003. Print.

Nambisan, Kavery. "Life Can be a Fairytale … Or a Mess." Interview by Swati Daftaur. *The Hindu*. August 2, 2014. Web. September 12, 2014.

———. *A Town Like Ours*. New Delhi: Aleph Book Company, 2014. Print.

Neely, Carol Thomas. "Women/Utopia/Fetish: Disavowal and Satisfied Desire in Margaret Cavendish's 'New Blazing World' and Gloria Anzaldua's 'Borderlands/ La Frontera.'" *Heterotopia: Postmodern Utopia and the Body Politic*. Ed. Tobin Siebers. Ann Arbor: U of Michigan P, 1994. Print.

"Odd-Even Scheme: Why Exempt Women, Two-Wheelers, Delhi High Court Asks." *The Times of India*. December 30, 2015. Web. January 28, 2016.

Pariyadath, Renu, "Bhopal (1984– ?): The 30th Anniversary and the Ongoing Disaster." Iowa City Foreign Relations Council. Unitarian/Universalist Society, Iowa City, IA. March 5, 2015. Lecture.

Topinka, Robert J. "Foucault, Borges, Heterotopia: Producing Knowledge in Other Spaces." *Foucault Studies* 9 (2010): 54–70. Print.

Warren, Karen J., ed., *Ecofeminism: Women Culture Nature*, Bloomington: Indiana UP, 1997. Web. November 10, 2014.

11 Delhi at the Margins[1]

Heterotopic Imagination, *Bricolage*, and Alternative Urbanity in *Trickster City*

Sanjukta Poddar

Trickster City, Writings from the Belly of the Metropolis, is Sweta Sarda's English translation of Cybermohalla Collective's Hindi work, *Bahurupiya Shaher* (2005), and it was published in 2009 by Penguin, which is one of the largest publishers of English writing in India. This crossover into the Anglophone literary establishment is a significant feat for a collaborative, nonfiction text written by twenty working-class youths from the *bastis* of Delhi, albeit under the auspices of an NGO and an influential research institution—Ankur Society for Educational Alternatives and the Sarai Program of the Center for the Study of Developing Societies, respectively.[2] The publication of the work in Hindi and, particularly, of its English translation, signals the emergence of hitherto underrepresented or even misrepresented voices of urban outcasts into the literary mainstream—of garbage-collectors, butchers, petty traders, semi-skilled artisans, laborers, delivery boys, and so on—and carries the potential to transform the discourse on Indian cities, as well as their representation.[3] The project began as multimedia documentation of practices of livelihood and everyday experiences in neighborhoods such as Nangla Machi, Yamuna Pushta, Dakshinpuri and LNJP Jhuggi-Jhopdi Colony. Many of these locales were under the threat of demolitions as part of the preparations for the Commonwealth Games (or CWG) of 2010, and in many cases, this came to pass.[4] Since then, the residents of these settlements have been rendered homeless or relegated to the outskirts of the city. Some of the most expressive voices of this text belong to Jaanu Nagar, Suraj Rai, Neelofar, Rakesh Khairalia, Yashoda Singh, Shamsher Ali, et al. This text is a testimony to the experience of the city by these urban outcasts.

As opposed to more popular, fictional treatments of life in slums, as in Salman Rushdie's *Midnight's Children* (1980), and Rohinton Mistry's *A Fine Balance* (1995), *Trickster City* is a first-person witness account, a narrative-from-below wherein the residents of these *bastis* express their experience of everyday life in unauthorized colonies, about the coercive evictions and demolitions, and being forced to move to the peripheries. These events were also catastrophic blows that resulted in a crisis of faith in the city and their place within it. At first glance, the marginality of these urban outcasts is seemingly all-pervasive and operates at several levels. For instance, the authors do not evoke it as a mere trope but an empirical reality, an affective subject-position that defines their relationship with the city, and finally, a representational space. However, the central claim of this chapter is that marginality is not a natural or given state, but, rather, a product of specific processes involving the state, as well as the bourgeois public. I argue that these urban outcasts, owing to their marginal or liminal location, on both the spatial and representational fringes of the city, are in fact, privy to an imagination of the city that counters the bourgeois imaginary. Thus, I employ the term "heterotopic imagination" to define this empowering locale and perspective. In other words, the mantle of marginality is constantly resisted and challenged through recourse to creative expression and self-representation. I contend that *Trickster City* reformulates our perception of the urban outcasts and that, viewed through their representative lens, the imagination of the city also undergoes substantial change so as to provide an alternative conception of what the experience of urbanity constitutes. Both form, what I term a *bricolage*, as well as content, which is creative, non-linear, and personal, are tactics which complicate their status as outcasts or to use the postcolonial term, subaltern. Finally, I argue that they present a more nuanced perspective of their lives and of the city, which also demands new strategies of reading from the self-conscious bourgeois reader.

In the first section, through an analysis of the form of the work and exploration of the writings of these urban outcasts, I explore further the concept of the margins and how that enables the perspective of their heterotopic imagination to emerge. In addition, I contend that marginality is problematized through novel strategies of literary representation. In the later sections, I examine the modes through which the writers stake their right to the city, and finally, how the urban is being redefined—spatially and culturally—through these literary innovations from the margins.

Marginality and the Heterotopic Imagination of *Trickster City*

As the introduction to this collection evinces, the editors and authors anthologized here are all writing in the context of the shift within urban studies that emphasizes the need to move beyond strait-jacketed modes of reading the urban as monochromatic narratives of a particular discipline, or of a certain class, or of privileged Western locales. This includes attention to the urban margins as dynamic spaces, particularly in the global south, that are no longer just recipients of the discourse on the urban. Instead, now the residents are also active agents participating in the discussion and reformulating what urbanity means for them. In order to understand how *Trickster City* functions in a similar way, I suggest that these *bastis* of Delhi can be read productively as Foucauldian heterotopic spaces.

Foucault conceptualizes heterotopias as a multitude of spaces that exist within the same site but are different from the mainstream.[5] He writes:

> There are also, probably in every culture, in every civilization, real places—places that do exist and that are formed in the very founding

of society—which are something like *counter-sites*, a kind of effectively enacted utopia in which the real sites, all the other real sites that
can be found within the culture, are simultaneously *represented, contested, and inverted*. Places of this kind are outside of all places, even
though it may be possible to indicate their location in reality. Because
these places are absolutely different from all the sites that they reflect
and speak about, I shall call them, by way of contrast to utopias, heterotopias. (3, emphasis mine)

These *bastis*, too, operate as counter-sites that have been forcibly pushed to
the margins and rendered placeless as compared to the rest of the city. Both
at the semantic and discursive levels, there have been attempts to classify
these sites as non-sites. For instance, the word "slum" deliberately reduces a
complex reality to a pejorative implication that the *basti*-dwellers are illegal
occupants, and, hence, have no claim to the land they occupy. However,
I contend that in this process of resistance, these locales successfully challenge their framing as non-sites to emerge rather as counter-sites. In fact,
self-representation is a strategy through which these sites are narrated as
dynamic parts of the city with a complex everyday life. This leads to the
representation, contestation, and inversion of both the *bastis* as well as the
"real sites," or the rest of the city. This happens at several levels, including
the forging of a representational space or emergence of what I term the
"heterotopic imagination" within the hierarchized and close-ranked literary
mainstream.

A quick glance at the publishing scenario will illustrate. Although Delhi has
occupied center stage as a site of literary production and publication since the
late 1980s for both Hindi and English-language publishing (Sadana 48–93),
I contend that the city and its everyday did not emerge as significant subjects
of concern until much later.[6] For instance, as recently as the early years of the
2000s, the domain of contemporary representations of Delhi was limited to
a few well-known texts such as *Delhi: A Novel* by Khuswant Singh and *City
of Djinns* by William Dalrymple. While an analysis of this purported lack of
a more significant corpus is beyond the scope of this chapter, I wish to draw
attention to a contrasting phenomenon witnessed in the last ten years. A substantial number of nonfiction writings on the city—representing a plethora of
genres such as travel writing, photographic and pictorial documentary, anthology of reflective essays, and narrative nonfiction—have radically altered the
discursive space of urban representation. Such a shift is perceptibly rooted in
changes in the economy in the post-globalization period and its influence on
print culture, and the growth of a new reading public, particularly in English
(Varughese-Dawson 25–40). Arguably, this trend constitutes a powerful section of the new literary mainstream. Within this wide range, I focus on nonfiction narratives (to which *Trickster City* belongs), and propose that this
form has emerged as an enabling idiom, which greatly expands on the limited
range of Anglophone fiction. Of yet more interest is the fact that, even within

this genre, *Trickster City* constitutes an alternative to this discourse and presents an instance of heterotopic imagination.

A reference to some of these recent, prominent works of narrative nonfiction on Delhi such as *A Free Man* (2011) by Aman Sethi, Rana Dasgupta's *Capital: A Portrait of Twenty-First Century Delhi* (2014), and Siddharth Deb's *The Beautiful and the Damned* (2010, which contains a section on Delhi), illustrates the limitations of recent non-fiction works.[7] I argue that these works represent one end of the spectrum of this upcoming genre whereas the other is occupied by its internal other, a collaborative text like *Bahurupiya Shahar*, written in Hindi by a group of authors from a different socio-economic, as well as cultural class from those like Sethi, Deb, and Dasgupta. To elaborate, all these texts do represent a concern with the margins, but on the one hand, the latter group of authors occupy the subject-position of curious but sympathetic observers and documenters of the underbelly of the city whereas on the other, the former constitutes that purported underbelly. Hence, the question arises—how does *Trickster City* aid or alter our understanding of the urban outcasts as well as the city as occupants of this rare socio-economic but also creative vantage point? First, the *bastis* themselves are found to emerge as spaces characterized by multiplicity and complexity, not as a statistical black-and-white situation. Thus, their stereotypical and reductionist framing is contested. For instance, the title itself is illustrative of the possibilities of alternative readings of the city as a tricky, cunning space but one that is full of both chances and pitfalls for its residents. The original Hindi title—*Bahurupiya Shaher*—extends this multitude of possibilities further. The phrase translates literally as "multi-faceted city," which is consistent with the multiple perspectives of its many authors. Incidentally, the word *bahurupiya* is also used to describe a performer or trickster who dons many masks and can play a variety of roles. Arguably, this can be stretched to include not just the nature of the city but could also be interpreted as a warning of being duped, tricked or put in danger by the various faces of the city. Each one of these interpretations emblematizes the tense but sensitive relationship between the authors and their city.

Evidence of such plenitude of perspectives is also visible in the book's subtitle: "Writings from the Belly of the Metropolis," which clearly defines the position which the authors consciously occupy and identify themselves with—not the underbelly, as the working-class is popularly designated—but rather the "belly," a central organ crucial to the smooth functioning of the city. Through this subtle linguistic maneuver, the authors argue that the lives documented in these pages, their own as well as those of their families and peers, are by no means marginal to the discourse on the urban. Instead, as the subsequent discussions will show, their concerns about love, friendship, family, the neighborhood, work, safety, and identity as citizens have equal claim to representation in popular and academic discourse. The text can be understood as a confident declaration that these working-class subjects are also self-representing creators who successfully re-inscribe the underprivileged subjects as imaginative, creative, and affective citizens, no less than their more visible bourgeois counterparts who live in gated enclaves, have access to state services such as water, sanitation, and electricity, can access education and employment opportunities, and present the dilemmas of their lives in mainstream discourse. I further suggest that this special text provides a unique perspective and a more broad-based engagement with the city which positions the authors not just as residents but also rights-bearing citizens who have an equal claim to the representation of the city and their own place in it. In this process, an alternative conception of the city emerges. In order to understand this perspective further and what it facilitates, an engagement with the complex form of *Trickster City* is necessary.

Urban *Bricolage* and *Bricoleurs*: Form and Authorship

Before I begin the discussion of *Trickster City*, I confess that, after nearly four years of close engagement with this text, the *bahurups,* or "many aspects" of this trickster still feel elusive and difficult to identify, nor is it easy to employ the usual kind of formal literary analysis. For one, this work seamlessly combines a variety of forms—documentary montages, reportage, journal entries, confessionals, and short narratives. Some of these pieces are written from the first-person perspective and deal with the authors' own experiences whereas other writers occupy an almost-detached, omniscient perch, delineating the events in the lives of others in the vicinity. The only narrative *telos* that holds this series of multifaceted reflections on the city together is the structure of seven loosely organized thematic sections: "Arrival," "En Route," "Repartee," "Whereabouts," "Incognito," "Encounter," and "Frontier." Thus, form, authorship, and (as I will discuss in subsequent sections) content, all throw up myriad challenges at each step, compelling the reader to employ novel practices of reading and interpretation. Such writing also demands a direct engagement both with the text but also its subject matter, the city, and the acknowledgment of multiplicity as the key characteristic of both. This is a feature of the heterotopic imagination at play, which uses representational techniques that do not always characterize other works on Delhi. One such technique is the use of unique voices, which speak about both the *bastis* and the rest of the city (the "counter-site" and the "real sites") as insiders, rather than speaking "about" or "to" these.

For example, the epigraph sets the tone of the text; it reads, "So that affection for the city endures," and functions both as tribute and satire. In fact, it is the first of many fine ironies that layer this rich text because every vignette belies how the city has rejected these citizens at various turns; yet, they continue to identify with it. Indeed, the writers engage with the city by internalizing, in the form and in the content, the plenitude and excess the city represents. One of the defining features of *Trickster City* is its collaborative nature, which eschews the dominant perspective of one author for the multiple voices of several authors. For instance, three authors discuss the same incident, such as a devastating incident of fire in a storage facility. However, there is no continuity between these various renditions, either in terms of an attempt to construct a continuous narrative or even in the form used to describe the event. Shamsher Ali's piece "Vanished in Smoke," a sympathetic but objective report, documents the sudden outbreak of the fire with a focus on Sunitaji's (one of the residents) experience. She has lost her home in the fire and she, along with her son, rummages through the ashes to retrieve their most precious belongings—official documents that verify their identity and proof of residence in the neighborhood (114–17). Suraj Rai in "The Guarantor," which is narrated almost like a mystery tale, takes up the aftermath of the fire a couple of chapters later. However, the fire appears only incidentally in this piece; the center stage is occupied by an informal committee, which runs a trust fund to cover emergencies in the absence of support from banks and other formal governmental institutions (122–5). The third mention of the fire is in passing, in the section "Evictions," wherein some of the authors take it up as an example of the dangers of living in areas not formally recognized by the government. What it facilitates for the reader is a multiplicity of perspectives that paint a far more complex portrait of the city than previously available.

To take a closer glance, the authors indicate here as well as throughout the text, how an incident of such stature affects the community as a whole and how lives led on the margins often rely on communal bonds, perhaps more so than in the case of documented citizens. As a stylistic ploy, one incident is explored from a variety of subject-positions to yield a layered, richer text, which functions as an emphasis on the shared nature of such experience, and hence, underscores the need for shared representation and authorship. This unique form of writing could be gauged better if viewed as a *bricolage*, a term borrowed from Jacque Derrida (when he reflects on structure and Claude Levi-Strauss' distinction between nature and culture), although he employed it in a somewhat different context. The French word *bricolage* indicates a work-in-progress; it constitutes the contingent, the ongoing, and implies the employment of the "means at hand," as opposed to the mythical, impossible nature of the totality and the finished discourse of the "engineer." Moreover, Derrida reads *bricolage* as operating outside the canonical codes of preferentiality, as "critical language" (360), which simultaneously challenges prior discourse and presents itself as an alternative discourse. Both these elements are noticeable in *Trickster City*, which undertakes a radical de-centering of the literary discourse on the city, mainly characterized by literary fiction, polished prose, the finished, and the complete. Instead, the *bricolage* of *Trickster City* presents fractals, fragmented experiences, and raw emotions; the unstructured voices work through the juxtaposition of images and contrapuntal discourses. Perhaps, the best instance of such episodes and its expression is evident in "Repartee." Its two sub-sections, titled "Daily Hurts" by Kulwinder Kaur (88), and

"Daily Acceptances" by Rakesh Khairalia (89–105), constitute several unrelated, seemingly random snippets and observations on people and their lives in the city, offered in no particular order. They function as photographs that offer staccato glimpses to be subjectively arranged and interpreted by the reader (or viewer, to continue the metaphor of photography) because each reading of the city is influenced by individual lifeworlds. This kind of bricolage makes possible a mode of understanding the urban outcast as creative, agentive, and multi-dimensional instead of being an object or recipient of other discourses.

If the form of this work is understood as *bricolage*, should the unified subjectivity of the author be replaced by a more apt term—*bricoleurs*—those who captures the radical instability of those who are attempting to forge a new, contingent idiom? On the other hand, their status as marginalized urban citizens—residents of *bastis* and permanent refugees, fringe claimants to the status of citizenship—also designates these urban homeless as the *new subalterns*, an evolution of the definition of subalternity that Gayatri Chakravorty Spivak indicates as a possibility in an interview on the shifting terrain of postcolonial studies ("New Subaltern" 330). She states that the earlier formulation of subalterns as the rural, agrarian class with little or no access to networks of power ("Can the Subaltern") could be extended to include the "metropolitan homeless" ("New Subaltern" 331). Exploring the contradiction between this twin status—self-representative, creative, *bricoleurs*, and new subalterns—and the dynamics of this interplay could help us understand the subject-position of these writers better. In fact, the classic definition of subalternity—deprivation and distance from networks of power—does not seem to operate for the Indian urban poor due to other structural causes as well.[8] In fact, what emerges in a creative text like *Trickster City* are unstable, plural subject-positions that bring the alleged subalternity into tension, thus creating new forms of expression which problematize their marginality. Writing, in fact, becomes an act of countering their status of subalternity. It constitutes an oppositional event—both to the imposed status of marginality as well as the identity of authorship—which reclaims the representative space and functions as an agential act. This mode of expression also produces a more comprehensive sense of the urban, which includes subjective expression, the affective, and creative, beyond the social science discourses that take only the empirical, objective modes of deprivation into account.

Thus, *bricoleurs* occupy the unique subject-position of self-representing writers who narrate experiences of their own life and that of others who have been pushed to the margins but do not accept marginality as a condition. For instance, butchers, courier delivery boys, budding authors, phone booth operators are all classes of voices who are only "represented" or spoken for and rarely get an opportunity to "present" themselves or to speak for themselves. Examples of such presentation are: when Lakshmi Kohli writes in "Missed Call," how the phone booth operator, Sonu, clings on to the memory of a momentary romantic encounter with a customer (70–6); Arif

Ali asks after two weeks of apprenticeship as a butcher, "Why do the hens have to be thrown around so much" (83). Here, the word "representation" is dialectically activated in another sense that encompasses self-presentation as well as to include fashioning themselves through writing and to forge themselves anew. This occurs both at the level of authorship and at the level of form. In fact, the city and the urban experience emerge as constituted by this plurality and multiplicity. Moreover, because the authors are from lower socio-economic backgrounds and residents of a uniquely liminal spatial zone, the analysis also seeks to take into account what the implications are of their voice being given expression. These concerns will be examined in the following sections.

Countering the Discourse of Space

One of the main causes, which have led to the marginalization of the urban homeless, is the discourse within which they are framed and explained. As Lalit Batra aptly points out, the entire discourse of a "world-class city" propagated by the bourgeois public, particularly since the liberalization reforms of the 1990s, hinges on the twin axes of environment and legality. This discourse and its informing imaginary claims that the unauthorized settlements are dirty, polluting and, in the case of Yamuna Pushta settlement, that it endangers the Yamuna by encroaching on its riverbed. Behind this desire lies the informing notion that only full citizens, in other words the propertied bourgeois, have a right to the city. Batra says in this regard that the idea of reclaiming the rights of the "citizenry" is directly linked to "the dispossession of the working classes" (27). The thin margin of cleanliness versus dirt, health versus pollution, and sanctioned versus unauthorized are used to demarcate the legitimate bourgeois citizen from those who are considered squatters and a burden on the rest of the city. Both these frameworks are challenged in a variety of ways in the text.

There are several instances in *Trickster City* that narrate how these so-called unauthorized settlers had claimed these spaces from the wilderness, which had been marked as wastelands in city maps, and created settlements over thirty-odd years. Three authors write about this process of reclamation of Nangla in "Evictions," in three reflections titled "Where …?," "What was Nangla?," and "It was heard …" One of the *bricoleurs*, Dilip Kumar, narrates the local *pradhan*'s version: "'Where Nangla is today, was once a dense forest. Snakes, monkeys, lions ruled the forest. Some people cut down the forest and made their homes here with the wood. And today it has taken the form of a dwelling'"(145). Jaanu Nagar reports other versions he has overheard, "'We gave everything … to make a dwelling out of it.' 'Not just our earnings, we have out the labor of our bodies to make this place'" (146). Thus, ignored by the state and by the bourgeois public, the working class and homeless of the city had claimed places like these for their own over the years. Notably, Yamuna Pushta was home to 35,000 working-class families and more than 1,500,000 people before the demolitions (Menon and Bhan 2).

On the other hand, the bourgeois citizens view these settlements as dens of criminals, an eyesore not befitting a world-class city, or, at best, makeshift residences of service providers who have long facilitated their world-class living at a low price. These citizens also feel that they have a right to all of the land in the city, including that which was reclaimed by the urban poor. However, the reality belies the falsity of these strident claims of the bourgeois public. Urban geographer and social thinker David Harvey's contention in this regard is pertinent. He observes that the availability of surplus capital often led to urban restructuring, as happened in the case of Paris and New York, which was then carried out and actualized through state-led violence.

> It has entailed repeated bouts of urban restructuring through "creative destruction", which nearly always has a class dimension since it is the poor, the underprivileged and those marginalized from political power that suffer first and foremost from this process. Violence is required to build the new urban world on the wreckage of the old.
>
> ("Postcolonial Critique" 33)

The threatening messages put up by the government, loudspeakers which ordered immediate eviction, the bulldozers which appeared overnight in these areas, and the deployment of the Rapid Action Force (RAF) or the riot-police force during the demolitions—repeatedly mentioned by the writers, especially in "Evictions"—are all testimonies to the coercion and violence that accompanies urban restructuring. Jaanu Nagar and Lakshmi Kohli write:

> Doors to every house were open. It seemed there were far more doors and too few walls in these lanes ... Police forces descended on the settlement like fog, settling over everything, changing everything ... in all these years, today was going to be the first time that a vehicle other than a bicycle was going to pass through it ... The "first vehicle" was going to be a bulldozer. And once it passed through, there would be no scope left for anyone else to pass through ever again. (143)

Further, urban planner Asher Ghertner contextualizes these acts of governmental violence in the case of Delhi, which also apply to any rapidly globalizing megapolis: "According to this *aesthetic* mode of governing, which I will show to be widespread in Delhi today, if a development project *looks* 'world-class', then it is most often declared planned; if a settlement *looks* *polluting*, it is sanctioned as unplanned and illegal" (286, emphasis mine). Ironically, the propertied section of the city often indulges in flouting its own famed claims of legality and environmentalism as they are also the prime champion of illegal constructions, such as massive temples, enormous malls, entertainment parks, and luxury housing like farmhouses and high-rise condos (Srivastava "Urban Spaces").

Conversely, the erections in demolished colonies are found to be neither makeshift, nor unhealthy, nor polluting. Social scientists who have studied the evictions, such as Kalyani Menon-Sen and Gautam Bhan in *Swept off the Map*, are consistent in their claims about how efforts were made to concretize and sanitize both the homes and its environments in these *bastis*. Several of the *bricoleurs*, too. mention how some of the houses were *pukka* two-story structures with well-built kitchens and toilets,[9] which are often considered signs of bourgeois status. As an unauthorized settlement that was built entirely without governmental support over a period of more than thirty years, there were buildings here in which generations of a family had invested their savings.

As the foregoing discussion shows, space, as envisioned by the writers of *Trickster City*, is more than just a territorial location. It is part of the larger social and geographical context, such as the neighborhood or the city. At the same time, it is also shaped by the various imaginaries and is simultaneously embedded within a specific set of discourses, such as that of the government, the bourgeois public, and the local. Therefore, one of the key conflicts on urban land use arises from the struggle over whose vision of the city dominates. Amita Baviskar writes about how space in Delhi has been reduced to the singular notion of monetary value that cuts down these multiple connotations:

> treated as a financial commodity, as land that can generate profit for private developers ... Space as a four-dimensional unity—light and air, trees and water, earth and dwellings, fellow beings—has been shrunk to the singular metric of money. (11)

As such, the ideological dimension of space as socially produced, as discussed by Henri Lefebvre, cannot be ignored. (Lefebvre) In Michel de Certeau's reading and revision of Henri Lefebvre's conception, space is also crafted through lived experience and the everyday that renders it into a place.[10] I argue that this broad-based reading of space can constitute a counter-discourse to the macro-narratives and plans of architects, planners, and urban policymakers.

Thus, after the demolitions, as the section "Incognito" shows, it is as if the space which had been excavated from nothingness, had returned to the same facelessness, erasing for the residents much more than just material life. This sense of placelessness and lack of claim is a recurrent motif in many of the pieces. In the context of this past rich life of the community, Suraj Rai, one of the *bricoleurs*, asks, "How is it that there are no sayings about the demolition? A story, or just a line that may express something?" (134). As mentioned earlier, this forcible marginalization and relegation of the *basti*-dwellers to placelessness, ironically, aids the rise of subjectivity as creative *bricoleurs*.

In the case of *bastis*, public memory has not merely been short but entirely uninterested. *Trickster City* highlights this *aporia* and questions the conscience of the bourgeois public, appealing not for pity but for understanding and inclusion within the city imaginary as well as urban planning. Clearly, the difference often lies in whose unauthorized settlement is under scrutiny. Therefore, it seems that the conflict is first and foremost over contested commons in the city and who has a right to the city.

To illustrate, the *bricoleurs* delineate with poetic finesse, choices made in terms of employment or livelihood, sometimes to take up work as a male model in fashion shows, a waiter at lavish parties thrown in the farmhouses of the rich, a phone booth operator in the neighborhood, or a butcher in the Chandni Chowk market. For the protagonists, each choice turns out to be an eye-opening and, often, cruel exposure to the city beyond the *basti*, reinforcing their sense of spatial and social marginalization. For instance, Rai recalls his "first experience of the city"—"Saturn had cast a malefic influence over the handicraft work we do from home. There was no sign of any new assignment. Papa had had to resume working at the *godown*. The doctor had warned him not to." (48). Only fourteen years old, he decides to quit school and take up work as a courier delivery boy who travels the city in his uniform, without which he would never be allowed to enter gated enclaves of the wealthy. These simple sentences encompass the entire nexus of drudgery, backbreaking labor, limited life choices and insecurity, which envelop lives in these areas. Moreover, this is also an insight into the city from those pushed to the peripheries. As the text reminds us, despite these hardships, the family once had some amount of security in the form of a stable living space. What remains unsaid in these accounts, but remains a spectral presence in each narrative, are the constant threats of demolition that become a reality all too often. As discussed already, in the case of the urban poor, loss of homes most often also implies the loss of livelihood, networks of support, and urban commons.

Claiming Right to the City

Apart from countering widely held perceptions about *bastis*, the text also makes substantive claims for the residents as rights-bearing citizens, as stakeholders rather than dependents. However, this claim is activated in a range of ways, not all of which choose to reply to the bourgeois discourse in its own empirical idiom. Instead, the *bricoleurs* claim the city and citizenship based on the experiential, emotive, and affective, as well as the right to cultural and literary representation. David Harvey, who coined the phrase "right to the city," similarly envisages this "right" as a broad-based term that extends not just to physical spaces and facilities, but also "the freedom to make and remake our cities and ourselves" ("Right to the City" 23).

One mode of reclaiming the city is through the narratives themselves. While demolitions, evictions, and resettlement are some of the key themes of the text, they are not the only reality to which this work testifies. Everyday life, lifeworlds, and affective relationship with the space and its people—neighbors and citizens—also come alive. Life, as it was before the demolitions, for these residents had its own rhythms and routines: Ramlila rehearsals, celebration of festivals, how the community opened up to strangers and made them their own, and how some went away never to return. At the same time, there is no attempt to shy away from the gruesome reality of how friends sometimes turn out to be criminals or run away to escape police brutality and torture. Each short account functions as yet another insight into life choices and everyday practice in the *bastis* of Delhi. What the text says is as much a reflection on the rest of city as on the *bastis*. Neelofar writes, "It seems Delhi is distancing itself from the whistle of the pressure cooker, the heat of the stove, the coolness of the earthen pot half buried in sand ... Delhi is becoming an expensive, beautiful, fragile showpiece, which will be picked up and put away carefully somewhere" (184). Thus, the *bricoleurs*, too, reinforce how the bourgeois urban imaginary seems to have become the dominant voice of urban expression whereas the earthy tones of the working class are ignored.

At several junctures in this book, the alleged lack of legality is severely questioned by the authors of *Trickster City* by citing the reams of official documentation and paper trails that families had maintained over generations as proof of their long-term residency. As mentioned in the case of Sunitaji, the most precious belonging is often official documents, "paper boats," as Shamsher Ali writes which were once considered "flimsy" but are now "firm support": "We are not recognised by our faces alone. We are asked to prove our identity ... frisked to ascertain who we are. If this search does not yield our documents, we are labelled 'unknown'" (116). Incidentally, these same documents also make them valuable to politicians as they are a substantial vote bank and might actually earn them a hearing when they petition for resettlement (Srivastava "Duplicity, Intimacy"). The writers are drawing attention to the fact that pieces of paper are often considered far more important than human beings, bonds, and lives.

Further, the writers also prove that they are not parasites that leech on the facilities bourgeois citizens pay for. Several details in the text reflect how self-sufficient communities made great efforts to improve their economic and social situation and outgrow the stigma of being a polluting slum. The descriptions of the everyday practices by the authors reflect how residents invested their hard-earned money to improve their living conditions and acquire the comforts that gave them a semblance of bourgeois life. Similarly, residents who have been given plots in lieu of their demolished houses, are found to have paid for them, just like they queue up to pay and access services such as

subsidized groceries from ration stores, education at government schools, etc.
Lakshmi Kohli writes that alternative support networks are autonomously
built and utilized by the community as a whole, for instance, the community loan system run by an elected committee (mentioned in the foregoing
section), rescue services, and help offered during the frequent fires that had
plagued the area. In fact, as Menon-Sen and Bhan discover, the *basti*-dwellers
often paid more than the due rate in an effort to illegally obtain civic services
offered easily and legally to the bourgeois citizens of Delhi. What this reflects
is the unwillingness and inadequacy on the part of the state to provide services that would allow the *basti*-dwellers to remain in the realm of legality.
Instead, this denial pushes them towards the hazy realm of para-legality and
forces them towards self-help in the form of *jugaad*.[11]

One of the reasons some residents agreed to shift to the new settlements
was due to the promise of legal, permanent residence in the city. However,
as the last section of the book, "Frontiers," testifies, the path to that stability
has proven to be both long and torturous. Families have been separated so
the men can stay on in the city to work and save time and money on the
transport; women have lost their jobs as domestic help due to a shift of
location and, with that, their precious independence, and children have no
schools to go to or lose valuable time in facing the hardships of a new settlement. As Menon-Sen and Bhan found in the resettlement colony of Bawana,
on several indices, the quality of life had worsened as compared to their
status in Yamuna Pushta. Most significantly, it goes against the declared
aims of the Delhi Master Plan 2021 and common sense, because migration
to the city is in the first place primarily related to livelihood (DDA). The
dislocation goes against this logic and re-creates the trials and traumas of
forging a home and livelihood in the city for residents who are already settled.[12] Rakesh Khairalia states in "Construction has Begun," that "Those
lives, which had once before transformed barren terrain by infusing it with
life-force and embellishing it, have now begun to descend on the land of
Ghevra,[13] to once again take on the challenge. Another struggle to give
direction to the wayward lines of time has begun" (277).

Finally, I suggest that in these locales, just as many aspects of life at
the margins and the rest of the city are reflected, inverted, and held up for
scrutiny, similarly, several aspects of the city are also imitated. One such
facet is the rapidly increasing desire for participation within the post-
liberalization consumerist scenario. *Trickster City* presents, how, in the
absence of employment avenues even for the educated, the community
invests in entrepreneurial ventures to generate employment or find work in
NGOs or in lower rungs of the service sector and MNCs. Also reflected in
these acts is the desire of the urban poor for upward mobility, however limited it may be. Joining the service sector is one such move, which evinces the
maximum utilization of their limited education, improving upon the labor
or factory-work background of their earlier generation.

As research by Srivastava in his study of the consumer practices in these *bastis* and similar spaces evinces, this might also take the form of *jugaad*, and participation in quasi-legal and borderline illegal financial schemes ("Revolution Forever"). Thus, the lifestyle created by the bourgeois vision of a world-class city, particularly with liberalization of the economy, is ironically shared by those it systematically marginalizes as undesirable. While research by sociologists like Srivastava provides several case studies of urban outcasts as desiring consumers and globalized citizens, this chapter has emphasized on their participation in the literary sphere of representation, which has now opened up as a result of similar processes.

By Way of Conclusion

To complete this discussion, it is important to comprehend why such a text found a reading public as recently as this millennium whereas demolitions, evictions, and fault resettlement policies have been part of the Indian urban climate for decades now. I contend that this has been possible, ironically, due to globalization. To cite Arjun Appadurai in this regard: "social exclusion is ever more tied to epistemological exclusion and ... the discourses of expertise that are setting the rules for global transactions, even in the progressive parts of the international system, have left ordinary people outside and behind" (2). The operative phrase here is "epistemological exclusion," which implies marginalization from both popular and academic discourses. Further, Appadurai is of the opinion that globalization opens up possibilities for the expression of vernacular discourses and micro-narratives. While I treat his overall optimistic assessment of the cultural facets of globalization with some caution, as it is not sufficiently anchored in an examination of the economic processes, his acknowledgement of the epistemic exclusion of the margins from academia and the literary forum, as well as the wider possibilities provided under global changes, nonetheless, do explain the emergence of a text like *Trickster City*. In other words, trends of globalization that have pushed the bourgeois rhetoric of world-class cities and global citizenship to a fever pitch (of which urban homelessness is a result), have unwittingly facilitated the emergence of counter-tales and micro-narratives. Thus, it is possible that the opposition to globalization could emerge most effectively from within the trend itself. It is within such a revised academic atmosphere that an erstwhile non-literary and non-Anglophone work such as *Trickster City* can be treated with due gravitas as a testimonial of the urban homeless and a product of alternative urbanity.

Noted urban theorist Ananya Roy, comments ironically on globalized cities like Delhi, "Of course, the urban poor have no place in the *good* city" (Roy 272, emphasis mine). However, *Trickster City*, a pioneering text, reflects how, at the discursive level, the urban poor can make their place in the city and intervene in the bourgeois public imaginary of the city. In this way, the urban poor have successfully brought the discussion of marginalized lives, led in spaces that are geographically part of the city but remain peripheral to the public imagination, into the literary and public spheres. Thus, this text is a testimony to the emergence of these urban outcasts as self-representing creative authors, and consequently, more confident, rights-bearing citizens of Delhi, statuses not allowed to them previously.[14]

Notes

1. The word "margins" is employed throughout the chapter to signify a general condition of liminality and deprivation that encompasses the spatial, social, economic, but, most significantly, the cultural and epistemological.
2. The Hindi word *basti* literally translates as "settlement" and, even though it could be used as an equivalent of the pejorative "slum," intrinsically it carries no such derogatory connotation. Kalyani Menon-Sen and Gautam Bhan in their research in one such resettlement colony of Bawana highlight the misconceptions generated by the pejorative connotations of the term slum, which reduce the residents "to a faceless mass of people who apparently have nothing in common with 'respectable citizens'"(3). Instead, they advise the use of the Hindustani term *basti*, which simply indicates a settlement.
3. *Pushta*, a Hindi word, means embankment. These settlements were spread on the banks of the Yamuna and, hence, led to the name.
4. The preparations for the CWG, as is often the case during such international extravaganzas, were used as an opportunity by the government to execute massive projects of urban renewal and infrastructure change to the cityscape, such as the building of stadia, housing facilities, roads, flyovers, and the beautification of the riverfront, among other changes. Both in rhetoric and scale, these reforms were reminiscent of the Haussmannian makeover of Paris, led to similar consequences, such as large-scale displacements of the urban poor living in unauthorized settlements. Baron Haussmann, the nineteenth-century architect, is responsible for the restructuring of medieval parts of central Paris, which stand to this day. To usher in modernity, he demolished much of the overcrowded parts and, allegedly, unsanitary parts of the city. However, these parts were also the hotbed of revolutionary fervor and demolishing them would be instrumental in controlling dissent. See Sennett for details (329–47).
5. From the Greek *hetero* or many and *topos* that translates as space.
6. Rashmi Sadana elaborates on the contention between Hindi and English, their various publishing houses, readership, cultures, and public spheres in her monograph *English Heart: Hindi Heartland*.
7. In fact, several other recent works in this genre may lend some credence to this argument. Pulitzer-prize winning author, Katherine Boo's important work on the Annawadi slum in Mumbai, *Behind the Beautiful Forevers: Life, Death and Hope in a Mumbai Undercity* (which won the National Book Award for Best Non-Fiction in 2012) is another such example.
8. Sociologist, Sanjay Srivastava, in his ethnographic work on these unauthorized colonies, finds that residents of urban *bastis* in Delhi also have been integrated into some aspects of the globalized network due to the neoliberal pattern of development followed by the state. As such, through their efforts to gain official identification and documentation—legally or extra-legally—and participation

in quasi-legal economic opportunities such as chit-funds, and pyramid or Ponzi schemes, *basti*-dwellers attempt to access legality and financial stability ("Duplicity, Intimacy").

9. *Pukka* is a Hindi word that means concrete.

10. In *The Practices of Everyday Life*, Michel de Certeau focuses on a socio-geographical approach, similar to that of Lefebvre. De Certeau opens up a new vista of reading the urban by observing and analyzing the micro-signatures left by individuals who map the city through their seemingly banal, routine, every-day practices. What I am proposing here is a dual technique of reading Lefebvre and De Certeau in a dialectical mode. On the one hand, a challenge to the macro-concept of socially and ideologically produced space is evinced in *Trickster City* and, on the other, we notice individual everyday practices in these spaces which to an extent, are able to leave their own tiny footprints on city spaces.

11. *Jugaad* is a Hindi word, which, in this context, implies informal arrangements, but also connotes an entire range of maneuvers that can be mutually forged between the state and the citizens within the realm of para-legality.

12. Among thousands who were displaced, only 6000 families were "resettled" on the outskirts of the city in areas like Madanpur Khadar, Bawana, and Savda-Ghevra (Menon-Sen and Bhan 2).

13. Ghevra is one of the resettlement colonies n the outskirts of Delhi.

14. I would like to thank the editors of this volume for their support, and Tavi Steinhardt, who patiently read and commented on several drafts of this chapter.

Works Cited

Appadurai, Arjun. "Disjuncture and Difference in the Global Cultural Economy." *Public Culture* 2.2 (1990): 1–24. Print.

———. "Grassroots Globalization and the Research Imagination." *Public Culture* 12.1 (2000): 1–19. Print.

Batra, Lalit. "Out of Sight, Out of Mind: Slum Dwellers in 'World-Class Delhi." *Finding Delhi: Loss and Renewal in the Megacity*. Ed. Bharati Chaturvedi. New Delhi: Penguin Books, 2012. 16–36. Print.

Baviskar, Amita. "Public Spaces and the Poor in Delhi." *Finding Delhi: Loss and Renewal in the Megacity*. Ed. Bharati Chaturvedi. New Delhi: Penguin Books, 2012. 3–15. Print.

Bohman, James and Rehg, William. "Jürgen Habermas." *The Stanford Encyclopedia of Philosophy*. Ed. Edward N. Zalta. Winter 2011 ed. 2011. Web. June 8, 2013. <http://plato.stanford.edu/archives/win2011/entries/habermas/>.

Chatterjee, Partha. *The Politics of the Governed*. Columbia UP, 2004. Print.

Dasgupta, Rana. *Capital: Portrait of Twenty-first Century Delhi*. Delhi: Penguin, 2013. Print.

Deb, Siddhartha. *The Beautiful and the Damned: Life in New India*. New Delhi: Penguin, 2010. Print.

De Certeau, Michel. *The Practice of Everyday Life*. Berkeley: U of California P, 1984.

Delhi Development Authority (DDA). "Introduction." *Delhi Master Plan-2021*. No date. Web. May 10, 2013. <http://dda.org.in/planning/draft_master_plans.htm>.

Derrida, Jacques. "Sign, Structure and Play." *Writing and Difference*. Trans. Alan Bass. London and New York: Routledge, 2005. 351–70. Print.

Eade, John and Christopher Mele. "Introduction." *Understanding the City: Contemporary and Future Perspectives*. Eds. John Eade and Christopher Mele. Oxford: Blackwell Publishers, 2002. 1–25. Print.

Foucault, Michel. "Of Other Spaces: Utopias and Heterotopias." Trans. Jay Miskowiec. *Architecture/Mouvement/Continuité*. October (1984). 1–9. Print.

Ghertner, Asher. "Rule by Aesthetics: World-Class City Making in Delhi." *Worlding Cities: Asian Experiments and the Art of Being Global*. Eds. Ananya Roy and Aihwa Ong. Wiley-Blackwell, 2011. 279–306. Print.

Harvey, David. "The Right to the City." *New Left Review* 53. September–October (2008): 23–53. Web. November 20, 2011.

———. "The Postcolonial Critique of Liberal Cosmopolitanism." *Cosmopolitanism and the Geographies of Freedom*. New York: Columbia UP, 2009. 37–50. Print.

Lefebvre, Henry. "Social Space." *The Production of Space*. Trans. Donald Smith-Nicolson. Blackwell, 1974. 68–168. Print.

Menon-Sen, Kalyani and Gautam Bhan. *Swept Off the Map: Surviving Eviction and Resettlement in Delhi*. New Delhi: Yoda P, 2008. Print.

Roy, Ananya. 2011. "The Blockade of the World-Class City: Dialectical Images of Indian Urbanism." *Worlding Cities: Asian Experiments and the Art of Being Global*. Eds. Ananya Roy and Aihwa Ong. Wiley-Blackwell, 2011. 259–79. Print.

Sadana, Rashmi. *English Heart: Hindi Heartland*. Berkeley: U of California P, 2012. Print.

Sennett, Richard. *Flesh and Stone: The Body and City in Western Civilization*. London: W.W. Norton, 1994. Print.

Sethi, Aman. *A Free Man*. New Delhi: Random House, 2010. Print.

Spivak, Gayatri Chakravorty. "Can the Subaltern Speak?" *Marxism and the Interpretation of Culture*. Eds. Cary Nelson and Lawrence Grossberg. London: Macmillan, 1988. 260–313. Print.

———. "New Subaltern: A Silent Interview." *Mapping Subaltern Studies and the Postcolonial*. Ed. Vinayak Chaturvedi. London: Verso, 2012. 324–40. Print.

Srivastava, Sanjay. 2009. "Urban Spaces, Disney-Divinity and Moral Middle Classes in Delhi." *Economic and Political Weekly* 44. 26 (2009): 338–45. Print.

———. "Revolution Forever: Consumerism and Object Lessons for the Urban Poor." *Contributions to Indian Sociology* 44. 1–2 (2010): 103–28. Print.

———. "Duplicity, Intimacy, Community: An Ethnography of ID Cards, Permits and Other Fake Documents in Delhi." *Thesis* (2012): 1–16. Print.

Tabassum, Azra, et al. *Bahurupiya Shahar*. New Delhi: Rajkamal, 2005. Print.

———. *Trickster City: Writings from the Belly of the Metropolis*. Trans. Sweta Sarda. New Delhi: Penguin, 2009. Print.

Varughese, E. Dawson. *Reading New India: Post-Millennial Indian Fiction in English*. New Delhi: Bloomsbury, 2013. Print.

Part IV

Forms of Urban Outcasting

12 Carl Muller's Palimpsestic Urban Elegy in *Colombo: A Novel*

Maryse Jayasuriya

Colombo. The capital. Seat of government; of commerce. It was capital to the British and the administrative seat of the Portuguese and Dutch. On the map it lies 7°N, 79°48'E. The British guarded it with some three hundred pieces of heavy cannon. Its Fort rang to the drunken revelry of the Dutch. It was fed by slaves and rose on the black backs and shoulders of the natives.
—Carl Muller, *Colombo* 7

Obviously there isn't a single Colombo, just as there isn't a single any city in the world I guess.
—Romesh Gunesekera "Sense of the City: Colombo"

Colombo is Sri Lanka's most populous, most diverse, and most politically, culturally, and economically influential city. It owes its preeminence in no small part to its development under the Portuguese, Dutch, and British colonizers of Sri Lanka into a colonial capital and a site through which transnational capital flowed during the colonial era and continues to flow now. Carl Muller, one of Sri Lanka's most prolific post-independence Anglophone novelists, has devoted much of his career to exploring the complicated colonial legacy of Sri Lanka, particularly by exploring the history of the Burghers (Sri Lankan Eurasians of Dutch and Portuguese descent) before and after independence. In one of his more unusual works, *Colombo: A Novel*, Muller presses against generic, temporal, and political boundaries in order to explore the persistence of violence, inequality, exploitation, and exclusion in Sri Lanka's commercial capital during the second half of the twentieth century.

Colombo: A Novel proclaims its commitment to the novelistic genre in its title, but most of the text seems to resist this claim: the book is largely nonfiction, and it moves among fictionalized vignettes meant to represent some of the most painful realities of life in the city, straightforward reportage, and editorial denunciation as it narrates the city's history and its late twentieth century present in a voice at once elegiac and wrathful. Muller thus structures his novel in a way that is palimpsestic both in its form and in its subject matter: the narrative shifts among various moments in the distant and recent past, and Muller shows that the violence and exploitation of colonialism resurfaces in the 1980s and 1990s in the long-running conflict between the Sri Lankan state and Tamil separatists, in the brutal war between the Janatha Vimukthi Peramuna (JVP) insurrectionists and the government death squads seeking to suppress them, in the patterns of sexual violence against women and children that are at least in part enabled by the inequalities between the upper and lower classes in Colombo and between Sri Lankan nationals and foreign tourists, and in the economic exploitation of internal migrants who come to the city seeking a living. Colombo, then, is represented as a location marked in multiple ways by violent exclusionary practices.

Muller makes these links evident at the outset, when he discusses Slave Island, which was once the place where the slaves of Portuguese and Dutch colonizers were quartered and is now one of the bustling commercial areas in Colombo. As the narrator reflects through Anton, the protagonist of the book's opening vignette, slavery appears to be only notionally a thing of the past for an internal economic migrant: Anton is on the ground level of Colombo society and surrounded by various forms of violence, exploitation, and exclusion. This initial reflection becomes an overture to the entire book, which condemns the crimes that disfigure the city while Muller's narration oscillates between the past and the present, documenting and mourning cycles of colonial and neocolonial violence. At the same time, Muller's laudable goals are tempered by the association of his work, here and elsewhere, with Sri Lanka's English-speaking elite, and by an impulse towards nostalgia for the colonial Colombo of his youth. In this way, Muller's work becomes symptomatic of central tensions within the broader representation of South Asian, postcolonial cities, thereby perhaps participating in—albeit in limited ways—the same kinds of exclusions he attempts to expose.

Muller's own positioning relative to Colombo's palimpsestic history is complex: he is a Burgher, the descendant of the Portuguese and Dutch who settled in Sri Lanka. Having worked as a navy signalman and as a reporter, he gained fame initially for his trilogy of novels about the Burghers in Sri Lanka (starting with *The Jam Fruit Tree* and followed by *Yakada Yaka* and *Once Upon a Tender Time*), for which he received the Gratiaen Prize.[1] It might seem surprising for the author of the rollicking, irreverent, bawdy and humorous set of novels about the Von Bloss family to have written the bleak and wrathful *Colombo*. But, as Minoli Salgado has asserted, Muller's entire oeuvre "repeatedly transgresses the boundaries of fact, fiction, and myth, personal and public history, employing in his Burgher trilogy, a mongrelized Sri Lankan English idiom that is explicitly related to his own hybrid status as a Burgher of mixed ancestry" (90). Salgado identifies in Muller's work a "double-codedness"—a "paradoxical melding of carnivalesque linguistic subversion and ideological conservatism" (90). This "double-codedness" appears in *Colombo* as in the Burgher trilogy, but the effect is significantly grimmer than that which he achieves in his earlier novels. Ultimately, *Colombo* is an expression of barely controlled fury and condemnation, in contrast to the gentler nostalgia of his earlier works.[2]

A Novel? Muller's Urban Form

The paradoxes of the postcolonial South Asian city insinuate themselves even into the ambiguous form of Muller's work. The title of *Colombo: A Novel* can seem misleading, or even perverse, once a reader is immersed in the text. There is no clear plot line, and the organization seems to be shaped more by the irregular topography and complicated history of Colombo than any overarching narrative structure. In certain ways, the book is reminiscent of Charles Dickens's descriptions of the dark underbelly of nineteenth-century London and his critiques of social ills in novels such as *Oliver Twist* and *Great Expectations*, or *Sketches by Boz* in its vignettes of various individuals, events, establishments and institutions in the metropolis. Unlike Dickens, Muller does not use any lighthearted humor—only bitter irony. He finds nothing to laugh about in the city's present incarnation, but he finds a great deal to criticize and lament, often in a mode that mixes bitterness with nostalgia.

Colombo's predominant focus on the sex, violence and corruption in a South Asian metropolis—and its undercity—makes a comparison to Suketu Mehta's depiction of Bombay in *Maximum City* or Katherine Boo's account of life in the Annawadi slums of Mumbai in *Behind the Beautiful Forevers* irresistible. Unlike the narrative nonfiction of Mehta and Boo, Muller's accounts are not based on extensive investigative reporting or interviews and interactions with the subjects; instead, he has created composite characters in plausible scenarios using archival research, observations, and imagination. This book could be called faction, instead of nonfiction, which, as Christopher Anyokwu puts it, is "a trend which tends to collapse fact into fiction, and, sometimes, vice versa. [...] an act of combining historical truth with 'poetic' or imaginative truth. By so doing, the ensuing or resultant art work benefits from the historical documentation of lived (and/or felt) experience as well as the imaginative freedom of pure fiction" (187).

Muller attempts to explain and justify this use of "faction" in his "Author's Note" at the beginning of the text. He acknowledges that

> While all historical, literary and journalistic references in this book are true and diligently accounted for, all incidents, characters and characterizations herein are fictitious and have no similarity whatsoever to persons living or dead. I have to state, however, that the episodal contents of this book have been narrated in support of the specific themes contained, and are based on real-term approximations to the typical city scenario of Colombo's nights. These are penned to draw attention primarily to the immensity of the many problems that would beset any crowded Asian city. I make no apology for the dark pictures I have painted since they have been deliberately included to underscore the way in which so many thousands would survive in a city that is quite implacable in demeanour and quite unable to offer any real show of hospitality. (ix)

Having dedicated his book "to the people of Colombo—the ordinary people with all their difficulties and the problems of day-to-day living," the author seems to anthropomorphize the city itself as the root of the problem here instead of specific socio-economic and political factors. In this disclaimer, Muller insists that he is not attempting "to speak for the whole of Sri Lanka, even for the whole of Colombo. I am a Sri Lankan and the land of my birth is very dear to me. As a country—and with Colombo as its capital—it has its share of virtues and diversities, the pepper as well as the salt" (ix). Although he talks about the city's "virtues and diversities," Muller—unlike Mehta in *Maximum City*— primarily focuses on the city as a nightmare, without the seductive capacity to draw outsiders in with hopes of a better, more success-ful or glamorous life. Acknowledging that he is writing an exposé of sorts, Muller claims that his goal is "not to defame but to use the tool of brutal honesty" to bring Colombo's "sins" to light (x)—perhaps anticipating cri-tiques like that of D. C. R. A. Goonetilleke, who has said that Muller is "like a crypto-colonialist" because he "demonizes the Sinhalese" and "run[s] down Colombo" in this text (276). At the end of the book, Muller includes a bibliography, a final chapter of so-called "props and crutches" on which he has leaned in order to relate Colombo's five-hundred-year-old history while admitting unapologetically to having been "opinionated" in his depiction of the current condition of the city.

Muller's approach in this book brings to mind Michel de Certeau's dedication of *The Practice of Everyday Life* to "ordinary people" and also de Certeau's emphasis in his seminal essay "Walking in the City" on seeing the city at the ground level, in all its diversity, rather than from a privileged and unified perspective. Muller likewise dedicates his book to ordinary people and seeks to tell the stories of those who are among the poor and lower-middle class. Muller's relation to de Certeau's approach is compli-cated, however, by the persistent strand of colonial nostalgia that crops up throughout *Colombo* indicating the writer's status as part of the Burgher elite, who benefited under British rule.

On the one hand, the fact that Muller writes for an Anglophone audience means that the "ordinary people" who are fluent in Sinhala or Tamil but not in English may be outside his audience.[3] Language issues have had significant political implications in Sri Lanka. The Sinhala-Only language reforms of 1956—ostensibly a post-independence attempt at decolonization but actu-ally a chauvinistic act meant to pander to the Sinhala-speaking majority that disenfranchised the Tamil-speaking minority—contributed substantially to the country's ethnic conflict. In addition, the English language continues to function as a marker of class privilege and has frequently been referred to colloquially by the Sinhala word "kaduwa"—literally, the sword, which divides the Westernized, culturally elite class, fluent in English, from every-one else in the country and "cuts down" anyone from the lower classes who aspires to economic and social advancement. Thus, language is a crucial issue for anyone writing in contemporary Sri Lanka, as Tamil-speakers have been marginalized in the postcolonial era by Sinhala speakers, and both Sinhala and Tamil speakers have suffered from lost opportunities in both the colonial and postcolonial eras if they lack a firm command of the English language. On the other hand, it is also important to note (as I do in my 2012 study *Terror and Reconciliation: Sri Lankan Anglophone Literature, 1983–2009*) that Anglophone fiction has much potential: English is the link language between speakers of Sinhala and Tamil, and there is a deep desire among Sri Lankans to learn or become more fluent in English.

The topography and history of the city contribute to the often erratic form of the text. Colombo, a city built by colonizers, is not well-planned, having evolved and sprawled over time, and the book mimics that sprawling lack of structure in its meandering. It begins with people who live in the city—lovers taking paltry refuge under an umbrella on Galle Face Green for their amorous encounters because no other, more private, space is available to them, a rapist stalking his prey, beggars using and abusing whatever—or whomever—they can to survive, hired assassins and paramilitary forces carrying out commissioned atrocities—but juxtaposes each of these vignettes with forays into colonial history and sociological studies about Colombo. A chapter describing the battles between the Portuguese and the Dutch to seize control of Colombo in the seventeenth century, for example, is followed by a chapter detailing the brutalities and trauma of the anti-Tamil pogrom of 1983 and the abduction by the police of a schoolboy who has participated in protests against the government during the second JVP insurrection of the late 1980s and early 1990s. Even within the same chapter, a broad theme is explored from different and somewhat surprising angles. In one chapter entitled "Fishers All," for instance, Muller juxtaposes the diurnal routine of poor people living around the polluted Beira Lake—once "Colombo's most scenic watermark" (324)—and eking out a living by fishing in the green and scummy waters with the endeavors of Portuguese, Dutch, and British missionaries who flocked to the city in the past to convert "the heathen" to Christianity. Another chapter entitled "Target—Colombo" contrasts an account of a Sinhalese king aiming to win back Colombo in 1563 from the Portuguese colonizers, with descriptions of the LTTE targeting the city using suicide bombers during the ethnic conflict that would last from 1983–2009.

Colombo is postmodern in the generic diversity of what it includes—from poems penned by Muller on the main focus of each chapter and the fictional figures that populate each vignette to news reports, historical accounts, travel writing about Colombo,[4] sociological analyses, and human rights reports. Muller has also compiled lists calculated to evoke outrage at privileges given to those already in possession of power in both the colonial and post-independence eras, such as the allowances and benefits provided to Members of Parliament in present-day Sri Lanka (373–81) and the Crown lands that were parceled out and allotted tax-free to British companies by the colonial regime between 1836 and 1841 "that made them owners of chunks of the city and its environs" (456–8).

A hidden source of Muller's form might be the numerous newspapers that are printed and disseminated in Colombo, which both provide a major source of material—sometimes seemingly undigested—for Muller's use, and resemble the chaotic slippage among genre conventions that often appears in Muller's work. Today's Sri Lankan English-language newspapers (for example, *The Daily Mirror*, *The Sunday Times* and *The Sunday Leader*) are very heterogeneous in nature, a vibrant mix of news reports, human-interest pieces, satiric columns, and letters to the editor, all of which seem to be mirrored in the pastiche that is Muller's book. By making use of journalistic form, Muller brings the text closer to the ordinary people to whom he dedicates it.

In one of the few consistent structural modes of the novel, Muller traces the violence that has happened in the city from the time it was founded—successive waves of colonial violence contrasted with the violence happening in the present of the text as a result of the ethnic conflict, the JVP insurrection, etc. He reflects, "The violence continues. It is asked, even casually, is this Colombo's inheritance? The city has seen immense blood-letting, monstrous battles, sieges, starvation, bomb attacks, massacres. It has stood witness to military and political treason, weathered the ruinous policies of political parties, stood in bread lines, rice lines and infant milk lines" (372). The emphasis on violence contributes substantially to the palimpsestic effect of the novel, but it also risks presenting a wholly negative "urban imaginary" (Edensor and Jayne 24): violence can appear like an essential part of Colombo's identity, rather than a contingent series of occurrences related to specific causes. This oversight becomes particularly pronounced, as we shall see, in Muller's treatment of the respective struggles of the JVP and the Liberation Tigers of Tamil Eelam (LTTE) against the government, because Muller does not do much to anatomize the sources of the conflicts.

Another consistent structural element is how Muller presents Colombo as a testament to exploitation—from the colonial era when the city "rose on the black backs and shoulders of the natives" (7) to the neocolonial present. As we shall see below, Muller identifies two sets of urban outcasts in Colombo. His main concern is the wretched, the impoverished, and the exploited masses, the economic outcasts who struggle to survive and who are frequently the victims of exploitation, both financial and sexual. He is also roused to pity by all who are affected by the violence between the state and its enemies and thus become outcasts within their own city as a result of the violence they can neither predict nor control. Although the unpredictability of political violence affects all classes, the poor are more likely to be victims of criminal violence, which further contributes to their status as outcasts.

The Postcolonial Metropolis: Raging Against "Colombo Nights"

Muller spends a substantial portion of the book critiquing the inequalities of Colombo's urban milieu and exposing the reality behind the image of

Sri Lanka as "a taste of paradise" (which was, in fact, the slogan of Sri Lanka's national airline at the time *Colombo* was written). Central to his critique of inequality is his decision to focus much of the book on scenarios involving urban outcasts—those who are excluded and marginalized because of poverty, social status, age, gender, or some combination of the above in Colombo. Muller highlights what he sees as the city's current degeneration, where "over sixty percent of Colombo's population still resides in tenements, slums, shacks and other plaguey dwellings which are both social and moral disasters" (451). He rages against political corruption and institutional indifference, uneven development and poorly thought-out and haphazard attempts at modernization, resulting in the ever-widening gap between the rich and the poor. He traces the way in which the poor have become so desperate that they will do anything to survive: parents feel compelled to sell or give away their children to prostitution or domestic slavery in middle-class homes where young children will be exploited and sexually abused. Beggars will maim their own family members to earn a few extra rupees.

Muller first provides the statistics: "Records reveal over 165,000 rapes and attempted rapes and over 120,000 cases of child abuse, where the average age of victims are [sic] a little over nine years" (19), and "child trafficking and child prostitution have become serious issues here. It is estimated that 500,000 children are in employment, many as domestic aids" (136). The numbers are followed by a series of episodes that humanize the reports in the most heart-rending way: Nelum is a little girl who runs away when she realizes that her poverty-stricken parents are considering selling her, only to be caught by a stranger who sells her to a brothel (138–41). Later, Nelum is hired out to two foreigners and two days afterwards, her "raped, battered body" is found in a canal (148). Jaya, a thirteen-year old boy who labors all day in a bicycle repair shop, finds that he is able to eke out more money by providing sexual services to local and foreign men (141–4). Lakshmi, another little girl whose mother is dead and who has been taking care of her younger siblings, steps in front of an oncoming vehicle in order to provide some relief to her father by reducing the number of mouths he has to feed (149–52). Eleven-year old Somalatha is promised an education and brought to live in Colombo by a middle-class family but then exploited as a domestic aid and raped by her employers' son (62–3). Boo, in her sustained narrative of the daily tribulations of slum children in Mumbai, gives a poignant first-person account of what she has witnessed; Muller's third-person omniscient factional accounts throw brief but brutal light on the abuse of the underprivileged.

Muller emphasizes that the poor and exploited cannot rely on assistance from public institutions. These institutions, as Muller depicts them, have become so corrupt and indifferent that there is no refuge to be found, whether in law enforcement or the justice system. Politicians hatch conspiracies to fan the flames of ethnic or religious or class hatred in order to ensure riots and pogroms that will enable them to extend the Emergency Law and the limits of their authority and immunity.

The corruption that Muller condemns also pervades the city's relationship to the wider world in Colombo's capacity as the center of government and commerce. The change in Sri Lanka from a state-regulated economy to an open economy in the late 1970s resulted in an influx of foreign investment in private enterprise, which made a small number of individuals extremely wealthy without necessarily benefiting the masses. Attempts at promoting Sri Lanka as a tourist paradise brought all types of foreign interests engaged in, among other things, the trafficking of young children to pedophiles and the smuggling in and selling of narcotics. In considering these matters, Muller touches on the neocolonial aspects of Colombo's urban crisis.

Exclusion and Violence in Postcolonial Colombo: The 1983 Riots, the JVP Insurrection, and the Neo-Colonial Metropolis

Kumari Jayawardena traces the rise of ethnic chauvinism in Sri Lanka to socio-economic factors relating to different groups having to compete for scarce resources; thus ethnic riots become "an expression of the economic and social discontent and frustrations of deprived sections of populations, fanned by propaganda arousing religious or ethnic animosity" (112). As Jayawardena's remarks suggest, the large-scale violence shaped by ethnic and class conflict is thus influenced by the same neocolonial socio-economic context that provides the backdrop for the criminality that Muller catalogues. Violence can provide a sense of agency to those who have been excluded, oppressed or outcast; it can also cause alienation and exclusion.

A major concern for Muller is the way in which outcasts are created in the city as a result of the waves of violence associated with the ethnic conflict and the JVP insurrection. Muller— writing before 9/11 and the era in which North American and Western European cities have become terrorist targets—emphasizes the daily uncertainties, frequent atrocities and resulting anxieties of people living in a city that is a constant target for attacks and counterattacks by perpetrators who are seldom held accountable:

> But war goes on today as it always did. The battles are more brutish. They come on bicycles and motorcycles. Their visors are tinted and there is death in their hands. Ministers, an admiral, even the President of the country, have died. Handbombs, grenades, timed explosives, machine pistols ... it is a thing of social and political expediency: to kill any man who stands in the way. (17)

The references here are to the assassinations in Colombo of political leaders like ministers Gamini Dissanayake and Lalith Athulathmudali, and President Ranasinghe Premadasa by the LTTE in the early 1990s. Suicide bombings in crowded areas of Colombo killed not only public figures such as those mentioned above, but also countless civilians. Survivors were left to cope with physical injuries and trauma while specific buildings and locations were either razed to the ground or marked by devastation.

The July 1983 riots that heralded the beginning of the ethnic conflict have formed an important feature of Sri Lankan Anglophone literature about the conflict and the violence and terror that have surrounded it. Among others, Shyam Selvadurai in *Funny Boy* and Jean Arasanayagam in *Apocalypse '83*, describe the atrocities from the perspective of the Tamil victims; Muller, however, in his vignette on the events of July 1983, focuses on the mixed reactions of the Sinhalese to the pogrom and the way in which they either continue to victimize, attempt to help, or ignore the Tamils: Agnes and Simon, a Sinhalese couple, give shelter to Mr. and Mrs. Rasa, their Tamil neighbors, whose house has been set on fire by Sinhalese mobs. Even as Agnes attempts to make her neighbors comfortable, she seethes with resentment at having to put herself and her family at risk for this importunate couple (177–82). Meanwhile, Palis, a Sinhalese man who set fire to a Tamil neighbor's house, finds that his own adjoining house has gone up in flames as a result and, ironically, feels victimized. Dr. Wimal, a Sinhalese doctor at a Colombo hospital, ignores the protests of Swarna, a bigoted Sinhalese nurse, and donates his own blood to save Thurai, a Tamil man severely injured in the pogrom, only to find that the latter dies from his wounds (183–5). This means that the urban subject that Muller portrays, when not Anglophone and elite, is typically Sinhalese and majoritarian, obscuring the fact that Colombo is a multiethnic, multi-religious city, and that in parts of the city like Wellawatte, for example, people of Tamil language and ethnicity form a substantial portion of the population. The events of July 1983 are followed by the long-running conflict between the Sri Lankan government and Tamil guerrillas: "Colombo's nights are long and uneasy. The war, spawned by massive ethnic misunderstandings and misapprehensions, has been waged unceasingly for over a score of years" (192). A reader might wish for more explication of the "ethnic misunderstandings and misapprehensions" Muller identifies.

The book deals with yet more uneasy nights in Colombo with its accounts of the second JVP insurrection. The Marxist-leaning, nationalistic insurgents carried out violent acts and assassinations against politicians and others they deemed to be "traitors" acting against Sri Lankan sovereignty. In retaliation, paramilitary forces of the government struck down anyone remotely associated, or suspected of associating, with the JVP, as well as those who sheltered them. Muller points out that

> War was a more straightforward business in the sixteenth century. But Colombo, today, walks a tightrope. There is an immediate and invisible threat to life which makes the city a nervous and dangerous

place. For the LTTE, and, at one time, the JVP as well as the killers who operated out of the shadows, threats against life and property are the means and the end. Vendettas are always savage. The erosion of respect for life is alarming. (258)

Muller is deeply sympathetic towards the people who are caught between the government, the JVP, and the paramilitary groups. In one episode, Sherriff, a Muslim man, and his twelve-year old son Hilmy, in the course of organizing an almsgiving at the local mosque, are in a bus that literally gets caught in the crossfire between government troops and the JVP, and the young boy is killed (193–5). In other episodes, people are scared into silence by the violence coming from all sides. When a couple living in the affluent area of Bambalapitiya hear shots outside their home in the middle of the night, they stay indoors and pretend not to hear anything for the sake of their own protection. The next morning they see the corpses of three young men and refuse to call the authorities—who, they suspect, might well be the perpetrators—or get involved in any way (106–9). Fear psychosis has settled in, and people tell each other: "Go home and lock the doors and be quiet," and "You don't go to ask questions" (108–9). An unsuspecting elderly woman, Mrs. Rosa, rents a room to a youth she believes is merely a young university student. The young man is later found dead and she herself is killed for giving aid to someone suspected of being a member of the JVP. Muller reflects, "What is never really dealt with is the peculiar position a city such as Colombo is in. Violence is met by the imposition of an Emergency Law. Then, a covert violence, infinitely worse, is unleashed" (372). The "covert violence" here refers to the paramilitary death squads that the state employed to crush the JVP. Through each of the above episodes, Muller highlights the traumatic effects of the violence between the state and its antagonists on non-combatants who are caught, all too often literally, in the cross-fire.

It is noteworthy that Muller does not comment much on the causes for either the ethnic conflict (the discrimination meted out to the Tamil minority in the post-Independence era, as S. J. Tambiah, A. Jeyaratnam Wilson and others have argued) or for the JVP insurrection (originally the class disparity that led university-educated youth to attempt a violent overthrow of the status quo in 1971 and then resistance to the Indo-Lankan Peace Accord and the presence on the island of the Indian Peace-Keeping Force [IPKF] in 1987, as Rajan Hoole, Asoka Bandarage and others have delineated).

Colonial Colombo: Waves of Conquest, Waves of Nostalgia

Much of Muller's tendency to simplify the violence in Colombo has to do with the urban nostalgia that pervades the work. There is a lot of yearning, but it is for the Colombo—leafy, green, salubrious, colonial—of Muller's childhood. Beyond this, there is nostalgia for an imaginary urban space of Muller's creation, which seems to be inevitably situated in the colonial past.

Like R. L. Brohier, an earlier Burgher writer and historian whom he quotes, Muller bemoans the way in which a modern city has come into being: "the concrete jungle which has taken up the body of old Colombo, shaken out its soul and cast aside its skin" (120). He contrasts this modern "jungle" with the colonial past when "centuries ago, the Portuguese were the first builders of the modern house in this country. And then the Dutch and the British ... and now the people who, like twenty-first-century magpies, forage quickly, nervously, to make nests of every modern scrap they can find" (120–1).

Muller reinforces this sense of the city as a lost paradise:

> It was a small, green city then. Then? When? Oh, about a hundred years ago, when life was so neat and leisured and there weren't the spectres of over-population, over-crowding, social dislocation, all the ills of today which sit like big black crows on our defeated shoulders. (207)

He goes on to say,

> It was so easy to see Colombo in the old days—day or night. Many of the fine sturdy Dutch buildings in Chatham Street have disappeared, and many of the other quaint old shops, usually limited to one floor, have also given way to the strident clamourings of modernity. (213)

If Colombo, as the author claims, was a garden city in some prelapsarian time, he implies that it has had its fall—it is no longer an Eden or a Paradise. "Colombo's soaring skyline represents, above all, a city on the make—a new Asian Babylon, sordid, greedy, lecherous, unbelievably corrupt. Here, high-rise and low life are synonymous" (121). At times, the nostalgia seems to function on the level of naming:

> The Victoria Park is today the Vihara Maha Devi Park. There was a bandstand, promenade, golf links, tennis courts, a circular carriage drive and a galloping course for riders then. Today it is a den of thieves, perverts, vagrants and prostitutes. (218)

A troubling dimension of this nostalgia is the degree to which Muller's lost paradise is a colonial, Europeanized city (that can contain a park named in honor of Queen Victoria), and the fallen present of Colombo is the Asian city it has become during decolonization (where "Victoria Park" becomes a park named for the mother of Dutugamunu, a Sri Lankan warrior king).

The writer seems to mourn the lack of knowledge about Colombo's historic past among the city's current inhabitants, who wander the streets

with little to no comprehension of significant historical sites. In the very
first chapter, the writer bemoans the fact that Anton—who has a rendez-
vous with his girlfriend Kusum every evening on Galle Face Green—has
no inkling of the role this expanse of land played in the colonial games of
the past:

> How would Anton know that he had just left *la plaine de Galle*
> where, close to where he had sat, fondling his beloved, M. Duperon,
> second engineer with the Dutch forces had, in 1795, mounted four
> eighteen-pounders. There was a defensive barrier then, as the Dutch
> prepared to meet the onslaught of the British. (6)

Muller's invocation of Colombo's history here is valuable, as it suggests
the ways in which Colombo's past shapes its present; its value is somewhat
vitiated by the fact that he does not make the next, necessary imaginative
leap of showing what M. Duperon's eighteen-pounders mean to Anton and
Kusum by fully connecting that history with the present in which the latter
are living.

Attending to topography as well as history, Muller writes of Colombo
in ways that enable the reader to actually follow the layout of the city,
mentioning specific roads and how they intersect and which noteworthy
buildings or sites can be found there. He even specifies where certain well-
known individuals have their private residences—for example, "Sir Arthur
Clark lives here now—in Barnes Place" and "In Rosmead Place is the official
city residence of the Bandaranaikes" (218). The different areas of Colombo
are described and accounted for—Slave Island; Cinnamon Gardens; Fort;
Pettah; Borella; Maradana. Part of Muller's lament for the earlier leafy city
is framed in terms of the expansion of the city itself:

> Colombo today is about ninety times as densely crowded as the rest
> of the island. It has also expanded. From an area of 9.45 square miles
> in 1881, it became 14.32 square miles in 1963. Today we consider
> what is known as the Greater Colombo Area which encompasses up
> to thirty-eight square miles. (448)

In one of the more troubling dimensions of Muller's critique of present-day
Colombo and his lament for the Colombo of his youth, Muller seems to
understand the expanding population—the presence of ordinary people
within the city to whom he dedicated the book—as part of the change he
regrets.

While Muller goes back and forth from colonial Colombo to the modern
metropolis, he keeps returning to the Portuguese, the Dutch and the British
Colombo, perhaps because Sri Lanka's commercial capital would not have
existed if not for its colonial past; thus, he is attempting to challenge the idea

that Colombo is *merely* a symbol of postcolonial modernity, and prevent what Rashmi Varma has referred to as the "occlusion of colonial history" of postcolonial cities (16). Gayatri Spivak has asserted that naming is an act of power. Muller traces the changes in names of streets and other sites in Colombo as a way of emphasizing the way in which power has changed hands over the centuries:

> The Portuguese insisted on saints' names for their roads; the Dutch recalled their Governors and places in Holland. [...] The British named the best roads after their Governors, then went on to commemorate the planters, government officials, Mayors, Councillors, engineers, doctors, the Royals of course, and other streets named after well-known places in England such as Ascot, Hyde Park, Kew, Kensington, et al. Thus did they turn Colombo into 'this other England' and there wasn't, by the turn of the century, any way in which the citizen of Colombo could escape the stamp of the Britisher. (460)

In an attempt at decolonization after gaining independence from the British in 1948, Sri Lankans have renamed those streets with Sinhalese, Tamil and Muslim names, leaving many Sri Lankans disoriented. Not just streets but also buildings were given new identities, and Muller carefully delineates these changes. The house of the last Dutch governor, for example, which was acquired by the British and renamed Queen's House, is, after Independence, renamed President's Palace (437).

A curious instance of this renaming relates to Slave Island, to which Muller gives considerable attention. "Slave Island" remains the name of the posh commercial center Muller describes in English, thus recalling the violent enslavement of Africans by the Portuguese and the Dutch in the distant past. Muller's Sinhala-speaking characters—such as Anton—would not necessarily be aware of this name, however, as the Sinhala name is "Kompannya Veediya,"—literally, "Company Street"—a nomenclature that effaces the locale's historical association with slavery, and merely reinforces its contemporary associations with commerce and trade. In this way, Muller's Anglophone history of the city has something to offer contemporary Sinhala and Tamil speakers that they might otherwise ignore, even as Muller himself at times seems to understate the gaps in English speakers' knowledge that need to be supplemented by speakers of Sinhala and Tamil for a thorough picture of the city to emerge: here again, Muller seems, rightly, to imply that the history of Slave Island's name matters to the Antons and Kusums of late twentieth-century Colombo, but is unable to take this insight to its conclusion, in part because of the linguistic gaps between English, Sinhala, and Tamil speakers in the city.

This omission has implications for Muller's broader project of mapping the varieties of urban outcasts in Colombo. Perhaps the most important missing piece in Muller's work is an explicit analysis of the connection between the violence of the colonial past and that of the postcolonial present (as of 1995).[5] This connection is everywhere implicit in *Colombo*, but is not explicitly interrogated. If as readers we seek these connections, they become increasingly apparent. Tensions between capital and labor in colonial Sri Lanka form the background for the tension and ultimate violence between the state and revolutionary organizations like the first incarnation of the JVP in the post-independence period. Colombo's status as a city of relative privilege when compared to the rural poor meant that the class-based war in the south between the government and the original JVP was in part a battle between the city and the educated but still disenfranchised Sinhala-speaking youth of the rural south. Meanwhile, Tamil-speaking youth in the north and east were locked out of government employment by Sinhala-Only legislation that had its roots in resentment resulting from colonial "divide-and-rule" policies that privileged one ethnic group over another. Making these connections could have made Muller's lament for Colombo's fractured present in 1995 all the more powerful.

Muller's work in *Colombo: A Novel* is at once valuable and flawed. Muller calls attention to such pressing matters as urban inequality, sexual exploitation, political violence, crime, governmental corruption, and the way in which all of these factors contribute to making urban outcasts in Colombo. He dramatizes these matters powerfully throughout the book. Ultimately, the gap between Muller's own complex subjectivity and those he seeks to map is such that the "ordinary" experiences of Colombo remain elusive, and the connections between the violence of the colonial past and the neocolonial present remain suggestive, but not fully articulated. In this sense, Muller's work constitutes both powerful social criticism of the contemporary Sri Lankan city, with its troubling aspects of marginalization, exploitation, and outright violence, and a symptom of why further critique is needed. Muller's palimpsestic elegy for Colombo is stirring and necessary, but also fragmentary and incomplete.

Notes

1. Muller's other works include an epic novel about the origin myth of the Sinhalese, *The Children of the Lion*, and a science fiction novel, *Exodus 2300*.
2. While *Colombo* has not received as much critical attention as did the Burgher trilogy, Muller's critique of violence, inequality, and sexual exploitation has drawn some favorable commentary. According to Biswadeep Ghosh, "Muller's is a kind of realism [...] that transforms the book into a mouthpiece for the under-privileged." Charles Sarvan asserts that "the anger of Carl Muller is born of love, pity and despair" (133). He sees "strength and power" in Muller's "courage to confront and re-present the truth; in the refusal to minimize or embellish; in declining to offer facile, heartwarming hope" (131). (Sarvan is

actually responding to Muller's *All God's Children*, a collection of short stories, poems and vignettes. Some of the accounts of exploited adults and children that appear in the collection have been repurposed by Muller in *Colombo*.) As Ghosh and Sarvan point out, Muller makes it impossible for his readers to be morally complacent about the exploitation and violence that are an unavoidable part of Colombo's story throughout his work.

3. Some English language writers, including the novelist Shehan Karunatilaka and the poet Vivimarie VanderPoorten, have worked to ensure that their works are available in Sinhala and/or Tamil translations, but *Colombo*, published in 1995, remains available only to an Anglophone audience.
4. Muller quotes from works by a variety of travelers ranging from missionaries like Harriet Wadsworth Winslow and writers such as Anton Chekhov, Mark Twain, Edward Lear, Paul Bowles, Frances Parkinson Keyes, Pablo Neruda, Nikos Kazantzakis, Premnath Moraes, Christopher Isherwood and W. H. Auden.
5. The works of certain other Sri Lankan writers present a contrast to that of Muller in this regard. In A. Sivanandan's novel *When Memory Dies*, for example, the author delineates the way in which changes implemented in colonial times contributed to postcolonial violence.

Works Cited

Anyokwu, Christopher. "May We Always Remember: Memory and Nationhood in Chimamanda Ngozi Adichie's Half of a Yellow Sun." *NTU Studies in Language and Literature* 20 (December 2008): 179–96. Print.

Arasanayagam, Jean. *Apocalypse '83*. Colombo, Sri Lanka: International Centre for Ethnic Studies, 2003. Print.

Bandarage, Asoka. *The Separatist Conflict in Sri Lanka: Terrorism, Ethnicity, Political Economy*. Colombo, Sri Lanka: Vijitha Yapa, 2009. Print.

Boo, Katherine. *Behind the Beautiful Forevers: Life, Death, and Hope in a Mumbai Undercity*. New York: Random House, 2012. Print.

De Certeau, Michel. *The Practice of Everyday Life*. Trans. Steven Rendall. Berkeley: U of California P, 1984. Print.

Dickens, Charles. *Great Expectations*. New York: Penguin, 2002. Print.

———. *Oliver Twist*. New York: Penguin, 2003. Print.

———. *Sketches by Boz*. New York: Penguin, 1996. Print.

Edensor, Tim, and Mark Jayne. "Introduction." *Urban Theory Beyond the West: A World of Theories*. New York: Routledge, 2012. 1–28. Print.

Ghosh, Biswadeep. "Oh! Oh! Colombo!" *Outlook* February 7, 1996. Web. July 17, 2015.

Goonetilleke, D. C. R. A. *Sri Lankan English Literature and the Sri Lankan People 1917–2003*. Colombo, Sri Lanka: Vijitha Yapa, 2005. Print.

Gunesekera, Romesh. "Sense of the City: Colombo." BBC News. August 5, 2003. Web. July 17, 2015.

Hoole, Rajan. *Sri Lanka: The Arrogance of Power—Myths, Decadence, and Murder*. Colombo, Sri Lanka: University Teachers for Human Rights (Jaffna), 2001. Print.

Jayasuriya, Maryse. *Terror and Reconciliation: Sri Lankan Anglophone Literature, 1983–2009*. Lanham, MD: Lexington, 2012. Print.

Jayawardena, Kumari. *Ethnic and Class Conflict in Sri Lanka: The Emergence of Sinhala-Buddhist Consciousness 1883–1983*. Colombo, Sri Lanka: Sanjiva Books, 2003. Print.

Mehta, Suketu. *Maximum City: Bombay Lost and Found.* New York: Vintage, 2004. Print.

Muller, Carl. *The Jam Fruit Tree.* New Delhi: Penguin Books India, 1993. Print.

———. *Yakada Yaka.* New Delhi: Penguin Books India, 1994. Print.

———. *Colombo: A Novel.* New Delhi: Penguin Books India, 1995. Print.

———. *Once Upon a Tender Time.* New Delhi: Penguin Books India, 1995. Print.

———. *Exodus 2300.* Colombo, Sri Lanka: Vijitha Yapa, 2003.

———. *All God's Children.* Colombo, Sri Lanka: Vijitha Yapa, 2004. Print.

———. *Children of the Lion.* New York: Penguin, 2011. Print.

Salgado, Minoli. *Writing Sri Lanka: Literature, Resistance, and the Politics of Place.* London: Routledge, 2007. Print.

Sarvan, Charles. "Carl Muller's Trilogy: The Burghers of Sri Lanka." *Sri Lanka: Literary Essays & Sketches.* New Delhi: Sterling, 2011. 25–39. Print.

Selvadurai, Shyam. *Funny Boy.* San Diego: Harcourt Brace, 1994. Print.

Spivak, Gayatri. *Outside in the Teaching Machine.* New York: Routledge, 1993. Print.

Tambiah, S.J. *Sri Lanka: Ethnic Fratricide and the Dismantling of Democracy.* Chicago and London: U of Chicago P, 1986. Print.

Varma, Rashmi. *The Postcolonial City and Its Subjects: London, Nairobi, Bombay.* New York: Routledge, 2012. Print.

Wilson, A. Jeyaratnam. *Sri Lankan Tamil Nationalism: Its Origins and Development in the 19th and 20th Centuries.* New Delhi: Penguin, 2000. Print.

13 The Fiction of Anosh Irani
The Magic of a Traumatized Community

Kelly A. Minerva

Bombay is a cross between a nightingale and a vulture: beauty and death.
— Anosh Irani, Interview, *Eclectica*

Everyone has a Bombay story, a Bombay they want represented. And everyone's Bombay is not the Bombay we thought we knew.
— Jerry Pinto and Naresh Fernandes, "Introduction:
The Lived City" *Bombay Meri Jaan*

Since the 1980s, Mumbai has increasingly been the subject of novels written in English; these novels are most often set before 1995, when the city was renamed, and depict the city as a main character who defines the identities of its residents, even as these inhabitants redefine the city.[1] These novels create a corpus of literature that constructs Bombay as more than just a mere backdrop to the plot, but as the beloved source of a character's identity and the reviled cause of their destruction. I argue that this genre can be characterized by its emphasis on Bombay's diverse population and overcrowding; by the struggles to define individual identity in a city that changes so rapidly and constantly; by clashes between individual identity, local communal identities, and national identities; and by the impositions of local city, state, and national politics on everyday life. Predominately male, first-person focalizers in Bombay novels reveal the imaginative constructions of Bombay created to assuage the alienation self-proclaimed Bombayites experience in their modern urban lives. The ever-growing list of Anglophone Bombay novelists contains diasporic and indigenous writers including, but not limited to Vikram Chandra, Amit Chaudhuri, Dilip Chitre, Boman Desai, Farrukh Dhondy, Anosh Irani, Cyrus Mistry, Rohinton Mistry, Jerry Pinto, R. Raj Rao, Salman Rushdie, Manil Suri, Shashi Tharoor, Thrity Umrigar, and Ardashir Vakil. These novelists depict the city Bombay as a place defined by the inherent contradictions between its magical possibilities and harsh realities; its extreme riches and extreme poverty; its industry and disease; and its service and inefficiency.

While all the protagonists of Bombay novels call the city "home," they do not all exercise the same level of political and social capital and often Bombay's economic outcastes remain relegated to literary margins. Increasingly twenty-first-century Anglophone Indian literature portrays Bombay's most under-privileged and often invisible communities through protagonists who challenge the conceptual divide between "home" and "house"[2] in a city plagued by housing problems. While earlier examples of Bombay novels like Rushdie's *Midnight's Children* and *The Moor's Last Sigh* depict protagonists safely housed within upper-class residences, later examples, like Manil Suri's *The Death of Vishnu* juxtapose a wider variety of Bombay's house-poor residents. Suri's middle-class families struggle to live in crowded apartments, while other characters sleep on stair landings; his characters may all be house-poor, but they are, ultimately, still able to define themselves based on the fact that they can call Bombay their home. They thus reveal how, in Bombay novels, physical and political alienation do not necessarily manifest as emotional or psychic estrangement from the city. In many other novels, like *Shantaram* by Gregory David Roberts, *A Fine Balance* by Rohinton Mistry, and *Sacred Games* by Vikram Chandra, the marginalized characters who fight for housing and to call Bombay home are slum dwellers—city inhabitants denied power over their houses by a city government that refuses to recognize them as legal residents.

Despite this focus on housing struggles in Bombay novels, the city's houseless, especially its beggars, remain in literary margins, little more than minor characters and stereotypes in narratives about Mumbai's housed. Although the struggles of beggars may be more widely represented in Dalit literature, this literature is primarily written in Marathi and is largely inaccessible to Anglophone audiences.[3] Indian-Canadian author Anosh Irani brings Mumbai's houseless beggar community to the foreground of Indo–Anglian literature, generally, and Bombay novels, specifically. Although he writes in a privileged language not necessarily accessible to Bombay's most oppressed communities, Irani gives voice to Bombay's urban outcastes and the unspeakable traumas they experience in Bombay's streets through his manipulation of magical realism.

In *The Cripple and His Talismans* (2004) and *The Song of Kahunsha* (2006), Irani reveals communities of urban outcastes whose traumatic experiences are far more violent and extreme than those of many other Bombay protagonists, but whose narratives reproduce the formal and thematic elements of Bombay novels and thus help define the city and the genre. In *Cripple*, Irani portrays an unnamed narrator's search to find his amputated arm. He wanders the streets of Bombay reminiscing about his childhood and searching for mythical answers from the wide variety of personages he meets in the streets, including a wide range of crippled beggars. Although beggars remain two-dimensional fictions and metaphors for his own personal journey, the narrator can see and hear them in a way he was unable to before he lost his arm and they populate his new Bombay as few other Anglophone novels allow. *Song* follows an orphan boy, Chamdi, who dreams of living in "Kahunsha," his imagined "world without sorrow." He runs away from an orphanage only to find himself lost—homeless and houseless—and at the mercy of Bombay's beggars. He is eventually taken in by a poor family of beggars and, under their tutelage, becomes part of a gang of beggars and thieves controlled by Anand Bhai. Irani's novels importantly expand the spectrum of protagonists in Bombay novels fighting to tell their stories of urban alienation. Like all Bombay novels written in English, Irani's novels investigate the complex relationships between Mumbai's local communal politics, India's national postcolonial politics and histories, and an individual's relationship to the spaces of everyday life. However, Irani's texts push us to understand these relationships through the city's outcastes.

Bombay/Mumbai: Narratives and Politics

As a genre, Bombay novels engage with a literary tradition of postcolonial writing in English that aims to redefine the identities of former colonies and their inhabitants. Salman Rushdie's *Midnight's Children*, a quintessential Bombay novel, is often used as an exemplar of Indian postcolonial fiction, which redefines India and Indianness through magical realism. While many literary critics have tried to tackle the complexities of Indian literary histories and, in particular, the role of the novel written in English within these histories, Chelva Kanaganayakam provides a formal comparison of Western and Indian literary traditions and genres without privileging either (unlike, for example, Meenakshi Mukherjee, Subha Rao, or Makarand Paranjape). Kanaganayakam argues that Rushdie's magical realism was not so much a break in the literary tradition, but one constituent component in the tradition of Indian writing in English, which uses "artifice as a central organizing principle" in its use of language and form (7). He calls this tradition "counterrealism" and argues that it is a literary, aesthetic, and narrative mode which departs from mimesis and verisimilitude. "Particularly in the study of fiction," he argues, "the focus has been on common themes or certain responses to social realities, but hardly any attention has been paid to formal innovation as a recurring pattern, or as a basis for typology" (13). Kanaganayakam disagrees with the critical tradition that would exile Indo–Anglian fiction from the canon of Indian literature because of its linguistic ties to colonialism. Instead, he argues, this decision to write in a language that is largely alien to the people and places described inspires a critical distance between reality and literary subjects that enables readers to understand the complex historical and political relationships depicted in literature, such as protagonists' struggles against Shiv Sena politics in both Rushdie's and Irani's novels. Through counterrealism, Indian fiction in English "acknowledges its own artifice, and in the process turn[s] the limitations imposed by language into strengths" (7). These novels, he argues, emphasize their constructedness and thus distance themselves from traditions of writing "that strive for the transparency of mimesis." Thus Kanaganayakam investigates the use of realism and experiment in Indo–Anglian novels to provide a reading strategy that does not depend upon linking the formal characteristics of Indo–Anglian literature with Western and/or Latin American narrative modes of magical realism, while he simultaneously interrogates the Indian literary tradition within which they also fall.[4] Indo–Anglian counterrealism may borrow from Western models, but it "is also insistently Indian" in its concern "with the quest for an Indian identity" (19). This identity quest conducted through counterrealist narratives is also a primary feature of Bombay novels.

Literary critics Roshan G. Shahni and Priyamvada Gopal also defend Anglophone Indian literature as an authentic part of India's literary history, but they do so by highlighting an additional category for consideration: the Bombay novel. Set firmly within this tradition of Indo–Anglian writing, Bombay novels create an alternative model for Indian identity based on the city's, rather than the nation's, plurality and contradiction. These novels inhabit a place simultaneously outside and inside India, its literary traditions and its cultural identities. Shahni argues that, as a genre, Bombay novels engage with themes of urban alienation caused by the city's economy and politics and reveal the struggle between cosmopolitanism and parochialism in the city. "The city's amorphousness," Shahani writes, "accentuates the terrifying sense of anonymity among its inhabitants" which also "permits a sense of freedom and privacy" in both characters and authors who are able to use Bombay's plurality "to liberate themselves from an essentialist view of the nation" (101). Gopal echoes the argument that Bombay provides writers the freedom to explore multiple definitions of Indian identity because the city offers a unique source of inspiration for novelists:

> Though all Indian cities can claim a certain constitutive diversity, Bombay is distinguished by the presence, in significant numbers, of a variety of minority or marginalized communities from Parsis, Muslims, and Jews (of different denominations), to Protestants, Roman Catholics, and Dalits. Their complex relationship to the larger project of "India"—at once integral but often sidelined—generates unique stories which can evince critical questioning attitudes to both nation and community. (117)

Thus Bombay helps authors "to assimilate the 'outside' while laying claim to a home 'inside' the nation" (116). These authors depict the city in a way that challenges readers to understand its inherent contradictory narratives—its colonial and its postcolonial features, its cosmopolitanism and its parochialism, or its poverty and its riches. Irani's Bombay novels in particular focus readers on urban outcastes who epitomize the city's poverty and degradation and whose stories rely on magical realist and/or fantastical re-imaginings of the city's harsh reality. Despite the fact that Irani's protagonists encounter and create Bombay's ethnic, economic, and religious diversity, they (like most urban protagonists) are alienated from the city they call home.

Urban literature, no matter its specific locale, is often defined by alienation and the erasure of the poorest members of society from its representations. In his seminal essay on urban studies, "The Metropolis and Mental Life" (1903), Georg Simmel argues urban alienation is *the* modern urban condition. Simmel posits that an individual gains power from his ability to distance himself from the everyday life in which he is entrenched. Despite the language of economy and commodity in urban theory, he eliminates the poorest urban residents from view and produces a model of modern urbanity that insists on a divide between aesthetically pleasing commodity and the grim realities of labor. Rashmi Varma explains that what was concealed by "these seductive arrangements of commodities was the real world of gritty and often unseemly human labor, and nasty relations of social economic exploitation" (3). "The contradiction between the real and the image," she summarizes, "between the glitter and the grime, between labor and commodity, produced what came to be theorized as the fragmented consciousness of modern subjectivity" (3). Irani's novels place this poverty and grime at the center of literary images of Bombay.

On the whole, Bombay novelists, including Irani, may appear to reproduce this center/periphery model, but they do so by also calling attention to the various historical and social conflicts that impact the city's identity through the act of writing in English—a language that emphasizes the history and effects of British colonialism and the ongoing struggle to define Indianness based on its modernity and tradition. They also all engage with the different forms of urban alienation that Bombay residents encounter and negotiate in their daily lives—from overcrowded housing and public transportation, to discriminatory politics. In other words, the postcolonial modernity of Bombay depicted in novels reveals individuals who must take advantage of their alienation from the city in order to establish the powerful distance between themselves and everyday life. This distance foregrounds the fictional constructedness of the narratives and makes it possible to read the magical realism of *Cripple* alongside the less magical counterrealism of *Song* and in the same tradition as the realism of Bombay novels by authors like Mistry and Desai. The narrative techniques, perspectives, and themes within these novels reveal the urban alienation in Bombay as a function of the intrusion of local, regional, and national political narratives into the everyday lives of individuals. Thus Bombay novels like Irani's produce Bombay as a conjunctural space, which "produces a critical combination of historical events, material bodies, structural forces and representational economies which propels new constellations of domination and resistance, centers and peripheries, and the formation of new political subjects" (Varma 1). Readers of Bombay novels can understand the conjunctural space through the historical and political forces that collide over the city's name change, an event portrayed in nearly every Bombay novel.

Bombay and Mumbai Collide: Defining Identity through Naming

The idea of cities as imagined places has dominated urban studies through-out the twentieth and twenty-first centuries. In Bombay, to a greater extent than most other cities, the imagined city has dominated historical and polit-ical rhetoric without always acknowledging the narrative artifice implicit in the construction of the city's identity. In *Mumbai Fables*, Prakash works to "unravel" the "fables" of how the city came to be (24). Prakash argues that deeply flawed "narratives of change" about "the rise and fall of the city" dominate textual depictions of it:

> Pick up recent novels on the city, read nonfiction writings, turn the pages in newspaper and magazine files, talk to people, and you will be confronted with a story that purports to tell us what the city was as Bombay and what it has become as Mumbai. (23)

Prakash is among a number of writers in disciplines as varied as anthropol-ogy, sociology, and cultural theory who have written about the complexities of Bombay's political landscape—focusing on the city's name change in 1995 as a moment which exemplifies the clashes over narrative constructions of the city. Writers like Arjun Appadurai and Rashmi Varma are among those who try to unpack the city's binaries by examining the ways that journalists, planners, writers, artists, filmmakers, and political activists engaged with and helped to construct the city's identities. The difficulty, Prakash explains, is that "Mumbai's everyday practice rejects history written as a linear story and presents it instead as a tapestry of different, overlapping, and contradic-tory experiences, imaginations, and desires" (348). It is therefore a city ripe for magical realist narratives that enable non-linear stories to be told about the complex city politics. In Mumbai, groups of individuals are often alien-ated from their environment by political pronouncements, which interfere with the daily experience of living in the city. Irani's characters thus join the legions of characters in Bombay novels whose narrative relationship to the city depends upon their distinction between Bombay and Mumbai. Before we look at Irani's portrayal of the name change, a brief historical overview is necessary.

The city of overwhelming urban growth and decay that politicians, filmmakers, and authors of both fiction and non-fiction try to understand through their writing is one that was officially renamed in November 1995 as the result of the Indian federal government's approval of a request by the Maharashtra state government to change the name of its capital city. The request was a seemingly benign part of India's complex national project of decolonization: the change marks a bureaucratic attempt to excise the city's colonial legacy from its present incarnation. At the very least, the 1995 name change solidified two particular definitions of the city—an English colonial city signified by the name Bombay and a Marathi anti-colonial city signified by the name Mumbai. As the capital of the film industry and home to a wide variety of manufacturing, finance, and service industries, it is a beacon of opportunity that attracts large numbers of immigrants who harbor dreams of prosperity. This is the city typically identified by the name "Bombay."[5] The large population of migrants and minorities has made it a culturally diverse, cosmopolitan city that is paradoxically a breeding ground for violent fundamentalist politics. Thus the city of promise has an alter ego defined by parochial politics, corruption, and poverty. These aspects of city life are often signified by the name "Mumbai."[6] "While 'Bombay' invoked the world of the colonial and the British-influenced, liberal, post-colonial middle class," summarizes Amit Chaudhuri, "'Mumbai' signifies the Post-Modern, contradictory city in which xenophobia, globalisation, extreme right-wing politics and capitalism come together" (16). When read in rigid, static binary terms rather than as coexisting narratives, the competition for dominance between the two conflicting identities of Bombay and Mumbai manifests as a violent struggle over identity formation. Each signifier of the city invokes a potentially pernicious signified—either at the cost of tradition and local culture for the sake of progress and modernity, or at the cost of multiculturalism and cosmopolitanism for the sake of localism and provincialization. The conflict over the city's name—unresolved despite the bureaucratic change—exemplifies the complex histories that engender the city as a palimpsest. Moreover, the political forces behind the name change become shorthand for the perniciousness of communal politics in Mumbai that threaten Bombay characters.

The driving force behind the official name change—the Shiv Sena—intended to reclaim from colonizing forces Maharashtra and its capital city for indigenous Hindu Marathi residents, regardless of their tenure in the city (or, for that matter, the tenure or size of other communities living within the city). The Shiv Sena is an organization founded in Bombay by Bal Thackeray in the 1960s, which typically espouses Hindu fundamentalist politics. The group aims to protect indigenous Hindu Maharashtrians from foreign colonizing forces. Similar to the national Bharatiya Janata Party (BJP), the Sena bases its platform on a call to an originary Hindu Indianness as a rallying cry for Indian nationalism, known as *Hindutva* and based on V. D. Savarkar's 1923 tract of the same title. In his in-depth study of the Sena's rise to political power, social anthropologist Thomas Blöm Hansen explains that "[t]he change of the name was a rather straightforward assertion of the nativist agenda of claiming Bombay and all its symbols of modernity and power to be the natural property of local Marathi speakers," a move which "efface[s] the fact that most Marathi speakers were as alien in the city as everybody else" (3). According to the Shiv Sena, the Maratha people rightfully possess Mumbai and Maharashtra because they descend from the warrior Chhatrapati Shivaji, who battled with the Portuguese and the British for control of the region in the seventeenth century. Ultimately unsuccessful in his military attacks, Shivaji's efforts did shape the architecture of downtown Bombay as the British built large military forts from which they could defend their territory. The name change thus evokes the history of the Kolis, but it also elevates the Marathi and Gujarati name Mumbai above the Hindi Bambai and the Tamil Bambaai, which were used just as commonly by city inhabitants as the names Mumbai and Bombay (Appadurai "Spectral Housing" 644; Patel 4). Although many political parties are guilty of making pronouncements about the city and its population that miscategorize the daily experiences of living in the city, the Sena and Indira Gandhi most often appear in novels as one-dimensional political forces responsible for the urban alienation characters experience.[7] Consider, for example, Rushdie's caricature of Bal Thackeray in *The Moor's Last Sigh* or his depiction of Indira Gandhi as a green witch in *Midnight's Children*.

The violence of the Sena's politics re-emerged in Bombay in 1992 and dominates Irani's second novel, *Song*, and Vikram Chandra's *Sacred Games*. The December 1992 destruction of the Babri Masjid in Ayodhya, followed by Hindu celebration rallies in support of its destruction, which inflamed Muslim residents, and the insensitive mishandling of the tensions by the police, caused widespread riots and bombings. Between December 1992 and January 1993 a series of riots left approximately 900 people dead in Bombay. The riots were followed by retaliatory bombings on March 12, 1993 which resulted in approximately 300 fatalities and 1200 injuries as 13 coordinated bombs exploded throughout the city. The Srikrishna Report, published in 1998 as the product of the government's inquiry into the riots, explains,

> For five days in December 1992 and fifteen days in January 1993, Bombay, *prima urbs* of this country, was rocked by riots and violence unprecedented in magnitude and ferocity, as though the forces of Satan were let loose, destroying all human values and civilized behavior [...] From January 8, 1993, at least, there is no doubt that the Shiv Sena and Shiv Sainiks took the lead in organizing attacks on Muslims and their properties.
> (qtd in Kumar 43)

These riots plagued Bombay but were not confined to the city.

Vikram Chandra shows the destruction of one particular slum during the riots as a metaphor for the lines drawn between Bombay's communities. The riots are depicted from protagonist Ganesh's point of view as he returns to the city to protect his gang's territory. Ganesh explains: "During a lull in my own war I had left my home, and came back to find my home the battleground for a larger conflict. They, somebody, had drawn borders through my vatan. My neighbours were now refugees" (366). Ganesh recognizes that although he had been fighting a gang war in the streets of the city, it had not disrupted the community. However, the communal riots alienated residents by allowing non-local anger to manifest itself locally: neighbors had drawn lines based on religion and had driven out certain members of their once-united community and thus Gopalmath is no longer the close-knit quilt he had described earlier. Chandra stresses the invisibility and fictionality of these communal lines by depicting Ganesh as viewing the riot-torn streets from above. Despite his elevated position, Ganesh gains neither insight into, nor control over, the situation. Flying into Bombay after the riots have begun, Ganesh feels that he is no longer a "king but an impotent clown," unable to protect the slum neighborhood that he helped create. He and his entourage look helplessly out the window as their plane descends:

> From the muddy coast-line emerged a scattering of islands, and then I could see clearly roads, buildings, the shape of colonies and the spreading brown patches of bastis. From behind [me] I could hear the boys arguing, "That's Andheri there." "Maderpat, where Andheri? That's Madh island, can't you see?" Then they were all quiet. A thick black snake of smoke grew from a coastline settlement and twisted in towards the centre, towards another dark, curving fume—the city was burning. (364)

From the airplane, Ganesh and his gang are powerless and ignorant—they can no more protect their neighbors from the flames than they can properly identify the city's districts without artificial map lines. Theirs is not the privileged, imagined view of Saleem Sinai winging across the city and able to name all the sites he passes. Instead of creating a Foucauldian panopticon or tower-perch from which to view the circumstances, Ganesh's elevated views reinforce the blindness that accompanies this height, thereby eliminating any suggestion that there is a power hierarchy to be ascended. Their impotence and the city's anonymity in this situation together reinforce the fiction of a power hierarchy drawn between local and global people or places. Instead, this scene reinforces the importance of visibility in transnational currents and acknowledging the existence of multiple Bombay narratives: from high above, all sections of the city are equally invisible to the viewer. Irani's characters, however, do not have access to protective heights from which to view their Bombay and, in *Song*, the main character becomes an unwilling but active participant in the violence. Although Irani's characters imagine multiple versions of the city, they are not able to draw clear lines between Bombay and Mumbai.

Chamdi, like every other protagonist in a Bombay novel, envisions two versions of the city: the violent city outside the walls of the orphanage and the sorrow-less city in his imagination. However, Chamdi's Bombay is both an ideal dream and a reality filled with the suffering typically associated with Mumbai, and he therefore needs to create a new signifier for his ideal city. Irani writes,

> In Chamdi's Bombay, children play cricket in the street with a red rubber ball and even if the batsman hits the ball hard, sends it crashing into a windowpane and the glass breaks, no one gets angry … He sees

people celebrating Holi [which they] have finally understood the true nature of ... and men, women, and children pass through their troubles with ease ... Every colour known to man comes to the people of Bombay as a friend, and the people become them all. (11–12)

In the tradition of urban renaming, Chamdi invents a new name for his Bombay without sadness because he knows "such a place must be known by some other name." Someday all sadness will die, he believes, and Bombay will be reborn as Kahunsha (12). The dual versions of Bombay—a space of gruesome violence and life-saving magic—exist for Chamdi not just as a metaphor for the name change, but also as a necessary pairing of reality and fantasy. In *Cripple*, the naming of the city more explicitly establishes the novel's magical realist form.

Irani juxtaposes realism and myth to depict Bombay's complex realities: instead of apposing the secular modernism of Bombay with the traditional religiousness of Mumbai in *Cripple*, he portrays modern Bombay as a modern spiritual world without a God. The novel begins with a prologue reminiscent of Christian and Native American creation myths: a boy alone in the universe creates the world in the image of a tree he envisioned—with many limbs "to branch out to become the roads of the world"—and populates it with a variety of forms from Man and Woman to Smoke and Snake (9). Then he tries to teach these forms how to use the paths of the tree in order to return to himself (God, presumably), but none of the forms listens. "I can see what is going to happen here," he prophesies, "There will be magic, poverty, thievery, music, pollution, dancing, murder, lust, and very little prayer" (11). Then Man not only confirms the place's identity, but actively banishes god from Bombay:

> "Leave me alone," said Man. "Promise me that you will never come here again."
> "First tell me what this place is called," said the boy, "so that I remember never to visit it, for it is no longer the place of the tree."
> "Bombay," said Man. "There is no other like it."
> "Thank God," said the boy.
> It was then that the boy realized who he truly was. He kept his promise never to return. (11)

Thus Irani establishes Bombay as a mythological and hopeless place: the traumas experienced and horrors witnessed by the unnamed narrator challenge the borders between magic, reality, and madness. In this secular magical realist novel, the narrator's faith and spiritual journey will not lead to a sacred reward. Instead, he and all of Irani's Bombayites are doomed and isolated, even among Bombay's overwhelming crowds. Unlike other Bombay protagonists who associate a similar pessimistic version of the city with the name Mumbai, Irani's characters cannot isolate their suffering from Bombay because, as outcastes, their Bombay has never been ideal. Furthermore, the isolation and alienation prophesied in the prologue define, but do not inhibit the formation of, a beggar community in either of Irani's novels. In both of Irani's novels, characters try to mitigate the trauma they experience in Bombay's streets through the magical elements in their narratives.

Unreal Meetings in the Streets: Irani's Bombay Novels

Irani's formal combination of magical realism, counterrealism, and trauma fiction to imagine Bombay enables him to place the city's outcastes at the center of his narratives. Formal devices such as word play, repetition, and the incorporation of the supernatural classify the novels as magical realist (or counterrealist, more generally) because they are used to "express the real that is beyond language," "to disrupt fixed categories of truth, reality and history," and to "create a space beyond authoritative discourse where the unrepresentable can be expressed" (Bowers qtd. in Mrak 5).[8] These are features which also coincide with the genre of trauma fiction, which provides narrative space to write about unspeakable violence and trauma.

As a genre, magical realism offers a narrative form that allows competing narratives to coexist, while using unreal elements to draw attention to the narrative artifice employed in the construction of identity. Rawdon Wilson explains that the hybridity of magical realist space depends upon the genre's juxtaposition of realistic and fantastical events side by side in a narrative voice that normalizes all the events. Magical realism aims to redefine "hegemonic discourse in order to accommodate alternative/marginalised/ ex-centric perspectives" (Mrak 2). It achieves this redefinition by obfuscating the distinction between magic and realism in order to express the "unexplainable according to the laws of the universe as they have been formulated by modern, post-enlightenment empiricism" (Faris 102). Similarly, trauma theory offers "a way of thinking about how some extreme event or experience that is radically non-linguistic, that seems even to negate language, is somehow carried across into language" (Berger 563–4). Trauma fiction uses metaphor to express the unspeakable. The unspeakable and the unexplainable parts of everyday life are often one in the same for Irani's outcastes, who thus show how fantastical storytelling can give voice to Bombay's silenced communities.

Magic realism in *Cripple* functions as a way to access the city and as a way to understand the traumas of loss experienced in and by the city. Irani's magical realism functions as a conduit—a linguistic and psychic tool that helps the narrator understand and recover from the trauma of his dismemberment. The unnamed protagonist's traumatic loss provides him a new way to see and understand the city and its inhabitants—the narrator has a new way to hear the voices of the people around him, although they never get control of the narration. The magic he sees in Bombay enables him to build new communities, as well as a new identity for himself, post-trauma.

For the unnamed narrator in *Cripple*, his traumatic dismemberment grants him the ability to see a community in Mumbai's streets that was previously invisible to him. "The moment I lost my arm, two months ago, I felt like a pariah in the company of normal people" he says (14). The trauma has quite literally silenced him: he did not speak to anyone for two months until the day his narrative begins when he speaks with Gura, a beggar who lives outside his new apartment. "It was as though my arm had done the talking before," he says. "It happened quite naturally," he tells us, "In my new physical state I recognized Gura as my equal—a beggar I could speak to," despite the fact that he had never noticed Gura before. This previously invisible individual begins to teach the narrator about the magic of the streets as a way to learn about his lost arm and how to deal with its absence. In other words, his unspeakable trauma requires a magical narrative. Furthermore, their riddled exchange exemplifies the fine line between magic and madness in Irani's Bombay:

> "There is an absence," he continued. "And you are not handling it well."
>
> Why should I? I thought. It is not as if I have lost my wallet. In fact, even when I lost my wallet I never handled things gracefully.
>
> Then he leaned toward me. "Now listen," he whispered.
>
> Gura scratched a boil on his thigh. He picked out flakes from his scalp. He bared his teeth to the sun until they got hot. He licked his lips, tweaked his eyebrows and crossed his arms.
>
> "Why are you staring at my face?" he asked.
>
> "You said to listen."
>
> "Not to me."
>
> "To whom, then?"
>
> "The street. All answers lie in its sounds. In the bicycle bell of a little boy also lies the wail of his mother, for she knows he will leave her soon when he is crushed by a speeding truck." (15)

The silences in their exchange emphasize the need to acknowledge the mundane but otherwise invisible individuals on Bombay streets. The horrors and losses witnessed here will not necessarily provide us with every invisible silenced Bombayite's story—the novel is not going to tell us Gura's story, the passage indicates—but Gura and others will help the narrator to find his voice as he learns to speak and see without his arm. Thus, Irani presents the world of beggars and cripples as an unreal, magical place that often resembles madness.[9] For example, nothing about his exchange with the chicken seller suggests that the vendor knows anything about the narrator's quest, and yet the narrator proceeds to buy all the chickens and "kill their king" to find his next clue (42–3). It appears in this scene that the protagonist's insanity causes him to see clues where none exist, and yet his lost arm and, later, the leper's amputated finger he carries do appear to guide him on his quest.

The lost arm and the found finger give him access to communities that had previously been invisible (or a hassle when they were visible) and to another way of seeing the world. This finger—a literal reminder of his own amputation and a metaphor for the violence of Bombay's streets—gives him the power to change situations, like hailing a taxi. Waiting on a median after his failed suicide and trying to discern the next part of his journey, the narrator watches a young boy beg for money at a taxi window. The narrator is able to witness the event both from the perspective of the woman in the taxi and from the perspective of the community of beggars:

> I have heard these words in the past and they meant nothing to me. It made me angry that small children begged. If I do not feed them, I thought, they will die and I will be doing them a favour. If we all stopped giving alms, dead beggars would fall on the streets like flies. It will help our government. If outside countries want to help, they should send planes so we can load bags of poor children on board. Then we will all feel better. (76)

But now, he hears the child's plea for money differently:

> At this moment, even though the boy's words are the same as they have always been, even though I take them in through the same ears, I do not want him dead. I am listening through the arm I do not have. (76)

The callous first perspective renders beggars invisible through a violent erasure and echoes commonplace global justifications for ignoring beggars by eliminating their humanity. Irani's narrator, however, becomes sensitive to these urban outcastes and makes them visible to readers who do not need to suffer the same dismemberment to hear their voices. Whether or not he is mad, however, is inconsequential once he actually meets Baba Rakhu in his warehouse of limbs. The idea of an economy of body parts and Bombay warehouses with arms and legs hanging from the ceiling which can be attached by "surgery" that uses neither "knives and blood, or any bogus rituals" (147), is at once horrifying and surreal. However, it is also terrifyingly real—the black market for internal organs is no more fantastical than the trafficking of human beings. This physical threat to individual lower-class bodies becomes a central focus again in *Song*.

Irani plants the violence of Bombay's streets firmly within reality, but the horrific events of Chamdi's tale border on the surreal, rather than the magical or fantastical. The novel also opens with a prologue, but this is no mythical beginning, it is a foreshadowing of one of the most vicious and gruesome events in Chamdi's young life. The only preparation Irani gives readers is a short introductory phrase before the violence begins: "Without warning, the man rams the iron rod into the face that peers through the window. There is a sickening crunch and the face disappears" (1). Chamdi, at the mercy of the unrelenting criminal and gang leader, Anand Bhai, must stand and watch a family perish, trapped in their burning home by a fire he is forced to set. The rest of the novel builds up to this climactic scene, a fictionalization of an event that was repeated throughout Bombay during the 1992–1993. In this novel, there is no magic to distance Irani's characters (or his readers) from the gruesome violence experienced by Bombay residents. While living in an orphanage, Chamdi dreamt of a city "without sadness"; when he leaves the orphanage, he learns that the sadness he knew before was only a small part of the immense sadness his life could hold. The traumas of loss dominate this counterrealist tale of an orphan who learns to beg, thieve, and eventually kill.

Chamdi does not have to suffer the dismemberment the unnamed narrator of *Cripple* does to access the voices of Mumbai's beggars and the magic to be found on its streets. Afraid that his parents will not be able to find him if he moves with his orphanage to Pune, he runs away and is homeless on Bombay's streets. Overcome with hunger and tiredness, he tries to rest and escape his surroundings: "he sits under the water tap and closes his eyes to the sounds of the street. He has no idea how sound will help him, but since his eyes are closed, sound is all he has" (62–3). Similar to the unnamed narrator who must learn to hear the beggars he had long ignored, Chamdi must learn to listen to the streets in a new way in order to uncover the traumatic stories of the child beggars. Alone in the crowded streets, Chamdi joins the invisible beggars whose stories are no longer silenced. His journey through the city will teach him how to walk the streets without ignoring others (he is given the sage advice to "look down" when he walks because he "might step on someone" [70]) and his story will become the story of so many of Bombay's oppressed children. Thus Irani makes visible urban outcastes and teaches readers to listen to the traumas of Bombay's street dwellers.

This is not to say that Irani presents Bombay's beggar community idealistically, in the way that many slums are discussed.[10] In both novels, Irani's protagonists are confronted by crowds of beggars who confront and prey on each other for entertainment and power. "The Games," where the unnamed narrator procures the leper's finger, features a fight between two lepers watched by an "army" of dismembered individuals. The narrator describes the scene and explains his (and thus our) complicity in rendering these individuals invisible:

> I look at their faces and I am not surprised that I recognize some of them. It is not a mystery that all beggars look the same. They *are* the same, floating beggars. You see them at one traffic light, asking for

money in God's name. You see them at another traffic light, pleading that one of their relatives is dead and money is needed for a funeral. You think: this beggar has a resemblance to the one seen in another part of the city, or at a previous signal. Clouds float, and when you look up from taxis, you can swear that they follow you. Beggars do the same.

The floaters come to the edge of the circle. Wheels scrape on concrete ... There are at least fifty people now, representations of everything that is wrong with the world, everything that will remain unchanged because normal people are in charge. (22)

His description parallels fears about the swarms of beggars who "harass" tourists and upper-class city residents.[11] When we witness this community without having to compare them to house-secure individuals (as we do when Saleem Sinai forays into slums and streets crowded with beggars in *Midnight's Children*), they are no longer mere foils emphasizing Bombay's extreme divide between its haves and its have-nots. Instead, they constitute a community with internal, political struggles for power that are not all that different from urban and national political power struggles—the potential for violence and trauma is just as great.

In *Song*, Irani again presents haunting, gruesome details of violence enacted against beggar children but every beggar is also given a name. The gathering of child beggars that Chamdi witnesses when he first meets Anand Bhai, the criminal leader who violently controls the child beggars, is peopled not by a faceless hoard grouped by impairment, but a number of named individuals. The brother and sister, Sumdi and Guddi, who are Chamdi's tour guides and teachers, introduce Chami to their community members and the reasons for each infirmity. As the square fills up, Chamdi is as overwhelmed as the reader: he "had not seen such deformity before, and to see it all in one place is too much for him" and he resolves that "No one will be deformed in Kahunsha" (146, 147). Anand Bhai's brutal domination over these children holds none of the humorous hyperbole of Baba Rakhu in *Cripple* and it threatens Chamdi's ability to dream of Kahunsha. In fact, the death of his friend Sumdi, and Anand Bhai's forcing Chamdi to throw the bomb that kills a Muslim family locked in their home, threatens to sever the connection entirely. In the novel's final pages, Chamdi has been struck dumb and Guddi begs Chamdi to talk to her, while he struggles to imagine that "police-tigers are inside his chest, and even though they are silent now, someday they will roar" (307). The small glimmer of hope at the end of *Song* occurs as the two friends sit together near the Gateway of Bombay and the Taj Mahal Hotel and look out on the sea and share a dream of one day sailing away from the city. For now, however, our struggle as readers is to recognize Chamdi, his companions, and Irani's unnamed narrator as Bombayites whose stories define the city just as loudly as Saleem Sinai's.

Ultimately, Irani's beggar communities change the way characters see the world of Bombay and demand that readers (re)consider the relationships between trauma, magic, and madness. Postcolonial literature raises the question of which disempowered communities get to tell their stories, trauma literature questions who has enough power over traumatic events to be able to tell their stories, and Indian literature investigates how we define Indianness; all these questions coalesce in Irani's Bombay novels. Through Irani's novels, Bombay's "underworlds" of cripples and beggars can be read as part of the city's defining contradictions. These urban outcastes are brought out of the urban and literary margins in Irani's novels and establish their Bombay stories alongside the tradition of Salman Rushdie's Muslim narrators, Rohinton Mistry's Parsi protagonists, and Vikram Chandra's gangsters and prove, once again, Pinto's and Fernandes' assertion that not everyone's Bombay "is the Bombay we thought we knew."

Notes

1. The name "Bombay" remains a prominent signifier in this body of literature and, for this reason, is also my dominant term when referring to the city depicted in novels; I use the name "Mumbai" to refer to the contemporary historical city.
2. I use the term "houseless" rather than "homeless" to avoid conflating an objective physical description of residence with a subjective imagined description of a person's relationship to the place he or she lives. Moreover, "houseless" is not necessarily synonymous with "beggar"; indeed many of Mumbai's houseless and house-insecure are formally employed. "Beggar" is a distinct category of houseless residents who lack both legal housing and legal employment (after the Bombay Beggar Act of 1959 criminalized begging).
3. Dalit literature often focuses thematically on rebellion against caste and class discrimination. Viyut Bhagwat explains that "the term was first used in the 1960s for the writing that has come chiefly from ex-untouchables" and represents "a rebellion in life as well as in letters against the white-collared Hindus who had up till then monopolized cultural expression" (113). "The word *dalit* means 'ground down', 'depressed,' 'oppressed,' 'broken,'" he writes, and "is intended to avoid the negative connotation of 'untouchable' and also the Gandhian expression 'Harijan' (children of God)."
4. The difficulty of defining magical realism is explored at length in Zamora and Faris.
5. The name "Bombay" is believed to have derived from the British pronunciation of the Portuguese phrase *bom bahia*, meaning "good bay." Govind Narayan, in his Marathi biography of the city written in 1863, also attributes the name to the Portuguese:

   It is said that there is no other place in all of India which has a harbor more amenable to trade and handling ships. In the Portuguese language, '*Bom*' means good and '*Bahia*' means harbor. It is commonly believed that '*Bombay*' was given as a descriptive name by the Portuguese because of this very same harbor. (59)

6. The name Mumbai is derived from the goddess Mumba Devi, worshipped by the Koli fishermen who were early inhabitants of the islands that became Bombay.
7. The Sena and the BJP are most often depicted as political parties with villainous agendas, but the Indian National Congress, for example, has also been accused of inciting riots for political gain.
8. Counterrealism, according to Kanaganayakam, may or may not also be magical, so long as it uses formal and linguistic artifice to break from verisimilitude and mimetic representations of history.
9. To this end, Irani's novel also invites a reading through the lens of disability studies, which I do not have space for currently.
10. See also Minerva "Slumbai: Mumbai."
11. With a callous deafness to economic inequalities and an abilist urban legend about willfully inflicted impairments, V. S. Naipaul in *An Area of Darkness* chastises Bombay's beggars as a community that has lost its value because of its growing size:

> The very idea of beggary, precious to Hindus as religious theater, a demonstration of the workings of *karma*, a reminder of one's duty to oneself and one's future lives, has been devalued. And the Bombay beggar, displaying his unusual mutilations (inflicted in childhood by the beggar-master who had acquired him, as proof of the young beggar's sins in a previous life), now finds, unfairly, that he provokes annoyance rather than awe. The beggars themselves, forgetting their Hindu function, also pester tourists; and the tourists misinterpret the whole business, seeing in the beggary of the few the beggary of all. The beggars have become a nuisance and a disgrace. By becoming too numerous they have lost their place in the Hindu system and have no claim on anyone. (57)

Works Cited

Appadurai, Arjun. "Deep Democracy: Urban Governmentality and the Horizon of Politics." *Public Culture* 14.1 (2002): 21–47. Print.
———. "Spectral Housing and Urban Cleansing: Notes on Millennial Mumbai." *Public Culture* 12.3 (2000): 627–51. Print.
Berger, James. "Trauma Without Disability, Disability Without Trauma: A Disciplinary Divide." *jac.* 24.3 (2004): 563–82. Print.
Bhagwat, Viyut. "Bombay in Dalit Literature." Patel and Thorner 113–25. Print.
Chandra, Vikram. *Sacred Games.* London: Faber & Faber, 2006. Print.
Chaudhuri, Amit. "Light, Colour and Real Estate." Rev. of *Love and Longing in Bombay* by Vikram Chandra. *London Review of Books* May 21, 1998: 16–18. Print.
Faris, Wendy B. "The Question of the Other: Cultural Critiques of Magical Realism." *Janus Head.* 5.2. (2002): 101–19. Print.
Gopal, Priyamvada. *The Indian English Novel: Nation, History and Narration.* Oxford: Oxford UP, 2009. Print.
Irani, Anosh. Interview by Elizabeth Glixman. *Eclectica Magazine*, Eclectica.org, Jul/Aug 2006. Web. February 2, 2015.
———. *The Cripple and His Talismans.* Raincoast Books: Vancouver, 2005. Print.

————. *The Song of Kahunsha*. Toronto: Doubleday Canada, 2006. Print.

Kanaganayakam, Chelva. *Counterrealism and Indo-Anglian Fiction*. Waterloo, ON: Wilfrid Laurier UP, 2002. Print.

Kumar, Amitava. *Bombay—London—New York*. New York: Routledge, 2002.

Minerva, Kelly. "Mumbai, Slumbai: Transnationalism and Postcolonialism in Urban Slums." *Transnationalism, Activism, Art*. Eds. Kit Dobson and Áine McGlynn. Toronto: U of Toronto P, 2013. 29–53. Print.

Mrak, Anja. "Trauma and Memory in Magical Realism: Eden Robinson's *Monkey Beach* as Trauma Narrative." [*sic*]—*A Journal of Literature, Culture and Literary Translation* 2 (2013): 1–15. Web. May 20, 2015.

Naipaul, V. S. *An Area of Darkness*. New York: Macmillan, 1965. Print.

Narayan, Govind. *An Urban Biography from 1863 (Govind Narayan's Mumbai)*. Ed. and trans. Murali Ranganathan. Foreword by Gyan Prakash. London: Anthem, 2009. Print.

Patel, Sujata. "Bombay and Mumbai: Identities, Politics, and Populism." *Bombay and Mumbai: The City in Transition*. Eds. Sujata Patel and Jim Masselos. New Delhi: Oxford UP, 2003. 3–30. Print.

Patel, Sujata and Alice Thorner, Ed. *Bombay: Mosaic of Modern Culture*. Bombay: Oxford UP, 1995. Print.

Pinto, Jerry and Naresh Fernandes, Ed. "Introduction: The Lived City." *Bombay, Meri Jaan: Writings on Mumbai*. New Delhi: Penguin, 2003. xi–xii. Print.

Prakash, Gyan. *Mumbai Fables*. Princeton, NJ: Princeton UP, 2010. Print.

Rushdie, Salman. *Midnight's Children*. 1981. Intro. Anita Desai. Rpt. New York: Everyman's Library, 1995. Print.

Shahani. Roshan G. "Polyphonous Voices in the City: Bombay's Indian-English Fiction." Patel and Thorner 99–112. Print.

Simmel, Georg. "The Metropolis and Mental Life." *Social Sciences III, Selections and Selected Readings*. Vol. 2. Trans. Edward Shils. Chicago: Chicago UP, 1948. Rpt. in Bridge and Watson *Blackwell*, 11–19. Print.

Suri, Manil. *The Death of Vishnu*. New York: Perennial, 2001.

Varma, Rashmi, "Provincializing the Global City: From Bombay to Mumbai." *Social Text* 81 22.4 (Winter 2004): 65–90. Web. 11 April 2007.

Wilson, Rawdon. "The Metamorphoses of Fictional Space: Magical Realism." Eds. Zamora and Faris 1995, 209–235. Print.

Zamora, Lois Parkinson and Wendy B. Faris. Eds. *Magical Realism: Theory, History, Community*. Durham, NC: Duke UP, 1995. Print.

14 New Capital? Representing Bangalore in Recent Crime Fiction

Anna Guttman

Sunil Khilnani argues in *The Idea of India* (1993) that Bombay and Bangalore are each "an avatar of the contrary potentialities of India's modernity" and "each manifests an exhaustion of the national imagination" (148). Khilnani fears it has become more advantageous for residents to identify as Maharashtrian or Hindu than Indian in Bombay. In the case of Bangalore, Khilnani imagines its exemplary resident as "the young MBA or software expert" for whom "India is merely one stopping place in a global employment market" (149). If Bombay risks falling into a dangerous parochialism and communalism, a process famously represented by Salman Rushdie in *The Moor's Last Sigh*, then Bangalore, according to Khilnani, risks falling prey to a deracinating globalism.

While the representation of Bombay has been the subject of considerable attention both in literature[1] and in literary criticism,[2] Bangalore has been comparatively neglected. To Ana Christina Mendes, Bangalore is simply "clichéd" as the "bustling city" (280). But in the last several years, this has changed radically. From Aravind Adiga's *The White Tiger* (2008) to Bharati Mukherjee's *Miss New India* (2011) and Brinda S. Narayan's *Bangalore Calling* (2011), to name just a few texts, Bangalore is finding a place in Indian fiction in English. As Bangalore is increasingly being imagined as a site for literary and economic production, it is also emerging as an important setting for recent crime fiction, a site for both capitalism and capital offences.

Capitalism, crime, and the notion of the urban outcast are intimately connected. In Loïc Wacquant's *Urban Outcasts*, the titular subjects inhabit

> "lawless zones", the "problem estates", the "no-go areas" or the "wild districts" of the city, territories of deprivation and dereliction to be feared, fled from and shunned because they are—or such is their reputation, but in these matters perception contributes powerfully to fabricating reality—hotbeds of violence, vice and social dissolution. (1)

At the same time, the processes of marginalization thought to create outcasts are intimately linked to class structures associated with capitalist expansion.[3] The simultaneous fear of and fascination with slums, ghettos, banlieus, and other areas of urban underprivilege and marginality that Wacquant identifies, invests those who inhabit them with a paradoxical imaginative authority over urban spaces. I argue that in contemporary Bangalore crime fiction, violent crime, and its ability to draw the middle-class detective (conventionally imagined as liminal and rootless) and reader into unseemly parts of the city, works to call into question the logic of capital, both local and global, while at the same time producing Bangalore as a culturally important subject of representation. In so doing, it positions the urban outcast as an authority on the city, whose presence and knowledge is paradoxically essential, both to the safety of Bangalore's middle- and upper-class inhabitants, and to the city's moral order. This authority and flexibility, however, is restricted to cis-male outcasts. Class and caste boundaries are therefore more easily traversed in these novels than gender norms.

Aravind Adiga's *The White Tiger*, which won the Booker Prize in 2008 and which charts the rise of the lower-class protagonist, Balram, from servant to venture capitalist via murder, epitomizes an outcast narrative insofar as its main character does not, and cannot, fit into existing class, caste or cultural structures, and whose life represents a daily defiance of social and legal norms. Though not a detective novel, I will demonstrate that the representation of Bangalore bears many similarities to those in more popular texts, and troubles existing theorizations of both the city and the outcast. I then move on to a reading of two detective novels by Bangalore-based authors: Anita Nair's *A Cut-Like Wound* (2014) and Zac O'Yeah's *Mr. Majestic: The Tout of Bengaluru* (2012). As David Schmid demonstrates, detective fiction offers "imaginative models of how the various spaces of a city are connected through acts of violence, and how these connections indicate the spatialization of power within the city" (243). Cast variously in the popular press as the nation's high-tech capital, the startup capital, and the suicide capital, contests over the nature and ethics of Bangalore's role reflect and refract larger debates about India's shifting place on the global stage.

While classic detective novels invited the reader to take pleasure in the identification and punishment of the guilty party, like other postcolonial detective novels, all three works discussed here challenge any "assumption of a good/evil dichotomy, and its unspoken complicity with (neo-) colonial law enforcement" (Chambers 34).[4] At the same time, detective fiction often brings into view urban subjects and events normally beyond the view of the middle-class city-dweller, such as the interiors of lower- and upper-class homes, street prostitution and criminal transactions. The detective not only reveals the existence of such subjects but also the capacity for the lives of outcast subjects to touch and intersect with those of the elite.

In *The White Tiger*, Bangalore plays a crucial role in the symbolic landscape of the text as the place to which the main character, Balram, escapes after murdering his employer to begin his life anew as a supposedly legitimate and successful businessman coordinating the transportation of call center employees to and from their place of work. From this location, Balram narrates his story in the form of letters to the Chinese Premier in advance of his visit, because, as Balram says, "If anyone knows the truth about Bangalore, it's *me*" (2). As in Bangalore crime fiction, it is an outcast character operating on the margins of law, caste, and social norms who is able to access and narrate the truth of the city. Though not a detective in the conventional sense, Balram therefore takes on the detective's role—revealing both the facts of an unsolved crime as well as a larger truth—and is certainly an urban outcast in all senses.

In Bangalore, Balram is no longer bound by rural caste relations and class relations, which had so fundamentally structured his early life. Balram also maps both Delhi and Bangalore into a larger symbolic geography of India: an India of light—encompassing urban spaces, and an India of darkness— the rural north in which he is born. In Bangalore, according to Balram, "if a man wants to be good, he *can* be good. In Laxmangarh, he doesn't have this choice" (262). In Lena Khor's reading, the space of capitalism is therefore ethically superior to that of feudalism in the novel. According to Robbie Goh, "[t]his spatialization [into light and dark, coastal and interior] ties India's hope for modernization and economic progress to its transnational connections" (337). This is reinforced in the novel by the fact that Balram's nephew Dharam is enrolled in an English language school in Bangalore where he learns the skills necessary to pass as an Indian elite and therefore to disassociate from vernacular culture. Balram may be an outcast, but Dharam is not.

Bangalore stands apart from the other areas of light that Balram lists in that, as Robbie Goh notes, it is the only location not on the coast. A landlocked city, the real and imaginative rise of Bangalore emphasizes that we are no longer connected solely by the sea but by the high-speed cables that run beneath it, and that the circuits of economic and cultural exchange for contemporary postcolonial culture are frequently electronic ones. If the global cities—London, Bombay, New York, Tokyo, Singapore, to name just a few—have largely been formed and imagined as ports, brought to prominence by the maritime movement of both goods and people, representations of Bangalore point to new possibilities for the twenty-first-century global hub. While the erstwhile symbolic light of India's coastal regions implies enlightenment and connotes access to education, health care, and voting rights unavailable to the subaltern subject, the light of Bangalore is repeatedly literalized in *The White Tiger* in the chandelier that hangs in Balram's office and in the glow of his computer screen.

The light under which Balram sits, as he composes the narrative that demonstrates his knowledge of the city, mirrors the light that the urban outcast symbolically shines on his terrain; it is the liminal subject who can traverse—and guide the reader through and around—Bangalore's darker streets and interiors. In *Mr. Majestic*, the titular character is an email scammer and tout who, through a series of mishaps and coincidences, is hired to track down an Indian–American woman named Maddy, lured to the subcontinent by one of his own email scams. Neither a legitimate business person nor a hardened criminal (with whom he is juxtaposed), Hari (aka Mr. Majestic) moves between spaces—both figurative and literal—in his ultimately successful quest to locate Maddy. Hari is a liminal figure not only because of his employment but also because of his familial circumstances. An abandoned infant found by a sweeper woman in a movie theatre, he is raised first by the single, Dalit woman who finds him and then, after she passes away, by her secret (caste) lover, whom Hari refers to as an uncle. Hari therefore lacks caste, as well as being the object of multiple familial and personal rejections. Uncle depends on Hari yet keeps the relationship hidden from his biological family. Along the way, Hari enlists the help of a police officer (whose son he helped cheat on his exams), his alcoholic uncle, and a drug-addled western tourist named Tord, all of whom also occupy outcast roles, though to varying extents.

The collision of wealth and poverty, religion and capitalism, and criminality and legality in the city is evident from the beginning of *Mr. Majestic*:

> Even the roads were known by their aliases in these parts. C.D. Road had a much longer official name, but ... [i]ts real name had fallen to disuse so long ago that Hari couldn't remember ever having heard it.
>
> The veranda afforded a panoramic view ... In the previous millennium ... the street used to be clogged with four-wheeler Ambassadors, three-wheeler auto-rickshaws, and two-wheeler bullock carts, but the city had changed, upgrading its cars and traffic jams simultaneously.
>
> The traffic had stalled, and at the center of attention was a brand new pink Porsche. It had hit a cow munching on plastic bags. Luckily, it wasn't possible to speed on the potholed roads, so the cow was more alive than the car and was limping undeterred into the middle of the road. A tired streetlamp lay on top of the Porsche. (9)

This twenty-first-century city is both wealthier and more decrepit than ever—and it is not simply a matter, as the juxtaposition of the oblivious cow and the dead Porsche demonstrates, of the new riding roughshod over the old. If the cow evokes a traditional, religious India, then it is one that collides with, but remains unharmed by, capitalist modernity. Indeed, it is fully integrated into the city's urban landscape. The Porsche itself, driven by an unlicensed local movie star, later disappears, thereby avoiding any legal scrutiny. The city itself is characterized by multiple and competing histories, emblematized by the competing vehicles, only partially visible, and prone to absurdity. Such an environment, which is continually in flux, challenges from the outset both the place and identity of outcasts and their others.

It is on this street where Hari first meets Jane, the American woman who hires him to locate Maddy. Contact with Jane brings Hari to parts of the city and region beyond his usual circuit between street, Internet café, and home (which is technically an office). The relationship between Hari and Jane destabilizes the relationship between insider and outsider. At first, Jane appears to be a disoriented tourist, whose presence on C.D. Road Hari interprets as accidental. Indeed, as a tout, Hari immediately begins to try to spin this supposedly chance encounter to his advantage. As the story continues, however, it seems less and less likely that their meeting was, in fact, accidental, and it becomes clear their relationship involves a complex struggle for both knowledge and power, rather than straightforward exploitation. Nowhere is this more apparent than when the two have sex in Jane's hotel room, while, unbeknownst to Hari, Jane's criminal associates observe from the next room. This is, simultaneously, a moment of intimacy, and of betrayal.

In *The Tout of Bengaluru*, each chapter is named after a location—whether a neighborhood, a bar, or a hotel room, making explicit its reliance on location. The places Hari visits are both more elite—a five-star hotel, a tourist café—and seedier—an illicit pornography business (run by a preschool director), a gym that is also the headquarters of a local crime syndicate—than his usual haunts. It is not just the call centers and multinational brands that declare Bangalore's place on the world stage; likewise, the "Bengaluru underworld was a genuine example of globalization" (92). Hari's adoptive mother, a single, slum-dwelling woman, "named him 'Hurree' which was auspicious. (She also used the Anglicized spelling of Hari because she wished him the best possible chances in a globalized world.)" (76). In this text, everyone is a global subject; there is not a tidy division between globalization from above and globalization from below. As the narrative unfolds, it becomes clear that Jane is also in cahoots with a local crime syndicate who may be tied to Maddy's disappearance. Therefore, the line between the criminal outcast and the law-abiding citizen is deliberately blurred. Hari may be as close as the novel comes to a moral center. In contrast, though Jane, unlike Hari, is never shown committing a crime, her association with criminality, and rejection by her family (which, biologically, is not her own) threatens to make her an outcast.

Yet Hari's morality is also largely accidental. Hari's success comes not as a result of any particular observational or other powers; this is a humorous text where the protagonist's haplessness produces much of the comedy. He compares himself to Sam Spade and like Spade, is often more confused than others assume and frequently on the receiving end of physical violence. Hari can straddle "different worlds with ease" (41) and is ultimately able to locate Maddy using his intimate knowledge of Bangalore and his ability to slip easily between its physical and social spaces. Bangalore is compared variously to Vancouver and Singapore but requires a local to properly navigate. Indeed, in contrast to foreigners like Jane, all the locals in Bangalore are polyglot (223). Even the road to the airport is "not quite India" (287). To Jane, worldly as she is, the middle-class neighborhood where Maddy is ultimately located appears to be a slum (232). Maddy, though Indian-born (her full name is Madhuri), shows herself even less apt, with her would-be lover Triplex driving her in circles, successfully convincing her that they are miles away from Bangalore when she has merely moved to a neighborhood beyond the usual tourist sites (227). This lower-class residential area is, in Wacquant's schema, the terrain of the urban outcast and therefore known to both Hari and Triplex but so mystifying and frightening to both Maddy and Jane that the former agrees not to leave the apartment while the latter fears to approach it even in broad daylight.

One of the few clues to Maddy's fate is the set of photographs on her recovered digital camera. Hari correctly identifies the particular café where one photo is taken (40), allowing him to trace her hotel room and thereby discover her last known address. Another breakthrough occurs when, through a series of improbable coincidences, Hari learns that his best friend, Triplex, who runs a small video bootlegging operation, is involved in Maddy's disappearance. Hari's less savory friends therefore prove just as important as his well-placed ones. Importantly, these friends are frequently in the same physical location. The police station where Hari interviews Triplex, thus finally solving the mystery of Maddy's whereabouts, is the same one where he successfully placates the police officer, Mrs. Pushpa, who Hari deferentially refers to as aunty (117). Hari also stashes his illegal gun at this same police station, thereby demonstrating that the line between those who break the law and those who enforce it is very thin indeed.

Rather than cemented into a subaltern position as an outcaste, who, though marginal, nevertheless has a defined position and community within Indian society, the urban outcast's flexible identity also reveals the underlying instability of caste and class identities at the periphery as well as closer to the center, both locally and globally. Mrs. Pushpa protects Hari because he had helped tutor her son, enabling the young man to pass his exams. Unable to afford further education himself, Hari nonetheless gains a sort of legitimacy, via his intelligence, which Mrs. Pushpa's own son lacks. Mrs. Pushpa risks scandal for her own participation in her son's cheating, which is surely out of place with her role as police officer. Hari's flexible position also makes at least somewhat viable his romantic pursuit of the much wealthier Maddy. Adopted as a child into an American family, and of uncertain biological origin, Maddy cannot fit tidily into fixed Indian social categories, yet has a degree of class privilege that makes such conformity unnecessary. Why then, the novel seems to ask, should conformity be expected of Hari?

Hari is of the city but doesn't master it. The city is characterized by uncontained excess (and compared to a tumor) (143), to which Hari contributes by bringing back a dog (who may be a rat) from the country. In the course of the novel, which takes place over only a few days, Hari navigates a riot, braves monsoon flooding, and participates in a high-speed auto rickshaw race all while moving within and between the city's many neighborhoods. Indeed, for Hari, life is best imagined as a train that criss-crosses cities, both dividing and uniting them, and is also vulnerable to becoming stuck in the mud created by monsoon rains (130–2). Many of the corners of the city that Hari visits might not be normally thought of as part of the urban landscape at all, such as an abandoned train tunnel and a field of (likely illicit) poppies, both of which prove useful hiding places that help him escape Jane's hired thugs.

Hari's mobility both defies Western ideas of the urban outcast—who is fixed within and by his or her underprivileged neighborhood of origin—and evokes India's distinct history and pattern of urbanization. As S. N. Sen noted of Calcutta in the mid-twentieth century, "[t]he slum areas are not concentrated in separate areas like the East End of London. They are to be found scattered all over the city, fashionable houses and *bustees* side by side" (quoted in Bonner 61). The same, I contend, is true of Bangalore in these texts. Phil Bonner points out that urbanization in India, more so than elsewhere, was characterized by flow across urban areas and between urban and rural areas, as a largely male workforce followed opportunities for short-term employment while their wives and children remained in or left for rural areas (74–6). Indeed, he argues that such mobility has a pre-colonial origin, with the sense of local place having become artificially rigid under colonization, much like the notion of caste (73). Hari's movements therefore point simultaneously to his transgressive global modernity as well as his connection to distinctively Indian social forms.

Anita Nair's *A Cut-Like Wound* is similarly fascinated with the transgression of boundaries within, and without, the city and also with the elusive presence and place of the outcast. The novel begins with an unnamed male transforming himself into a woman, and then setting forth into the Bangalore night. Within a few pages, there has been a murder and the bodies keep piling up. The main character in this novel is Borei Gowda, a once-promising police detective gone to seed, with a track record of pursuing cases destined to remain unsolved and defying his superiors. Although a member of the official law enforcement, Gowda, too, has a record of professional and legal transgressions, which have left him languishing in a small rural station, lacking the means or opportunity to solve major crimes despite his exceptional abilities. Borei's personal life, too, is one of transgression, and the story of the case is interspersed with an account of his burgeoning extramarital affair with his college sweetheart Urmila.

Borei's peers complain that he thinks of himself as "bloody Sherlock Holmes and Inspector Madhukar Zende rolled into one" (34). Holmes, of course is both a hero and an outcast—a socially isolated drug addict—whose powers come from a flair for observation, disguise, and an ability to traverse social and geographical boundaries, maintaining allies and helpers both on the streets and in the corridors of power. Zende, a police inspector in what was then Bombay, achieved fame in the mid-1980s for his role in the apprehension of Charles Sobhraj, a notorious serial killer who had broken out of prison (Ganguly). Borei is therefore imagined potentially as pretentious and a throwback to an earlier era but also as having both Western and Indian antecedents, bringing into proximity the high and the low. It is only Santosh, the younger detective, who enters the newer steel and glass cafés, geared to those whose wages are being paid by multinational corporations and whose tastes are being shaped by Westernized consumer culture. Even so, he feels uncomfortable not only because his salary makes the coffee on offer seem unduly expensive but because of his own lack of belief that he belongs.

Indeed, Santosh imagines that he is traversing not just a geographical landscape, but also an ideological one, as he moves through the city. As in *The White Tiger*, it is the city itself that harbors the truth, which is the object of the detective's quest:

> The truth was the city was beginning to scare him. The truth was his job was beginning to feel like it was beyond him ... as the lights changed, SI Santosh took a forbidden U-turn ... Somewhere in this locality he would discover what Samuel had hinted at. And with that he hoped to find his faith again: the belief that had brought him this far that the world would allow itself to be righted. That all was not lost even in this cold, heartless, city.
>
> (Nair 115)

Santosh and Borei are linked by a shared idealism, which, while seemingly of the past, is ultimately necessary to, and triumphant in, the present. Importantly, this idealism is not a form of knowledge, nor is it something that can be unveiled through rational investigation or moral commitment. Rather, Santosh is required to acknowledge his own potential for, and acts of, transgression, before he can make any progress in the case or in the city's traffic.

The murder victims, united only in their vulnerability to the charms of Chikka/Bhuvana (the transgender killer), also illustrate Bangalore's global landscape. A call center worker with political connections, a drug-addicted street youth, an older factory owner, a waiter recently immigrated from a neighboring state, and very nearly, a police officer, are all among the victims, demonstrating the interconnectedness of the social classes. Each murder even occurs in a different part of the city (126). Chikka/Bhuvana's crimes not only demonstrate the scope of the outcast's movements but also his/her ironic centrality, both in Bangalore and beyond. Globalization is expressly linked to the breakdown of the rigid social and class hierarchy that, in Western theory, and in Hindu theology, holds the outcast(e) in place.

While Santosh and Borei are arguably more skilled investigators than Hari (who bumbles haplessly from one beating to the next), they, too, rely on knowledge of the city. When one victim turns out to have a regional Keralan snack food in his stomach at the time of death, Santosh displays his ability to locate the restaurant that serves just this snack at the requisite time of day, using a combination of skill and tenacity (260). Santosh is also aided by Samuel who photographs the scene of the novel's first murder and is a key witness in the investigation of that crime. As a photographer, Samuel is also a liminal figure and tasked with knowing the city, often by traversing its boundaries, from elite social events to dark alleyways. No surprise, then that he provides a break in the case by offering Santosh an essential tip. Borei also confronts a city official at an exclusive country club to which the detective manages to gain admission despite his own more humble status. Santosh and Borei visit a home specifically for Hijras, an African migrant home, an abandoned factory, the opening of a photography exhibit, and a "piazza" (213). The presence of both the African migrants at the piazza reinforces the fact that Bangalore is a global city, but the limits of Borei's own global citizenship are reinforced by his inability to pronounce the Italian word.

Borei must reimagine his own life and his 'home' to reclaim his career as a detective in the changing city, which requires that he reject and fight existing prejudices—against those who are sexually and racially other—as well as repair his own personal relationships. Borei's crucial break in the investigation, for instance, occurs only because he agrees to offer his support to an organization campaigning for the rights of Hijras, an act which also brings him closer to Urmila. In becoming more sympathetic to Hijras and their plight, Borei begins to reconsider what values are most compatible with Indian identity, and therefore, refigures the nature of Indianness. As the imaginative center of a new India, literary representations of Bangalore and its urban spaces produce new discourses about India and Indianness, with the potential to reconfigure received paradigms of race, gender, caste, and class in the process.

The workplaces and homes depicted in these novels are highly permeable. The opulent home of the corporator, a municipal official, is situated behind high walls and, is in stark contrast to the slum, a "second-hand hole" (84). But the walls provide only an illusion of separation (84). In fact, not only are the occupants' origins humble, but those who live in the opulent home remain intimately tied to the world of poverty outside, which regularly streams through the gate. The call center worker and scammer alike are situated in a virtual workspace, whereas the police officer, like the gangster, is at work throughout the city's interiors and exteriors. This permeability both empowers and corrupts. While a character such as Michael Hunt in *A Cut-like Wound*, who enjoys unsettling fellow Indians with the contrast between his light skin and his fluent Tamil and Kannada, points to the ways in which Indian culture has long been globalized, global India, as epitomized by Bangalore, can also be a place of nationalist retrenchment, as is evident even in the title of Bharati Mukherjee's *Miss New India*.[5]

As Ines Detmers explains, with reference to *The White Tiger*:

> The "New India" and the "New Metropolis" represent both decentred and decentring sites of an allegedly re-formed ethno-racial identity bracketed by the reciprocal dynamics of colonial influence and post-colonial response. In this regard, the concept of the New Metropolis

clearly diverges from that of the postcolonial metropolis, as the former at the same time articulates a mistrust of the values and evaluation of liberation and dismisses the ethos of ethnic equality as nothing more than a mere comforting—in a post-Marxian sense—"neo-bourgeois" fiction. (538)

This, I contend, gets to the heart of both the representation of Bangalore and of outcast identity, in all three texts. All playfully deconstruct identity and demonstrate that the identities of the elite and the outcast alike are at least partly fictive and unfixed. In the case of *The White Tiger*, Ana Christina Mendes demonstrates that "Balram and his 'reality' are strategically inauthentic: through intentional self-contradiction and ironic character development, Adiga's failure to achieve (an in itself untenable) authenticity is deliberate" (284). The same is arguably true of Hari in *Mr. Majestic*. Not only does his name and tragicomic origin story preclude a simplistic authenticity, but his role as Internet scammer also requires him to take on many different identities and stories, which, at times, he struggles to keep straight, to comic effect. *A Cut-Like Wound* ends before the text can resolve one of the major questions around Borei's identity, which helps drive the plot: can he, and will he, reconcile with his wife, to whom he is bound by marriage and tradition, or will he be drawn into the exciting (and more elite, westernized world) of his new lover Urmila?

Furthermore, *The White Tiger*, *Mr. Majestic* and *A Cut-Like Wound* all privilege narrative perspectives that view and navigate the city from a perspective decidedly opposed to the "neo-bourgeois," who are represented by Jane, Urmila, and the city's young business process outsourcing employees, among others. All three protagonists reject traditional attitudes towards career advancement, and, despite their different relationships to law and order, all break it with enthusiasm. In all three cases, the crime itself originates with the elite, whether in the form of caste discrimination, corruption, or personal vanity. In the case of the missing Maddy in *Mr. Majestic*, it is Jane who has falsely claimed to be a sister, when she is in fact a stepmother. Rescuing Maddy turns out to involve keeping her away from Jane, as much as it is helping her away from the disgruntled would-be pornographers and their gang, from whom she is trying to flee. In *A Cut-Like Wound*, it is the house of the wealthy corporator (a city official) that shelters the murderer, and the corporator, himself, is associated with many crimes. In *The White Tiger*, Balram's employer is similarly corrupt, and it is his repeated acts of bribery, along with systems of caste and class-based discrimination, that arguably generate Balram's own criminality.

If, as Detmers suggests, Bangalore is not a postcolonial metropolis, insofar as it rejects both the promise of nationalism and identity politics more broadly, is it a global one? As Claire Chambers and Graham Huggan point out, global cities and postcolonial cities are situated differently within contemporary theory, with the former situated in terms of recent economic developments, and the latter imagined in terms of older, colonial social orders, producing disparate theorizations of the 'same' urban space (4). Indeed, as A.D. King points out, the very idea of a postcolonial city may privilege an outsider's, rather than an insider's, view (2). Globalization theory, on the other hand, has a privileged focus on larger cities and tends to flatten out regional differences. To imagine Bangalore as a global city, therefore, necessarily reconfigures that category, especially when viewed through three novels that, though written in English, also strongly emphasize vernacular culture, and position crucial narrative events outside the city. Global cities, according to Suman Gupta, are more:

> than their locations and boundaries and physical geographies; their populations flow over definitions and constitute a sort of world-in-itself. They represent the accruals of history, which are not understood through any limited progression of history, which push such cities into an apparently unhistoricizable complex present. They offer boundaries of ethnic and racial conflict, of segregation and stratification, or marginality and centrality, only so that all of these are criss-crossed and interpenetrated even while being reified in the process. (43)

It is, I contend, the emphasis on simultaneous reification and transgression of boundaries that unites all of these novels and all of their versions of Bangalore. In this context, the outcast, and the outcaste, remain necessary categories of analysis, even as outcast and outcaste individuals and communities exceed and reconfigure their marginalized positions.

Saskia Sassen argues that in the late twentieth century, cities such as London, New York and Tokyo functioned:

> first, as highly concentrated command points in the organization of the world economy, second, as key locations for finance and for specialized service firms ... third, as sites of production, including the production of innovations, in these leading industries; and fourth, as markets for the products and innovations produced. (3–4)

These characteristics, for Sassen, are constitutive of the global city. In the novels discussed here, Bangalore now occupies this role. In all of the texts I have discussed the presence of business process outsourcing, and the influx of foreigners into Bangalore (both official and unofficial), demonstrate Bangalore's global economic importance. The role of the workers as consumers—of coffee, clothes, food, cellular phones and more—is also heavily emphasized. I, therefore, contend that global India's ethnoscape (the flow and distribution of peoples and cultures) and financescape (the flow and distribution of money and wealth) are increasingly refracted through its technoscape (the flow and distribution of technologies).[6] Hari, of course, dwells on C.D. Road, which privileges both technology and globality in its reference, even though it is the urban terrain of the outcast subject.

The same technology that gave rise to the call centers is what allows Hari in *Mr. Majestic* to both use and be used by the internet in his own shady dealings (the Nigerian woman with whom Hari works is also a would-be lover, and she may or may not be conspiring to harm him after he breaks off their relationship). This is not, however, a simple allegory of the dangers of technology—because digital technology also offers Hari romance, as well as the opportunity to find Maddy. Nowhere is this more apparent than in *A Cut-Like Wound*. At the end of the novel, it is only Santosh's mobile phone, and his knowing use of that device, that allows Borei to trace his whereabouts, thus rescuing him from death. Unbeknownst to Bhuvana, Santosh has set his mobile phone to record audio so that the truth of his fate will be known, and so that Borei will be assured of correctly identifying the real criminal. The technology, which links the globe, is therefore fully incorporated within, and necessary to, Bangalore's own internal order. If, as Dick Hebdige claims, technological objects are "brought down to earth ('mediatised') by being made to function as differential elements—as markers of identity and difference—organized into meaningful relations through their location within cultural/ideological codes" (86–7), then the computer and the mobile phone in these texts assert both a connection with a particular location—as indicated through their GPS functionality—and a connection to the globe. In this way, even those characters, such as Hari and Gowda (who must learn how to text in the course of the narrative), who never have, and perhaps never will, leave India, are nonetheless hybridized and globalized subjects both because and despite of their outcast status.

The city, however, remains assuredly male in all three texts, thereby pointing to the gendered limits of the outcast(e)'s flexibility and authority. Indeed, there are potential outcast identities that remain reified and immobile.[7] *The White Tiger* is a conversation between two men, in which women hardly figure. All the victims in *A Cut-Like Wound* are male, and the border crossing of both the murderer and the investigators in this text is available exclusively to those sexed male. Since Chikka/Bhuvana appears to seduce the victims before murdering them, both victimhood and criminality are associated with non-normative sexuality and gender performance. In contrast, Borei's ideas on gender and sexuality are resolutely normative. He recalls his previous experience working with a female colleague who embarrassed him because of his own failure to avoid staring at her chest. Borei is explicit about only being able to work with other men (30). Yet he remains unmoved by Bhuvana, who Santosh finds very attractive.

While in *A Cut-like Wound* Borei and Santosh both explore new urban spaces, Urmila remains firmly fixed within her own elite social sphere for most of the text. She does, however, drive Borei to an abandoned factory in the final chapter thus making possible his just-in-time rescue of Santosh. It seems that an emergency, and a man's sanction, is therefore required for women to be mobile. Indeed, the link this text forms between Chikka's cross-dressing and his serial murders (all of which are committed in female guise) recalls familiar stereotypes, which associate non-normative gender and sexuality with criminality.[8] Transgender individuals remain outcasts in this text with only tentative attempts to better recognize them—all of which take place outside the city itself. If Hari, in *Mr. Majestic*, is Sam Spade, then Santosh, in *A Cut-Like Wound*, is Philip Marlowe, whose hetero/homosexual orientation allows him to apprehend the killer, but also places him in danger as he unwisely follows Bhuvana to an isolated location, seduced by her charm and attractiveness (Langham 148). Indeed, Bhuvana's antics also threaten her sibling, the corporator, whose wealth can neither protect Bhuvana, nor stave off the dangers of scandal for the family.

Mr. Majestic's attitude towards gender is perhaps even more disturbing. Hari's only previous girlfriend was also transgender, a fact that, in the text, has rendered him emasculated, and he proves unable to capture Maddy's romantic interest, despite his many attempts. His exclusion from hetero-sexuality, more so than his caste or class, means that he must remain a marginal, outcast figure. While Maddy's ability to escape her class and caste origins may initially make it appear as though she is a flexible and mobile subject, she is severely punished for doing so, and in a specifically gendered way. Maddy's gang rape (she is kidnapped and drugged by Jane's criminal associates after Hari 'rescues' her) is played for laughs as Hari drops her off afterwards at the hospital so she can have "her stomach pumped, her vene-real diseases treated, and … be fed massive doses of abortion pills" (284). Maddy has attempted to occupy locations and roles not normally available to tourists or to middle-class Indian women, and she has paid a very heavy price, one which the text does not fully acknowledge. Nor is she assured of future protection, given that Jane, her stepmother, may control Maddy's access to the wealth of her adoptive father. She, like Hari, is an outcaste and outcast from her own family and community, but she cannot make a home in the city or on the street as he has. Hari ends the novel with more money in his pocket, his community connections reaffirmed, and an adventure under his belt. Maddy, in contrast, exits the novel battered and alone as she boards a plane back to the United States. Whether she will see either Jane or Hari again remains unknown.

Thus, while contemporary detective fiction challenges earlier represen-tations of Bangalore and may require a reconsideration of what constitutes a globalized city, these texts do little to challenge gendered conventions in either detective fiction or globalization discourse. In *The Tout of Bengaluru* and *A Cut-like Wound*, moral order is restored to the city by removing ren-egade women (Bhuvana, Jane, Maddy) from it. Yet women are also absent from domestic life. Globalization is often figured in the language of rape "as the penetration (or imminent penetration) of capitalism into all processes of production, circulation and consumption, not only of commodities but also of meaning" (Gibson-Graham 120). This seems to be replicated rather directly in both O'Yeah's and Nair's work. This is rather ironic, given that the rise of business process outsourcing in Bangalore—touched on in all of these texts—which is closely tied to the city's global status, has affected women's lives at least as much as men's, providing new opportunities for work, domestic arrangements, and consumer spending.[9]

Rashmi Varma argues that the city has historically been a "site of masculinist and colonialist publics" (5). The contemporary, globalized city may no longer be colonial, but, for both Nair and O'Yeah, it remains at least somewhat masculinist. This is not, however, an inevitable feature of the detective genre, or of the city of Bangalore. The power and importance of Sherlock Holmes's adversary, Irene Adler, for instance, demonstrates that there has long been at least some room for complex women within the genre. Clearly, both men and women inhabit the urban terrain that Wacquant identifies as that of the outcast. Indeed, women are, on average, more marginalized in urban areas than men on most measures (Wacquant 107). Yet there are women in virtually every public space in these novels—from the café, to the call center, to the street. Their narrative marginalization is, therefore, not an eternal inevitability. The fact that Urmila's, Jane's and Maddy's stories remain unfinished points to further narrative possibilities both for a globalized Bangalore, and for the lives of its gendered, globalized, and outcast citizens.

Notes

1. Well-known examples include work by Salman Rushdie (*Midnight's Children* and *The Moor's Last Sigh*), Rohinton Mistry (*A Fine Balance*) and Vikram Chandra (*Love and Longing in Bombay*).
2. Rashmi Varma devotes a substantial section to Bombay in her monograph, *The Postcolonial City*. Caroline Herbert also focuses on Bombay in "Postcolonial Cities."
3. The term outcast was varyingly defined in sociology. Pierre Bourdieu imagined himself as an outcast because his schooling was at odds with his class origins, which creates tension with other young people of all classes (see Gartman). As Nikita A. Kharlamov, points out, this definition is not usually used today. Instead, the outcast is characterized by a marginal position vis-à-vis an imagined mainstream, and is often associated with poverty, criminality, and isolation. I use this latter definition throughout the chapter.
4. Gordon R. Kelly extensively analyzes the sources of pleasure in reading detective fiction in *Mystery Fiction and Modern Life*. The reader's pleasure is linked to diverse factors, including realism, morality and engagement with problem solving.
5. In that novel, after being sexually assaulted, Anjali, a young Hindu woman, refuses an arranged marriage and runs away to Bangalore to make a career for herself in that city's call center industry. Her prejudices against South Indians, Indian Christians, and Indian Muslims are never challenged, even as her status as the representative of the new India is reinforced. Anjali, herself unemployed,

New Capital? 271

receives Girish's protection and offers her body in return. She, too, is arguably an urban outcast, whose adventures through the city yoke a fascination with its westernized elite with a tour of its seamy underbelly, which includes: prostitution, terrorism and petty theft, among other things.

6. I am, of course, following Arjun Appadurai's definition of these terms laid out in *Modernity at Large*.
7. While this may seem unremarkable, considered solely in terms of detective fiction's nineteenth-century origins, this is by no means the norm in twenty-first-century detective fiction, which increasingly features detectives of diverse race, gender, and sexuality.
8. As T. L. Ebert explains this history in detail.
9. As J. K. Tina Basi discusses at length, women have made substantial inroads into India's business process outsourcing industry, a fact which has brought both opportunities and challenges to gendered norms.

Works Cited

Adiga, Aravind. *The White Tiger*. New York: Free Press, 2008. Print.

Appadurai, Arjun. *Modernity at Large: Cultural Dimensions of Globalization*. Minneapolis, U Minnesota P, 2005. Print.

Basi, J. and K. Tina. *Women, Identity and India's Call Centre Industry*. New York: Routledge, 2009. Print.

Bonner, Phil. "Labour, Migrancy, and Urbanization in South Africa and India, 1900–1960." *Journal of Asian and African Studies* 44.1 (2009): 69–95. Print.

Chambers, Claire. "Postcolonial *Noir*: Vikram Chandra's 'Kama.'" *Detective Fiction in a Postcolonial and Transnational World*. Eds. Nels Pearson and Marc Singer. Surrey, Ashgate, 2009. 31–46. Print.

Chambers, Claire and Graham Huggan. "Revaluating the Postcolonial City." *Interventions: International Journal of Postcolonial Studies*. n. pages. Web. January 15, 2015.

Detmers, Ines. "New India? New Metropolis? Reading Aravind Adiga's *The White-Tiger* as a 'Condition-of-India Novel.'" *Journal of Postcolonial Writing* 47.5 (2011): 535–45. Print.

Ebert, T. L. "Detecting the Phallus: Authority, Ideology, and the Production of Patriarchal Agents in Detective Fiction." *Rethinking Marxism: A Journal of Economics, Culture and Society* 5.3 (1992): 6–28. Print.

Ganguly, Arghya. "After Charles: Mumbai's Dons feared him, but Madhukar Zende is more Famous for Having Caught Sobraj Twice." *Business Standard*. N. pages. Web. June 16, 2012.

Gartman, David. "Bourdieu and Adorno: Converging theories of culture and inequality." *Theory and Society* 41.1 (2012): 41–72. Print.

Goh, Robbie B. H. "Narrating 'Dark' India in *Londonstani* and *The White Tiger*: Sustaining Identity in the Diaspora." *Journal of Commonwealth Literature* 46.2 (2011): 327–44. Print.

Gupta, Suman. *Globalization and Literature*. Cambridge, UK: Polity, 2009. Print.

Hebdige, Dick. *Hiding in the Light: On Images and Things*. London: Routledge, 1988. Print.

Herbert, Caroline. "Postcolonial Cities." *The Cambridge Companion to the City in Literature*. Ed. Kevin R. McNamara. Cambridge: U Cambridge P, 2004. 200–14. Print.

Kelly, R. Gordon. *Mystery Fiction and Modern Life*. Jackson, U Mississippi P, 1998. Print.

Kharlamov, Nikita A. "Boundary Zone between Cultural Worlds or the Edge of the Dominant Culture? Two Conceptual Metaphors of Marginality." *Journal of Intercultural Studies* 33.6 (2012): 623–38. Print.

Khilnani, Sunil. *The Idea of India*. London: Hamish Hamilton, 1997. Print.

Khor, Lena. "Can the Subaltern Right Wrongs?: Human Rights and Development in Aravind Adiga's *The White Tiger*." *South Central Review* 29.1–2 (2012): 41–67. Print.

King, A. D. "Postcolonial Cities." *International Encyclopedia of Human Geography*. Eds. Rob Kitchin and Nigel Thrift. Philadelphia, Elsevier, 2009. Web. 1–5.

Langham, Jeffrey. "Subject to Interrogation." *Multicultural Detective Fiction: Murder from the "Other" Side*. Ed. Adrienne Johnson Gosselin. New York: Garland, 1999. 143–64. Print.

Mendes, Ana Christina. "Exciting Tales of Exotic Dark India: Aravind Adiga's *The White Tiger*." *Journal of Commonwealth Literature* 45.2 (2010): 275–93. Print.

Mukherjee, Bharati. *Miss New India*. Toronto, Harper Collins, 2011. Print.

Nair, Anita. *A Cut-like Wound*. London, Bitter Lemon Press, 2014. Print.

O'Yeah, Zac. *Mr. Majestic: The Tout of Bengaluru*. Gurgaon: Hachette India, 2012. Print.

Sassen, Saskia. *The Global City: New York, London, Tokyo*. Princeton, Princeton UP, 1991. Print.

Schmid, David. "Imagining Safe Urban Space: The Contribution of Detective Fiction to Radical Geography." *Antipode* 27.3(1995): 242–69. Print.

Varma, Rashmi. *The Postcolonial City and its Subjects: London, Nairobi, Bombay*. New York: Routledge, 2012. Print.

Wacquant, Loïc. *Urban Outcasts: A Comparative Sociology of Advanced Marginality*. London: Polity, 2007. Print.

List of Contributors

Nazia Akhtar works as an ad-hoc faculty member (temporary Assistant Professor) at the Centre for Comparative Literature at the University of Hyderabad, where she has taught courses on cultural studies, narrative, literature and social movements, and Comparative Indian Literature. She also conducts research on literary and journalistic representations of Hyderabadi women and is currently translating into English the Urdu short stories and essays of two Hyderabadi writers, Najma Nikhat and Zeenath Sajida.

Maswood Akhter is an Associate Professor of English at the University of Rajshahi, Bangladesh. He has edited an anthology titled *Musings Post Colonies* (2012) and published in journals including *The Sri Lanka Journal of the Humanities, Spectrum, Rajshahi University Journal of Arts and Law, Asiatic: IIUM Journal of English Language & Literature, South Asian Review* etc. Dr. Akhter co-edits the research journal of his Department, *Praxis*. Recently he received the University Grants Commission of Bangladesh Award in the category of best research work in Arts and Humanities.

Umme Al-wazedi is Associate Professor of Postcolonial Literature in the Department of English and Co-Program Director of Women's and Gender Studies at Augustana College. Her research interest encompasses (Muslim) women writers of South Asia and South Asian Diaspora, Partition Novels, Trauma Theory, Standpoint Feminist Theory, and Muslim and Third World Feminism. She has published in *South Asian Review, South Asian History and Culture, Sycamore Review, The Clearing House* and *Research Journal* (Bangladesh). She co-edited a Special Issue of *South Asian Review* with Madhurima Chakraborty entitled "Nation and its Discontents."

Amit R. Baishya is an Assistant Professor in the Department of English at the University of Oklahoma. He is completing a book manuscript on violence, terror and survival in contemporary literature from Northeast India. He teaches courses in postcolonial literature, film and comic books.

Sourit Bhattacharya is a doctoral candidate in English and Comparative Literary Studies at the University of Warwick, UK. He works in historical crisis and literary realism in the post-independent Indian novel. He has an M.Phil. and M.A. from Jadavpur University, Kolkata, India. Sourit's broader areas of interest remain in political fiction (especially state of emergency texts), postcolonial and world literatures, materialist aesthetics, and environmental studies. His work is either forthcoming or published in journals such as *ARIEL*, *South Asian History and Culture*, *Rupkatha*, and in edited books. Sourit also co-edits *Sanglap: Journal of Literary and Cultural Inquiry.*

Madhurima Chakraborty is Assistant Professor of Postcolonial Literature at Columbia College Chicago. Her teaching and research interests include Postcolonial, South Asian, Indian Diaspora, and British Literature. With Umme Al-wazedi, she guest edited a special issue of *South Asian Review* on "Nation and Its Discontents." She has also been published in *Journal of Postcolonial Writing*, *Literature/Film Quarterly*, *South Asian Review*, and *Journal of Contemporary Literature.*

Claire Chambers is a Lecturer at the University of York, where she teaches contemporary writing in English from South Asia, the Arab world, and their diasporas. She is the author of *British Muslim Fictions: Interviews with Contemporary Writers* and *Britain Through Muslim Eyes: Literary Representations, 1780–1988*. Both texts in this two-book series are published by Palgrave Macmillan, and supported by funding from the British Academy and Arts and Humanities Research Council. Claire has also published widely in such journals as *Postcolonial Text* and *Contemporary Women's Writing*, and is Co-editor of the *Journal of Commonwealth Literature.*

Anna Guttman is a Professor of Postcolonial Literature in the English Department of Lakehead University, Canada. She is the author of *Writing Indians and Jews: Metaphorics of Jewishness in South Asian Literature* (2013), *The Nation of India in Contemporary Indian Literature* (2007) and co-editor of *The Global Literary Field* (2006).

Nishat Haider is Associate Professor of English at the University of Lucknow (India). She is the author of a book titled *Contemporary Indian Women's Poetry* (2010). Recipient of the Meenakshi Mukherjee Award (2016), C. D. Narasimhaiah Award (2010) and Isaac Sequeira Memorial Award (2011), she has presented papers at numerous academic conferences and her essays have been included in a variety of scholarly journals and books. Her research interests include Postcolonial Studies, Popular Culture and Gender Studies. Her recent publications have appeared in *Culture in Aphasia: The Language Loss of the Indigenous*, edited by G. N. Devy, Geoffery V. Davis and K. K. Chakravarty (Routledge), the *South Asian Review* 2015 (Vol. 35 No. 3; Vol. 36 No.1), a/b: Auto/

Biography Studies (Volume 30, Issue 2, 2015), *Contemporary Women Writing in India*, and *Gender, Space and Resistance* 1st Edition (1 July 2013), edited by Professor Anita Singh (D.K. Print World Ltd).

Maryse Jayasuriya is Associate Professor in the Department of English and Associate Dean for the College of Liberal Arts at the University of Texas at El Paso. She is the author of *Terror and Reconciliation: Sri Lankan Anglophone Literature, 1983–2009* (Lexington, 2012). She co-edited a Special Issue of *South Asian Review* (33.3) entitled *Sri Lankan Anglophone Literature*.

Lauren J. Lacey is Associate Professor of English and Director of Women's and Gender Studies at Edgewood College in Madison, Wisconsin. She is the author of *The Past That Might Have Been, the Future That May Come: Women Writing Fantastic Fiction, 1960s to the Present* (McFarland, 2014).

Kelly A. Minerva is an Assistant Professor in the Department of English and Foreign Languages and affiliate faculty in the Center for Global Studies and Social Justice at Avila University in Kansas City, MO. She researches the narrative construction of urban identities in contemporary South Asian literature. Her work has appeared in *University of Toronto Quarterly* and *Transnationalism, Activism, Art*.

Payel Chattopadhyay Mukherjee received her Ph.D. from the Humanities at the Indian Institute of Technology Gandhinagar. Her interests are in Cosmopolitanism, South Asian literature, Subaltern and Postcolonial theories.

Joy E. Ochs is a Professor of English and Director of the Honors Program at Mount Mercy University. Her interest in theories of city and space are reflected in her work with the National Collegiate Honors Council developing pedagogies of place-based learning, including City-as-Text. She has published articles on place-based pedagogies in the monographs *Honor Spaces* (2015), *Writing on Your Feet* (2014), *Partners in the Parks: Field Guide to and Experiential Program in the National Parks* (2010), and *Shatter the Glassy Stare: Implementing Experiential Learning in Higher Education* (2008). She received a grant from the National Endowment for the Humanities in 2013 and one from the Mellon Foundation in 2014 to travel to India in order to incorporate elements of place-based pedagogy in the teaching of Indian and Anglo-Indian literature.

Sanjukta Poddar is a doctoral student in the Department of South Asian Languages and Civilizations at the University of Chicago. She studied at St. Stephen's College, Delhi, and the University of Delhi where she completed an MPhil in English. She has taught at Indraprastha College for Women, St. Stephen's College, and at the Centre for Writing and Communication, Ashoka University. Sanjukta has published in Postcolonial Text and in *Interrogating the Nation* (New Delhi: IGNOU, 2014) and has also published poetry.

Jay Rajiva is an Assistant Professor of Global Anglophone Literature at Georgia State University. His research focuses on the narrative structure of representations of trauma in postcolonial and world literature, and has appeared in *Research in African Literatures* and *Angelaki: Journal of the Theoretical Humanities*. His current book project, *Postcolonial Trauma: Literature, Narrative, and the Ethical Tactility of Reading*, interrogates the representation of trauma in literature of the late apartheid in South Africa, the partition in India, and the civil war in Sri Lanka. Examining narrative structure through the critical lens of trauma theory and phenomenology, his project reconfigures the practice of reading postcolonial and world literature as an ethically significant act.

Arnapurna Rath works as Assistant Professor in Humanities at IIT Gandhinagar. Her research interests are in the fields of Comparative Literature, South-Asian narratives, Critical Theories, and Creative Writing.

Ragini Tharoor Srinivasan is a doctoral candidate in Rhetoric at the University of California, Berkeley, where she conducts research on literary and archival mediations of Indian globality. Her essays and articles have been published in over two-dozen scholarly and journalistic publications including *Public Books*, *Women & Performance*, *South Asian Review*, *The Caravan*, *HimalSouthasian*, *Verge: Studies in Global Asias*, and *Studies in South Asian Film and Media*. Ragini was also Editor of *India Currents* magazine from 2007–2009 and has written an award-winning, syndicated column for that publication since 2001.

Koshy Tharakan is a Professor of Philosophy at Goa University. His area of research interest is Philosophy of Social Sciences and Phenomenology. His publications have appeared in journals including *Indian Philosophical Quarterly* and *Journal of Indian Council of Philosophical Research*, and various edited anthologies. Currently he is also a guest professor at the Indian Institute of Technology Gandhinagar.

Index